DAILY FOCUS®

A Devotional *for* Homeschoolers *by* Homeschoolers

TO

_____

FROM

_____

DATE

_____

DAILY FOCUS®

A Devotional *for* Homeschoolers *by* Homeschoolers

Alpha Omega Publications®

JANET TATMAN

ISBN 978-0-7403-1475-9

Published by Alpha Omega Publications, Inc.
804 N. 2nd Ave. E., Rock Rapids, Iowa 51246

www.aophomeschooling.com

Printed in the United States of America.

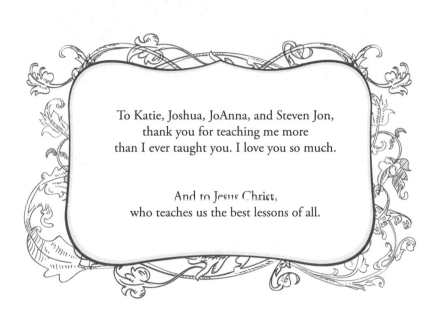

To Katie, Joshua, JoAnna, and Steven Jon,
thank you for teaching me more
than I ever taught you. I love you so much.

And to Jesus Christ,
who teaches us the best lessons of all.

The Passion of Homeschooling

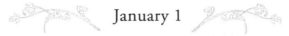

January 1

"Thou compassest my path and my lying down, and art acquainted with all my ways" (Psalm 139:3).

What makes people invest 20 years or more of their lives to homeschool their children? Ask any homeschooling parent, and they'll tell you it's for the joy of seeing their children learn. Watching your child discover God's creation creates a passion that transcends any cheap shot from uninformed critics. Daily, you have the opportunity to discover, play, and learn what God would have for your family. You share love, devotion, loyalty, and faithfulness, as you work toward educational goals and a deeper faith in Christ. Perhaps the question should be, who wouldn't want to experience a life homeschooling their children?

As Christians, Christ desires a far greater passion from us as we live for Him. Lukewarm love is something He detests in His children (Revelation 3:15-16). Every day we have the opportunity to love and learn from the Most High as we read His Word and pray. Confessing our sins daily (1 John 1:9) keeps our hearts close to the Father, so the Holy Spirit can guide and fill us with His presence. God's jealous love desires an intimacy with us that transcends any love known in this world.

Have you experienced the passion of Christ? He gave His life for your sins and wants to give you an abundant life full of His love. "I am come that they might have life, and that they might have it more abundantly" (John 10:10b). Why not rediscover the joy of being called His child this new year and yield yourself to His Lordship? "And he that loveth me shall be loved of my Father, and I will love him, and will manifest myself to him" (John 14:21b).

Jesus, thank You for Your wondrous love and the joy of being in Your family. Teach me to love You more fully, and help me yield my life to You in every area. In Your name I pray, Amen.

 Share your thoughts about this devotional at **aophomeschooling.com/001**

Mirror, Mirror on the Wall

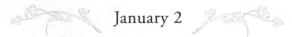

January 2

I stood looking at the photographs pasted on the outside edge of my daughter's bedroom mirror. What had started as a few pictures of a look-alike movie star had now turned into a collage of movie-star photographs that left only one small space for her reflection in the middle of the mirror. I sighed as my heart cringed.

Apparently, the homeschooling curriculum I had used to teach my daughter her value in God's eyes wasn't working. Satan's lies were convincing my daughter to identify herself with the world's definition of beauty. I cried as I thought of the depression she seemed to display each morning. "No wonder," I said to myself. "Who could compare to each of these air-brushed beauties?" How could I teach her that Proverbs 31:30 was true. "Favour is deceitful, and beauty is vain: but a woman that feareth the LORD, she shall be praised."

If there ever was a beauty in the Old Testament, Esther was it! Chosen from the most beautiful women in Persia to be the wife of King Ahasuerus, the meaning of her name came true: she was a "star." Although she wasn't in a major motion picture, God cast her for a part that would save the entire nation of Jews. The true beauty of her character, which lay in her faithfulness to Jehovah God and His people, shone when she chose to listen to God instead of her fears and claimed, "If I perish, I perish"(Esther 4:16).

Someday I look forward to meeting this beautiful woman in heaven, for it was her story that turned my daughter's life around. Praise God for the wisdom to teach our children the truth and for the mighty power of His Holy Word that is tested and sure, never returning void. "So shall my word be that goeth forth out of my mouth: it shall not return unto me void, but it shall accomplish that which I please, and it shall prosper in the thing whereto I sent it" (Isaiah 55:11).

Jesus, make my heart sensitive to my children's needs and lead me as I teach them Your truths. The world's ways seem so much stronger at times, and it is only by Your hand that I know what to do. Thank you, Jesus, for being the most beautiful thing in our lives. In Your precious name, Amen.

The Dangers of Disrespect

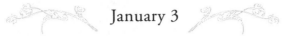

January 3

"Honor thy father and thy mother, as the LORD thy God hath commanded thee" (Deuteronomy 5:16a).

Disrespectful actions of children, no matter their age, are abhorred by God, and there's no place that's worse to see the disrespectful actions of children than in a homeschooling family. This serious offense robs parents of their authority to teach and destroys the family unit. Repeatedly, God warns children to honor their parents with loving hearts of obedience (Exodus 20:12, Ephesians 6:2). Mouthy and sarcastic children who demean or belittle their parent's leadership and decision making are clearly on a path to destruction.

King David's son, Absalom, is one such example in the Bible. The tragic story of this young man's disrespect toward his father is recorded in 2 Samuel 15-18. Absalom not only disrespected his father by defying him, but he also attempted to usurp David's reign as king. Secretly, he won the hearts of the people and eventually drove David from Jerusalem in fear of his life. The total defiance of Absalom toward his father culminated in the public act of sexually violating his father's wives on a roof top. Fortunately, King David had enough loyal followers to stop his foolish son, but at the cost of his son's life.

What about your children? Do they know the boundaries between respectfully disagreeing and disrespect? Because homeschooling families interact together 24/7, we have even more opportunity to let this problem begin in our relationships. As parents, God wants us to deal with this form of rebellion in our children as soon as it arises. After all, if children cannot learn to respect their parents, chances are they will also have difficulty respecting the Lord.

Father, sometimes it seems easier to look the other way or laugh it off when my children fail to respect me. Help me to realize the importance You place on correcting this problem when my children challenge me in ways that are inappropriate. In Jesus' name, Amen.

Spiderman

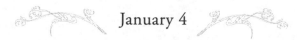

January 4

"I will praise thee; for I am fearfully and wonderfully made: marvellous are thy works; and that my soul knoweth right well" (Psalm 139:14).

We were expecting company one night for supper and were a long way from getting a meal prepared. In fact, I hadn't even bought the groceries yet. I decided a quick trip to the grocery store was necessary during our afternoon homeschool break to save myself from being unprepared for our evening guests.

When I returned home from the store, I noticed the house was unusually quiet. A red flag went off in my mind, and I checked on my children. Three of them were all fine and busy doing the work I had left for them. But when I went into my oldest son's room, I found a surprise that was quite unbelievable. Even today, I am not quite sure how he managed to accomplish it.

We had been studying about spiders in our science lessons that week. He had read his workbook, answered his worksheet questions, and studied for his quiz the next day. He had even turned an old aquarium into a nice little home for two, big barn spiders he had found. But today he went one step further. He wanted to know what being like a spider really felt like. Using every spool of thread in my sewing can, he had weaved a web within his entire room. The web extended in all directions from the ceiling to the floor, and he really looked like a spider waiting for some unsuspecting prey as he sat on his bed in the middle of the room. Smiling, he quoted from Mary Howitt's poem, "Will you walk into my parlour?"

My first inclination was to be upset at the wasted thread, but then I had to smile back at my son. He had done a far better job of teaching himself about spiders than I had done. What's more, I learned another valuable lesson that day—my son didn't learn like his sisters and brother. God had uniquely created him to learn differently. My lesson plans were going to have to change, and fast, to match him!

Father, what an awesome God You are! How can You create so many people in the world and not have even two who are alike? I humbly come and ask for the wisdom I need to teach each of the children You have given me. Thank You for the unique blessing each one is to our homeschooling family. In Jesus' name, Amen.

Prove It!

January 5

Finding all the necessary documentation for my daughter's admission to college was a nightmare. Not only did we need two forms of identification, proof of health insurance, long-lost medical immunization records, GED, and ACT scores, but now we also needed an "official" high school transcript. Thankfully, I had saved her grades during the past four years, and had prepared a "transcript" in the event we needed it. Sorting through my files on the computer to find the transcript, I shook my head and thought, "Why do I still need to prove my daughter's high school grades when she received such great ACT scores?"

God is also no stranger to providing proofs to an unbelieving world. Some people wrestle with believing God exists, even though creation has shown He does exist (Romans 1:19-20). Others, like the people in Christ's day, refuse to believe unless they see the proof of "signs and wonders" (Matthew 12:38-39 and John 4:48). Then, there are those who think they no longer need any proof of God at all because they have simply declared, "God is dead."

But unbelievers are not the only people who foolishly place a burden of proof on the Lord. Sometimes we Christians demand proof. Our fragile faith causes us to also ask God for "signs and wonders" before we will step out and do what He clearly commands in the Scriptures. Repeatedly, we miss the blessings of being used because we are still waiting for some additional sign from God. God must shake His head in heaven and think, "I've given them the truth of my Holy Word, the example of my Son, and the guidance of the Holy Spirit. What other proof do they need to obey me?"

Have you been asking the Lord for more proof before you will serve Him (Deuteronomy 6:16)? Dear child of God, the burden of proof doesn't lie with God, it lies with you. God uses those who are willing to believe and obey Him. Won't you prove you are not only a hearer of the Word, but also a doer? "But be ye doers of the word, and not hearers only, deceiving your own selves" (James 1:22).

Lord, forgive me for doubting Your provision to do all that You ask. Increase my faith and help me follow You each day in the truths You teach through Your Word. In the name of Jesus, Amen.

Homeschool Bed and Breakfast

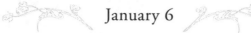

January 6

"Jesus saith unto them, Come and dine" (John 21:12).

One of my greatest pleasures as a homeschooling mother was giving my children a hot breakfast, along with a warm "good morning" each day. My sense of nurturing was satisfied as I watched sleepy-eyed yawns turn into energetic smiles. Cornbread, pancakes, waffles, omelets, French toast, apple muffins, and the like provided the necessary "brain power" for them to learn their homeschooling lessons. But just as important as the nourishing food, was the encouragement and love expressed when the food was served with a hug and a kiss.

Jesus knew all about the encouragement that comes from a good, hot breakfast. In one of His appearances after His resurrection, he had a great breakfast cooking for the disciples after their long, hard night of failed fishing. In the twilight, the disciples didn't recognize Jesus at first when He asked about their catch. But when Christ performed a miracle and filled their empty net, John realized it was Jesus. How wonderful they must have felt to see their Lord again as they shared a morning meal together!

Someday, the Lord will be serving another important meal. Christ is coming back for everyone who has trusted in Him as Lord and Savior, and we will share in His kingdom forever. "And he saith unto me, Write, Blessed are they which are called unto the marriage supper of the Lamb" (Revelation 19:9). I can only imagine the joy of fellowshipping with my Lord every morning and throughout eternity with the warmth of His love. What about you? Is your name on the invitation list? "Behold, I stand at the door, and knock: if any man hear my voice, and open the door, I will come in to him, and will sup with him, and he with me" (Revelation 3:20).

Jesus, how I long for the day of Your return! What indescribable joy there will be when I see You face to face! Use me to lead my children to You, so together, we can experience Your love forever at Your marriage supper. In Your holy, loving name, Amen.

A Mother's Fury

"The LORD preserveth all them that love him" (Psalm 145:20a).

If you want to see a homeschooling mother riled, just let someone ridicule her child for being homeschooled. Between being protective and having a firm belief in the value of homeschooling, even the most loving and gentle of us feel "the hair rising on our back" when our children are mocked. As a homeschooling mom, I also found myself saying, "Let people criticize and attack me for homeschooling all they want, but don't mess with my children!"

Moses' mother, Jochebed, felt more than just the rejection of her son by Pharaoh. She was facing her baby boy's death sentence and needed to use all of her motherly instincts to protect him (Exodus 2). God honored Jochebed and spared her son's life. Through an unusual rescue by Pharaoh's daughter and the clever bravery of his sister, Moses and his mother were reunited and able to spend more years together before he went to live in the palace.

Do you know that God is keeping you in His care today? Even though you may feel alone as you homeschool, He hasn't left you. Like a mother who cannot forget her nursing child, He wraps His arms of love around you and provides the strength you need to face the criticisms of homeschooling. The trials may seem great, but God knows and cares about every battle you face. "The LORD shall preserve thee from all evil: he shall preserve thy soul. The LORD shall preserve thy going out and thy coming in from this time forth, and even for evermore" (Psalm 121:7-8).

Lord, thank You for Your loving kindness toward me every morning. Strengthen me today to fulfill the call You have placed on my life to homeschool. Set Your hedge of protection around our family, and save us from those unseen evils that seek to destroy us. In Jesus' name, Amen.

Disciplines

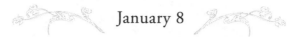

January 8

"It is good for me that I have been afflicted; that I might learn thy statutes" (Psalm 119:71).

Mopping the kitchen floor and washing dishes have always been my two least favorite jobs. Because of the obvious health hazard and the fact we needed to reuse them, I daily set my mind to rid the kitchen counters of the accumulated piles of dishes. However, procrastination would set in when the time came to mop the kitchen floor, especially during the snowy days of winter. I justified my laziness with the demands of homeschooling and counteracted with vacuuming daily and passing the "take your shoes off at the door" law. Unfortunately, even this new rule failed to eliminate the need for a daily, if not semi-daily mopping of footprints and sticky patches from spilled food. If the teaching role had been reversed and my young children had graded me on this task, I definitely would have received an "F."

My laziness and procrastination affected other areas of my life as well. Scripture memory was incorporated into my children's Bible curriculum, but disciplining myself to "hide God's Word in my heart" was an area in which I was sorely lacking. Again, I justified myself by saying, "I make time for daily prayer, Bible study, and devotions; I can't do everything as a homeschooling mom, there isn't time!" But God didn't simply give me an "F" in Scripture memorization and leave me alone. He challenged me with His truth in Psalm 119:99-104 and led me to a topical memory system of memorizing His Word. I soon discovered the blessing of really knowing God's Word and its power to change my life and others. In fact, He even showed me how to memorize Bible verses easily—by combining mopping and Scripture memory at the same time!

When was the last time you've memorized a new Bible verse? You'll never start if you don't make a lesson plan for yourself. Why not find an accountability partner (maybe your own child) to memorize Scriptures with and discover the strength of God's Word in your heart and mind? "Study to shew thyself approved unto God, a workman that needeth not to be ashamed, rightly dividing the word of truth" (2 Timothy 2:15).

Lord, please forgive my laziness in handling Your Word. Teach me again to love Your Word and to meditate on its truths. In Jesus' name, Amen.

One Day at a Time

January 9

"Take therefore no thought for the morrow: for the morrow shall take thought for the things of itself. Sufficient unto the day is the evil thereof" (Matthew 6:34).

The best advice I received when I first started homeschooling was, "Take one day at a time!" These words were easy to say, but very hard to do. Borrowing tomorrow's trouble is a learned family trait, and many times I had to come before the Lord in repentance. Many people like to think they are organized and prepared for the unknowns in life, but homeschooling four children has a way of changing that mindset. Each day I needed to erase the failures from yesterday, and realize that God was providing His strength and creativity—one day at a time.

Seeking God daily for strength is a lesson the people of Israel had difficulty learning as well. Each day for forty years, God rained manna from heaven to feed the Israelites (Exodus 16:4). The "organizers" in the group thought they could run ahead of the Lord and gather extra, possibly planning ahead for those unknowns. However, any amount the people gathered that was more than they needed for that day, spoiled. God's provision of manna was not only for nourishment but also a test. God wanted to see if the people would obey his commandments and trust that He would provide for their daily needs. God had commanded them to collect only enough manna to last for one day's needs—no more. Only on the day before the Sabbath had God commanded the people to gather twice the amount.

One other motivating factor also played a part in the gathering of this "daily bread"—the people had to gather the manna before the heat of the day (vs. 20-21). In this way, God showed them that they needed strength before the day's problems began.

Do you miss the joy of homeschooling your children today because you've run ahead to tomorrow? If you continue to look only at the "forest" of your child's academic goals, you will miss the many wonderful moments of the "trees" today. Perhaps that is why Jesus taught His disciples to pray, "Give us this day our daily bread" (Matthew 6:11).

Jesus, you are the bread of life, and without You I can do nothing. Teach me to wait on Your daily provision of strength and help me to find the blessings in homeschooling every day. In Your name, Amen.

Share your thoughts about this devotional at **aophomeschooling.com/009**

The Bigger Picture

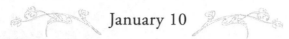

January 10

The year was 1981, and for two weeks I had been struggling with an important writing assignment. Enrolling my children into a homeschool satellite program to escape truancy charges from the public school was dependent on this "statement of homeschooling faith." Although I was frustrated with how much time and effort preparing this statement required, this document became my doctrinal guideline for homeschooling for the next twenty-five years. Frequently, I referred back to my God-given declarations contained in its pages and reminded myself why we were teaching our children at home.

The Bible contains many examples of individuals who verbalized or wrote their convictions down to solidify their commitments. Jacob made a verbal covenant with Laban by setting up a stone altar in Genesis 31:44-45. Joshua set up a memorial of stones from the Jordan River to serve as a testimonial of God's provision to future generations (Joshua 4). Greatest of all, God set His Word literally in stone for Moses and the nation of Israel when He carved the Ten Commandments into two tablets (Exodus 24:12).

Do you know why you are homeschooling? Really? Isn't there a bigger purpose than just simply getting your children out of public school for academic or safety reasons? Have you formulated God's purpose for your homeschooling, so you are not tossed around by each obstacle that comes your way? Perhaps writing a declaration of homeschooling might also help you bring all your thoughts together into one single-purpose statement. Maybe the beginning of our family's statement might help you get started—"As Bible-believing Christians, we are convicted that the ultimate responsibility for our children's education is ours, the parents" (Deuteronomy 6:5-7).

Father, whenever we do Your will, we face opposition from Satan. Help me to see clearly the purpose You have for our family's homeschooling, and guide me to preserve that message for our strength in the days ahead. In Jesus' name, Amen.

Dead Pencils

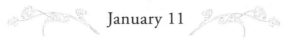

January 11

"Even so faith, if it hath not works, is dead, being alone." (James 2:17)

My children hated pencils without erasers. Being a thrifty homeschool parent, however, I couldn't understand the thought of throwing away perfectly good pencils just because they didn't have an eraser. Purposely, I left these "partial performance pencils" in the supply cabinet, but each morning when we started to homeschool, I would hear my children rummaging through the pencil can until they found a pencil with at least part of an eraser. Even though I bought new replacement erasers to put on the ends, nothing changed. The substitute erasers would crack or fall off within a few days and, unfortunately, I had to admit my children were right—there was simply no use for a pencil that couldn't both write and erase.

Like pencils without erasers, so are Christians who have lost their saltiness. Christ tells us in Matthew 5:13 and 16 that we are the salt of the earth and that we should demonstrate our faith in Christ to the world through acts of love and service. If we don't, we are as useless as salt without taste or pencils without erasers. The only thing they are good for is to be thrown out and trampled. "Ye are the salt of the earth: but if the salt have lost his savour, wherewith shall it be salted? it is thenceforth good for nothing, but to be cast out, and to be trodden under foot of men" (Matthew 5:13).

What about you? Are you known like Dorcus in Acts 9:36b for being "full of good works and almsdeeds?" Even though your days may be full as a homeschooling parent, God still desires for you to share your faith with your hands, as well as your lips. Why not let the Lord use you today to bless someone in need? "But whoso hath this world's good, and seeth his brother have need, and shutteth up his bowels of compassion from him, how dwelleth the love of God in him? My little children, let us not love in word, neither in tongue; but in deed and in truth" (1 John 3:17-18).

Lord, so many days my energy is gone after homeschooling, and I have nothing left to give to anyone else. Give me the desire to see the needs of others, and fill me with Your strength to reach out in love. In Jesus' name, Amen.

Share your thoughts about this devotional at aophomeschooling.com/011

Spicy Motivation

January 12

Developing strategies for motivating your homeschooled child is like being a good cook with the right spices. The basic "salt and pepper" seasonings of affirmation and discipline need to be added to every homeschooling day, but ingenuity and divine inspiration are required when motivating your child to learn challenging subjects. Although some homeschooling families may disagree, I never felt guilty about motivating my children with the special spices of a well-deserved gift or a day off from school when completing a difficult assignment or lengthy unit study.

God tried to motivate His people with an extra incentive when they faced the difficult challenge of conquering the Promised Land. He instructed Moses to send out spies to survey the land, and the fruits they found proved that it was indeed a land flowing with milk and honey (Numbers 13). In fact, one cluster of grapes was so large it needed to be carried on a pole between two men (vs. 23). However, because the difficulties of this assignment seemed larger than the promises and blessings, the people of Israel shied away from conquest.

God knows what you need, too, to stay motivated when facing the difficult challenge of homeschooling your children for twelve or more years. Sometimes God's recipe for your homeschooling day will include the basic salt and pepper joys of seeing your children learn and play together as a family. Other times, God will give flavorful opportunities to take unusual field trips or meet unique individuals to inspire both you and your children. Best of all, God will sprinkle the spice of the Holy Spirit into your heart to motivate you to face the major "giants" of homeschooling—mountains of laundry, disorganized school rooms, and a shortage of personal time. But like the nation of Israel, you have a choice to either respond to God's continued loving motivation or to turn away in fear and discouragement. Which will you choose? "O taste and see that the LORD is good: blessed is the man that trusteth in him" (Psalm 34:8).

Lord, only Your sweet love can keep me motivated to face the enormous challenge of homeschooling. Please let me see Your hand at work again today and whet my appetite to enjoy each of your blessings. In the name of Jesus, Amen.

 Share your thoughts about this devotional at **aophomeschooling.com/012**

Balancing Acts

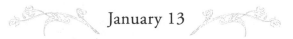

January 13

"Withhold not good from them to whom it is due, when it is in the power of thine hand to do it" (Proverbs 3:27).

I'm sure if someone had peeked through my windows during my first years of homeschooling, they would have laughed at my antics. Many days, I felt like the circus performer who balances the spinning plates on top of a pole, as I attempted to balance the needs of each person in my homeschooling family. On any given day, I tried to spin my husband's plate with affection and undivided attention as he came through the doorway after work. I also worked hard to spin my creative son's plate with assistance in science experiments and in finding interesting projects to hold his interest. I knew I needed to stop the wobbling of my oldest daughter's plate and run to the kitchen to help her as she learned how to cook. And to top it all off, there were always toddlers fussing and needing their plate spun with a clean diaper and companionship for playtime. I knew that at some point I was going to run out of energy trying to keep each of their plates spinning and wondered, "Who's going to spin my plate to keep this whole homeschooling act going?"

Praise God, the plates never did crash, but I did learn how to keep them spinning with someone else's energy other than my own. That someone was Jesus, and it was to Him that I ran each morning for the power to keep my own plate spinning. Knowing I only had so much strength, He showed me when and how to spin the plates of the family members who needed it most. I realized, too, that as much as I loved and wanted to help each member of my family, I was not responsible for making them happy or for fulfilling every one of their needs. The power was simply not in my hands! Just as I had gone to the Lord for strength; they, too, needed to learn to cast their cares on Him. "Cast thy burden upon the LORD, and he shall sustain thee" (Psalms 55:22a).

Do you feel like you're teetering on the edge of disaster in homeschooling your children? If so, you may need to hand off those spinning plates into the hands of someone who can balance them much better than you. "Now unto him that is able to keep you from falling, and to present you faultless before the presence of his glory with exceeding joy" (Jude 1:24).

Jesus, I'm so tired from trying to make our homeschooling successful in my own strength. Help me find the balance I need to meet each of my family's needs with Your wisdom and strength. In Your name, Amen.

Share your thoughts about this devotional at aophomeschooling.com/013

That Little Voice

January 14

"The spirit of man is the candle of the LORD, searching all the inward parts of the belly" (Proverbs 20:27).

My normally outgoing son had been acting sheepish for two days. He had been avoiding me as much as you can in a homeschooling family, and he was definitely dealing with "something."

I could see the Holy Spirit working on his conscience, so I prayed my usual "sick'em" prayers—you know, asking God to work on your child's heart until he turns back to Him in repentance. I wondered how long my son would struggle and if he would hide, ignore, or confess his problem. I didn't have to wait long. The very next day, the Holy Spirit's conviction weighed so heavily that he couldn't take the stress any longer.

"Mom," he said. "I need to tell you something."

"Yes," I responded. "What is it?"

"I took some money from your purse without asking you," he quietly confessed.

As Christians, we avoid God, too, after we've sinned. However, the Holy Spirit's job of convicting us of sin (John 16:8) brings us back to a right relationship with God. Even King David, "a man after God's own heart" (1 Samuel 13:14), attempted to ignore his conscience when his lust first caused him to sin with Bathsheba, and then set up her husband's untimely death on the battlefield (2 Samuel 11). David finally yielded to God's correction when the Holy Spirit convicted David's conscience through a prophet and a touching story that reached his ex-shepherd's heart.

What about your conscience? Is it sensitive to God's correction and leading, or have you hardened your conscience with unconfessed sin? Aren't you tired of the anxious tension that has replaced your fellowship with your loving heavenly Father? If God has been speaking to you about your speech, your anger, or your thought life, stop running away from Him. Since He already knows your sin, run into His arms instead. He's just waiting for you to listen to "that little voice" and rediscover the strength of living in obedience to Him. "If we confess our sins, he is faithful and just to forgive us our sins, and to cleanse us from all unrighteousness" (1 John 1:9).

Lord God, I confess today that I have been living in disobedience to You. Forgive my rebellious heart and discipline me in Your love. Lead me back to You and restore to me the joy of my salvation. In Jesus' name, Amen.

 Share your thoughts about this devotional at aophomeschooling.com/014

Daily Walks

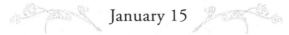

January 15

"If we live in the Spirit, let us also walk in the Spirit" (Galatians 5:25).

Taking a walk after supper became a guarded ritual for our homeschooling family. Each night, the entire family walked together down our country road to a creek a quarter mile away. Since our youngest daughter wasn't capable of such a long hike, we improvised and included her in this family time by pulling her along in our little red wagon. As we walked, we talked about whatever came to mind and observed the wonders of God's creation in nature. We never knew where the conversation was headed or what discoveries we would see along the way. We simply enjoyed the exercise and looked forward to this unhurried time of being together as a family.

One morning during my usual rushed devotion time with God, the Holy Spirit spoke to my heart and convicted me. I cried as I realized I had been shortchanging my time with God and quenching the intimacy of His love. Instead of a quiet, unhurried walk with my God in Bible study and prayer, I had been running "down the road" to the day's activities and problems. I had given up fellowshipping with my loving Lord for feeling more organized and in control of my day. I shook my head at my stupidity and said, "If my daily walks with my home-schooling family on earth are important for maintaining a close relationship, my daily walk with God is certainly even more important!"

What about you? Do you hurry through your quiet times with the Lord to get a jump on the busyness of the day's activities? Take a bit of hard-learned advice; learn the lesson of walking daily with the Lord. He really is so much fun to be with as you relax in His love. Best of all, you never know where the conversation may lead and what new spiritual truths He will give you to face each day. "Furthermore then we beseech you, brethren, and exhort you by the Lord Jesus, that as ye have received of us how ye ought to walk and to please God, so ye would abound more and more" (1 Thessalonians 4:1).

Lord, slow me down and teach me to walk hand in hand with You as I homeschool my children each day. You are the most important thing in my life. Help me to treasure every moment of every day with You. In Jesus' name, Amen.

God's Increase

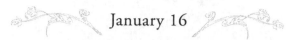
"For the administration of this service not only supplieth the want of the saints, but is abundant also by many thanksgivings unto God" (2 Corinthians 9:12).

When you discover the joy of homeschooling your own children, God usually gives you a burden to teach other children about His love, too. Many homeschooling parents can be found teaching children other than their own in Sunday school, mid-week church youth groups, vacation Bible school, or backyard Bible clubs. Maximizing your efforts by first teaching a Bible lesson to your own children and then sharing it with others only makes sense. Like the young boy who brought the two small fish and five loaves of bread to Jesus (Matthew 14:19), God is able to take the lesson you prepared for your family and use it to bless many more children as well.

Many times while Jesus was teaching His disciples on earth, His message blessed more than the twelve chosen men. His parables and sermons not only instructed His faithful followers, but they also taught the same truths to the multitudes who were within hearing distance (Matthew 5-7). The lives of many hurting bystanders were changed, and seeds of hope and faith were planted in their hearts. Even the outcast Gentiles were blessed as they heard and saw the power of God in Christ's miraculous healings and teachings.

You may not realize this fact, but same Bible story you've taught your children may be waiting to be heard by hundreds of other boys and girls. Whether it's a Bible story about Zaccheus, a topical lesson on salvation, or some aspect of Christian growth, the knowledge you've learned from the Holy Spirit during your study and preparation time is possibly the exact truth needed by the boys and girls in your church or neighborhood. Won't you share that same lesson God has given you for your own children with other young people who desperately need it? "How then shall they call on him in whom they have not believed? and how shall they believe in him of whom they have not heard? and how shall they hear without a preacher" (Romans 10:14)?

Jesus, as I homeschool, I see the spiritual needs of so many children from other families. Like the disciples, I don't know how to feed them all. Please take the Bible lessons I've prepared for my family and use them for Your glory. Help me to be faithful in sharing Your message of love and forgiveness wherever and whenever You give me the opportunity to teach. In Jesus' name, Amen.

Strength under Fire

"The LORD is my light and my salvation; whom shall I fear? the LORD is the strength of my life; of whom shall I be afraid" (Psalm 27:1)?

An emergency in my brother's family required me to give up our normal homeschooling day to watch his children. Looking out the window, I observed his children and mine playing together in the big tractor tire sand box. Considering that seven children were crowded into one small area, they were getting along quite well. Then, the inevitable happened—one of my brother's sons got upset because his space was violated, and he pushed my oldest daughter out of the sand box. Amazingly, my four-year-old son stepped up to defend his big sister. Raising himself to full height, he said, "You can't treat my sister like that!" My son never even considered the consequences of defiantly challenging his older cousin. The love for his sister filled him with a righteous courage that was ready to take on someone twice his size!

Defending our family is something we all experience as homeschoolers. Although we don't intend to take a defensive posture, many times the world pushes us around or throws punches that require us to take a stand. However, in Christian love, we must allow the Lord to be the One who speaks through us. Like Jehoshaphat as he stood before the armies of Moab and Ammon in 2 Chronicles 20, we defend ourselves from those who oppose homeschooling in God's strength instead of our own. "Thus saith the LORD unto you, Be not afraid nor dismayed by reason of this great multitude; for the battle is not yours, but God's" (2 Chronicles 20:15b). When the Lord is in the battle, all we need to do is sing the praises of homeschooling and let God do the defending.

Has homeschooling put you in the middle of a battle? Maybe you're ready to take things into your own hands to protect your family from unkind remarks or attacks. Don't let Satan tempt you to fight in the flesh. Let the Lord give you the words to say and the wisdom to respond in a way that will glorify Him. "And the servant of the Lord must not strive; but be gentle unto all men, apt to teach, patient, In meekness instructing those that oppose themselves" (2 Timothy 2:24-25a).

Father, thank You for being a mighty God that is perfectly capable of protecting my family. Give me the wisdom to know what to say and how to respond when others do not understand homeschooling. In the name of Your Son, Amen.

 Share your thoughts about this devotional at aophomeschooling.com/017

Mother of the Year

January 18

"For do I now persuade men, or God? or do I seek to please men? for if I yet pleased men, I should not be the servant of Christ" (Galatians 1:10).

Sometime after the third or fourth year of homeschooling, I finally gained enough confidence to believe I was capable of teaching my children at home. I could see my children were actually learning, and I was excited to be involved in their day-to-day learning adventure. Everything was clicking with our curriculum, and we actually seemed to be in a rhythm with our daily routine and homeschooling schedule. But something was missing, or so I thought.

As I gave in to my doubt, depression began to cloud my thinking with "poor me" thoughts like: "No one appreciates you," "You're just a mom," and "Everyone thinks you're nuts and could care less about what you're doing!" My self-defeating talk continued and many times was substantiated by attitudes and remarks of those in the community who didn't approve of homeschooling. Each day I seemed to take one step forward and two steps backward in recognizing my value as a homeschooling mom. Wasn't there any reward, recognition, or encouragement for faithfully loving and homeschooling my children?

Then, God's gentle rebuke spoke to my heart one morning during devotions. "Why are you still seeking the world's approval instead of mine?" He asked. Ashamed, I wondered how many times I would need to learn the lesson of Colossians 3:23-24: "And whatsoever ye do, do it heartily, as to the Lord, and not unto men; Knowing that of the Lord ye shall receive the reward of the inheritance: for ye serve the Lord Christ."

Feeling renewed after confessing, I walked into the kitchen to prepare breakfast. There sitting on the counter was a carefully wrapped package from my loving husband and children. Surprised, I opened the gift and found a sparkling, professionally-made plaque engraved in gold. Below my beautifully scripted name read the words, "Mother of the Year—in recognition for selflessly loving your family." Tears filled my eyes as I hung the trophy on the wall. Satan was wrong! I was valuable to God and to my family, and that was enough.

Father, I praise You for the constant reminder of Your love in Your Word. Teach me to always run to You first when I feel discouraged and to claim Your promises as my strength.
In Jesus' name, Amen.

Share your thoughts about this devotional at **aophomeschooling.com/018**

Death at My Door (Part 1)

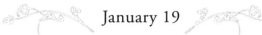

January 19

"What time I am afraid, I will trust in thee" (Psalm 56:3).

One evening after hosting a Bible study for homeschooling friends around a campfire, my observant son noticed a small amber-colored bottle lying on the ground. Walking up to me with the bottle in his hand, he began to read the letters on the bottle's torn label, "S-t-r-y-c-h . . . what's this, Mom?" he asked.

The next five minutes were a blur. I had seen a white powder on my two-year-old daughter's clothes and assumed she'd been in the ashes of the campfire. However, I quickly realized the white powder on her clothes matched the contents of the bottle that my son had just found. My heart stopped as I spelled out the letters again, S-t-r-y-c-h . . . . Strychnine! This was an old bottle of poison my grandfather had used years ago to kill rats on our farm! Somehow, we had missed seeing it when we had cleaned out the old shed before converting it into a playhouse. "Oh my!" I cried. "My daughter's been playing with poison!"

Every mom knows toddlers are forever putting things into their mouths, and I could only imagine how much of this poison my young daughter had ingested. Running into the house to call 911, I frantically prayed, "Please, help me Lord!" The anxious tone I heard in the voice of the poison control person gave me no reassurance. "Get her to the hospital as fast you can," he said. "Strychnine doesn't lose its potency!" Looking at my husband's frightened face, I knew he was thinking the same thing as me—our precious baby girl was going to die!

(To be continued in tomorrow's Daily Focus)

Father, when disaster looms, I run to You, my Rock and my Strong Tower. Show me how to trust You even in the worst of circumstances. In Jesus' name, Amen.

Share your thoughts about this devotional at **aophomeschooling.com/019**

Death at My Door (Part 2)

Somehow we arrived at the hospital within minutes, even though it was twelve miles away. We ran through the hospital doors to the emergency room and found the doctor waiting for us. Immediately, he began force feeding our daughter a charcoal mixture to neutralize the strychnine's effects. Since strychnine is normally fast acting, the next half hour was agonizing as my daughter suffered through gulping more of this mixture in between terrified sobs. Expecting the worse, we all watched and waited. After two more hours of this treatment, the doctor believed our daughter was out of danger. No visible effect of the poison was apparent in my daughter's body, and we became hopeful she was going to be all right. Miraculously, her condition seemed to indicate she hadn't swallowed any of the poison. However, the doctor gave strict instructions to monitor her through the night.

A sleepless night followed after returning home from the hospital as I observed my daughter for any effects of the poison. With the morning light, I was deeply thankful to God that my daughter was still alive. As I stepped outside for some fresh air, I saw it—the answer to what saved our baby girl from a sure death. Lying dead near the back door of our house was my young daughter's favorite kitten. Apparently, after opening the bottle of poison, my young daughter's fingers had been wiped cleaned from petting the kitten's fur. The kitten then licked itself and died from ingesting the poison left on its fur.

My daughter's near death experience changed the way I viewed life forever. I saw the demands of homeschooling in a new light, and I realized that academics were really of low importance in comparison to the hearts and souls of my children. My children's lives were precious to God, and He was giving me the privilege of teaching them about Him. Every moment we shared together was His gift, and I had no right to assume or expect that tomorrows would be guaranteed. God's Word tells us our lives are but a vapor (James 4:14); and that, at best, a mere breath (Psalm 39:5). Are you living and homeschooling with the passion that today might be your last day to tell those you love about Christ? "So teach us to number our days, that we may apply our hearts unto wisdom" (Psalm 90:12).

Lord, we are so frail and our very breath is held in Your hand. Teach me to number my days and to use every moment to guide my children to You. In the name of Your dear Son, Jesus. Amen.

The Proof Is in the Pudding

January 21

I take a strong stand in the beliefs I hold about homeschooling. Perhaps after twenty-five years of educating my children at home, I have earned the right to stand on my soap box and state clearly why I know homeschooling works. I know it works because my children have proved it works. They have graduated from college with honors, they know how to socialize, and they are able to function well in the work world and in their community. More importantly, each of them knows the Lord Jesus Christ as Savior and the truths of His Word.

Anyone is capable of teaching his children at home if he really wants to. I have found that if you really want to follow the Lord and do what He asks, He will even overcome homeschooling obstacles like being a single parent, financial limitations, or a physical handicap. As God's Word says in Romans 8:31, "What shall we then say to these things? If God be for us, who can be against us?"

Are you questioning today whether or not to continue homeschooling? Perhaps you are in your first or second year of schooling and thinking, "Maybe there's something better that I could be doing with my life?" I encourage you to remain faithful in homeschooling. You are making a difference in this world—you're loving your family and teaching them to follow Christ. Your purpose for being a homeschooling parent is treasured by God. The rewards will come, but you must be faithful. Don't give up! "Therefore, my beloved (homeschoolers), be ye stedfast, unmoveable, always abounding in the work of the Lord, forasmuch as ye know that your labour is not in vain in the Lord" (1 Corinthians 15:58).

Jesus, just getting through this homeschooling day, let alone the year, seems like an enormous task. Please empower me again by the Holy Spirit to stand firm in what You have shown me to do. In Your name I pray, Amen.

 Share your thoughts about this devotional at aophomeschooling.com/021

Who's Your Child's Hero?

"And ye became followers of us, and of the Lord" (1 Thessalonians 1:6a).

Who are the role models in your child's life? Who do they wish to emulate—movie stars, sports heroes, rock stars? Homeschooled children are no different from other children. They can also gravitate toward today's personalities and assimilate their qualities and characteristics. However, the people who stand out in the media often reflect values and beliefs far different from those we wish to see in our children.

So where do you go to find positive role models who will influence your children's minds for good? One place we chose was from the pages of history. Using God's Word, which is filled with examples of great men and women of faith in Hebrews 11, and historical biographies of famous church leaders, missionaries, scientists, and explorers, we found ample material to fill our children's minds and hearts with godly inspiration. In fact, our oldest daughter was so inspired by the story of Florence Nightingale that today she is a registered nurse!

However, perhaps the greatest role model who will ever affect your child's life is you! Whether you are aware of it or not, you are being watched every day. Your attitudes and character (good or bad) are being imitated and incorporated into your children's life. Such accountability to live a godly life challenges homeschooling moms and dads to a higher standard in their Christian walk. Are you able to say like Paul in 1 Corinthians 11:1, "Be ye followers of me, even as I also am of Christ?" If not, why not recommit yourself and your home to the Lord and watch a new generation of super Christian heroes be born!

Lord, what an awesome responsibility to be a parent! As I teach my children, make my actions and words a reflection of You. Please direct me to those people who will influence my children in Christ-like character. In the name of Jesus, Amen.

Undeserved Love

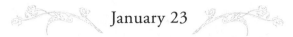

January 23

"But by the grace of God I am what I am" (1 Corinthians 10:15a).

The email was waiting for me when I arrived at work. The message was short, sweet, and simply read, "I love you forever, Mom!" Instantly, I was taken back in time to my blond, blue-eyed, five-year-old daughter as she stood in front of me with pigtails, a toothless smile, and a book tucked under her arm. I smiled and thanked God again for the privilege of homeschooling my children. What a blessing they had been and were continuing to be in my life!

Tears filled my eyes as I read again my daughter's expression of love. This time, my thoughts flew back to another young girl who had treated her parents quite differently. Painful choices and foolish rebellion had put her parents through misery. I was that young girl, and I heard again the hateful words I had said to my father in anger. My past actions stood as a stark contrast to my daughter's declaration of love. I realized again how deeply I had hurt my family. How undeserving I was to have been given a daughter who was such a joy!

Does Satan ever remind you of your shameful past to make you feel unworthy of love? You don't need to listen to his accusations any more! No sin is bigger than the depths of God's love and grace. "There is therefore now no condemnation to them which are in Christ Jesus" (Romans 8:1a). If you have confessed your sin before God in repentance and received His forgiveness, your sins are removed as far as the east is from the west, and God remembers them no more (Psalm 103:12). Praise God for the immeasurable grace He freely gives to all who are in Christ Jesus! "In whom we have redemption through his blood, the forgiveness of sins, according to the riches of his grace" (Ephesians 1:7). The next time Satan comes to remind you of your past, just remind him of his future and Christ's blood that was given for you!

Jesus, thank You for dying on the cross for me and lifting my burden of sin. I stand amazed at the many undeserved blessings You've given me and humbly worship and thank You for Your forgiveness. In Your holy name, Amen.

Homeschooling Blunders

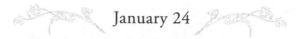

January 24

"And a fool's voice is known by multitude of words" (Ecclesiastes 5:3b).

My daughter glared at me from across the room, and I knew I had done it again. I had embarrassed her by speaking for her when my friend asked her what she had learned in school that day. This violation of her individuality and personhood ranked quite high on her top-ten list of homeschooling blunders, and Mom was the worst offender! As she informed me that day, "Mom, I am 13 and perfectly capable of answering questions on my own!"

Speaking on our children's behalf is a common offense of many homeschooling parents. Perhaps the teacher in us births an over-exuberant desire to convince others of homeschooling's benefits, or the mother in us seeks to protect our child from any uncomfortable confrontations. Regardless, this blunder robs our children of the opportunity to express themselves and can cause future problems in their adult lives. The ability to formulate an opinion and express one's views is a quality every child needs in order to live a successful life.

Christians make similar blunders in their spiritual walk with God. Many times, we attempt to speak for God and expound our knowledge on doctrines and theologies when helping people in need. With no thought of the person we are speaking to, we impart our wisdom on Biblical topics and fail to speak to the needs within that person's heart. People hear wonderful words of "Christianese," but never hear the words that will lead them into a relationship with the Creator of the universe. Instead of allowing the Holy Spirit to speak through us, we puff up our flesh and speak on God's behalf with our own human understanding.

What about you? Do you repeatedly make spiritual blunders and speak to others on God's behalf? Are you sharing your own thoughts and problem-solving remedies, or do you pray for God to speak through you with the right words? "A word fitly spoken is like apples of gold in pictures of silver" (Proverbs 25:11).

Lord, forgive me when I run ahead of You and talk on Your behalf. Teach me to pray first and to listen to You before I speak to the needs of those who are hurting. In Jesus' name, Amen.

 Share your thoughts about this devotional at **aophomeschooling.com/024**

Making Do

January 25

"Let your conversation be without covetousness; and be content with such things as ye have" (Hebrews 13:5a).

Contrary to public opinion, you can homeschool your children without having to spend a large amount of money. Like most homeschooling parents, I considered "cheap" and "free" my favorite two words when looking for curriculum and resources for our homeschool. Many times I was forced to make my own teaching aids for phonics, math, and science concepts. Surprisingly, my children never minded my "homemade" visuals. In fact, they became inspired to design their own teaching tools for playing games together.

Making the most of what you have is a missionary mindset the Apostle Paul illustrated well in Philippians 4:11-12, "Not that I speak in respect of want: for I have learned, in whatsoever state I am, therewith to be content. I know both how to be abased, and I know how to abound: every where and in all things I am instructed both to be full and to be hungry, both to abound and to suffer need." Paul had learned the art of being content no matter what material blessings God provided. At times, God provided for Paul's needs by giving him the opportunity to earn his own living (1 Thessalonians 2:9). Other times, God used the charitable giving of Christians to meet Paul's needs. Whatever the situation, Paul knew God would provide if he was in the middle of God's will, even if God's will placed him in the middle of a sinking ship (Acts 27)!

God promises that you will not lack concerning the work He has for you to do (2 Corinthians 9:8). If He has called you to teach your children, He already knows the costs involved and the resources you need. Don't get into trouble financially by falling for the "bigger and better" mentality in regard to purchasing homeschooling supplies. Pray and seek the Lord's choices for teaching your children. Perhaps you're failing to notice the untapped resources He has already given you. Isn't the Bible (the best curriculum any child can use) the best place to start?

Lord, forgive my greediness in wanting homeschooling trips and resources I cannot afford. Open my eyes to see the provisions You've clearly laid before me to teach my children what they need to know. In Jesus' name, Amen.

 Share your thoughts about this devotional at **aophomeschooling.com/025**

Reflections

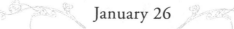
"Not that we are sufficient of ourselves to think any thing as of ourselves; but our sufficiency is of God" (2 Corinthians 3:5).

As my eight-year-old son and I observed the craters on the moon for science class, his simple observation of the moon's reflection left a profound teaching on both our minds.

"Mom," he asked. "The moon really has no light of its own, does it?"

"No," I replied. "It simply reflects the light from the sun. If the sun was gone, the moon wouldn't shine either."

Thinking deeply, he looked at me and said, "That's the same way we would be without Jesus."

Amazed at his understanding of the two concepts, I answered, "Yes, that's right honey."

As homeschooling parents, we like to think that we are the ones who teach our children. But anyone who has homeschooled for more than a few years knows this fact—apart from Christ, we are totally inadequate to teach our children. No college degree, teaching certificate, or earthly intelligence can prepare you to teach your children the right lesson at the right time or how to incorporate into your lesson the true wisdom that comes from above. Like the moon without the sun, we have no understanding on our own to impart the truths that will forever change our children's lives.

However, the good news is that you have Christ, the "Light of the world" in you (John 9:5). Not only are you filled with His presence for teaching your children, but you also have the ability to reflect God's love to others by shining hope and encouragement into a very dark world. Just as Moses needed his shining face veiled after being with God (Exodus 34:29-35), your challenge as a homeschooling parent is to live in close obedience to God to reflect His light into your family and the world. "Arise, shine; for thy light is come, and the glory of the LORD is risen upon thee. For, behold, the darkness shall cover the earth, and gross darkness the people: but the LORD shall arise upon thee, and his glory shall be seen upon thee" (Isaiah 60:1-2).

Lord, let me reflect Your love and wisdom as I homeschool my children. Reveal any sin in my heart that would block Your light from shining in my life. In Christ's name I pray, Amen.

 Share your thoughts about this devotional at **aophomeschooling.com/026**

Test Days

January 27

"The LORD trieth the righteous" (Psalm 11:5a).

Test days brought varying responses from my homeschooled children. My oldest daughter was ready to tackle whatever was thrown at her with aggressive confidence. My oldest son faced his tests pensively and held a quiet, inner confidence as he matched his knowledge against the written questions. With the fearful apprehension of a person facing the gallows, my youngest daughter dreaded the challenge, and my youngest son just shrugged off the pressure and simply gave tests "his best shot." Surprisingly, test days not only revealed what my children knew academically, but it also revealed their character.

The tests in life also have a way of showing a person's character. Christ's disciples proved that to be true when Jesus was arrested in the Garden of Gethsemane. Peter boldly came at the temple soldiers with a sword as he cut off the ear of the high priest's servant (John 18:10). John quietly stood back and followed Christ to the high priest's court to see what would happen to his beloved Lord (John 18:15) The other frightened disciples ran away fearing a sure death for following Christ (Mark 14:50), and Judas' greed was shown when he betrayed the Lord with a kiss (Matthew 26:49).

What do the tests that come from those who oppose homeschooling reveal about your character? Are you defensive and ready to attack? Do you quietly sit back and do your own thing and hope others will leave your family alone? Does fear make you constantly worry about possible problems with difficult school authorities? If God is in control of your homeschooling, He wants you to reflect His character to the world. When the infamous socialization and legality questions are thrown at you and you're tempted to "speak your mind," trust God instead to give you the right answers. Only He can make you shine like Christ as you tell an unbelieving world of the joys of homeschooling. "But sanctify the Lord God in your hearts: and be ready always to give an answer to every man that asketh you a reason of the hope that is in you with meekness and fear" (1 Peter 3:15).

Lord, sometimes I get so tired of defending our homeschooling. Help me to seek Your wisdom and love in responding to those who don't understand the blessings found in homeschooling. In Jesus' name, Amen.

Homeschool Fears

Satan really takes advantage of homeschoolers. When you jump into something different, like teaching your own children, you become susceptible to his attacks of doubt and fear. Unsure of your abilities, you second-guess your decisions and desperately look for affirmation and direction. Added to those doubts are questioning remarks and comments from those who don't homeschool, and soon you begin to think, "I could really mess up my children's lives if I do this wrong!" The multiple battlefronts of spiritual, emotional, and physical attack call for reinforcement from the Lord. Only His divine strength, wisdom, and power can counteract Satan's fears.

The apostle Paul understood what being attacked by Satan felt like. When addressing the church in Corinth, he stated in 2 Corinthians 7:5, "For, when we were come into Macedonia, our flesh had no rest, but we were troubled on every side; without were fightings, within were fears." I'm sure at times Paul must have questioned if he was doing the right thing when he went on his missionary journeys to establish the early churches. Not only did the other apostles criticize his work with the Gentiles, but he also suffered at the hands of his fellow Jews and from the unbelieving communities he tried to reach. Add to those fears the beatings, shipwrecks, and other persecutions from without, and it's no wonder he was afraid. Still, Paul continued to trust in Jesus for every need and even his very life.

Are you tired from Satan's attacks? Does it seem like when you find victory over one fear another one develops? Dear one, I wish I could tell you things will get better, but that might not be the case. The battles will probably remain. You see, if Satan can't keep your family from believing in Christ, his next goal is to keep your family from living for Christ. If you're feeling weary today, run to your Commander and Lord and let His love empower you to face every fear. In Christ's name and by the power of His blood, you will defeat Satan. Besides, the worst way you could mess up your children's lives is if you don't fight. Don't let the fears win over you! "Be sober, be vigilant; because your adversary the devil, as a roaring lion, walketh about, seeking whom he may devour: Whom resist stedfast in the faith" (1 Peter 5:8-9a).

Lord God, I recommit myself and my family to You today. Strengthen us to stand strong against the fears and discouragement that Satan brings to our homeschool. Let me see the plans and purpose You have for us and may our lives glorify You. In the dear name of Jesus, Amen.

Unanswerable Questions

January 29

"He shall call upon me, and I will answer him: I will be with him in trouble; I will deliver him" (Psalm 91:15a).

Do your younger children drive you crazy with all their questions each day? With an insatiable desire to know "why," they ask a barrage of unending questions that homeschooling parents are forced to answer as best they can. Some questions like "Why is the sky blue?" and "Where do babies come from?" might set us back for a few minutes as we think of the best way to answer. But other questions like, "Why did Grandpa die?" and "Why did God let my sister get cancer?" pose a much bigger challenge. Sometimes, questions are simply unanswerable and the "whys" of life's problems have no answer keys for us to use.

Like little children, countless men and women in the Bible also asked questions when they struggled through the "whys" of life's difficulties. Job's life is one such example. After suffering horrific loss of belongings, family, and health, he sat down and asked God "why" in Job 31. God never gave Job an outright answer, but He did counteract Job's question with a few questions of His own, like "Where were you when I created the world?" Confessing his ignorance in questioning a Holy God, Job reached the point of submissive humility and brokenness. "Who is he that hideth counsel without knowledge? therefore have I uttered that I understood not; things too wonderful for me, which I knew not" (Job 42:3).

Are you looking for some answers to the "whys" in your life? Is the pain and suffering that you're experiencing causing you to wonder, "Where is God, doesn't He know what is happening to me?" Perhaps God is taking you to a new level of trusting in Him or He is trying to teach you a deeper truth. Either way, God has not left you. He sees your every tear and will deliver you in His time. Will you continue to hope in Him and wait for His answer? "Why art thou cast down, O my soul? and why art thou disquieted within me? hope in God: for I shall yet praise him, who is the health of my countenance, and my God" (Psalm 43:5).

Lord, I acknowledge that You alone are God. I lay my burden at Your feet and ask You to strengthen me to face this problem in my life. Even if I never know "why," I will continue to trust in You and Your love for me. In Jesus' name, Amen.

Cleaning Day

January 30

About once a month I would shake my head in despair when I looked into our homeschooling supply closet. "How does this get messed up so quickly?" I would think. "I just cleaned this out a few weeks ago, and now it looks like a tornado hit again!" Staying organized and keeping things put away were endless tasks for me as a homeschooling parent. Multiply four children times six to eight subjects apiece with accompanying teacher guides, quiz and test papers, and answer keys (plus endless art and daily school supplies), and it's no wonder I couldn't keep ahead of the mess. Even though I tried to pick up and straighten things out daily, the added monthly task of a major clean-up day was always necessary.

God understands the necessity for major overhauls, too. Once a year, He commanded Aaron the high priest to come before the Holy of Holies and offer a sacrifice for himself and the sins of Israel (Leviticus 16). Using a live scapegoat, the high priest would lay his hands on the goat, confess the sins of the people, and then send the goat away into the wilderness. Even though individual sacrifices were observed by the people for their sins, the Lord also required this yearly sacrifice to clean up the nation's spiritual mess. Years later, God would fulfill the need for all sacrifices by sending His son, Jesus, as the final payment. "Neither by the blood of goats and calves, but by his own blood he entered in once into the holy place, having obtained eternal redemption for us" (Hebrews 9:12).

Does your spiritual life need a major clean-up? Have you allowed seemingly "little" sins to enter your daily life? Some actions like telling half-truths, laziness, and over-indulging in shopping or eating may appear "acceptable" in your eyes at first, but if unconfessed for too long, they may begin to make a total mess of your daily walk with God. Isn't it time to clean up your actions with the Lord's forgiveness and to reorganize your spiritual walk with Bible study and prayer? "Having therefore these promises, dearly beloved, let us cleanse ourselves from all filthiness of the flesh and spirit, perfecting holiness in the fear of God" (2 Corinthians 7:1).

Father, how did I get back into this place of spiritual apathy again? Forgive me for not coming before You each day in prayer and seeking the strength I need from Your Word. In Jesus' name, Amen.

 Share your thoughts about this devotional at aophomeschooling.com/030

Commissioned to Serve

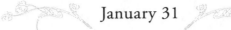

January 31

"And whosoever of you will be the chiefest, shall be servant of all" (Mark 10:44).

When was your defining moment of deciding to homeschool your children? Mine came one day as I stood over the kitchen sink washing dishes for the fourth time. After running all day to keep up with my preschoolers and the housework, I felt as limp as the dish rag I was holding. I had been thinking about homeschooling, but quite frankly, the thought of being a homeschooling parent for the rest of my life wasn't too appealing right then. As my children entertained themselves with one of their favorite Christian music tapes, the words to the song they were playing echoed in my thoughts. In that moment, something happened. The Holy Spirit convicted me and said, "Are you willing to be my servant?"

"Yes," I replied.

"Then teach these children about Me," He said lovingly.

"But I don't know how, God," I cried.

"Trust me," He said in return.

Throughout my homeschooling experience, no other moment was quite as powerful as that one. Taking God at His word, I began to learn that you can't be a good homeschooling parent without learning how to be a servant first. God gave me a new love for my children and the wisdom to use my spiritual gifts of teaching, administration, and exhortation to benefit the people I loved most, my family. Although plenty of "rag days" were still to come, I knew I was serving my Lord right where He wanted me to be!

Learning how to be a servant doesn't come easy for any of us. Our selfish flesh screams so loudly, "What about me?" Homeschooling may take you to a new dimension of sacrifice, but it will never be as great as Christ's sacrificial love for you. His death on the cross washed away every mess you will ever make, and He never complained once while doing it. With Jesus as your role model, will you pick up your towel and continue serving the Lord in your homeschool? "For even the Son of man came not to be ministered unto, but to minister, and to give his life a ransom for many" (Mark 10:45).

Jesus, help me to hear Your voice today instead of the "What about me's?" Thank You for Your wondrous love that sacrificed so much for me. Give me a servant's heart and teach me to follow You. In Your precious name, Amen.

 Share your thoughts about this devotional at **aophomeschooling.com/031**

Ahead of His Time

February 1

"Whosoever shall receive one of such children in my name, receiveth me" (Mark 9:37a).

I could hear my youngest son preaching to his older brother and sister in the living room. Earnestly, he was telling them to behave and stop fighting. However, like a bucket of water on a raging forest fire, his words had no effect. Frustrated, he tried again to get their attention, quoting Bible verses stating why they shouldn't be arguing. His strong leadership qualities (his siblings called them "being bossy") and sense of right and wrong would not allow him to walk away from the problem. Unfortunately, because he was their "little brother," both his brother and sister refused to listen to his counsel.

Being young has its disadvantages when witnessing to those who are older. The Apostle Paul warned young Timothy of the challenges in 1 Timothy 4:12, "Let no man despise thy youth; but be thou an example of the believers, in word, in conversation, in charity, in spirit, in faith, in purity." Mistakenly, older Christians tend to think they have a market on spiritual understanding and wisdom. Although experience does give older Christians an edge, it is often the passionate drive of youthfulness that keeps a body of believers vibrant and alive.

What about you? Do you consider your children's faith in God immature and not worth listening to? As a homeschooling parent, you may think you have all the answers concerning spiritual matters, but you don't. If you will humble yourself to learn from your children's faith, you will see again how the Lord wants you to approach Him with your own worship—intense, passionate, and full of hopeful enthusiasm and praise! "And Jesus called a little child unto him, and set him in the midst of them, And said, Verily I say unto you, Except ye be converted, and become as little children, ye shall not enter into the kingdom of heaven" (Matthew 18:2-3).

Father, forgive me when I become a stumbling block to my children's faith. Help me to follow their example and freely give You all my love and praise. In Jesus' name, Amen.

I Can Only Imagine

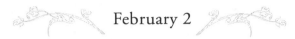

February 2

"I will walk within my house with a perfect heart. I will set no wicked thing before mine eyes" (Psalm 101:2b-3a).

I can still picture my two little daughters playing their favorite game during recess time from homeschooling. With the "Little House" books written by Laura Ingalls Wilder as their inspiration, they loved becoming "Mary" and "Laura" whenever playing alone or together with friends. Since we had read the entire series several times during our nightly story time, I shouldn't have been surprised this was their favorite game. Living in the heart of the Midwest made the stories even more alive in their imagination.

Time and again I saw the influence of a story or book on the hearts and minds of my children. The literature they read was not only processed as information, but also became the seedbed for their imagination in play. Therefore, choosing the right books became crucially important since their character development was affected by them. Thankfully, there was always one book we could rely on to communicate a message we wanted our children to hear. My young children never tired of hearing the Old Testament stories of Moses, Joseph, Gideon, Samson, David, and the like.

What about you? As a homeschooling parent, where do you go with your imagination when you have time for yourself? Does your imagination lead you into the spiritual truths you've learned from the Bible, or does it play tempting "what if" games with the ungodly mental pictures you've seen in magazines, books, movies, and TV? Today, the influences for evil in the world are everywhere; but God's Word exhorts us to take every thought captive to the mind of Christ, including our imagination (2 Corinthians 10:5). Wouldn't you hate to imagine what you may become if you don't? "But every man is tempted, when he is drawn away of his own lust, and enticed. Then when lust hath conceived, it bringeth forth sin: and sin, when it is finished, bringeth forth death" (James 1:14-15).

Father, forgive me for using my imagination for evil instead of good. Expose those secret places in my thoughts that I think You, don't see. Show me again how to meditate on Your Word to live in a way that pleases You. In Jesus' name, Amen.

Godly Legacies

February 3

"The righteous shall be in everlasting remembrance" (Psalm 112:6b).

"And he did evil in the sight of the Lord," read my youngest son out loud as we studied the kings of Israel and Judah in our homeschool Bible curriculum. After reading the same sad statement in regard to three or four more kings, my son looked at me with a sober face and said, "Mom, weren't there any kings who did good in the sight of the Lord?"

"Yes," I replied. "As a matter of fact, there was a king named Josiah, and he was only eight years old when he became king. The Bible says he was different than the evil kings before him, 'and he did that which was right in the sight of the LORD, and walked in all the way of David his father, and turned not aside to the right hand or to the left' (2 Kings 22:2). Because he brought the people of Judah back to God and destroyed all the false gods they had been worshipping, King Josiah is forever remembered as a good king."

I could see my young son deep in thought before he turned to me and said, "Wow, I wonder what they'll write about me in the Bible after I'm dead!"

The story of King Josiah's life is an inspiration to all who read it because when Josiah heard the Word of God, he repented and made a covenant with God to serve the Lord with all his heart and soul and to obey God's holy law (2 Kings 23:3). Because of his decision, the people also entered into the same covenant, and the nation was cleansed from its ungodly practices.

Legacies are not only for kings in Old Testament times. As a Christian, someday you will leave a legacy behind, too, when God chooses to take you home to heaven. If the story of your life was included in the Bible, how would you be remembered—as a man or woman who served the Lord faithfully with all your heart and soul, or as someone who did evil in the sight of the Lord? "Wherefore seeing we also are compassed about with so great a cloud of witnesses, let us lay aside every weight, and the sin which doth so easily beset us" (Hebrews 12:1a).

Father, thank You for preserving Your written Word, so I can learn from those who went before me. Help me to remain faithful in homeschooling and in serving You, so I can leave a godly legacy to all those who come after me. In Jesus' name, Amen.

Share your thoughts about this devotional at aophomeschooling.com/034

Helping Hands

February 4

"She stretcheth out her hand to the poor; yea, she reacheth forth her hands to the needy" (Proverbs 31:20).

I brought home more than our fourth child from the hospital when I gave birth that day. I also brought home a whole new set of anxieties about homeschooling and my ability to meet the demands of a family of six. Feeling weak and tired, I knew my energy supply was running low. I simply couldn't take care of a new baby, maintain a house, and homeschool, too.

Little did I know, God was already preparing a blessing that would help me with the extra work. A fellow homeschooling friend arrived the next day with a gift that was not only timely, but so incredibly sacrificial that it made me cry. Even with her own responsibilities as a busy, homeschooling mom, she came and delivered a delicious, home-cooked meal. Humbly she said, "I thought you could use a helping hand for awhile. You don't have to worry about supper for the next two weeks. I'll be bringing them over every night about this time." Since I didn't have to prepare meals, I was able to use the little energy I had to homeschool at least half days, as I slowly regained more strength.

The Bible tells of another man who was incredibly thankful for the helping hands of his friends. The lame man's friends in Luke 5:18-25 were not deterred by the crowds that surrounded Jesus. Because of their faith and willingness to go the extra mile, they tore a hole in a roof to lower their lame friend, who was lying on a stretcher, in front of Jesus. That day, the lame man found both healing and salvation because of his friends (vs. 24).

Do you know a homeschooling family who might need an extra hand? Maybe life has put them into a stressful situation that seems insurmountable. Since you homeschool, you know their needs best. Even if it's only a small thing, your helping hand might be the life-giving answer to help them through this difficult time. Why not go the extra mile and show them the love of Christ?

Lord, give me compassion to see the needs of other homeschooling families. Show me how to be a blessing and use my hands to minister to them however I can. In Jesus' name, Amen.

Share your thoughts about this devotional at aophomeschooling.com/035

Misgivings

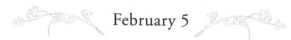

February 5

"Hold fast the confidence and the rejoicing of the hope firm unto the end" (Hebrews 3:6b).

Do you ever feel like you haven't accomplished a thing at the end of your homeschooling day? Do you look around and see even more piles of projects to finish and messes to clean up than when you started? Have your children learned a new set of multiplication tables today, but entirely forgot the historical facts they learned about George Washington yesterday? Some days you may wonder if you can be your children's teacher. Maybe they would be better off if they went to school. Stop! Think about what just went through your mind. Where are those thoughts coming from—from the one who called you to teach your children and promised you the strength to do it, or from the one who would see you fail?

Every homeschooling mother second guesses herself from time to time. After a difficult day, we all question whether we heard God right when He asked us to homeschool our children. We're not alone. Even great men of God faced similar doubts when God called them to difficult tasks. Men like Moses, Gideon, and David all struggled with their anxieties in serving God, too. But God knew their hearts, and He provided the confirmation and the assurance they needed to remain faithful in doing what He asked. "I called upon the LORD in distress: the LORD answered me, and set me in a large place" (Psalm 118:5).

God is waiting to do the same for you today. If you're wondering how you are going to get through homeschooling today, simply take a moment now and pray something like this:

Father, my faith is weak, Please fill me with Your presence and confirm again to me that I am doing Your will in homeschooling our children. Strengthen me to follow You in obedience and help me commit this day to You for Your glory. In the name of Your dear Son, Jesus, Amen.

Share your thoughts about this devotional at aophomeschooling.com/036

Back by Popular Demand

"God hath chosen the weak things of the world to confound the things which are mighty" (1 Corinthians 1:27b).

In all my years of teaching, "popular" was one word I never heard used to describe home-schooling. Sure, I had heard words like illegal, over-protective, and crazy, but popular? Never! Going against the norm in the educational realm led to some hot debates, even within my own family. When talking to relatives who were "certified" teachers, I never heard phrases like, "Oh, how interesting!" or "That's great, how can I help you?" Instead, my ability and sanity was questioned, and I was warned about the practicality of such an undertaking. Even today, twenty-five years later, people still think having homeschooled my children is odd.

Being unpopular is difficult for any young homeschooling mother. Your need for acceptance is strong, but your need to temper your emotions with God's perspective on popularity is more important. Rarely did God use the popular person to do His will. A serious Bible study would reveal that God usually used the unloved, unwanted, and broken person most. Leaders like David and Moses, prophets like Jeremiah and Jonah, and even common women like Rahab and Ruth were chosen by God over the popular counterparts of their time. Even Christ felt the rejection of the crowds and religious leaders who wanted to crucify Him.

Are you feeling the pain of being unpopular today because you homeschool? Does your single income leave little money for trendy wardrobes (or even new clothes for that matter)? Do others treat you with disdain because you're "just a mom?" Have friends stopped calling because they don't understand how homeschooling limits when you can talk on the phone? You may not be popular in the world's eyes, but in God's, you are a precious jewel for obey-ing His call to teach your children. He treasures you and wants you to find your value in Him. Even if you are never popular because you homeschool, will you hold fast to the One whose acceptance is all that matters? "The LORD is on my side; I will not fear: what can man do unto me" (Psalm 118:6)?

God, I feel so lonely. Show me how to be obedient when others don't understand our choice to homeschool and to find comfort in Your arms of love that surround me. In the name of Jesus, Amen.

Blame Game

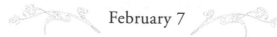
"OK," I asked my daughter. "Where is the book report you were supposed to have done today?"

"Oh, that was due today?" she responded innocently.

"Yes, you knew it was due today. I reminded you last week, remember?" I replied.

I could see another excuse beginning to form in her mind, and from past experience, I knew what was coming.

"Yes, I remember," she answered, "but I had to do all those extra chores last week because the other kids were sick, so I didn't have time to finish writing my book report."

Not letting her off so easily I said, "But what about all the extra time you seemed to have to read other books and go for bike rides?"

"Oh, yeah, I guess I could have done it then," she reluctantly admitted.

Looking for someone else to blame when things go wrong in life is a common escape route from accountability. King Saul's response to Samuel in 1 Samuel 15 is a classic example. God had commanded Saul to utterly destroy everything when he went to war against the ungodly nation of Amalek. Instead, Saul kept livestock and other spoils for himself and the people. When Samuel heard the bleating sheep and asked Saul if he had obeyed God's command, Saul put the blame for his disobedience on the people. Eventually, when his back was against the wall, Saul admitted he was responsible for disobeying God's command.

Do you blame others for your foolish actions and bad choices? Do you point the finger and say, "If they hadn't been so . . . I wouldn't have . . .?" Whether in friendships, marriage, or homeschooling, God holds you accountable to faithfully obey Him in what He has commanded you to do. Blaming others is really trying to hide your own failings from God. The blame game first started in the Garden of Eden with Adam and Eve, but you don't have to keep playing it in your home. Why not confess your sin instead and be healed? "He that covereth his sins shall not prosper: but whoso confesseth and forsaketh them shall have mercy" (Proverbs 28:13).

Father, thank You for Your forgiveness You freely give to me. Help me to acknowledge that the fault lies with me when I sin and to keep my heart clean before You. In the name of Jesus, Amen.

Count Your Blessings

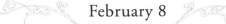

"He brought me up also out of an horrible pit, out of the miry clay, and set my feet upon a rock, and established my goings. And he hath put a new song in my mouth, even praise unto our God: many shall see it, and fear, and shall trust in the LORD" (Psalm 40:2-3).

How is your homeschooling starting today? Has another late night and early morning drained your energy level and given you an attitude that is less than positive? Fatigue can make cowards of us all and turn the daily housework into mountains and the homeschool responsibilities into huge obstacles. Just when you think you can't take anymore, you need to step back and regain your focus. Your children need you to bring a positive perspective to their learning experience.

Seeing the day through God's eyes instead of your own will change your attitude and possibly the results of your day. A close homeschooling friend blessed me with a cross-stitched version of the poem below. (I think she knew I needed to see it every day!) Its constant reminder encouraged me to be thankful for all we had and changed many a bad morning into a good one as I reflected on its message. I pray this poem will do the same for you.

Count Your Blessings
Author Unknown

Count your blessings instead of your crosses;
Count your gains instead of your losses.
Count your joys instead of your woes;
Count your friends instead of your foes.
Count your smiles instead of your tears;
Count your courage instead of your fears.
Count your full years instead of your lean;
Count your kind deeds instead of your mean.
Count your health instead of your wealth;
Count on God instead of yourself.

Father God, lift the heavy burdens off my heart and let me see this new day as You do. Give me strength to stand against the discouragement that weighs me down and help me defeat Satan's lies with praise to You for Your blessings. In Jesus' name, Amen.

 Share your thoughts about this devotional at **aophomeschooling.com/039**

Homeschool Seedlings

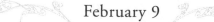

February 9

How many times have you been accused of sheltering your children from the real world because you homeschool? After experiencing this confrontation numerous times, I finally realized an important fact my accusers were ignoring—they sheltered their children from the real world, too. Most caring parents draw a line and set limits on what they allow their children to experience. The only difference between my sheltering and theirs was that I had simply drawn our children's line in a different place. R-rated movies, magazines and books that promoted sex outside of marriage, violent video games, and other activities that violated God's Word were not a part of our family life. The standards I wanted to set were for training in righteousness, not for training in the ways of the world.

Learning how to be in the world but not of it is difficult for Christians—young or old. The unbelieving community sees us as trying to live "holier than thou," but sometimes we must allow God to sanctify us by removing ourselves from the temptations that would lead us into sin. God even commands us to run away (flee) from idolatry (1 Corinthians 10:14) "and have no fellowship with the unfruitful works of darkness, but rather reprove them" (Ephesians 5:11). However, Jesus also gave us the example of reaching the lost by meeting them in their homes and on the streets. Finding the balance between loving the lost and not getting caught in sin takes discernment and wisdom that comes from studying God's Word, prayer, and listening to the Holy Spirit.

So how much do you shelter your children from the evil in the world without quenching the redemptive work of Christ? After all, as Christians, we are to be salt and light. My answer to that question came one day while gardening. The Master Gardener showed me that if I transplanted my seedlings that had been started inside the house into the outside garden too soon, they would die from the exposure to the elements. However, if I moved them at the right time and carefully nurtured the seedlings for a time with extra protection and fertilizer, they would grow into strong, healthy plants that would not only resist bugs, heat, and hail, but also produce an abundance of fruit. Don't let anyone's "sheltering" argument convince you to transplant your precious homeschooling seedlings too early!

Lord, give me discernment to hear Your voice on how to homeschool my children so they are effective witnesses for You. Help me ground them in Your Word and fertilize them with Your truths so they not only survive in the world, but also flourish and change it. In Jesus' name, Amen.

 Share your thoughts about this devotional at **aophomeschooling.com/040**

Money to Burn

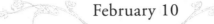
"For every beast of the forest is mine, and the cattle upon a thousand hills" (Psalm 50:10).

Can you imagine what your homeschool would look like if you received the same amount of money that public education receives for one child? At the current rate of $7500 per child, you could buy state-of-the-art computers for each of your children, expand your library with quality reference books, take unlimited field trips, purchase tons of curriculum, buy your own copier and office equipment, purchase high performance microscopes for science, hire tutors to help with high school level subjects, and still have money to burn. Such would be the dream of every homeschooling parent!

Ironically, we do have a storehouse in heaven for all our homeschooling needs that far outweighs any earthly fortunes. God's Word tells us in Psalm 50:10 that God owns everything. We are simply stewards of the abundant blessings which He chooses to bestow. Our heavenly Father has unlimited resources, and like the birds of the air and flowers of the field, He provides for every need of our children. How reassuring to claim the truth in Matthew 6:8b, "For your Father knoweth what things ye have need of, before ye ask him!"

How about you? When your checkbook balance makes you anxious, do you worry and fret, or do you run to the Creator God for help? If you are living in obedience to His Word, you can trust Him to be there for you. That doesn't mean you'll receive every homeschooling "bell and whistle" on the market or every "extra" for your home that you desire, but He does promise to provide for our needs if we follow the truths in Matthew 6:33: "But seek ye first the kingdom of God, and his righteousness; and all these things shall be added unto you."

Lord, you are a great and mighty God! Open my eyes to see the many blessings You've already given me and help me to trust You for every financial need we have in the future. In Jesus' name, Amen.

Flea Friendships

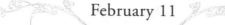

February 11

"Withdraw thy foot from thy neighbour's house; lest he be weary of thee, and so hate thee" (Proverbs 25:17).

When we first started homeschooling, receiving support and encouragement from other homeschooling families was crucial. Without it, we might have given up in our attempts to teach our children at home. However, as time went on with our small homeschooling support group, I noticed there seemed to be one or two families who always wanted someone else to do the work of homeschooling for them. They loved their children and the idea of homeschooling, but they repeatedly left their children in someone else's care or advocated having other homeschooling families educate their children in a co-op class. Although I was happy to help, I realized later that these families were simply taking advantage of others. When the problem repeatedly robbed my family of the care and homeschooling they deserved, I said "no" more often.

The apostle Paul experienced a similar problem when he exhorted the Thessalonians in 2 Thessalonians 3:10: "For even when we were with you, this we commanded you, that if any would not work, neither should he eat." Paul used his own disciplined life as an example of working hard to not be a burden to others. Paul furthers his exhortation to those who look for the easy way out with a definite command in vs. 12: "Now them that are such we command and exhort by our Lord Jesus Christ, that with quietness they work, and eat their own bread." Although Galatians 6:2 tells us to bear one another's burdens, we must realize there is also a difference between helping and enabling. Sometimes, love must be tough enough to say no.

What kind of homeschooling friend are you? Do you take more than you give? Maybe today you should consider running to the Lord with your insecurities and needs instead of automatically going to another homeschooling family. People do love and care about your burdens, but we all have our own homeschooling cross to bear. Homeschooling is hard work and takes an enormous amount of time, energy, and prayer. The Lord wants you to depend on Him first because in Him, you will find the true strength you need.

Jesus, help me to discipline my life so our homeschooling will be a blessing to others instead of a burden. Teach me to bring my problems to You first and to spend as much time talking to You about them as I do with others. In Your name I pray, Amen.

Share your thoughts about this devotional at **aophomeschooling.com/042**

Surprise, Surprise

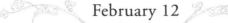

February 12

"And what is the exceeding greatness of his power to us-ward who believe, according to the working of his mighty power" (Ephesians 1:19).

One thing you know for sure as a homeschooling parent is that you can never be sure what your children are going to say or do. Every day holds a surprise or two that makes teaching your children anything but boring. At least that's what I reminded myself as I walked into my son's room one day. Always the practical joker, my son had made a look-a-like mannequin with his clothes and placed it in the middle of his bed. With the mannequin's back facing the door, I thought it was really my son sitting on his bed studying until I touched its body and the head rolled off. If someone had visited our home and walked in the door at that moment, they would have heard me scream and thought our homeschooling family was crazy. For me, it was just another day of laughing with my children and enjoying their creative imaginations.

As a Christian, walking with the Lord is never boring either. The disciples discovered that fact as they followed Jesus while He was on earth. They saw Christ control the wind, heal the diseased and lame, feed the multitudes, and even bring people back to life from the dead. The disciples learned that Jesus was capable of anything, and they were continually surprised at His unlimited, mighty power.

What surprises does God have for your family today? He knows the homeschooling day that lies ahead, and has already orchestrated divine encounters and blessings just for you. Your challenge is seeking His wisdom and then obediently leading your children into that divine plan. What an awesome adventure you'll experience as you learn to expectantly follow the Lord! "Call unto me, and I will answer thee, and shew thee great and mighty things, which thou knowest not" (Jeremiah 33:3).

Father, you are life itself and without You, there is no meaning or purpose. Thank You for the many surprise blessings You give each day that reveal what a loving God You are.
In Jesus' name, Amen.

Overwhelmed

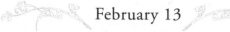

February 13

"My confusion is continually before me" (Psalm 44:15a).

Do you ever stand over your young children while they are sleeping and feel that overwhelming sense of love for them? Their sweet, innocent faces conjure up deep feelings to cherish and protect each moment together. However, when the morning light comes and you are in the middle of another homeschooling day, you may also feel another overwhelming sense. This time you are overwhelmed at your inability to be their teacher. Who can keep up with their energy level and all of their questions while they learn?

If anyone ever had the right to feel overwhelmed by his inabilities, it was Moses. Imagine being given the responsibility to lead millions of stubborn, foolish people hundreds of miles to a new country. Yet, Moses learned the secret to staying sane in the midst of this chaos— to continually pray for wisdom to make each decision. Because of Moses' obedience, God parted seas, provided food and water, and performed miracles time after time to deliver His cherished people from their difficulties. Moses' continuous trust in God stands as a shining example for those who feel overwhelmed when homeschooling.

Do you look ahead into the future and feel overwhelmed at the thought of homeschooling for the rest of this year, next year, or for the next twelve years? Take a step back and look again to your pillar of cloud by day and pillar of fire by night (Exodus 13:21-22). Let the presence of the Holy Spirit light your path and protect you from the unknown as you take this homeschooling journey. "When my spirit was overwhelmed within me, then thou knewest my path" (Psalm 142:3a).

Lord, I stand in awe of You and the task You have given me to do. Help me to look to You for every answer I'll need to homeschool my children the way You want. In the name of Jesus, Amen.

Looking for Love

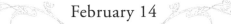

This wasn't the first time my teenage daughter had brought up the topic of boys. Like any normal, healthy young woman, she dreamed of the day when she would meet "Mr. Right!"

"Mom," she began. "How am I ever going to meet anyone if we're homeschooling?"

Remembering my own daydreams of meeting someone special who loved only me, I tried to be patient as I answered, "Don't you think God is big enough to bring the right person to you at the right time? If you're supposed to meet someone, homeschooling won't stop God's plan. In fact, it may even help you meet a young man who truly loves and cares for you."

Young girls are constantly bombarded by the media's hype to be loved and wanted, and they envision their prince arriving someday on his white horse to whisk them away to "happily ever after." They're encouraged to paint and decorate themselves all in the hope of attracting that special someone. However, God's Word has something different to say about attracting someone with only our outward appearance in 1 Peter 3: 3-4: "Whose adorning let it not be that outward adorning of plaiting the hair, and of wearing of gold, or of putting on of apparel; But let it be the hidden man of the heart, in that which is not corruptible, even the ornament of a meek and quiet spirit, which is in the sight of God of great price." God wants us to care about the way we look since we are the temple of the Holy Spirit (1 Corinthians 6:19), but the best way for a young girl to make herself truly beautiful is to develop inner character qualities that reflect the beauty of Christ.

As a Christian homeschooling mom, what message are you communicating to your teenage daughter about love? Has your daughter learned to care more about the clothes she wears and the way she does her hair to attract a young man than caring for the things of the Lord (Matthew 6:33)? Have you shown your daughter where to find true love? End her search and point her again to the One who already thinks she is beautiful: Jesus. His love is true, and He will meet every need she has for love.

Father, help me teach my daughter to listen to Your voice and to find the love she's looking for in You. Convict me of anything I'm doing that communicates the wrong message about the true meaning of love. In the name of Jesus, Amen.

Time Out for Mom

February 15

"I will cry unto God most high; unto God that performeth all things for me" (Psalm 57:2).

Did you wake up this morning wishing you could just have a few hours or an entire day to yourself before homeschooling? Imagine the possibilities with that amount of unscheduled time! You could read a book, soak in the tub, actually fold the clean clothes on the couch and put them away, polish your shoes, weed the flower bed, window shop, take a friend you haven't seen in months to lunch, or spend a full hour with the Lord in prayer for your loved ones.

Every homeschooling mother treasures moments for herself when they come, but the problem is they rarely come on their own. If we want to stay emotionally and spiritually healthy to enjoy homeschooling our children, then we must make taking time for these moments a number one priority. Without them, we shrivel up and die within, and homeschooling becomes one repetitious day after the next. The Lord Jesus Christ needed timeouts to get through His day (Luke 5:16). Often, He left the disciples and the crowds to be alone and find strength from His Heavenly Father. A wise homeschooling mom will say no to the false guilt she feels for "stealing" a few hours for herself and learn from Christ's example. Besides, your children will enjoy homeschooling much more, too, with a content, happy teacher.

Is today your day to rejuvenate and find yourself again? Don't wait for the help to fall from the sky. Humble yourself and ask for it. Call a fellow homeschooler and ask her if you can trade watching each other's children every other week. Maybe your parents or grandparents have promised to teach your children a new skill and today's the day to cash in on that promise. Maybe you could ask your husband to use half a vacation day and homeschool the children (Don't worry—they'll still learn, even if he doesn't teach them the same way as you!) God knows you can't homeschool all on your own. Trust Him for the right answer to help you take a "timeout" for Mom! "Blessed be the LORD, because he hath heard the voice of my supplications. The LORD is my strength and my shield; my heart trusted in him, and I am helped" (Psalm 28:6-7a).

Father, take my tired spirit and provide the moments I need to be filled with Your strength. Please send someone today who will help support me in homeschooling. In Jesus' name, Amen.

Running Ahead

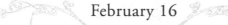

February 16

"I waited patiently for the LORD; and he inclined unto me, and heard my cry" (Psalm 40:1).

My daughter's riding lesson had gone well that day. I was proud to see her riding correctly at both a walk and trot, and I knew she was looking forward to cantering soon. As she circled the arena for the last time, I shouted, "It's time to quit for the day so we can finish the rest of our schoolwork. Bring her in and we'll brush her down together."

As my daughter turned her horse back toward the paddock, she replied, "OK, Mom, but watch this." Thinking she was ready to handle the extra speed, she cued her horse into a canter. I shook my head "no" at her, but her horse was already moving so fast she could barely hang on. As her horse took control and increased its speed to a full gallop, I knew my daughter was in trouble. Quickly, I ran in front of the gate to slow down her horse by waving it off. Instead, her horse applied its full brakes and stopped dead in its tracks. However, my daughter didn't stop. She flew through the air and hit the fence with her chest. As I picked her up, she couldn't breathe, and I thought her windpipe had been broken. Fortunately, only the air had been completely knocked out of her lungs, and she was OK after several anxious minutes. "I'm sorry, Mom," she said when she was finally able to speak. "I thought I could handle the speed."

The real lesson my daughter learned that day deals with the same pride that causes many of us Christians to fall. Not willing to wait on the Lord, we too run ahead and attempt to take the reins. We forget who is in control and make unsound financial decisions or foolish choices based on our emotions, not expecting to be hurt in the process! God may even tell us no, but we ignore Him and let our pride tell us we can handle it. We run into problems and pain we could have avoided if we had just waited on the Lord.

Are you struggling with waiting on God today? Is your anxious attitude becoming like the world's that says, "I can't take this anymore. I'll take care of it myself?" Be careful! Running ahead of God may find you lying on your back someday as you struggle to pray and ask Him for help. "The LORD is good unto them that wait for him, to the soul that seeketh him" (Lamentations 3:25).

Lord, teach me to "be still" and know You are God. Help me to trust in Your answers instead of my own and to wait for the best You have planned for me. In the name of Jesus, Amen.

Birth Order Blues

A great controversy exists in psychology regarding the relationship between a child's personality development and their birth order within the family. After homeschooling my children, one theory I do agree with is the first-born syndrome. My 18-month-old daughter initially displayed her first-born characteristics when I brought home her new baby brother. Setting him next to her in the recliner, I could see that look which told me she was not about to share her parents' attention with this new intruder. From that time on, she was always "top dog" in our homeschool family. In schoolwork or in play, she was always the leader and in control. Although her brother, standing six feet tall, finally outgrew her, the thought to take over never occurred to him. Her rank and authority as the first in the family dictated an unspoken respect and overpowered even his size.

Although the first born may not always be the leader in every family, many stories in the Old Testament do illustrate the importance of the first-born's position within the family. Stories such as Jacob stealing Esau's birthright, the sacrifice of the Passover lamb for the first born of every Hebrew family, and the principle of the double portion of inheritance found in Deuteronomy 21:17, clearly reveal the special blessings and responsibilities given only to the first born. Christ Himself, the Son of God, is called the first born in Colossians 1:15: "Who is the image of the invisible God, the firstborn of every creature."

How do you treat the first born in your homeschooling family? Like most parents, you probably strive to treat each of your children equally, but do you find yourself disciplining your oldest more strictly? Subconsciously, you may feel that you must make an example of your first child so the rest of the children turn out right. Perhaps it's time we gave credit to our first born children, instead of focusing on the responsibilities they bear in being the oldest like helping more with chores and bearing the brunt of our parenting and homeschooling mistakes. Although each child is precious within the family, why not take a moment today to acknowledge the special blessing of your oldest child who is the beginning of your strength (Deuteronomy 21:17)?

Lord, thank You for the blessing of each child You have given to our family. Give me wisdom to acknowledge my oldest for his place in the family and show me how to teach him to follow You. In Jesus' name, Amen.

To God Be the Glory

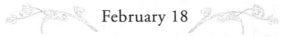

February 18

"So then neither is he that planteth any thing, neither he that watereth; but God that giveth the increase" (1 Corinthians 3:7).

One reason for the success of our homeschooling was the fact that my husband and I complimented each other in our personalities and abilities. He was the explorer and adventurer who loved to take the children on impromptu field trips to see and experience new things. I, on the other hand, loved staying home by the stuff with the comfort and familiarity of the day's homeschooling schedule. Our children loved both aspects of this team-teaching approach—the secure, repetitive learning environment of my teaching and the surprise learning experiences Dad created. Homeschooling was never a one-man show. We both shaped our children's lives, and we both felt the rewards of seeing their educational success.

The Apostle Paul realized, too, that he was not the only one who successfully preached the Gospel message to the early churches. Although he certainly could have taken credit for much of the work, Paul recognized the work of Apollos and other disciples. Rebuking the Corinthians for taking sides, Paul said, "Who then is Paul, and who is Apollos, but ministers by whom ye believed, even as the Lord gave to every man" (1 Corinthians 3:5)? Each did the work God gave him to do, "but God gave the increase" (I Corinthians 3:6b).

Are you ever tempted to think your family's homeschooling success lies solely on you? Just as the responsibilities are not yours alone, neither are the blessings. As a family, you come together and learn from each other and from God. The credit for whatever success comes from your homeschooling efforts really belongs to God. He is the One who gives the increase and the One who should receive the glory!

Lord, help me humbly remember I am only a vessel used by You to teach the hearts of my children. You are the reason we homeschool, and the reason for our success. I praise You and give You all the glory. Because of Jesus, Amen.

 Share your thoughts about this devotional at **aophomeschooling.com/049**

For the Long Haul

Faithfulness can be described as being true to one's word, promises, or vows. Faithfulness, then, according to homeschooling, is persevering in teaching your children even when you're criticized by a well-meaning person who is worried about your child's socialization. Faithfulness also means spending countless hours preparing for daily lessons, teaching a concept until your child "gets it," learning to live on less sleep and money, giving more of your time to your family than to yourself, and following the one who gives you the strength to do it all: Jesus.

God's Word provides many examples of people who remained faithful to the Lord in their work or call, but God Himself is the best definition of this character quality. As creator God, faithfulness is an attribute of His very nature. He demonstrates that attribute each day as He lovingly cares for us and meets our needs. The Bible describes God's faithfulness as infinite (Psalm 36:5) and everlasting (Psalm 119:90). Every morning, the Lord's faithfulness is new (Lamentations 3:23) and unfailing (Psalm 89:33). Even when we fail to be faithful to God, He remains faithful to us (2 Timothy 2:13).

Faithfulness is a character quality not easily found today. Homeschoolers, as well as Christians in general, approach too many commitments with the option of, "Well, if this doesn't work, I can always get out." When life gets tough, we are tempted to escape from our responsibilities, but faithfulness means not forgetting the Lord in the good times, and not blaming Him in the bad. No matter where we go, we will have difficulties of some kind. What about you? Are you in this homeschooling journey for the long haul?

Father, only You can give me the strength I need to remain faithful in homeschooling. Fill me again this day with Your power and help me remain true to You and the commitment of teaching my children. In Jesus' name, Amen.

One Step Behind

"That I may make it manifest, as I ought to speak" (Colossians 4:4).

My youngest son was in trouble, and I didn't know how to help him. Daily, he tried to communicate with his older brother and sisters in a group setting during our homeschooling, but he always seemed to be going in different directions in his conversation. Because he processed information more slowly, his contributions to the discussion seemed disjointed and off topic. Frustrated, he began to withdraw and keep his thoughts to himself.

I knew I had to do something to help him with his communication skills, but I didn't know what. As I prayed and asked the Lord for guidance, He gave me the perfect visual to help my young son. Using a basketball, I simultaneously passed the ball and said, "OK, we are going to practice a speaking skill today that will help you better communicate. As you pass this ball back to me, you have to say something back in response to what I've just said."

"OK, Mom, I think I get it," he said as he passed the ball back. For the next ten minutes we talked and communicated easily as he learned to pass the "conversational" ball back and forth. Next, I told him that if he was going to change direction and introduce a new topic, he needed to clearly indicate that before he passed the ball; otherwise, I would drop it. At that point, he understood the difficulty other people were having in following his conversation. After practicing this exercise several times, my son finally gained the understanding and confidence he needed to effectively communicate.

As Christians, we can also drop the ball when telling others about Christ. How many times have you been frustrated in not knowing how to explain salvation to others? Although the Holy Spirit does the leading, you also need to be prepared with memorized Scriptures and a clear presentation of the Gospel. If you're tired of seeing that confused look on people's faces as you attempt to tell them about Christ, ask a pastor for guidance or read a Christian book on witnessing. Acquiring the necessary skills to be an effective witness for the Lord just takes a little practice! "That therein I may speak boldly, as I ought to speak" (Ephesians 6:20b).

Lord, I know I've failed so many times in sharing who You are with others. Lead me to the help I need to clearly communicate the message of Your love and forgiveness. In Jesus' name, Amen.

Packing Light

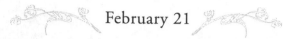

"So likewise, whosoever he be of you that forsaketh not all that he hath, he cannot be my disciple" (Luke 14:33).

"OK, I think we are just about ready to go," I said to my husband as I set the last backpack and the lunch cooler down by the front door.

Looking at all the items that needed to be loaded into the car, he shook his head and said, "Do we really need all this stuff just to go on a field trip for the day?"

"Yes," I replied. "The children need to work on their schoolwork in the car, and you never know what we might need once we get there. This way we will be prepared for whatever comes along."

Reluctantly, he carried each of the items to the car, even though he knew they would probably be carried back into the house without being used.

The early disciples of Christ were much better at traveling than I am. They packed nothing as they went out two-by-two preaching the good news of the kingdom of God. Leaving the comforts of home behind, Jesus specifically told them, "Carry neither purse, nor scrip, nor shoes" (Luke 10:4a). Freed from the weight of personal baggage, they came and went quickly as they preached and healed others in the name of Jesus. Their ministry was much more effective without the burden of lugging "stuff" around, and they discovered a total reliance on the Lord for everything they needed.

As homeschoolers, we can carry extra baggage that weighs down our homeschooling efforts. Instead of trusting the Lord for what we need to teach our children, we compare ourselves to other homeschooling families. We see what they are doing and complicate our lives by adding their activities and events to our day and rob ourselves of simple homeschooling joys. Although these activities may be good in themselves, we risk losing the spontaneity in teaching our children because we are locked into a full schedule. Why not leave the suitcases in the closet and rediscover your freedom in homeschooling?

Lord, forgive me for placing such a burden on myself and on my children with all our activities. Help us to prayerfully consider all that we do as we homeschool, so we don't lose the joy in the homeschooling journey. In Jesus' name, Amen.

The Power of Prayer

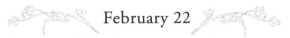

February 22

"But we will give ourselves continually to prayer" (Acts 6:4a).

Did you really pray for your children today? Although you may be the first to say that your prayers are important, how much time did you actually spend praying—one, five, ten minutes? Were your prayers more than "bless them" and "keep them from harm" prayers? As homeschooling parents, we forget that prayer is the most important thing we can give our children each day. More than our human love, more than academics, earnest prayer will help our children more than anything else in this life.

My routine and unimpressive prayer life was challenged when my children and I studied the life of David Brainerd, a missionary to the American Indians in the early 1700s. David Brainerd usually spent several hours a day in prayer and frequently devoted an entire day fasting before the Lord. As my children and I read his biography and diaries, the example of his selfless life challenged my personal lack of prayer for my own family and others. In one diary entry on June 14, 1742, Brainerd wrote about fasting and praying so fervently for an ingathering of souls that he was completely covered in sweat. Obviously, this man's passionate prayer life was something I needed to emulate in my life.

What about you? Are you willing to come before the Lord of the universe in the middle of the night or earlier in the morning to intercede on behalf of your children and your homeschooling? Don't wait for a crisis or tragedy to find yourself in the place where God wants you to be every day—on your knees in prayer. "Praying always with all prayer and supplication in the Spirit, and watching thereunto with all perseverance and supplication for all saints" (Ephesians 6:18).

Lord, forgive me for not taking prayer seriously. Teach me to pray and help me to earnestly intercede on my family's behalf. In the name of Jesus, Amen.

Share your thoughts about this devotional at **aophomeschooling.com/053**

The Hidden Meaning

February 23

"Give me understanding, and I shall keep thy law; yea, I shall observe it with my whole heart" (Psalm 119:34).

My young daughter was only six years old when she began to memorize poetry. She loved the rhythm and rhyme in poems and never had difficulty in understanding their meaning. Metaphors and similes were her favorite "pictures" and she digested the words like a chocolate delicacy. My son, however, was exactly the opposite. Poetry was one subject he avoided as much as possible, and he especially hated reciting any verse out loud. Because of their length, he was overwhelmed by poems like "Hiawatha," "The Lady of Shalott," and "Snow-bound," and felt they were written in some language he never quite understood. Frustrated, he would say, "Why don't they just come out and say it? Can't they just talk normally so you know what's going on?"

Compared to poetry, God's Word may seem even more difficult to understand. Filled with its own books of poetry, as well as history, prophecy, and other types of writing, we need help in discerning its truths. Because we have finite minds, we don't always understand how the Bible relates to us. However, 1 Corinthians 2:14 tells us, "But the natural man receiveth not the things of the Spirit of God: for they are foolishness unto him: neither can he know them, because they are spiritually discerned." Since the Bible is from God, to understand its truths, you must be born of the Spirit (John 3:6) and filled with the Spirit (Ephesians 5:18). Therefore, we must always ask the Holy Spirit to be our teacher when we read the Bible.

Do you avoid reading the Bible because it seems too difficult to understand? Preachers and seminary students are not the only ones who can know its truths. Guided by the Holy Spirit, you are perfectly capable of understanding Bible principles and sharing those principles with everyone you meet. Best of all, God will help you apply its principles to every homeschooling challenge you face, including teaching poetry to your son!

Heavenly Father,

My heart sings with praise to You
For the blessings in Your Word so true.
Teach my mind this day to know
Wisdom from You that will make me grow. Amen.

Stricter Judgment

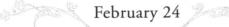

February 24

"My brethren, be not many masters, knowing that we shall receive the greater condemnation" (James 3:1).

Just when I started to feel good about my teaching abilities as a homeschooling parent, God's Word challenged me again. After reading Romans 12:7 and 1 Corinthians 12:29, I realized that teaching was more than a job. It was a spiritual gift that James 3:1 says is subject to God's stricter judgment. Knowing this, validating the accuracy of what I was teaching became of utmost importance. Someday the Lord would hold me accountable for what I had taught my children about Him, and I wanted to prove myself as an unashamed teacher when handling the Word of Truth (2 Timothy 3:16).

As I looked to the Bible for examples of great teachers, the life of Moses stood out. Moses had done so much to help the people of Israel know their God. I could never understand then, why he was not allowed to enter the Promised Land. Why couldn't God cut Moses a little slack when he failed to speak to the rock as God commanded (Numbers 20:8-13)? Meditating on this, I realized that Moses was held accountable with a stricter judgment because he was a teacher, as well as a leader. His disobedience affected not only him, but all the people who looked to him for wisdom and knowledge in following God.

As a homeschooling parent, do you realize the importance of correctly teaching your child the Word of God? Your child may receive Scriptural teaching in church and Sunday school, but his foundational understanding of God will come from your biblical knowledge. No one knows all the answers, but you must be prepared to teach God's Word. Teaching the Bible requires time, effort, and serious lesson preparation. "For unto whomsoever much is given, of him shall be much required: and to whom men have committed much, of him they will ask the more" (Luke 12:48b).

Lord, thank You for the gift of teaching You have placed on my life. Give me wisdom to understand Your Word so I can impart its truths to my children. Help me make the Bible the first subject to study in our homeschooling day. In the name of Jesus, Amen.

Share your thoughts about this devotional at **aophomeschooling.com/055**

The "Home" in Homeschooling

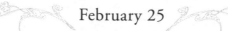

February 25

"For we brought nothing into this world, and it is certain we can carry nothing out" (1 Timothy 6:7).

Another typical day had started for our homeschool family, but as it progressed, we noticed the weather changing drastically. The northwest sky looked unusually dark and threatening, and by 2:45 p.m., we knew no ordinary storm was approaching. Hurrying outside, my son covered the garden and flower beds with old blankets, my daughter quickly herded the animals into the barn, and I drove the cars inside the garage and shut the door. As we finished and ran back to the house, the storm let loose with all its fury. Quickly, we ran down the basement steps to my daughter's bedroom and huddled in the corner of her closet. As we watched debris fly by my daughter's small bedroom window and heard the deafening noise of baseball-sized hailstones, we hung on to each other for dear life.

Normally, these storms only lasted a few minutes, but this one went on for almost an hour. When the worst was finally over, we opened my daughter's bedroom door and what we saw made us sick. Glass and hailstones were littered throughout the house and water damage from the rain was everywhere. The force of the wind had embedded pieces of glass into the woodwork, and every window on the north side of our home was completely shattered.

What we saw when we walked outside was even worse. Every tree and shrub on our seven acre farm had been completely defoliated. Our roof was missing half of its shingles plus, there were places where the hailstones had gone completely through the plywood sheeting. Holding each other, we thanked God we were safe, but we knew our home was going to be unfit for living and homeschooling for many days.

That awful day our house was damaged, we learned a new definition for the word "homeschooling." As we cried over the damage, we realized that homeschooling wasn't dependent on a house with four walls and a roof. As long as we had each other and our faith in God, we were still a family and could homeschool anywhere, any time.

Lord, each day I take my home for granted and forget that it too is a blessing from You. Thank You for all the comforts my home provides and help me to use it to minister to my family and others. In Jesus' name, Amen.

 Share your thoughts about this devotional at **aophomeschooling.com/056**

Following Directions

"Therefore we ought to give the more earnest heed to the things which we have heard, lest at any time we should let them slip" (Hebrews 2:1).

What was I going to do? My son had studied all week long for this test, and if I accepted the way he had answered the questions, he would receive a score of 100%. However, there was one huge problem troubling my grading—he hadn't followed the directions.
Although I had reminded him to read the instructions thoroughly, he had written his response in the blank instead of circling the correct answer. So what was more important, the fact that he knew the answers or that he had failed to follow the directions?

After praying, I decided to let my son be his own judge. Surprisingly, he was tougher on himself than I would have been and said, "Mom, it wouldn't be fair for me to get an A on this test." Together, we decided he should be penalized by receiving one grade lower for his failure to pay attention to the directions.

Not following the directions usually has a more severe consequence in real life. That fact was first discovered by Adam and Eve in the Garden of Eden. When dealing with a Holy God, you simply can't skip over important details in His directions like don't eat from "the tree of the knowledge of good and evil" (Genesis 2:17). Today, Christians continue to skip God's commandments when they feel it restricts their way of life. Thinking they're able to do God's will their own way, they fail God's test because they didn't follow His directions.

Is your life one that reflects God's divine instructions from His Word? Do you skip over those passages that test your character like "Wives, submit yourselves unto your own husbands, as unto the Lord" (Ephesians 5:22), and "Love not the world, neither the things that are in the world" (1 John 2:15a)? God doesn't give instructions to make your life more difficult. He gives directions because He loves you and wants you to succeed in living for Him. Will you choose today to follow His direction in those areas you've been avoiding and receive His grade of "well done, thou good and faithful servant" (Matthew 25:21)?

Lord, forgive me for thinking I can ignore Your directions and not suffer as a result. Cleanse my life today of those things that shame Your name, and help me to walk in a manner worthy of Your love. In the name of Jesus, Amen.

From the Beginning

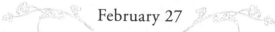

February 27

Every mother is a teacher. I was no exception. God used me to teach our baby how to eat with a spoon, say words, play catch, and dress himself. Daily, I taught our little one everything he needed to know to succeed at home. Then, the school years arrived, and I doubted if I would be able to teach him everything he needed to know to succeed in school. I wanted to homeschool, but people intimidated me about obeying God's call to homeschool. When they said, "You're not smart enough to teach your child," I was tempted to believe them. After all, I didn't have a four-year college degree. Disregarding their comments, however, I decided to relinquish my fears and trust Christ for the wisdom and knowledge necessary to continue teaching my child from home.

Fear is a successful tactic Satan uses to make Christians disregard God's call on their lives. It causes them to doubt God's love and provision, even though they started out strong in their faith. The inspiration given by Jesus to walk on the water is lost, and like Peter, believers find themselves sinking under the waves.

What about you? Are the waves of opposition getting high and beating fear into your decision to homeschool? If you've been walking on "water" and experiencing God's blessings in teaching your child at home, don't look down now. Keep your eyes on Jesus and cry out like Peter, "Lord, save me!" Jesus knows what you need, and you can trust Him to offer His loving hand to lift you to safety. After all, hasn't He been right there with you as you've taught your child from the very beginning? "And Jesus said unto him, No man, having put his hand to the plough, and looking back, is fit for the kingdom of God" (Luke 9:62).

Lord, forgive me for doubting You and listening to the lies of the evil one. Give me Your hand of strength and lift me above these fears as You calm my heart to faithfully homeschool. In Jesus' name, Amen.

The Truth of the Matter

OK, so here it is, straight up. If you homeschool your child, there is no 100% money-back guarantee he will turn out to be a straight "A" student with prestigious colleges knocking on his door when he's finished with high school. That scenario could happen, but it might not! As much as you want the best this world has to offer your child, God may have something different planned for his life. Your child could go to the mission field or work at an "ordinary" job living a faithful, God-honoring life in his home and community.

I had over-exaggerated expectations for my children's futures until my husband rebuked me one day while homeschooling. "Why are you pushing so hard?" he asked. "What if the girls just want to be stay-at-home moms like you? Is that so bad?" As I began to think about my husband's question, I realized that my dreams for my children and God's dreams for them were two different things. I wanted them to be intelligent and successful, but God's main concern was that they be obedient and Christ-like. My foolish pride had taken me off God's straight and narrow homeschooling path for my children's futures.

How do you envision your child's life at the end of your homeschooling days? Are you teaching him to follow God's will for his future or yours? A good way to double-check is to ask yourself this question: "Is my child more concerned about pleasing me and trying to live up to my expectations or to God's?" Be careful that your dreams for your child are not leading him off God's path for his life. "Trust in the LORD with all thine heart; and lean not unto thine own understanding. In all thy ways acknowledge him, and he shall direct thy paths" (Proverbs 3:5-6).

Lord, help me to see my child's future as You do and give me wisdom to lead him in the direction You seek. In the name of Jesus, Amen.

Smooth as Honey

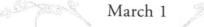

March 1

"Deliver the poor and needy: rid them out of the hand of the wicked" (Psalm 82:4).

I heard voices quietly talking in my daughters' bedroom as I put the laundry away in the hall closet. My oldest daughter was coercing her younger sister into trading something with her. Because I couldn't see what was going on, I assumed they were trading old stuffed animals or some other inexpensive toy. As I walked past the door to their room, however, I saw my younger daughter replacing her piggy bank on the shelf. Questioning the transaction, I went on with my work and waited until my older daughter left the room. When my younger daughter was alone, I quietly asked, "What did you just trade with your sister?"

"Oh, she just traded a whole dollar for my new doll!" she replied excitedly in her little girl voice.

"What?" I cried. "Your new doll was worth more than $1.00, and your sister knows that!" Disgusted, I called my older daughter back into the bedroom. Our homeschooling was going to have to wait. Apparently, a discussion time on deceitfulness was of first importance today.

Taking advantage of the young, old, innocent, or the less fortunate is detestable in God's sight. Joseph's brothers discovered that fact after their aged father suffered emotionally from their lie. For years, they had let Jacob believe Joseph had been eaten by a wild animal (Genesis 37:33). God eventually exposed their sin and deception in selling Joseph into slavery and brought a similar mental anguish into their lives as they stood before an angry official in Egypt. Not knowing the official was their brother, they feared for their lives as Joseph dealt severely with them after they had come to Egypt to buy grain.

What about you? Do you look for ways to protect the needy from being taken advantage of by others? Have you taught your children to do the same? Greed, jealously, and lust are powerful forces that cause others to use people for their own gain. God needs you to stand in the gap when you see little ones or the elderly being mistreated. Will you be their advocate today? "Open thy mouth for the dumb in the cause of all such as are appointed to destruction. Open thy mouth, judge righteously, and plead the cause of the poor and needy" (Proverbs 31:8-9).

Lord, thank You for the loving protection You provide our family each day. Use us to shield and shelter those who are unable to defend themselves from being mistreated by others. In Jesus' name, Amen.

 Share your thoughts about this devotional at **aophomeschooling.com/060**

Flexible Forgiveness

March 2

"I, even I, am he that blotteth out thy transgressions for mine own sake, and will not remember thy sins" (Isaiah 43:25).

I was always thankful as a homeschooling parent that God designed children to be flexible. Every day I saw my children survive falls and painful bruises that would have made me ache for days. Their ability to bounce back physically from rough and tumble wrestling matches and foolish dare-devil antics was amazing. Even more amazing, however, was the way my children bounced back from emotional hurts. When the stress of the homeschooling day "got to me," I repeatedly found myself seeking their forgiveness for my unloving words and impatient actions. Each time my children would quickly say, "That's OK, I understand," and everything would be forgotten. Humbled by their gracious words, I knew my forgiveness wouldn't have come so easily if someone had treated me the same way.

As wonderful as a child's forgiveness may be, the forgiveness we receive from our heavenly Father is far greater. The sacrificial death of Jesus on the cross makes forgiveness of sin possible, but only those who receive Christ's forgiveness have the privilege of being called God's children (John 1:12). Each day God's immeasurable grace is poured out to us, and we receive the blessing of knowing our sins are remembered no more.

Are you dealing with an emotional hurt that has been causing you severe pain? Is your heart flexible enough to bounce back and forgive the person who has wronged you? If not, learn the lesson of flexible forgiveness from your children and extend the same hand of grace that was given to you. "And be ye kind one to another, tenderhearted, forgiving one another, even as God for Christ's sake hath forgiven you" (Ephesians 4:32).

Father, thank You for Your forgiveness that also forgets my sin. Please help me give that same love and forgiveness to those who have wronged me. In the name of Jesus, Amen.

 Share your thoughts about this devotional at **aophomeschooling.com/061**

Nothing Sacred

March 3

The wear and tear on our house was one thing I never considered when we first began to homeschool. Because we lived at home 24 hours a day, everything from the plumbing to the carpet took an extra beating. My husband regularly came home from work and found a frustrated wife with a request to fix another worn out or broken "whatever" in our house. After several years of homeschooling, we both came to the realization that our dream for a "showcase" house was simply not going to happen.

As Christians, we forget that our possessions are given to us by God. He makes us stewards of houses, cars, and "things" to accomplish His will, not just to look good. The rich, young ruler couldn't grasp that fact and loved his possessions too much to follow Christ. In 1 Timothy 6:18, the Apostle Paul exhorts those who are rich in this world to be generous, ready to share, and rich in good works. Like the story of the widow and her two small coins (Luke 21:1-4), even the poor have something they can sacrifice to further the kingdom of God.

Do you have possessions and belongings that are sacred to you—things you would never consider giving up for the cause of Christ? Ironically, the things we hold on to so tightly are the very things that begin to possess and hang on to us. You may think you've earned them or have a right to them, but your possessions really belong to God. Will you use them today for His glory instead of your own? "Sell that ye have, and give alms; provide yourselves bags which wax not old, a treasure in the heavens that faileth not, where no thief approacheth, neither moth corrupteth" (Luke 12:33).

Lord, my very life is Yours. Everything I am and everything I have belongs to You. Use me and what You've given me to be a blessing to others. In the name of Jesus, Amen.

Ask and You Will Receive

March 4

What would you ask for as a homeschooling parent if you could have anything you wanted? Most homeschoolers might ask for more curriculum, a maid, or even unlimited hours to sleep. As wonderful as receiving each of these requests might be, the great responsibility we have in teaching our children should move us to ask for something of far greater value—wisdom. After all, who of us can ever teach and lead our children with only our limited understanding?

King Solomon in the Old Testament realized his limitations in leading the nation of Israel, too. When God visited Solomon in a dream in Gibeon, He told him to "Ask what I shall give thee" (1 Kings 3:5). Solomon could have asked for long life, for his enemies to be destroyed, or for riches untold, but he didn't. Instead, Solomon asked for an understanding heart and discernment to judge the people (vs. 9). God was so pleased with this request that he not only gave Solomon the wisdom he asked for, but also gave Solomon what he could have asked for as well.

Do you ever wake up in the morning and wonder what you should teach your children? Homeschooling requires time and effort in preparation, but it also takes a supernatural wisdom that only comes from God. He knows the lessons that are most important for your children to learn and wants to lead you as you teach them. God gives a wonderful promise in James 1:5 for those who lack wisdom in homeschooling: "If any of you lack wisdom, let him ask of God, that giveth to all men liberally, and upbraideth not; and it shall be given him." Why not claim His promise today? Ask, and you will receive more wisdom and blessings than you can imagine.

Lord, thank You for the privilege of teaching my children. I humbly come before You and acknowledge that I need Your wisdom. Fill me with Your understanding and show me the best way to homeschool my children. In Jesus' name, Amen.

 Share your thoughts about this devotional at aophomeschooling.com/063

Dinner Disciplines

March 5

The life of a homeschooling parent requires discipline. Unfortunately, two areas that were totally undisciplined in my life were cleaning and organizing my home. At the end of each homeschooling week, my house was the perfect reflection of that lack of discipline.

There seemed to be no solution to my problem until God gave me a new motivation to care for my home. Because we desired more social opportunities for our children, we began a Sunday noon ritual of inviting guests for pot roast lunch. Our children took turns inviting their friends over, and we all benefited from the time together. Our children enjoyed playing with their friends, we developed friendships with their friends' parents, and my house was cleaned and organized in the process. When it was time for deeper cleaning, God disciplined me further by using extended stays of visiting family members to motivate me to spring clean.

Living a godly life as a Christian also requires discipline. We all struggle with areas that cause us to stumble in our walk with God. However, God knows the discipline we need to overcome these temptations and find the victory that will glorify Him. Satan would have us continue living in the dirt and clutter of our fleshly lusts, but God commands us to be controlled by the Holy Spirit (Galatians 5:16). Like cleaning and organizing, no discipline seems to be pleasant, but God's Word does promise that discipline will yield the fruit of righteousness after we have been trained by it (Hebrews 12:11).

How disciplined are you? How you teach is closely related to how disciplined you are in following God. Homeschooling will force you to make changes in your spiritual life as you depend on God for wisdom and strength. Perhaps, that is one reason why God called you to homeschool in the first place.

Lord, thank You for the blessing of homeschooling my children and the discipline it brings to my life. Fill me with the Holy Spirit and teach me to stay close to You as we walk together on this homeschooling journey. In the name of Jesus', Amen.

What Are You Waiting For?

March 6

My children were looking forward to their grandparents' visit one weekend. They had worked hard homeschooling all week, and by Friday noon, they had completed all of their assignments. As I started to prepare supper for my parents' arrival, I decided to make good use of time and straighten up the living room, too. To my surprise, I found my youngest daughter sitting on the couch looking out the window.

"What are you doing?" I asked.

"I'm waiting for Grandpa and Grandma," she replied.

"Oh honey, they're not going to be here for another five or six hours," I said.

"I know Mom, but can I just sit here and wait?" she asked.

Returning to the kitchen to finish my preparations for supper, I stole a glance from time to time to see how my daughter was doing. Most six year olds have trouble sitting still five minutes let alone five hours, but each time I looked, I was amazed as my daughter sat staring out the window awaiting her grandparents' arrival.

Waiting is not something any of us do well in today's world. In our fast-paced lives, we expect immediate responses to our daily needs. Fast food, fast lanes, and fast everything make us a nation of impatient people. Unfortunately, we carry that same philosophy over to our spiritual lives, and we want fast answers from God, too. However, God is in control, and He has His own timetable. As agonizing as it may seem, waiting is actually beneficial to us spiritually because it forces us to focus on God instead of our request.

Have you been waiting for a long time for God to answer one of your prayers? Maybe you have a family member who doesn't know Christ as Savior or you have a financial burden or physical illness that seems overwhelming. The Lord may want you to focus your attention completely on Him, so He can reveal His power to you at just the right time. Will you let Christ redirect your thoughts so He becomes the center of your focus while you wait? "My soul waiteth for the Lord more than they that watch for the morning: I say, more than they that watch for the morning" (Psalms130:6).

Lord, forgive my impatient heart that fails to wait on You for the answers to my problems. Let my anxious prayers turn into praise as I remember what a mighty God You are and what You can do. In Jesus' name, Amen.

 Share your thoughts about this devotional at **aophomeschooling.com/065**

Homeschool Messes

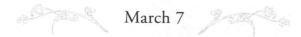

March 7

"Who can say, I have made my heart clean, I am pure from my sin" (Proverbs 20:9)?

Do you ever feel like you pick up messes all day? As a homeschooling parent, I quickly learned not to wait until the end of the day to clean the house. Walking through each room throughout the day, I continually organized and put a few things away as my children were studying. If I didn't, I knew I wouldn't have enough energy left to tackle the mountains of laundry, dishes, and clutter before bed.

Keeping our lives clean from the messes of sin also takes a continual effort. In the Old Testament, only the clean were allowed in the temple to worship before the Lord. Today, we must come before the Lord daily and allow Him to cleanse us of all unrighteousness. (1 John 1:9) Keeping short accounts with God keeps the messes of sin from building into mountains and destroying our relationship with God.

Is your spiritual life full of clutter and mess? Are there issues that God has prompted you to clean, like seeking forgiveness from a family member or disciplining yourself to live a healthier lifestyle? Don't wait until tomorrow, next week, or next year to start obeying the Lord. Start today and rediscover the joy, power, and strength that come from living a clean life before the Lord. "But if we walk in the light, as he is in the light, we have fellowship one with another, and the blood of Jesus Christ his Son cleanseth us from all sin" (1 John 1:7).

Father, forgive me for letting the messes build up in our relationship. Please speak to me again and show me those areas in my life that need to be cleaned by Your forgiving love. In Jesus' name, Amen.

Totally Discouraged

March 8

"And the LORD, he it is that doth go before thee; he will be with thee, he will not fail thee, neither forsake thee: fear not, neither be dismayed" (Deuteronomy 31:8).

Homeschooling can bring out the worst and best in you. As I sat on the kitchen floor crying, I knew that today was one of the worst. I had put the children to bed early and my husband was working late. I was hoping a good cry would relieve my stress from the week of teaching, responsibilities, and housework. My inabilities to be supermom seemed immensely larger than the homeschooling blessings, and I felt like I was constantly disappointing someone—my husband, my children, my extended family, or myself. Failure waved its ugly banner over me, and I was tempted to cut my losses and give up. God seemed far away, and I felt alone.

Just when my pity party peaked, I felt a pair of little hands touching my face. Looking up, I saw my youngest daughter looking at me with deep blue eyes and concern on her face. "Mommy," she said, "Don't cry. I love you." In that moment, I sensed the Lord encouraging me through my little daughter's love. Homeschooling was for her and my other children. God would strengthen me to teach them.

Is today one of your bad homeschooling days? Have the failures seemed greater than the successes? Don't lose sight of the reason for homeschooling. God has called you to teach your children, and He has promised, "I will never leave thee, nor forsake thee" (Hebrews 13:5b).

Lord, help me to remember You are everything I need. Show me again how to claim Your strength to homeschool and to sense Your encouragement every day. In the name of Jesus, Amen.

 Share your thoughts about this devotional at aophomeschooling.com/067

Walking It Out

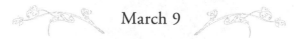

March 9

"Cause me to hear thy lovingkindness in the morning; for in thee do I trust: cause me to know the way wherein I should walk; for I lift up my soul unto thee" (Psalm 143:8).

Walking saved my life as a homeschooling parent. Each morning, before my spouse left for work, I spent one hour rejuvenating with prayer and exercise. As I walked, I listened to inspiring music and God spoke to my heart with encouragement for the day. Negativity and discouragement from yesterday's problems were pounded out with each footstep, and the fresh air and beauty of God's sunrise were taken in with each stride to uplift my weary spirit. However, whenever I allowed laziness or other distractions to rob this morning routine, my attitude and our homeschooling day suffered greatly. My daily walk with God became my refuge and the most important time of the day.

The Bible has many verses that illustrate the spiritual importance of how we are to walk with God. We are to walk in truth (Psalm 86:11), in newness of life (Romans 6:4), by faith (2 Corinthians 5:7), in the Spirit (Galatians 5:16), in the light (Psalm 89:15), according to His commandments (2 John 1:6), and as children of light (Ephesians 5:8). As we walk with God, He provides the strength and guidance we need to face the enormous task of homeschooling our children.

When was the last time you went for a walk? Let the physical discipline of exercising your body lead you to the spiritual discipline of exercising your soul. Then you will be able to say with the Psalmist, "I will walk within my house with a perfect heart" (Psalms 101:2c).

Lord, I need You so much. Thank You for being there each day to walk with me and guide me through all the homeschooling problems. Give me the wisdom and strength I need again this day. In Jesus' name, Amen.

Shaping the World

March 10

Did you wake up this morning thinking, "Wow, what I do during our homeschooling today could shape the world?" Probably not, but that doesn't negate the fact that every homeschooling decision you make influences your child. Homeschooling parents can easily forget the important, long-term effect of their teaching and the potential it has to shape the world. Like a hybrid seed, God will someday use the academics you teach, the beliefs you instill, and the character you nurture in your child to change the world. Hundreds, if not thousands, of lives will feel the impact of your child's godly actions due to your faithfulness in homeschooling. Yes, what you do today as a homeschooling parent has a far-reaching effect and really does make a difference now and for eternity!

As Christians, God commands us to go out into the world and be salt and light. Satan would rob us of our small acts of Christ-like love to others by convincing us they don't really matter. After all, what difference does it make to call your elderly neighbor to tell them you're thinking of them or to bring freshly baked cookies to the working mother who lives next door? Each act really does illuminate the world with God's love, now and for eternity.

Do you realize how much your Christian charity changes the world? Your faithful, small acts of love bring help, hope, and encouragement to many. If you doubt the importance of your loving acts, imagine for a moment what the world would look like if all the Christians were gone. "Now he that ministereth seed to the sower both minister bread for your food, and multiply your seed sown, and increase the fruits of your righteousness" (2 Corinthians 9:10).

Father, thank You for placing me in this world to glorify You. Give me wisdom to homeschool my children so they will also bear much fruit for You and bring Your light to a dark world. In the name of Jesus, Amen.

Lost

March 11

"For this my son was dead, and is alive again; he was lost, and is found" (Luke 15:24a).

The day had started expectantly for our family as we left on a field trip to Denver, Colorado. My children were looking forward to visiting the planetarium and seeing artifacts and rocks on display at the museum of natural history. Wonderfully, the entire day had lived up to our hopeful expectations, and only one stop remained before beginning our long drive back home. With a time limit of one hour or less, my husband dropped us off at the Christian bookstore.

My three oldest children left for the music department to listen to CDs, while my four-year-old son and I proceeded to shop for gifts for upcoming birthdays. Normally, I'm very attentive to my children's whereabouts while shopping, but after reading the verses in several cards, I looked down and saw that my son was gone. Thinking he had rejoined his older siblings, I began to look around for the four of them, but neither they nor my young son were in sight. After scanning the store, I located my older children, but our perfect day came to a terrible end as I realized what every mother fears most—my son was lost!

Circumstances in life can change so rapidly. One day we think we are safe and secure with money in the bank and food on the table, and the next day brings devastating problems that bring us to our knees. Like Job in the Old Testament, problems can hit us like a tsunami and wipe out all our joys in a single moment. Fortunately, my tidal wave of terror ceased that day. After searching with my three oldest children for over an hour, we finally found my youngest son asleep in the back seat of our car with his father fast asleep in the front.

Are you filled with uncertainty while you homeschool? Do you feel on top of the world one day and down in the valley the next? If you are just beginning to homeschool, it may seem like a rollercoaster ride for several months, or even a few years. Hang on! God will help level out your teaching days with His loving care and guidance, and He will help you find your way. "O LORD God of hosts, who is a strong LORD like unto thee? or to thy faithfulness round about thee? Thou rulest the raging of the sea: when the waves thereof arise, thou stillest them" (Psalm 89:8-9).

Lord, here I go again. I feel so lost in our homeschooling. Teach me to trust You for the wisdom I need to be the best teacher I can be for my children. In the name of Jesus, Amen.

 Share your thoughts about this devotional at **aophomeschooling.com/070**

Unfair Labels

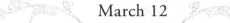

March 12

What labels have been placed on your children because they homeschool? During our years of homeschooling, my children faced innuendos that ranged from mental retardation to religious fanatic. Today, the media still portrays homeschoolers as naive, unfashionably-dressed nerds. Even though studies prove the contrary, public educators also insist that homeschoolers are deprived of proper socialization. Why does the phrase "homeschooling" bring out such nastiness in people?

Unfair labels are nothing new. When Christ lived on earth, He suffered form being misunderstood by the multitudes, Jewish leaders, and even His friends and family. Unfair labels like trouble maker, demon-possessed, and foolish fanatic were placed on Him as He told the world about the Kingdom of God and His love. Although the label placed above Christ's head on the cross was intended to mock Him, it was the one label the world got right when it read, "THIS IS THE KING OF THE JEWS" (Luke 23:38b).

So how do you live in a negative, anti-homeschooling world and not become negative yourself? As Christian homeschoolers, we seem to receive a double whammy from the world—unfair labels for our faith and unfair labels for our homeschooling. As hurtful as these labels can be, Christ can help us forgive and move beyond the painful remarks when they come. Jesus' example of love on the cross shows us the way when He said, "Father, forgive them; for they know not what they do" (Luke 23:24).

Lord, strengthen me to stand against the world's opinion of homeschoolers. Teach me to love as You loved when You died on the cross. In Jesus' name, Amen.

The Right Answer

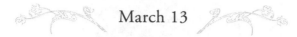

March 13

"He that answereth a matter before he heareth it, it is folly and shame unto him" (Proverbs 18:13).

I learned an important homeschooling secret after many years of teaching—it's more important to ask the right questions than it is to give the right answers. Too many times I piled tons of information on my children that was neither of interest or necessary. My "be prepared" teaching philosophy, which attempted to include every detail on a subject, was burning out my children's love of learning. Clearly, one carefully worded question sparked my children's interest far more than providing all the answers.

Needless to say, this same flaw also caused difficulty for me when witnessing to others. Because the Bible is the answer to people's problems, I attempted to provide all the facts and answers to show them their need for Christ. As I began down the "Romans Road" or shared the "Gospel Hand," I quickly spat out verses thinking I would change their lives. However, the Holy Spirit showed me that it is He who does the convicting in a person's heart. I needed to be sensitive to His leading when witnessing to others. Asking a person carefully worded questions is much more effective in leading someone to the Lord than providing all the right answers.

Do you have a tendency to give more information than necessary when you witness to others? Instead of trying to convince people of their need for Christ with your biblical answers, why not listen to the Holy Spirit instead? He is the one who has the perfect question to ask that will spark someone's interest in our loving Lord.

Jesus, lead me as I tell others about Your saving love. You have the right answers to everyone's problems, including mine. Help me to ask the kinds of questions that will spark others' interest in You. In Your name, Amen.

Lessons in the Garden

March 14

Do you realize how many homeschooling lessons can be learned from gardening? From biology to Bible, gardening provided our family more opportunities to learn truths than any other activity. Such was the case the year my son prepared to win the grand champion purple ribbon at the county fair with his home-grown vegetables.

Earlier that spring, my son and I had carefully planned and planted our garden. Throughout the growing season, his thriving tomatoes were the best of all his vegetables. Deciding to focus his attention on their care, he applied exact amounts of fertilizer and built cages to protect the vines from the wind. As the tomatoes began to form, we knew the timing for harvesting them would perfectly match the date of the fair. Excited, he could already see the purple ribbon hanging on his bedroom wall.

Two weeks before the fair, our garden received a mysterious nighttime visitor. Some four-legged fiend ransacked my son's tomatoes and broke off most of the vines. In hopes that we could save my son's tomatoes, we attempted to repair the remaining damaged vines. However, only a few days passed before we noticed the life-giving nutrients were not reaching the tomatoes. My son was devastated when he realized his dreams for that year's prize had been thwarted. He had learned the hard lesson of John 15:5, "I am the vine, ye are the branches: He that abideth in me, and I in him, the same bringeth forth much fruit: for without me ye can do nothing."

Have you considered planting a garden this year with your homeschoolers? Whether you grow one for fun or for feeding your family, the blessings God will give and the lessons God will teach will make all the work worth the effort. After all, gardens have been the best place to learn God's lessons since He first placed man in one when He created the world! "For as the earth bringeth forth her bud, and as the garden causeth the things that are sown in it to spring forth; so the Lord GOD will cause righteousness and praise to spring forth before all the nations" (Isaiah 61:11).

Lord, what an awesome God You are and how dependent we are on You for everything! Teach me the lessons from Your creation and Your Word that will make me more like You. In Jesus' name, Amen.

 Share your thoughts about this devotional at **aophomeschooling.com/073**

By Hand

March 15

"Examine me, O LORD, and prove me; try my reins and my heart" (Psalm 26:2).

When my four children reached long division in their math curriculum, several weeks of resistance and conflict resulted during our homeschooling days. The painstaking process seemed unending and laborious to my high-tech children. "Mom, why do we have to do this by hand?" they cried. "Why can't we just figure this out on the calculator?" Taking the time and effort to "show their work" on every quiz and test in division was even more agonizing. To them, the quick and easy method of using the calculator's brain instead of their own seemed the best answer to solving math computations.

Taking the easy way out is common for today's Christians. Most saved people consider the testing of their faith something to be avoided or eliminated. Instead of walking through life's trials with God, many bypass the challenge and supersede God's will with manmade answers. However, James 1:3-4 gives us God's perspective for trials: "Knowing this, that the trying of your faith worketh patience. But let patience have her perfect work, that ye may be perfect and entire, wanting nothing."

Is homeschooling stretching you to the limits and trying your patience? God is working in your life and your children's lives. He knows how demanding each day can be and wants you to trust Him "by hand." Place your hand in His today. Waiting on God for answers is never easy, but the spiritual lesson of endurance is only learned by going through the process. Will you let Him teach you to "let patience have her perfect work, that ye may be perfect and entire, wanting nothing" (James 1:4)?

Lord, how quick I am to give up when homeschooling gets hard. Teach me endurance and to be patient with myself and my children as we learn academic and spiritual lessons together. In Jesus' name. Amen.

Pity Parties

March 16

Self-pity is a common temptation faced by many homeschooling parents. After all, we have such a heavy burden to bear, right? If the daily duties of homeschooling are not enough, we also face ridicule and a lack of appreciation for the hard work of teaching our children. Our martyr syndrome assumes we're the only ones who really care about our children's education. Foolishly we say, "No one else sacrifices or suffers for what they believe like we do." Sadly, we actually believe these lies from Satan and sink into homeschooling despair because of them.

God doesn't want us to feel sorry for ourselves, and He teaches us that lesson with the stories of two pouting prophets in the Bible. Consider Elijah and the great demonstration of God's power at Mount Carmel. When Elijah prayed, the Lord proved Himself mighty to the prophets of Baal (1 Kings 18:20-39). Forgetting what God had just done, Elijah ran for his life to Mount Horeb to hide out in a cave because the evil Queen Jezebel threatened him. When God asked why he was there, Elijah claimed, "And I, even I only, am left; and they seek my life, to take it away" (1 Kings 19:14b). Or what about Jonah who preached to the city of Nineveh and watched as the entire population repented of their sins? Jonah became so angry at God for sparing them he said, "It is better for me to die than to live" (Jonah 4:3b). Both these prophets went from tremendous highs to the depths of despair as they felt sorry for themselves and forgot God's deliverance.

What about you? Are you having a one-person pity party to celebrate your homeschooling difficulties? Why be like a foolish prophet who's forgotten the mighty miracle of God's blessing? Rejoice instead in the precious opportunity God has given you to teach your children. Enjoy the wonderful gift of having fun together as a family. After experiencing the joys of homeschooling, why not throw a different party tonight and celebrate all that God has done for you?

Lord, I praise You for the love You show me each day. I am so thankful to be my children's teacher and rejoice in the blessings of homeschooling. I recommit my heart and thoughts to You today. In Jesus' name, Amen.

 Share your thoughts about this devotional at aophomeschooling.com/075

School Spirit

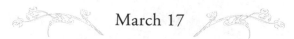

March 17

We never had a mascot for our homeschool and my children never knew the excitement of school pep rallies. However, what we lacked in school spirit for team sports was made up by the Holy Spirit in Christian ministry. As we reached out to others, the presence and power of the Lord filled us to accomplish His will. Being used by the Lord and seeing His mighty power displayed was much more exciting than any football, baseball, or basketball game.

When Jesus gathered His team of twelve players, He taught them about Himself and His heavenly Father. However, Christ also knew His disciples were going to need more. To remain His faithful witnesses on earth after His return to heaven, He knew they were going to need a new team spirit. Before He ascended, He strictly commanded them to wait in Jerusalem until the Holy Spirit came upon them (Acts 1:4). At Pentecost, the disciples were baptized and empowered with the Holy Spirit to begin evangelizing the world.

Does your homeschooling seem to be missing something? Do you commit each day to the Lord and ask the Holy Spirit to control your schedule and activities? God knows you need more than just your own wisdom and determined spirit to be a homeschooling winner. Successful homeschooling requires a school spirit that comes from above. Only the Holy Spirit's power can help you find the victory for every homeschooling challenge. "But ye shall receive power, after that the Holy Ghost is come upon you" (Acts 1:8a).

Father, I would be so lost homeschooling without Your power and constant care. Fill me today with the Holy Spirit and use me to accomplish Your will. In the blessed name of Jesus, Amen.

Lessons from a Goose

March 18

"A man's heart deviseth his way: but the LORD directeth his steps" (Proverbs 16:9).

I was on my daily walk and trying to organize my thoughts for a long homeschooling day. I stopped to observe the sunrise in the spring sky, and noticed a large flock of geese heading north. Captivated by the sight, I laid down on the ground to watch their movements. Watching them fly in their traditional V shape, I observed the lead goose as he dropped back to find a new spot in the formation. The goose that had been directly behind him assumed the lead, and the entire group continued flying. Twice more, I saw the same process take place before the flock was completely out of sight.

Reflecting on what I had just seen, I knew God had spoken to my heart with a new homeschooling philosophy. Since I didn't have the energy or the wisdom, God's divine plans for my children's education included others besides me. Sometimes God moved my husband into the lead position to teach art, physical education, or life skills in mechanics and carpentry. Other times, God provided homeschooling friends to share their expertise in a particular subject during a co-op homeschool group lesson. God even allowed me to drop back and catch my breath with field trips supervised by Grandpa and Grandma and high school tutors for biology and chemistry labs. Although I was ultimately in charge of my children's education, I found great relief in God's occasional provision of a new lead goose.

Have you made the mistake of believing you're in this homeschooling decision all by yourself? Blazing the homeschool trail is difficult, especially when you're teaching more than one child. God knows the rest you will need and has already planned for others to come along and help. Just pray and ask God to show you which goose to follow.

Lord, thank You for the joy of homeschooling. Forgive me for thinking I'm the only one capable of teaching my children. Lead me to those people You have prepared to help train them and teach me to relax and enjoy the time of rest. In Jesus' name. Amen.

 Share your thoughts about this devotional at **aophomeschooling.com/077**

Corporate Worship

March 19

"And they continued stedfastly in the apostles' doctrine and fellowship" (Acts 2:42a).

For several months I had noticed my teenage son's reluctance to go to church. Thinking we would leave him behind, he was always the last one to wake up on Sunday morning and painstakingly took his time in getting ready. After he had caused the entire family to be late for church several Sundays in a row, I knew I needed to speak with him about his actions. The next day during our homeschool devotions, we discussed the topic of worship and my son blurted out, "I don't need to go to church to worship God. I can worship Him at home just as well as at church!"

"Yes, that's true," I responded. "We can worship God anywhere at anytime, but the Bible tells us to worship together as a group of believers to encourage each other."

"Well, I just don't get anything out of it anymore," he replied roughly.

After further discussion, his real reluctance in attending church was revealed. After a long week of homeschooling and work, he simply didn't want to get up early on Sunday morning, too.

If left to ourselves, most of us would sleep in or play instead of remembering to keep the Sabbath Day holy (Exodus 20:8). Unfortunately, the world does exactly that and sees Sunday as a day of relaxation rather than a day set apart to worship God. People go to the beach, the park, or the mountains to "get away from it all" and completely forget about worshipping or serving God.

What about your homeschooling family? Are you disciplined in church attendance? Not only do you have opportunities to encourage and be encouraged by other believers, you also hear the Word preached and worship God as you sing and give gifts corporately. Yes, you could worship the Lord just as easily at home, but is that really where He wants you to be on Sunday morning? "And let us consider one another to provoke unto love and to good works: Not forsaking the assembling of ourselves together, as the manner of some is; but exhorting one another: and so much the more, as ye see the day approaching" (Hebrews 10:24-25).

Lord, thank You for giving me a separate day each week just to worship You. Help me to faithfully be in Your house on Sunday and convict me to set a good example for my children. In the name of Jesus, Amen.

Share your thoughts about this devotional at aophomeschooling.com/078

Blinding Problems

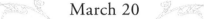

March 20

"When my spirit was overwhelmed within me, then thou knewest my path" (Psalm 142:3a).

We should have never started out on our three-hour trip home after attending my oldest daughter's college graduation. The further we traveled, the lower the visibility became from the blinding snow. Eventually, we couldn't see the road at all. Since turning back was just as far as traveling to the next town, we continued down the road. The close homeschooling relationship between my husband and son was soon to be tested. Sticking his head out the passenger window to see the white line on the road's edge, my son started giving directions to my husband and said, "Move a little left," or "Move a little right." For the next hour, my husband put his total faith in my son's navigation and literally drove blind in the raging blizzard.

Trusting the Lord when you can't see the way through life's difficulties is even a greater challenge than a blinding snow storm. Emotional pain and hardships blind you to God's love and rob you of your faith. You are tempted to believe that God has left you and you doubt His loving care. Instead of trusting in His promises, you start out on your own to escape the pain and fail to stay in the middle of His will. Trusting in your own human understanding, you head for the ditch and destruction.

Is homeschooling testing your faith in God in a way you never imagined? Are you wondering why He started you down the path of teaching your children when it is so difficult to see the daily obstacles and hazards? God knows what lies ahead, and He will tell you if you need to move a little left or right. He hasn't abandoned you and promises to help with parenting problems, financial problems, and even loneliness. Homeschooling works—don't give up the faith! "That the trial of your faith, being much more precious than of gold that perisheth, though it be tried with fire, might be found unto praise and honour and glory at the appearing of Jesus Christ" (1 Peter 1:7).

Father, I cry out to You for help with my homeschooling. I am lost and in need of Your guidance. Show me the way, so Your perfect will is accomplished in my children's lives. In Jesus' name, Amen.

Share your thoughts about this devotional at aophomeschooling.com/079

Put Off Until Tomorrow

March 21

"To day if ye will hear his voice, harden not your hearts" (Hebrews 4:7b).

Prioritizing my workload as a homeschooling parent was difficult because everything seemed urgent. The baby needed to be bathed and fed, the clothes needed to be washed, the meals needed to be kept on schedule, and daily school lessons needed to be completed. Too many days I felt like Peter robbing Paul, as I juggled each of these activities. Anything that could be put off until tomorrow usually was, including grading school papers, quizzes, and tests.

I didn't realize my children's annoyance with my grading delay until my daughter said, "It's been over a week since I took that history test! I studied so hard! When are you ever going to grade it?" My failure in giving instant feedback not only caused frustration and a lack of motivation in our homeschooling, but also eliminated the opportunity to correct errors immediately to prevent them from being repeated in future lessons. Sadly, my children's schoolwork suffered for several years from my inability to prioritize.

Accepting Christ as Savior is also a decision many people will put off until tomorrow. The busyness of life takes priority and people fail to take time to consider the serious, life-changing gift of eternal life. Like the foolish man who stored up more and more treasures for himself on earth (Luke 12:18-20), they miss making the most important decision in life.

Do you have family members, friends, or even fellow homeschoolers who don't know Christ as Savior? God's Word says in Hebrews 3:13, "But exhort one another daily, while it is called To day; lest any of you be hardened through the deceitfulness of sin." Don't wait to tell of Christ's love and forgiveness to those you love. Tomorrow may be too late.

Lord, use me today to reach those people who have yet to put their trust in You. Show me their needs and help me to share clearly the message of salvation. In the saving name of Jesus, Amen.

Giant of Despair

March 22

I had no idea homeschooling would involve the spiritual battles I faced. Daily, I was challenged to maintain a godly attitude under the pressures of teaching and maintaining a home. Foolishly, I thought I could stay ahead of Satan's discouraging attacks with a few Scripture verses and my own strength. After a particularly difficult homeschooling day, I finally reached an emotional rock-bottom experience. Tired and drained, I decided tomorrow was the day to give up teaching my four children. Going to bed early that night, I had resolved to call the school district in the morning to enroll my children.

That night, I had the most unusual dream. In my dream, I saw a large, dark figure approaching our farmhouse from across the field. I sensed the evil coming from this "thing" and knew that if he reached me, I would be killed. As he came closer, I quickly looked for a way of escape and saw a reinforced cage lying on the ground next to me. Thinking I would be safe, I climbed inside. Sneering, the dark figure picked up the cage and shook it violently. I felt the painful blows from hitting the sides as he banged me around inside the cage. Looking down, I noticed several articles of padded clothing that would protect me, and as I struggled to reach them, I woke up.

I never had a dream that seemed so real. I immediately prayed to ask God if there was some special meaning. Amazingly, God led me to Ephesians 6:10-18, and after reading this passage of Scripture, I understood my dream. I had failed to put on the whole armor of God each day, and Satan was beating me up in my homeschooling efforts. My cage of salvation had kept me alive, but without the full covering of God's armor to protect myself during the daily spiritual battles, I would continue to be defeated. Enlightened and empowered with God's truth, my spiritual walk and my homeschooling changed.

Are you facing the giant of despair and feeling beat up in your homeschooling? If your temper is short and you feel frustrated and angry at God, your children, or yourself, perhaps you've forgotten to dress this morning with God's protective armor. Don't wait for a near homeschooling defeat before you realize the true source of your strength in homeschooling. Turn to God now and discover His power for victory. "Finally, my brethren, be strong in the Lord, and in the power of his might. Put on the whole armour of God, that ye may be able to stand against the wiles of the devil" (Ephesians 6:10-11).

Jesus, you are my King, and I surrender all that I am to You. Fill me mightily today with Your presence and power to defeat the lies of the evil one before they rob our family of the blessing of homeschooling. In Your precious name, Amen.

 Share your thoughts about this devotional at **aophomeschooling.com/081**

Parent and Teacher

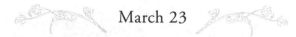

March 23

"For whom the Lord loveth, he chasteneth, and scourgeth every son whom he receiveth" (Hebrews 12:6).

Like most homeschoolers, the first few years were a struggle as I taught my children at home. The initial problems were not from a lack of quality curriculum, lesson planning, or teaching methods. Rather, the problems that tempted me to quit came from poor parenting skills. My children had the upper hand. I was bombarded with laziness, silliness, selfishness, and uncooperative spirits, and unfortunately, there was no super nanny to call to set things right. I needed to enforce the rules so my children could learn to the best of their abilities. Boundaries needed to be set with a firm, but loving hand of correction. When I finally realized that parenting and teaching were synonymous, our homeschooling changed for the better.

Many times Christians slide backwards in their faith because they fail to understand God's nature as both a loving, heavenly Father (1 John 4:8) and a lover of justice (Psalm 37:28). We quickly see God as "the big meanie" when He corrects us in our foolishness and sin. Wanting to bask in His love as friend and "Abba" Father, we forget that God is also holy and just. When we realize God is all powerful and disciplines us because He wants us to share in His holiness (Hebrews 12:10), our spiritual understanding of God's love changes for the better.

What about you? Do you doubt God's love because you're suffering from the consequences of a past sin? God cares more about making you more like Christ than letting you have your own selfish way. Why not turn to Him and learn the lesson He is setting before you today? "For they verily for a few days chastened us after their own pleasure; but he for our profit, that we might be partakers of his holiness" (Hebrews 12:10).

Lord, you hate sin, and I know You want me to be more like Christ. Work in my heart and change my bitterness and doubt to praise and trust in Your goodness and love. In Jesus' name, Amen.

Precept upon Precept

March 24

"Whom shall he teach knowledge? and whom shall he make to understand doctrine? them that are weaned from the milk, and drawn from the breasts. For precept must be upon precept, precept upon precept; line upon line, line upon line; here a little, and there a little" (Isaiah 28:9-10).

I'm not sure what I expected from my children when we first started homeschooling. I guess I thought they would be accomplished mathematicians and readers by the time they were in second grade. As we continued schooling each year, however, I realized that children grow intellectually the same way they grow physically—a little bit at a time. Even though I felt like we weren't accomplishing much each day, every new phonics rule, spelling word, grammar rule, or math fact was actually building upon itself and laying a foundation that would lead to their educational success.

Spiritual maturity is a step-by-step growing process as well. Too many times we look at older, more mature saints and wish we had their walk with God. However, we fail to see the years of lessons (sometimes painful lessons) that brought them to their point of maturity. Each lesson learned in faith, prayer, and Scriptural truths builds upon the last to produce a shining, godly character.

What about your spiritual life? Does it seem like there are so many lessons to learn before you become a person of faith? Maybe you even find yourself relearning the same lessons like patience, a pure thought life, or gratefulness over and over again. God is the master builder of all things (Hebrews 3:4), and He is setting the bricks of your faith one at a time. Trust Him and you'll become a shining example of His love to your homeschooling family and to the world. "Being confident of this very thing, that he which hath begun a good work in you will perform it until the day of Jesus Christ" (Philippians 1:6).

Lord, thank You for each lesson You've used to teach me more about You. Increase my faith and keep teaching me that my life might glorify You. In the name of Jesus, Amen.

Litter Bugs

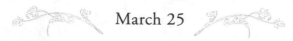

March 25

"Righteousness exalteth a nation: but sin is a reproach to any people" (Proverbs 14:34).

Every spring after the snow thawed in the ditches near our home, the ugliness of winter's past sins would be revealed. An endless disarray of empty glass liquor bottles and aluminum beer cans lined both sides of our country road for more than a mile. Looking at the mess, my young son shook his head in disgust. "Mom," he said. "Why do they have to throw their garbage in our ditch?"

Understanding his displeasure, I replied, "I don't know, but can you imagine the mess their lives are in if what they've left behind looks like this!"

The Bible doesn't pull any punches when it reveals God's attitude towards sin's ugliness. The Scriptures say sin is an abomination to the Lord (Proverbs 6:16) and that He hates those who do iniquity (Psalm 5:5). No matter if the sin is great or small in our mind, we suffer when we choose to disobey God. Our sinful actions and choices trash not only our lives, but also the lives of everyone they touch.

As a Christian homeschooling parent, do you take your sinful failings seriously? Proverbs 14:9 says, "Fools make a mock at sin." Each time you choose to lose your patience, make unloving remarks, or fail to discipline your children, you leave a mess in your own family, as well as the world. Left unchecked, sin's filthy effect will split your family apart and give the world cause to look on homeschoolers and Christians with disgust. Will you start picking up the mess by coming before the Lord today and seeking His cleansing from all unrighteousness (1 John 1:9)?

Father, forgive me for not hating sin like You do. Help me to deal with those seemingly "little" sins that make my life ugly and ruin Your best in my life. In Jesus' name, Amen.

Share your thoughts about this devotional at **aophomeschooling.com/084**

Daffodil Days

March 26

"Honour the LORD with thy substance, and with the firstfruits of all thine increase" (Proverbs 3:9).

Every year the daffodils were the first to push their green leaves through winter's cold earth in our flower bed. My daughter and I both looked forward to their annual spring arrival after homeschooling all winter. Not only were we blessed as the army of bright yellow blossoms began to form, but we anticipated the joy of sharing their beauty with others. Short on finances, giving away our daffodils was one simple, but welcomed way our homeschooling family could bring hope and love to family and friends. Our motivation to keep them fertilized and free of weeds came from the promise of future smiles we would see from those who would receive a bountiful bouquet.

Using what we have to be a blessing to others is a reoccurring theme found in the Bible. As a homeschooling parent short on money, but big on ideas, I loved encouraging my children to bless others with the resources at hand. My favorite Bible stories to illustrate this lesson came from the widow who fed Elijah bread with the last of her flour and oil (1 Kings 17:12), the poor widow who had only two small coins to give to the church treasury (Luke 21:1-4), and the young boy who gave his two small fish and five loaves of bread to Jesus to feed over five thousand people (John 6:9). Each is a clear example that God can use anything to bless others if we simply give it to Him.

Do you feel like you have nothing to give toward Christ's work because your finances are limited from homeschooling on one income? Don't despair! Look around instead and open your heart to God's creative ideas. Maybe you can bake fresh homemade meals, sew or crochet handmade kitchen towels, or just give sacks of your children's outgrown clothes to a needy family. Let the Lord lead and use what you have to be a blessing to others. When you see a smile appearing on a face, you'll realize you've received the greater blessing.

Lord, thank You for the blessings You've given to my family. Help me to teach my children to think of others and open our eyes to see the storehouse of resources You've made available to bless them. In Jesus' name, Amen.

 Share your thoughts about this devotional at **aophomeschooling.com/085**

Counting the Cost

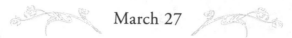

"For whosoever will save his life shall lose it: and whosoever will lose his life for my sake shall find it" (Matthew 16:25).

Sometimes learning a new skill and information requires a painstaking effort. Such was the case when my five-year-old son saw the new phonics chart hanging on the schoolroom wall. Looking at all the phonics rules he had to learn and memorize, my son looked at me with wide eyes and said, "Mommy, there's too many. Can't we skip some and just do the first ones?"

"No, honey," I replied. "Each one is important in helping you become a better reader. Just think, after you learn them all, you'll be able to read really hard books."

Looking at me skeptically, he answered, "Can I just learn to read easy books, Mom?"

Whether you're learning to become a better reader or a follower of Jesus Christ, you must count the cost and recognize the sacrifices involved. In Matthew 26:6-13, Jesus rebuked His disciples for their indignation toward a woman's sacrificial act of love. Instead, Jesus commended her for bringing a vial of very costly perfume and pouring it on his head, even though the poor would have benefited from its value. Giving such an expensive gift probably cost this woman everything, but what a perfect picture for us! There is a great cost involved in becoming a disciple of Jesus Christ.

What has it cost you to homeschool your children? Are you thinking now that the price is too high? Like the honor given to the woman for her costly gift (Matthew 26:13) or the reward promised for being Christ's disciple (Luke 18:29-30), God will honor your faithful homeschooling sacrifice of time, energy, and money. Will you hold fast to what God has shown you to be true? "So likewise, whosoever he be of you that forsaketh not all that he hath, he cannot be my disciple" (Luke 14:33).

Lord, convict me of my need to give back all that I am to You. Guide me as I homeschool today and remind me that this sacrifice is nothing compared to Yours when You died on the cross for me. In Jesus' name, Amen.

Unhealthy Competition

March 28

"And whosoever of you will be the chiefest, shall be servant of all" (Mark 10:44).

I never encouraged competition between my four children while homeschooling, but it happened anyway. In fact, I only wanted my children to give their best each day and suggested forgetting grades altogether. However, their need to rate themselves against each other and also against other children their age dictated a request for a report card. Their human need to know where they were in the scheme of things filtered its way into their mindset and manifested itself during schoolwork. They simply had to know if they were smarter or better in a particular subject than their siblings or someone else.

Christ's disciples were no different. When following Jesus here on earth, a great debate arose between them. Wanting to know where they fit into the future scheme of things, James and John, the sons of Zebedee, foolishly asked Jesus if they could sit on either side of Him in heaven (Mark 10:37). Hearing this request, the other ten disciples became indignant, and Jesus took the opportunity to teach them all a valuable lesson in servanthood.

Are you comparing your homeschooling performance to other families, or are you simply giving your best and expecting the same from your children? God has uniquely designed your family with gifts and abilities, and your success in homeschooling isn't dictated by what other families are doing. God only expects you to seek His guidance and obey Him so He can show you how to let go of unhealthy competition and focus on serving others instead.

Father, forgive me for trying to compete with "The Jones'" homeschool down the street. Teach me to listen to the Holy Spirit and to depend on the truths of Your Word as I homeschool each day. In Jesus' name, Amen.

Who Do You Believe In?

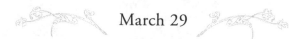

March 29

"Verily, verily, I say unto you, He that believeth on me, the works that I do shall he do also; and greater works than these shall he do; because I go unto my Father" (John 14:12).

When people attain a measure of success in the public spotlight, what words do you normally hear them say when they are interviewed? That person usually says, "Because my _____ (fill in the blank—grandmother, mother, father, sister, friend, whoever) believed in me, I was able to accomplish what I've done." Amazingly, one person's faith in another person's ability inspires great achievement.

Christ demonstrated this fact when He chose Peter as a disciple. Recognizing his potential (Matthew 16:16-20), Jesus challenged Peter to follow Him. After Christ's death and resurrection, the Lord's words about Peter were fulfilled when the Holy Spirit transformed his life at the day of Pentecost. Even though Peter was uneducated and untrained, his confidence and willingness to die for the sake of the Gospel amazed the elders, rulers, and scribes (Acts 4:13-14). Because Christ patiently loved and encouraged Peter, he was able to perform miracles and change the world with the message of Jesus' love and forgiveness.

Does this same underlying principle lie at the root of every homeschooler's success? Since most homeschooling parents only have a high school education, what else could account for the incredible results in academic success? Apparently, learning is only part of the equation in a child's ability to achieve great things. The other part lies within a loving parent's heart. When you see God's potential within your child and then encourage him to reach out and obtain it, you'll be amazed at what your child achieves, too.

Lord, forgive me for limiting my child because of my unbelief in his abilities. Help me inspire him to greatness by believing whom and what You've created him to be. In Jesus' name, Amen.

The Deepest Need

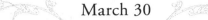

March 30

"The LORD is on my side; I will not fear: what can man do unto me" (Psalm 118:6)?

If someone gave you a blank piece of paper and said, "Write down your greatest needs as a homeschooling parent," what would you write? Would you write a few short sentences, or would you fill the entire page with a huge list of items? As unique as each homeschooling parent's needs may be, if you truly look inside your heart, chances are you'll discover your deepest homeschooling needs are love, significance, and acceptance. These needs aren't easily met, however, since the world considers homeschoolers "different" and shies away in rejection. Even your own family can fail in giving you the encouraging positive feedback necessary in homeschooling. So where do you go to fill your emotional void?

Praise God we have a loving heavenly Father who is more than enough to meet our deepest needs. The story of Noah in the Old Testament is a perfect example. Imagine the rejection and ridicule he must have experienced for obeying God when building a boat bigger than a football field! In a world filled with violence and corruption (Genesis 6:11), I'm sure Noah was probably threatened as well. But Noah had it right, didn't he? Even though the people probably mocked him for days, it wasn't Noah who was on the wrong side of the door when it began to rain! God's acceptance of Noah's faith was demonstrated when He spared Noah and his family from the flood.

Have you been building your homeschooling ark, but still find yourself being mocked by the world? Take courage. God's acceptance, approval, and love are all you need. Even though others will never understand the many benefits and blessings of homeschooling, you know the truth. Remain steadfast in teaching your children about the Lord, so when He returns, you'll be standing on the right side of the door. "What shall we then say to these things? If God be for us, who can be against us" (Romans 8:31)?

Father, some days, teaching my children seems as huge a task as building an ark. Thank You for Your love and acceptance that encourages me to go on homeschooling. Please strengthen me to hear Your voice clearly each day. In the name of Jesus, Amen.

 Share your thoughts about this devotional at **aophomeschooling.com/089**

Farmer Boy

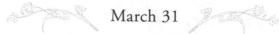

March 31

"Behold, the husbandman waiteth for the precious fruit of the earth, and hath long patience for it, until he receive the early and latter rain. Be ye also patient; stablish your hearts: for the coming of the Lord draweth nigh" (James 5:7b-8).

I think every parent secretly hopes his children will share his passions. My passion was gardening, but each year gardens came and went with only a limited interest from my older children. Yes, they enjoyed the flowers and the fresh vegetables, but I never saw that "look" in their eyes when they surveyed a freshly-tilled patch of ground. Years went by before God surprised me with my youngest son's interest. When he was old enough to start helping, I saw that far-off look that sees a future garden flourishing and yielding its fruit. I saw the excitement that says, "Let's try a new variety this year," or "Can we till up another patch of dirt to plant more?" For the next several years, my son and I happily pursued our "green thumbs" together.

As Christian homeschooling parents, we have a deep desire for our children to share a far greater passion. We desire them to share our same love for the Lord. Like a faithful gardener tending his crops, we take our children to church, teach them Bible stories and memory verses, and pray for the day when they realize their need of Christ as Savior. When that day finally arrives, we rejoice as we see the Holy Spirit's sparkle in our children's eyes. Plus, we share the excitement of serving the Lord in this life as a family. Best of all, we share the hope of a future home in heaven for all eternity.

What about you? Are you still waiting for your homeschooler to make a personal decision to receive the Lord Jesus Christ as Savior? Don't give up! Keep planting those things into his life that will yield the fruit of righteousness in due season. Most of all, don't lose that passionate look in your own eye when you speak of Christ's forgiving love. Your children are watching and waiting to see what you really love most.

Lord Jesus, thank You for the privilege of being a homeschooling parent and teaching my children about You. I lift up their lives to You and pray for Your divine touch to bring them into a personal relationship with You. In Your holy name, Amen.

Who's the Biggest Fool?

April 1

"But a foolish son is the heaviness of his mother" (Proverbs 10:1b).

We experienced a problem in our homeschooling family as my oldest son grew into his teens. Wanting to be accepted, my son started associating with a new group of friends. At first, I was happy to see my introverted son making new buddies, but then I noticed the beginning of undesirable qualities in his character. My son became more reckless and started showing off by taking foolish risks with his personal belongings, including his car. When my son started "fooling" me to participate in activities we wouldn't allow, it was time to address the situation. I realized I had been the biggest fool for not putting a stop to his foolishness sooner.

God's Word has nothing positive to say about fools or foolishness. Endless Scripture passages in Proverbs verify that claim as well as a story in Acts. Apparently, the new believers in Christ had been fellowshipping and sharing their belongings (Acts 4:32). Barnabas, one of the believers, decided to sell a portion of his land to help the group and gave the money to the apostles. Two other believers, Ananias and his wife, Sapphira, did the same thing, but for whatever reason, they decided to keep a portion of the money for themselves (Acts 5:1-10). Attempting to fool the apostles, Ananias and Sapphira told them that they had given the full amount. God's response to this deception was quick and severe. Within three hours, both Ananias and Sapphira fell over dead for trying to fool the Holy Spirit.

What about your homeschooling family? Have you noticed any foolishness creeping into your children's actions? Be careful! Foolishness left unchecked has the potential to destroy your child's life. Although the world may celebrate a day when people deceive and pull embarrassing practical jokes, God's Word says something entirely different about foolishness—"The thought of foolishness is sin" (Proverbs 24:9a).

Lord, show me how to discipline my children when they start acting foolishly. Give me the wisdom to train their immaturity into responsible actions that will glorify You. In Jesus' name, Amen.

If Walls Could Speak

April 2

"For I know that in me (that is, in my flesh,) dwelleth no good thing: for to will is present with me; but how to perform that which is good I find not" (Romans 7:18).

If your homeschool walls could speak, what would they say? What secrets would they tell others about your homeschooling family? My walls would tell of quiet times reading books, excited times when science experiments went "south," creative times of nightly puppet shows from behind the couch, and joyful times when a child received a hard-earned A+ on a semester test. Unfortunately, my walls would also tell secrets of not-so-nice times when conflicts led to unloving acts or when laziness led to procrastination.

Every homeschooling parent knows he falls far short of being the perfect Christian parent. The temptation to allow selfishness, greed, jealousy, and even laziness to take over our lives is strong. Homeschooling is only successful when we listen to the Lord instead of our flesh and submit to His constant love and guidance.

What about you? Have you been focusing on your failures more than your successes? Take heart! We all fail in our efforts to be the best parent and teacher of our children. The true battle that turns our defeat into a homeschooling victory lies in saying no to the flesh, so the Holy Spirit can control our every thought and action. "I am crucified with Christ: nevertheless I live; yet not I, but Christ liveth in me: and the life which I now live in the flesh I live by the faith of the Son of God, who loved me, and gave himself for me" (Galatians 2:20).

Lord, thank You for providing the way to have a homeschooling family who glorifies You. Teach me how to say no to my whiny flesh and to listen to You and Your promises instead. In Jesus' name, Amen.

Share your thoughts about this devotional at aophomeschooling.com/092

You Can't Have It Both Ways

April 3

"No man can serve two masters: for either he will hate the one, and love the other; or else he will hold to the one, and despise the other. Ye cannot serve God and mammon" (Matthew 6:24).

Our children were often frustrated when we first started homeschooling because they didn't know who to listen to, Dad or Mom. Our team-teaching approach was seriously lacking, and after the first year, we realized the problem. Although my husband wanted to help with teaching, he simply didn't know where the children were in their studies. When he attempted to answer their questions in the evening, he actually made things more confusing. Making adjustments, my husband and I decided he should be in charge of teaching only one or two subjects and leave the rest to me.

Having two masters in charge rarely works, but serving more than one master is even harder. According to Luke 16:13, there are no fence riders in the kingdom of heaven. The choice is plain and simple. Either we choose to submit our lives to Christ, or we live for money and the pleasures it provides. Ironically, the lack of money can actually make homeschooling parents value money as much as a greedy person living in abundance. By making every penny count, we overdevelop our focus in purchasing necessary items for our home. We also begin to see our husband's paycheck as our salvation, instead of trusting the Lord for provision. Money becomes our master—not because we have it, but because we don't.

How much time do you spend thinking about money during your homeschooling day? Do you wonder how you will make ends meet? If you're anxious or overly concerned about your financial situation, you'll only waste valuable teaching and family time. God knows what you need. Let His Word from Matthew 6:31-32 encourage you again this day: "Therefore take no thought, saying, What shall we eat? or, What shall we drink? or, Wherewithal shall we be clothed? (For after all these things do the Gentiles seek:) for your heavenly Father knoweth that ye have need of all these things."

Lord, you know I am trying to handle our finances carefully. Forgive me for stressing out and putting too much importance on "where the next meal is coming from." You've always provided, and I choose to look to You again for all that I need. In Jesus' name, Amen.

Boundaries

"For thou hast been a shelter for me" (Psalm 61:3a).

Growing up in the country, my children spent just as much time outside as inside when homeschooling. For their safety and my sanity, we established an invisible boundary around our farm where they could play and explore without my supervision. Expanding upon this concept, we decided to apply this same principle when visiting Grandpa and Grandma's lake home. Since my four-year-old son was still learning how to swim, his boundary had been set within the beach area only. After one reminder, we let him play in the sand while we continued to observe him from my in-laws' porch only a few feet away.

However, as every parent knows, children are notorious for testing boundaries. Seeing his older brother and sisters enjoy the water slide attached to the dock, he couldn't resist going out to join them. Each time he started down the dock, we yelled out his name and firmly said, "No!" Frustrated, he waited several minutes and then tried once more. This time, I said to my husband, "Wait, let's not do or say anything and see what he does." Agreeing, we watched as our son approached the spot on the dock where we had told him no. Expecting us to tell him no again, he stopped, turned, and said, "What?" before we could do or say a thing. Laughing inside, we saw that even a four year old is capable of knowing his boundaries and disciplining himself to observe them.

God gives adults boundaries, too. He knows our sinful nature and has given us loving guidelines to keep us safe from evil. As Christian homeschooling parents, we have an even higher need to discipline ourselves from Satan's tantalizing tidbits. However, keeping ourselves pure from sexual sins, greed, jealousy, and other sins is getting more difficult. The world continues to move the boundaries to remove their guilt for participating in these activities. What about you? Will you observe God's boundaries and stop, turn, and say, "What will you have me do, Lord?"

Father, you are a holy God who hates sin. Thank You for giving me such wonderful blessings within the confines of Your loving law. Help me to understand Your boundaries are a good thing and not to resent the disciplines necessary in following You. In Jesus' name, Amen.

Juliette

April 5

"For there is no respect of persons with God" (Romans 2:11).

Of all the cats my family loved during our homeschooling years, there was never one we loved quite like Juliette. If ever a cat could be perfect, she was. Unlike most cats that are somewhat indifferent and independent, Juliette was a socialite and loved being right in the middle of the action. Best of all, she never played favorites. Juliette made the rounds and spent equal time loving everyone in the family. One moment we would find her faithfully sitting on my older children's laps as they read their school assignments, and the next moment we would find her being dragged around the house by my toddlers as they played with her like a doll. At nighttime we would find her snuggling in the bed covers as she made the circuit from one bedroom to the next. Wherever and whomever she was with, Juliette loved them pur-r-r-fectly by giving them her utmost devotion.

Although Juliette was only a cat, God used her loving ways to teach me a valuable spiritual lesson. God's love is equally available to all mankind, and He shows no partiality (Galatians 2:6). In Christ, there is no distinction between rich and poor, Jew and Greek, or male and female (Galatians 3:38). God desires that everyone come to repentance and be saved (2 Peter 3:9). Unfortunately, this simple lesson was easier for a cat to learn than it was for me. Although I was a Christian, I found myself turning away from sharing God's love with those who were different, unlovely, or broken. Praise God that the unequal treatment and rejection I experienced when homeschooling showed me how foolish I was. In wanting others to love and accept me, I finally realized the same need in the hearts of those whom I had been ignoring.

Do you find it difficult to minister to the people the world rejects? While Christ was here on earth, He spent His time loving people whom others forgot. Just as Christ's unbiased love took Him to the cross for everyone's sin, He wants you to love impartially. Don't let someone's social status or appearance keep you from extending a hand of love. Reach out and let Christ's golden rule be your guide. "And as ye would that men should do to you, do ye also to them likewise" (Luke 6:31).

Lord, forgive my selfish pride and preconceived ideas that keep me from seeing each person through Your eyes of love. Please help me lay down my fears and misconceptions and to be willing to share Your love with everyone I meet. In the name of Jesus, Amen.

The Best Medicine

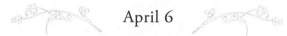

April 6

"A merry heart doeth good like a medicine" (Proverbs 17:22a).

To a child, there is only one thing worse than being sick in the winter, and that's being sick during the summer. After all, who wants to lie on the couch when everyone else in the family is having fun playing outside? As I looked at the purple, yellow, and red bottles of medicine in my bathroom cabinet, I heard my young son cry out from the living room couch, "Mom, please don't give me any of those terrible tasting things. They're just going to make me sicker." Although he had been running a fever through the night, I realized my patient wasn't as ill as I previously thought. Ignoring his pleas, I continued to administer the necessary medicine and turned to go back to my work in the kitchen. Grabbing my hand, my son said, "Mom, do you think you could just sit with me for awhile?"

"Sure," I replied. "How about if I read one of your favorite books to you?" Nodding his head in agreement, I proceeded to sit on the floor in front of the couch and spent the next half hour reading *Pilgrim's Progress*. After reading several chapters and talking with my son, I noticed a smile on his face and his relaxed posture. "Are you feeling better now?" I asked.

"Oh yes, Mom," he responded cheerfully. Giving him a hug and a smile, I realized the best medicine I had given him that morning was a happy attitude, my time, and love.

Everyone needs someone to sit and listen when life brings difficult times. Whether it's facing an illness or some other problem, an understanding ear and a kind word go a long way in relieving the suffering of a friend. Unfortunately, that type of medicine can't be purchased from a store. Rather, it comes from a sensitive and loving heart that truly cares about the needs of others.

Is there someone you know who is ill or hurting from life's problems? Chances are you're the nurse God could use to make that person well. Go to the medicine chest of God's Holy Word to find just the right encouragement, and then sit and take all the time necessary to administer the best tasting medicine they'll ever need. "Pleasant words are as an honeycomb, sweet to the soul, and health to the bones" (Proverbs 16:24).

Lord, you are the Great Physician who knows all our hurts and pains. Please help me bring Your healing words of love and encouragement to my family and friends today. In the name of Jesus, Amen.

Share your thoughts about this devotional at **aophomeschooling.com/096**

No Place like Home

April 7

"In my Father's house are many mansions: if it were not so, I would have told you. I go to prepare a place for you" (John 14:2).

When it comes to schooling, there's no place like home. To a homeschooling family, home is more than just a school; it is a church, a playground, a museum, a rest area, a trauma unit, a business office, a hospitality center, a safe place, and more! The home is the hub of the family, and a place where we live life together.

The home is really God's idea, a wonderful structure that Satan has worked hard at destroying. The evils and perversions of a sinful society have eradicated God's perfect plan of one man and one woman marrying and living together under His authority with their children. Refusing to believe the mandates in God's Word, the world conjures up theories and philosophies (based on human reasoning) and sidesteps the issue by counterattacking with offensive statements directed towards "intolerant" Christians.

Thank God no human can redefine the home in heaven that God has prepared for those who love Him. Next to salvation, Jesus' promise to prepare a place for us to live with Him in eternity has to be the greatest hope for every Christian (John 14:3). Each night that we lay our head on our pillow, we can have the peace of knowing that tomorrow brings no fear — we either spend it walking with Him on earth or walking with Him in heaven. Life is simplified when you remember that heaven is your true home.

Have you forgotten about your home in heaven? Homeschooling has a way of pulling your eyes off the One who is preparing a mansion just for you. Don't let the cares of lesson plans, household chores, and endless tasks make you forget who is waiting for you at home!

Lord, You are beautiful and marvelous, and I can hardly wait to get home to see You. Thank You for this opportunity to make a home here on earth for the family You've given me. May we always glorify You in our homeschooling and in our daily lives. In the name of Jesus, Amen.

Share your thoughts about this devotional at **aophomeschooling.com/097**

Hide and Seek

April 8

"Be sure your sin will find you out" (Numbers 32:23b).

One of my favorite rewards of being a homeschool parent is that we had so many opportunities to play games. Of course, the usual game our younger children chose was "Hide and Seek." With the help of their older siblings, my little ones actually became very good at hiding completely out of view. However, even though they managed to hide their bodies, they usually couldn't control their giggles when I said, "Come out, come out wherever you are!" After locating their hiding place, it was my turn to laugh when they asked, "Mommy, how did you find us so fast?"

Although we may smile at the innocent attempts of our children to hide, God the Father does not. Ever since Adam and Eve ate of the Tree of Knowledge in the Garden of Eden, man has been trying to hide his sin from God's almighty view. In fact, like Adam, we play games with God and foolishly think He doesn't see us when we sin. Worse still, we even try to play Adam's great cover-up game and cloak ourselves in the flimsy leaves of good works. Although we continue in our silly, sinful ways, God never sees our sin as funny. When He calls out and asks, "Where are you?" as He did to Adam, we feel the conviction of the Holy Spirit. With our sin revealed, we learn that there's no place man can hide from an all-knowing and omnipresent God. King David expressed it best when he said, "Whither shall I go from thy spirit? or whither shall I flee from thy presence" (Psalm 139:7)?

Are you playing games with God right now? Is there some known sin in your life you think He doesn't see? Maybe you've lied to your children or deceived your spouse on what you spent on homeschool curriculum this year. However big or small the sin, confess it to Him now before you quench the Holy Spirit's work in your life. Stop playing the game! Come out of sin's shadows and be found in the light of Almighty God.

Lord, how foolish I must seem when I sin and try to hide from You! Today I confess my sin that I might be close to You. In Jesus' name, Amen.

Too Much Love

April 9

Every morning I wondered what new discoveries lay ahead for my children as we home-schooled. Although I had the day's schedule planned, God always seemed to lead with His divine lessons. As my son and I walked to the barn for chores one spring morning, we noticed several cocoons hidden beneath the boards on the door. The cocoons were large, and as we examined one of them more closely, we saw a slight movement. Slowly, the cocoon began to crack open, and we could see something struggling to get out. "Mom, what is it?" cried my son. "Let's cut the rest of the cocoon so it can get out!"

"No, honey," I replied. "You don't want to do that. If we interfere, the creature inside will be hurt. We have to let it struggle on its own." Postponing my scheduled lessons, we sat and observed the beginning of this new life. Over an hour went by as we watched it emerge from its winter home. Still unsure what exactly was inside, we were totally surprised when the creature burst through the cocoon's covering. There, in all its glory, was a huge cecropia moth! We watched as the moth vibrated its velvety red and brown wings in the sun. The five-inch wingspan was impressive, and the whole scene was a breathtaking sight that my young son would never forget.

I know my son learned a valuable science lesson that day, but I learned a valuable lesson, too. As I watched the struggling moth, I understood how my past actions of motherly love had interfered with our homeschooling. I realized that I needed to be firm and expect my children to do their own schoolwork without asking for help on every question.

Do you ever find yourself trying to "help" your children more than you should? Your children's education can suffer if you don't learn to balance the dual role you play as teacher and parent. Spelling out every answer will be detrimental to the development of their reasoning and thinking processes. Be careful. Don't destroy the new life God is using you to shape. "Train up a child in the way he should go: and when he is old, he will not depart from it" (Proverbs 22:6).

Lord Jesus, thank You for the privilege of teaching my children. Show me how to educate them with a healthy balance of love and discipline and to not remove the struggles that will cause them to grow in knowledge. In Your name, Amen.

 Share your thoughts about this devotional at **aophomeschooling.com/099**

Kids to the Rescue

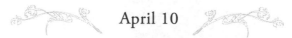

April 10

What do you do when you homeschool and the teacher gets sick? Not long after we first started homeschooling, I woke up one morning with an aching fever. "Great, now what am I going to do?" I thought to myself. My parents were out of town, and realistically, caring for my two toddlers was all I could handle for the day. Calling my two older children into my bedroom I weakly said, "Mom's really sick today. You'll have to work on your schoolwork by yourself or just read books and play."

Not batting an eye, they surprised me when they replied, "That's OK, Mom. We can take care of everything." What was even more surprising was that they did! Throughout the day they brought me juice and medicine and helped me keep their younger siblings happy. When the babies and I took an afternoon nap, my seven and eight year old grabbed their school materials and did all the work they could by themselves. Smiling, I realized my children were learning more than academics in our homeschooling. They were learning character qualities like responsibility and kindness.

Children are great helpers, and throughout the Bible, we read stories of when God used them in special ways. Consider young Samuel serving God in the temple (1 Samuel 3), Naaman's servant girl who directed him to Elisha for healing from his leprosy (2 Kings 5:2-3), the boy who shared his lunch with Jesus to feed five thousand (John 6:9), and little Rhoda who told the other believers that Peter was knocking at the door after his angelic escape from prison (Acts 12:13-16). Although they may seem small and insignificant, each act was great in the eyes of God.

Are you ever tempted to underestimate the value of your child's obedience and faithfulness to the Lord? Every time he speaks with kindness to a sibling, or remembers Grandma with a special hello when she comes to visit, or invites a friend to Sunday school, he is doing God's work on a grand scale. Like the disciples who thought the little children were wasting Jesus' time, don't become a stumbling block to your child's small acts of love. "But whoso shall offend one of these little ones which believe in me, it were better for him that a millstone were hanged about his neck, and that he were drowned in the depth of the sea" (Matthew 18:6).

Father, thank You for my children. Forgive me for underestimating what You can do through their prayers and acts of love, and help me encourage them to love You more. In Jesus' name, Amen.

Share your thoughts about this devotional at **aophomeschooling.com/100**

Homeschooling Comfort

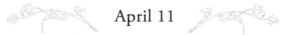

April 11

"Who comforteth us in all our tribulation, that we may be able to comfort them which are in any trouble, by the comfort wherewith we ourselves are comforted of God" (2 Corinthians 1:4).

Let's face it. Some mornings you wake up as a homeschooling parent and say, "If I have another day like I did yesterday, I'm going to lose it!" Between your little ones fighting and your older children taking the lazy way out of their schoolwork, you're tired of being a policeman. Ironically, those discouraging days seem to be the very ones when someone calls wanting your encouragement to start homeschooling. You feel like the proverbial blind leading the blind and think to yourself, "If they only knew!"

The stressful pressures of life can tempt anyone to give up. The Apostle Paul discovered that fact about his situation when he wrote in 2 Corinthians 1:8, "For we would not, brethren, have you ignorant of our trouble which came to us in Asia, that we were pressed out of measure, above strength, insomuch that we despaired even of life." Clearly, Paul was out of his comfort zone, but he didn't quit. Trusting God for everything he needed, Paul learned how to rise above his circumstances, even when facing death! With the comfort he received from God, he encouraged others to remain faithful in suffering for Christ (2 Corinthians 1:4-5).

Are you experiencing a "crunch time" in your homeschooling? Hang in there! Many have gone before you and survived the stress of being a homeschooling parent. The difficulties you're experiencing will get easier and someday the pressures won't feel as strong. Even when you feel like you can't cope, God's presence is with you to guide you and give you comfort. "Now our Lord Jesus Christ himself, and God, even our Father, which hath loved us, and hath given us everlasting consolation and good hope through grace, Comfort your hearts, and stablish you in every good word and work" (2 Thessalonians 2:16-17).

Lord, your Word says I can do all things through Christ who strengthens me. Strengthen me today and help me obediently follow You to accomplish Your will in our family. In the name of Jesus, Amen.

Bitter Roots

April 12

"The heart knoweth his own bitterness" (Proverbs 14:10a).

"I can't believe it, Mom!" cried my son. "Look at this!" Walking to the flower bed where my son was standing, I looked down and shook my head. Sure enough, the noxious weed that we had been trying to eradicate was back in our flower bed again. Frustrated, I realized the problem was my fault. When we had first moved to our home several years before, I had thought this weed was a flower. Unfortunately, after watching the other flowers choked out by this weed's entwining, tubular roots, I knew I had made a mistake in letting it grow.

"OK, that's it!" I said exasperated. "Let's dig two feet down and turn over the soil and maybe we'll find all the roots to kill it this time." For the next two years, our flower garden project for homeschooling suffered as my son and I attempted to prevent this weed from damaging any more of our tulips, irises, columbines, and other perennial flowers.

The Bible warns Christians of another root that can destroy in a far greater way—the root of bitterness. In Hebrews 12:15b, the writer says, "Lest any root of bitterness springing up trouble you, and thereby many be defiled." As believers, we must forgive those who hurt or offend us. When we refuse to forgive, bitterness grows, intertwines itself around our Christian witness, and chokes out our joy in Christ. Our lives become sour, and we see the world through critical eyes and speak with skeptical and sarcastic remarks. Not only is the Holy Spirit grieved, but also those we touch with the ugliness of bitterness.

Has bitterness taken hold in your life? Perhaps you have a family member or friend who has hurt you deeply and you've refused to forgive him. Be careful that the anger you're holding onto doesn't lead to bitterness. Why not let God uproot the pain and renew your bitter heart with a flowering heart of forgiveness and love? "And grieve not the holy Spirit of God, whereby ye are sealed unto the day of redemption. Let all bitterness, and wrath, and anger, and clamour, and evil speaking, be put away from you, with all malice: And be ye kind one to another, tenderhearted, forgiving one another, even as God for Christ's sake hath forgiven you" (Ephesians 4:30-32).

Lord, I know I need to deal with the hurt and anger I feel. Give me the strength and desire to forgive as You forgave me. Please help me lay the pain at Your feet to find Your peace and joy again. In Jesus' name, Amen.

Share your thoughts about this devotional at aophomeschooling.com/102

I Forgot

April 13

"I will meditate in thy precepts, and have respect unto thy ways" (Psalm 119:15).

How many times have you heard your homeschooler say, "I'm sorry, but I forgot to read that lesson," or "I forgot to get my assignment done?" When my children were little, saying "I forgot" meant exactly that. Their young minds were still developing and learning how to organize and remember. However, as my children grew older, I realized that "I forgot" was more often an excuse for being lazy or procrastinating. The unintentional forgetfulness they experienced during childhood stood in stark contrast to the "forgetfulness" of sidestepping their responsibilities as an adult.

The nation of Israel is a perfect example of a people who chose to "forget" the Lord their God. Time and again, the Scriptures state, "And when they forgat the LORD their God" (1 Samuel 12:9a). I can only imagine God's displeasure with His forgetful children. After blessing them and proving Himself with mighty miracles, they still disobeyed and forgot to follow His commands (Psalm 78:10-11). Not valuing God's provision, they made their excuse and followed their own desires instead of keeping their commitment to the Lord.

As Christian homeschoolers, "forgetting" to stay in the Word of God daily can ruin your spiritual walk with God, too. Homeschooling is hard enough without having God's Word to guide you. Don't allow laziness, procrastination, or even the daily diversions of life to rob you of the strength you need for each day's tasks. There is simply only one way to combat forgetting, and that is remembering. "Beloved, I now write unto you; in both which I stir up your pure minds by way of remembrance: That ye may be mindful of the words which were spoken before by the holy prophets, and of the commandment of us the apostles of the Lord and Saviour" (2 Peter 3:1b-2).

Father, without Your Word to guide me, our homeschooling is doomed for failure. Help me to prioritize and make time to remember the truths of Your commandments. In Jesus' name, Amen.

 Share your thoughts about this devotional at **aophomeschooling.com/103**

Dandelion Bouquets

April 14

The money shortages we experienced while homeschooling gave our family plenty of opportunities to discover life's simple pleasures. My husband and I enjoyed inexpensive dates and found activities for our children that cost very little money. One spring-time activity we enjoyed was walking barefoot through new green grass while having the first picnic of the year. The grass felt so good under our feet after a long winter, and our children loved creating craft projects from the dandelions. My oldest daughter especially liked making dandelion rings and stringing them together for a dandelion necklace. My son made war paint from the pollen found in the blossoms and streaked his face with yellow marks. My youngest daughter, however, simply enjoyed picking as many dandelions as her little hand could hold and giving them to me as a beautiful bouquet. Years later, when listening to my children talk about their childhood memories, I found that they remembered these ordinary things most.

Learning to be content with what you have is a secret few discover in this life. The Apostle Paul is a wonderful example of someone who knew the contentment of having much or little when he said in Philippians 4:12, "I know both how to be abased, and I know how to abound: every where and in all things I am instructed both to be full and to be hungry, both to abound and to suffer need." The success of his ministry to the Gentiles wasn't dependent on his paycheck from tent-making; it was dependent on God. In today's language, Paul learned to be happy eating steak or eating macaroni and cheese for supper. Either way, he knew God was with him providing exactly what he needed.

Would you like to feel more content homeschooling? Learn the art of appreciating life's simple pleasures. If you constantly struggle to give your child the biggest and best, you'll not only deplete your pocketbook, you'll deprive your children from enjoying ordinary, everyday blessings. Adding more outside educational activities to supplement your curriculum is not always the answer either. Spending time loving each other with the blessings God has already given is the homeschooling joy you and your children will remember most.

Lord, please give me wisdom to understand what my children really need. While we homeschool, help us to enjoy each other's love and the simple things you provide. In Jesus' name, Amen.

I Think I Can, I Think I Can

Like the little blue engine, my chant each morning during my early years of homeschooling was "I think I can do this!" I'm sure if anyone had heard my thoughts, they would have laughed. Trying to gain the confidence I needed for homeschooling, I thought that if I said the words enough, I would eventually believe them. Truthfully, I wasn't quite so sure I could homeschool. The idea of teaching my five-year-old seemed easy enough, but that was before I started teaching phonetic sounds. Since I had learned to read with sight words, teaching phonics was a whole new experience. Already, I was facing a roadblock of insecurities and my homeschooler was only in kindergarten! What was I going to do when we got to high school?

Joshua knew the insecurity of facing new challenges in his life, too. Taking over where Moses left off, he inherited the responsibility of leading God's people into the Promised Land (Joshua 1:1-2). Can you imagine how overwhelmed he must have felt following in Moses' footsteps? Understanding his fears, God reminded Joshua three times to be strong and courageous (Joshua 1: 6, 7, and 9). Encouraging him further, God also told Joshua, "There shall not any man be able to stand before thee all the days of thy life: as I was with Moses, so I will be with thee: I will not fail thee, nor forsake thee" (Joshua 1:5).

Are you feeling insecure today while you lead your children in their education? If God has led you to homeschool, the same words He spoke years ago to Joshua apply to you as well. You can become a courageous homeschooler, but it won't come from tooting your own whistle and saying, "I think I can." Instead, you must realize that God is the One who powers your engine to climb any homeschooling hill. In His strength, you'll arrive at the wonderful destination of successfully homeschooled children. "Have not I commanded thee? Be strong and of a good courage; be not afraid, neither be thou dismayed: for the LORD thy God is with thee whithersoever thou goest" (Joshua 1:9).

Lord, some days, being responsible for my children's education scares me. Remind me that You alone give the strength and wisdom to stay on track. Please encourage me now and help me to be courageous in the Holy Spirit's power. In the name of Jesus, Amen.

Side by Side

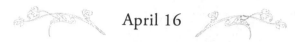

"Bear ye one another's burdens, and so fulfil the law of Christ" (Galatians 6:2).

Would you like to know a successful homeschooling secret? My children did their best schoolwork when I sat next to them as they completed their assignments. Sounds too simple, doesn't it? I thought so, too, until I tested my theory. No matter their age, the difference was remarkable between the days when I quietly sat nearby and the days when I was busy with chores in another room. Apparently, my presence empowered them with the reassurance that I was there to help if they had a question.

Having someone by your side to help you through life's problems is a blessing from God. In Exodus 17:8-13, Moses was blessed to have two men by his side, his brother Aaron and Hur. When Moses sent Joshua to fight the Amalekites, the Israelites prevailed in the battle as long as Moses held up God's staff in his hand. However, as the day progressed, Moses' hands became so heavy he could no longer hold them up alone. Sitting him down on a rock, Aaron and Hur stood by Moses' side and held up his hands until sunset. Without their help, Moses' hands would have dropped and Israel would have surely been defeated.

Do you feel alone in facing your homeschooling battles today? Praise God, His love and strength are as close as your next prayer. When you need an extra "hand" to get through a particularly tough day, He knows and cares. God loves you so much that He'll send the exact person you need to help hold you up. If you find yourself in a heavy situation right now, pray and watch as God proves Himself mighty in sending the encouragement you need. "Though he fall, he shall not be utterly cast down: for the LORD upholdeth him with his hand" (Psalm 37:24).

Father, thank You for watching over me and taking care of my every need. I lift up these home-schooling problems to You! Please, help me. In the name of Jesus, Amen.

 Share your thoughts about this devotional at aophomeschooling.com/106

To the Finish

April 17

The end of the school year was getting closer. The calendar wasn't the only source that revealed that fact. The quality of my children's schoolwork was also an indicator. With the finish line in sight and carefree summer days just ahead, my children rushed through their lessons. Poorly written compositions, half-answered history questions, and math papers with high percentages of incorrect answers confirmed that spring fever had hit our homeschool! I needed to find something to motivate my children to finish the school year working to the best of their abilities.

Christians can also suffer from a time of "spring fever." Being tempted to compromise God's standards of holiness, we half-heartedly obey and "slack off" when it comes to maintaining the spiritual disciplines of prayer and Bible study. Living the Christian life in our own strength, we fail to see our vulnerability and fall prey to Satan's temptations. "Wherefore let him that thinketh he standeth take heed lest he fall" (1 Corinthians 10:12). To run in the heavenly race in which God has placed us, we must run with self-control and discipline. To finish the race, we must buffet our bodies and run in such a way as to receive the prize—a crown incorruptible (1 Corinthians 9:25).

What about you? Your children are looking to you as an example of how to finish this year's homeschooling race. If spring fever is tempting you to be lazy and lax in disciplining your day's schedule, you can't expect your children to be much different. Pray and ask God to replace your lost motivation with a new fervor to finish the homeschooling task He has given you to do. "Know ye not that they which run in a race run all, but one receiveth the prize? So run, that ye may obtain" (1 Corinthians 9:24).

Lord, thank You for the joys of homeschooling my children. Please help me maintain our focus to accomplish Your best for this year and give me the strength to finish strong. In Jesus' name, Amen.

 Share your thoughts about this devotional at aophomeschooling.com/107

Painful Reminders

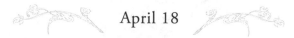

April 18

"Be ye not unequally yoked together with unbelievers: for what fellowship hath righteousness with unrighteousness? and what communion hath light with darkness" (2 Corinthians 6:14)?

The morning started with the warmth of a spring sun and God's prompting to take the children outdoors. Winter had been long, and I knew their spirits needed refreshment. Calling homeschooling off for the afternoon, I sent each child his separate way to enjoy his individual interest. My youngest set out to watch the ants as they built their new home, my oldest started down the road for a bike ride, and my two middle children walked to the paddock for a leisurely horseback ride.

After working in my garden for a few minutes, I looked up to see a riderless horse running past me with broken reins dangling from its bridle. As I wheeled around to find my children, I saw my son running toward me with a panicked look on his face. Just then, my daughter appeared holding what was left of the reins in her hands. Staggering and incoherent, I quickly took her inside the house to help her lie down. As my son followed us, he proceeded to tell me what had happened. Deciding to ride bareback together, my daughter rode in front with my son sitting behind her. However, as they started to trot, my son lost his balance and fell, grabbing his sister as he went down. Together, they had slipped off the horse's back, and in the fall, my daughter had struck her head on a large rock. After a visit to the doctor, we spent the next three days anxiously watching as my daughter recovered from a concussion and amnesia.

Many things contributed to my children's accident that afternoon. Their horse was overly frisky, they failed to ride with a saddle, and most of all, they shouldn't have been riding double since my son was an inexperienced rider. My daughter's painful lesson was verbalized when she recovered and said, "Sorry, I wasn't thinking. I should have never let him ride with me."

Too many Christians have also learned the same painful lesson—yoking yourself to the wrong person is sure to bring you down. Although we are to reach the lost with the love of Christ, God exhorts us to remember that we are His temple (2 Corinthians 6:16). There's only one way to reach the world yet remain separate and holy unto God. We must yoke ourself to Him. "Take my yoke upon you, and learn of me" (Matthew 11:29a).

Father, teach me how to love the lost without losing my love for You. Purify my life and use me for Your glory. In the name of Jesus, Amen.

 Share your thoughts about this devotional at **aophomeschooling.com**/108

Daily Chores

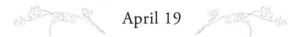

April 19

What chores have you delegated to your children to keep the homeschooling wheels turning in your family? To save electricity and money, my youngest daughter's chore was hanging up the clothes to dry. Each morning after breakfast, she either hung the clothes outside in the fresh summer air or inside on the drying rack during the winter months. With six people in our family, this task grew into a time-consuming chore. Early on, she discovered that no amount of complaining or procrastinating would relieve her of the responsibility. Learning to face the task with resolve and determination, she acquired a work ethic that has since served her well in the work place.

In living the Christian life, you too may face "chores" God has given you to do. Serving on church committees, hosting backyard Bible clubs, and teaching Sunday school can seem like added burdens to an already full homeschooling schedule. Although the extra discipline required to minister to others may seem daunting at the time, you'll discover it develops a Christ-like character that glorifies the Lord.

What about you? Are you complaining about the chores God has given you to do or have you learned to submit to the lesson of servanthood? Make no mistake, God will keep leading you back to what He last asked you to do until you say, "Yes, Lord. Here I am, send me." Embrace the responsibility and see the task for what it is—an opportunity to glorify your Lord and bless others. Is there anything better you could be doing with your life? "Even as the Son of man came not to be ministered unto, but to minister, and to give his life a ransom for many" (Matthew 20:28).

Lord, forgive me for complaining and shirking the responsibilities You've given to me. Open my eyes to see the joys of blessing others with Your love and let me serve You today with a totally devoted heart. In the precious name of Jesus, Amen.

Early Morning Singers

April 20

"O sing unto the LORD a new song: sing unto the LORD, all the earth" (Psalm 96:1).

Their greeting surprised me that morning. As the sun rose, their warbling song filtered through the window and lifted my spirit with the hope of spring. My patience had been running thin for the past several weeks, and God knew I needed a boost to finish our homeschooling year. With their joyful melodies ministering to my soul, I listened in amazement and smiled as I watched them sing. Their tiny bodies shook and resonated with sound, appearing as if they used their entire being. "Amazing," I thought to myself. "These little wrens do a better job of praising the Lord than I do."

Of all God's creation, humans seem to have the hardest time consistently praising God. Homeschoolers grow tired near the end of the school year and forget God is in control. With impatient hearts and complaining spirits, we trudge on in our own effort as we push to the final homeschooling days before summer. Instead of singing praises to God for the homeschooling joys He has given, we forget our blessings and simply focus on getting through our schoolwork. Satan smiles as he realizes he has succeeded in robbing us of our song.

How about you? Has it been awhile since God heard a song of praise from your lips? If you're experiencing difficulty in finding joy during these last days of homeschooling, you would do well to learn the lesson of praising the Lord from God's little wren. "The LORD is my strength and my shield; my heart trusted in him, and I am helped: therefore my heart greatly rejoiceth; and with my song will I praise him" (Psalms 28:7).

Lord, forgive me for failing to praise and thank You for Your many blessings. Put a new song in my heart today and let me rejoice in the goodness of Your love. In the name of Jesus, Amen.

Flying High

April 21

"Unto thee, O LORD, do I lift up my soul. O my God, I trust in thee: let me not be ashamed" (Psalm 25:1-2a).

The annual kite flying day was only two weeks away for our homeschooling group. My oldest son was looking forward to winning the category for the highest flying kite. For several months, he had been preparing the perfect design. Using the old box shape, he believed his kite would fly higher and better than any other kite in western Nebraska's strong, spring winds. His balsa wood frame was tightly wrapped in light-weight flour sack cloths, and with his father's help, he had tested the kite's lift/drag performance several times.

When the anticipated day finally arrived, we set out for a fun day of picnicking and kite flying with our homeschooling friends. The wind was steady and blowing at 15 to 20 mph. After a wonderful lunch and game time, each child brought out his kite for the contest. When my son ran down the pasture's gentle slope, his kite lifted effortlessly. Eagerly, we watched his kite climb farther and farther into the blue sky. A smile grew on his face each time he let out more of his line, and we all sensed the outcome. His hours of effort and work were paying off, and when he reached the end of his line, everyone cheered. His kite was flying hundreds of feet above the rest.

Watching God bless my son that day, I learned a spiritual truth from the Lord. Homeschool worries had been dragging me down. Were my children learning what they needed? Was my husband's paycheck going to be enough? Would I ever have time to feel pretty again? As the breeze blew against my face, I sensed the Holy Spirit saying, "Let out your line, and let Me show you just how good homeschooling can be." Trusting His promises, I said, "Yes, Lord." I realized then how intimately God wanted to be involved in our daily homeschooling. After I took that step of faith, I saw a new view of my children's futures from God's heights.

How about you? Are you weighted down from homeschooling in your own effort? Why not fly high and trust God for His perfect plan for your family? "For in thee do I trust: cause me to know the way wherein I should walk; for I lift up my soul unto thee" (Psalm 143:8b).

Lord, you are my King, and I bow my knee to Your holy name. Praise to You for releasing me from the doubt and fears that plague my homeschooling heart. Lift me above the problems and help me to trust You for everything we need. In the name of Jesus, Amen.

 Share your thoughts about this devotional at aophomeschooling.com/111

High Waters

April 22

"Therefore be ye also ready: for in such an hour as ye think not the Son of man cometh" (Matthew 24:44).

We had seen the dark cloud in the distance. Knowing we were in for another soaker, our family prepared for a torrential downpour. Just as we completed our preparations, however, it seemed like some invisible hand reached out and moved the cloud. After not even receiving a drop of rain, the sun came out and we thought the storm was over, until we heard a flash flood alert on the radio. Apparently, eight inches of rain had fallen in the neighboring town, and a three-foot wall of water was headed our way.

Looking out the window, I saw our neighbor working in his low-lying pasture. Knowing he was unaware of the strange events taking place, I sent my son on his bicycle to warn him. Having recently moved his herd of cows and newborn calves to the fresh green grass near the dry riverbed's edge, we knew they were right in the flood's path. As I continued to home-school my other children, my son soon returned and said, "Mom, I tried to tell him, but he wouldn't listen." Thinking we were overreacting, our neighbor ignored my son's warning and went about his business repairing the pasture fences.

A few minutes later, we watched as the fast-moving flood waters approached. From our ranch's hill-top view, we saw the wall of water etch its way toward our neighbor's cattle. Frightened and running in all directions, most of the cattle barely escaped as they ran to higher ground. However, several calves became disoriented in the confusion and found themselves being carried away in the water's swift current. Saddened by the scene, my son turned to me and asked, "Mom, why wouldn't he listen?"

"I don't know," I replied. "But this reminds me of what it will be like when Christ returns."

Someday Christ will bring judgment on today's sinful world. Those who have ignored the message of salvation are in great danger. Like the people in Noah's day, they go about their business and assume they have everything under control until it's too late. Are your loved ones ready for the day when Christ returns as King of Kings and Lord of Lords? "For as in the days that were before the flood they were eating and drinking, marrying and giving in marriage, until the day that Noe entered into the ark, And knew not until the flood came, and took them all away; so shall also the coming of the Son of man be" (Matthew 24:38-39).

Lord, someday You will return as King. Please use our homeschooling family to share the good news of Your forgiveness with as many people as possible before that day comes. In Jesus' name, Amen.

 Share your thoughts about this devotional at **aophomeschooling.com**/112

Going for the Gold

April 23

"Beareth all things, believeth all things, hopeth all things, endureth all things" (1 Corinthians 13:7).

My oldest son loved the old west stories in our U.S. history curriculum. He seemed to identify with the early settlers who left the comforts of home and family in the east for adventure and gold in the west's unknown frontiers. Because my son's interest in this chapter of history ran deep, we decided to celebrate his tenth birthday with a tour of a working gold mine in Colorado.

My son's eagerness to experience "panning" and extracting gold from rock was contagious. Exchanging our caps for hard hats, our entire family accompanied him as he proceeded down the mine. Our guide's expert commentary gave my son a new understanding of the methods used in locating and extracting gold underground. Although the first prospectors easily became rich, many who followed faced hours of difficult work to compile even an ounce of this precious metal. At the tour's conclusion, my son was given a pan to search for his own gold in a nearby riverbed. After panning in several spots for more than an hour, hoping to find his "fortune," he looked at me and said, "Mom, they sure had to work hard for just a little bit of gold, didn't they?"

Finding the gold in homeschooling also takes time. The first years usually involve sifting out mistakes like using the wrong curriculum, over-scheduling activities, and becoming intimidated by homeschooling opponents. However, if you faithfully continue teaching in God's strength, you'll soon discover the sparkling flakes of educational knowledge and Christ-like character shining in your child. So don't give up! Go for the gold and discover the best your homeschooling family can be! "And I will give thee the treasures of darkness, and hidden riches of secret places, that thou mayest know that I, the LORD, which call thee by thy name, am the God of Israel" (Isaiah 45:3).

Father, nothing of value ever comes easily. Please give me the strength and wisdom to remain faithful while You show me the gold You've placed in my child's life. In the precious name of Jesus, Amen.

The First Loaf

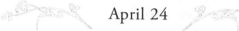

"And the patient in spirit is better than the proud in spirit" (Ecclesiastes 7:8b).

My daughter's first attempt at baking bread in our home economics class served as a stark reminder of the importance of patience. Although she carefully measured and followed the recipe's directions when making the dough, her lack of patience in waiting for it to rise paid a stiff penalty. Thinking she could hurry the process along, she only let the dough rise 15 minutes instead of an hour. Later, as she removed the bread from the oven, she discovered the consequence of her actions. Each loaf was flat and too hard to eat.

Patience is more than a virtue; it is a fruit of the spirit that must be developed in our children's character (Galatians 5:22). As we teach our children to discipline their selfish emotions, they learn to wait on God and to trust Him for all their needs. However, leading our children through this growing process requires a patience of its own. As homeschooling parents, we may find ourselves failing to demonstrate the very patience we are attempting to instill.

What about you? Are you speaking crossly, acting perturbed, or responding negatively to your child's request for help during the day? Homeschooling requires an intense amount of love and patience that only comes from walking with the Lord. The next time you find yourself growing cross after a long homeschooling day, remember that impatience can ruin more than just a loaf of bread. It can also ruin your relationship with your children and your home. "I therefore, the prisoner of the Lord, beseech you that ye walk worthy of the vocation wherewith ye are called, With all lowliness and meekness, with longsuffering, forbearing one another in love." (Ephesians 4:1-2)

Father, help me to practice what I preach and to demonstrate patience with those I love. Let my words be seasoned by Your grace and let me rise above the homeschooling problems in the power of the Holy Spirit. In Jesus' name, Amen.

Cutting Remarks

April 25

"If ye be reproached for the name of Christ, happy are ye; for the spirit of glory and of God resteth upon you" (1 Peter 4:14a).

If you've ever been slandered by someone as a homeschooler, you know the difficulty in forgiving hurtful words spoken in ignorance. As a homeschooling parent, rising above cruel remarks was a constant battle. Dealing with misinformed statements like, "Homeschoolers don't educate their children; they simply brainwash them and turn them into non-thinking Christian zombies," required the supernatural love and forgiveness of God. Unfortunately, many years went by before I finally realized the lesson God was teaching me—how to love others in the face of opposition.

While Christ lived here on earth, He was repeatedly reviled by the world. People slandered Christ's holy name and works and stated that He was a drunkard (Matthew 11:19), a blasphemer (Matthew 9:3), and a rebel (Luke 23:2,5). Christ warned the disciples that they also would be reviled and suffer verbal attacks for their faith in Him. In Matthew 5:11, He stated, "Blessed are ye, when men shall revile you, and persecute you, and shall say all manner of evil against you falsely, for my sake."

Are you hurting inside today from someone's malicious gossip? Slander never feels good, but God knows your pain. He cares about your feelings and will send the loving encouragement you need to keep homeschooling. Don't let someone's foolish talk rob you of the wonderful joy of teaching your children. "Be ready always to give an answer to every man that asketh you a reason of the hope that is in you with meekness and fear. Having a good conscience; that, whereas they speak evil of you, as of evildoers, they may be ashamed that falsely accuse your good conversation in Christ" (1 Peter 3:15b-16).

Father, help me to forgive others when they put down our homeschooling. Show me how to respond with a heart motivated by love and to keep my conscience clear as I represent You. In the name of Jesus, Amen.

Hen and Peck

April 26

"Likewise, I say unto you, there is joy in the presence of the angels of God over one sinner that repenteth" (Luke 15:10).

One of our homeschooling family's favorite spring-time activities was visiting the local feed and seed store to see the new baby chickens and ducks. Every year the store converted several small aluminum water tanks into warm, cozy homes for these little creatures. My children never tired of watching their antics and especially enjoyed their baby peeping noises. As my young daughter leaned over the tank to pet their soft downy feathers, she looked at me with questioning eyes and said, "Mom, can I have one?"

Normally, I would have said no, but this year I sensed the Lord leading in a different direction. Smiling, I said, "Yes, honey, you and your brother can pick one of the baby chicks to take home." My daughter's delight in my reply knew no bounds, and she and her brother set about choosing the perfect new little friend. Before we left the store that day, Hen and Peck were aptly named and adopted into our family.

New life is always a cause for rejoicing, especially when it's in the family of God. Whenever a person repents of his sin and receives new life in Christ, the Bible says the angels rejoice. Imagine, thousands of excited angels shouting and praising the Lord for the new life that has just been recorded in the Book of Life (Revelation 20:15). What a glorious time that must be!

As a Christian homeschooling parent, you have the wonderful privilege and responsibility to lead your baby "chicks" to the Lord. Every Bible lesson, Scripture verse, and godly character trait you teach your child leads to the moment when they, too, are born again into God's family. When the Holy Spirit convicts and your child prays, "Lord, forgive me. I'm a sinner," a new life in Christ begins. However, one question remains. Who will be rejoicing the most, you or the angels in heaven?

Father, thank You for the awesome responsibility and joy of teaching my children about Your forgiving love. Please touch their hearts with the conviction of the Holy Spirit so they too will experience the joy of a new life in You. In the saving name of Jesus, Amen.

Putting Down Roots

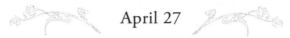

April 27

After you've lived somewhere like the windy, western plains of Nebraska, you begin to appreciate the value of a tree. Inspired by the founding father of Arbor Day, Julius Sterling Morton, my young son decided to make some changes in our barren landscape. Using seeds from his grandparents' ash trees in northwest Iowa, he planted hundreds in different locations on our ranch for a homeschool science project. My son faithfully watered each seed for several months, but soon discovered the climate and poor quality of soil were unfit for starting a new tree. Discouraged, my young son said, "I guess Iowa seeds simply won't grow unless they're in Iowa dirt."

Having the right soil is also important when planting spiritual seeds. In the parable of the sower in Matthew 13, Jesus taught His disciples the principle of planting God's Word in people's hearts. Many individuals with hard-packed hearts; rocky, shallow faith; or thorny, overcommitted lives miss the benefits of God's blessings. Only one soil is fit to nurture the seeds of God's truth. With the good soil of repentant hearts, these people experience salvation and forgiveness and bring forth thirty, sixty, and even a hundredfold harvest for the kingdom of God (Matthew 13:23).

What about you? Have you noticed any spiritual harvest in your life since you were saved? If not, perhaps it's time to take a soil sample to evaluate the content for PBS (Prayer and Bible Study). Only as you spend time in the Word and on your knees, will God enrich your life and give you the strength to remove rocks and pull weeds. "Now he that ministereth seed to the sower both minister bread for your food, and multiply your seed sown, and increase the fruits of your righteousness" (2 Corinthians 9:10).

Father, forgive me for not bearing the fruit You desire. Plant those things in my life that give You glory and cleanse me of any rocks and thorns blocking Your will. In the name of Jesus, Amen.

Focused Homeschooling

April 28

"Pray without ceasing" (1 Thessalonians 5:17).

Distractions. Every day you face them as a homeschooling parent. Although some may seem good in themselves, they can steal time from your family and destroy your homeschooling schedule. Learning to recognize each interruption as either a divine rescheduling or an evil diversion takes discernment that only comes from the Holy Spirit. Whether it's a long phone call from your mother or sister, or an invitation to enjoy an impromptu outing with another homeschooling family, you must prayerfully consider what daily activities are God's best for your family.

Going with the flow and failing to pray for guidance caused many problems for people in the Bible, too. Even Joshua, God's chosen leader after Moses' death, was distracted and made the mistake of believing the Gibeonites. After seeing the destruction of Jericho and fearing for their lives, the Gibeonites sent representatives disguised as travelers from a distant land to make peace with Joshua. Instead of coming before the Lord in prayer to verify their story, Joshua made a covenant with them, not knowing they were his neighboring enemies (Joshua 9:14-15). Held to his oath, Joshua was forced to let them live. He made them "hewers of wood and drawers of water for the congregation, and for the altar of the LORD" (vs. 27).

Have you learned how to discern God's will for your homeschooling day? Only as you walk in the power of the Holy Spirit will you be able to know the difference between a dangerous detour and God's window of opportunity. Taking the time to pray for wisdom each morning and throughout the day will save your homeschooling from disaster. "Yea, if thou criest after knowledge, and liftest up thy voice for understanding; If thou seekest her as silver, and searchest for her as for hid treasures; Then shalt thou understand the fear of the LORD, and find the knowledge of God" (Proverbs 2:3-5).

Father, only You know what's best for our homeschooling today. As we face distractions, please help me to discern what is Your perfect will for us and to adjust our homeschooling schedule accordingly. In Jesus' name, Amen.

Share your thoughts about this devotional at **aophomeschooling.com/**118

The Joy of Children

April 29

"As arrows are in the hand of a mighty man; so are children of the youth. Happy is the man that hath his quiver full of them" (Psalm 127:4-5a).

Call me crazy, but I just love kids. Therefore, making the decision to homeschool our four children wasn't difficult—it was simply a result that grew out of love. What did seem crazy, however, were the countless, negative remarks I received from people who felt bogged down by the responsibilities of parenting. Such comments like, "Why in the world would you want to stay home with your kids?" or "I can hardly wait until they're ready for school so I can enjoy my life again," seemed as crazy to me as my homeschooling did to them. In response I thought, "Why wouldn't you want to spend time with the people you love most?"

Treasuring the blessing of children is a foreign concept to most. Although many couples love and enjoy their children, there are couples who view children as an inconvenience. Wanting to "get ahead in the world," they only have time to enjoy their children in small doses and pass off the major responsibility for their children's care, education, and entertainment to others. However, God's view on children is different. He calls them blessings and "rewards" (Psalm 127:3). And they are! Through the eyes of children, you appreciate the wonder of God's world and maintain a heart that is soft and compassionate. Children also teach you to forgive easily, love unselfishly, and enjoy the blessings of the moment.

How are you feeling about your children today? Do you view each of them as a blessing even in the toughest times? Admittedly, homeschooled children are a huge responsibility that requires a great deal of self-sacrifice. However, even in the worst of your homeschooling moments, the blessings they bring far outweigh any burden involved. Ask any parent who has been homeschooling more than a few years, and they'll tell you the same story—their children are their greatest treasures. What about yours?

Father, forgive me when I take the world's view toward my children. Just as You treasure me as Your precious child, humble my heart and teach me to love my own children, too. In the name of Jesus, Amen.

 Share your thoughts about this devotional at aophomeschooling.com/119

The Lone Tree

April 30

"And he shall be like a tree planted by the rivers of water, that bringeth forth his fruit in his season; his leaf also shall not wither; and whatsoever he doeth shall prosper" (Psalm 1:3).

Attempting to find a few moments with the Lord before the beginning of our homeschooling day, I hiked the ragged bluffs in the pasture near our ranch. As I walked through the dry stubble, sage brush, and yucca plants, I came across a small cottonwood tree. With no other trees of any kind close by for miles, it looked completely out of place. The rocky ground in which it grew offered little nourishment, and I knew months had passed since any rain had fallen. "How does this little tree stay alive out here all by itself?" I asked myself.

Reflecting on the tree's life, I began to see it as a symbol of my own. For the past ten years, I had been homeschooling our children and feeling much like a loner. Not only was homeschooling going against the flow, it was completely out of the main stream. I found no encouraging nourishment from family or church friends, and wondered, like I did about this little tree, how much longer I could survive. But then the Holy Spirit spoke to my heart and showed me something amazing. I noticed a difference in the soil's color near the tree's base. As I looked closer, it became evident that this tree's roots went down many feet below the surface. I remembered then what my son and I had learned when studying the topography of the area. Deep below the surface, there was an aquifer, an underground river bringing life-giving water to this little tree. I smiled and said, "Thank You, Lord," as I learned God's lesson for the morning.

For the next several years, I remembered the lesson of the lone tree whenever I felt lonely or homeschooling became difficult. Each time I felt used up and dry, I stretched my roots of faith a little deeper and found the nourishment and life-giving water of God's love. Even though I couldn't see Him, the Holy Spirit's peace was always present. Best of all, this isn't just my story. If you are a homeschooler finding yourself alone in the middle of a dry day, the same life-giving water is waiting to bless you, too. "But whosoever drinketh of the water that I shall give him shall never thirst; but the water that I shall give him shall be in him a well of water springing up into everlasting life" (John 4:14).

Lord, thank You for refreshing me when I am empty. Teach me to reach for You whenever homeschooling leaves me feeling afraid or lonely, and fill me with Your strength and love. In the wonderful name of Jesus, Amen.

 Share your thoughts about this devotional at **aophomeschooling.com**/120

Kudos to You

"Wherefore seeing we also are compassed about with so great a cloud of witnesses, let us lay aside every weight, and the sin which doth so easily beset us, and let us run with patience the race that is set before us" (Hebrews 12:1).

Homeschooling is a challenge, a commitment, and a lifestyle of love and devotion. As a fellow homeschooling parent, my heart goes out to those who continue to faithfully teach their children at home. You are not alone in your efforts. I, along with thousands of home-schoolers who have run this race and reached the finish line, cheer you on. At times, homeschooling can be tiring and seem like a thankless job as you face hurdles of opposition. But those of us who have run the race know what you're doing is important. With great respect, we pray you'll keep going to the end to experience the wonderful blessing of helping your child rise to his gifting by God.

As Christians, Hebrews 12:1 tells us that we also have another crowd cheering us on. The great men and women of faith in Hebrews 11, along with thousands of other believers are cheering you on in your spiritual race. This "cloud of witnesses" watches and knows the blessings waiting for you in this life and in heaven. Like young Timothy following in the footsteps of Paul, "Fight the good fight of faith, lay hold on eternal life, whereunto thou art also called, and hast professed a good profession before many witnesses" (1 Timothy 6:12).

Is your faith being tested today? Do you feel like giving up instead of standing firm in what you know to be true according to God's Word? Don't despair, you have a great "cloud of witnesses" who have gone down this same path before you. Let the Holy Spirit and the encouragement of their faithful lives fill you with the strength you need to finish your spiritual race.

Lord, thank You for the countless lives of missionaries, martyrs, and believers who have remained true to You and Your Word throughout time. Encourage me today to take heart and stand strong as I face the daily battles of homeschooling. In Jesus' name, Amen.

The Microscope

May 2

"And be not conformed to this world: but be ye transformed by the renewing of your mind, that ye may prove what is that good, and acceptable, and perfect, will of God" (Romans 12:2).

My children weren't the only ones who learned character lessons during the course of our homeschooling. Daily, I came under the same instruction as my children, and I struggled to show patience, kindness, and love in my actions. One particular day of character building (or the lack of it) stands out clearly in my mind. I had just given my son an expensive hand-held microscope for his birthday. I envisioned him enjoying hours of inspecting bugs, plants, and rocks with this new educational toy, but my dreams were short-lived. As I walked into my son's room that afternoon, I found the microscope lying on his desk completely disassembled. Parts were everywhere, and before my son could offer any explanation, I immediately accused him of ruining the microscope. When my barrage of hurtful comments chastising him to be more responsible ended, he looked at me and said, "I'm sorry, Mom. I took it apart to use the light bulb in my science experiment. I was going to put it back together when I was done."

The ability to live godly is something every Christian seeks to attain. As I examined my actions that day under the light and focus of God's Word, I realized how undisciplined I was in showing patience. My tongue was severely in need of being bridled (James 3), and I found myself coming to God and my child to ask forgiveness for my sinful foolishness. Although I could have hidden behind fatigue and other excuses, the clear picture of whom I was without the Holy Spirit was more than evident.

What about you? Have you taken a good look lately at your attitude and actions during the course of your homeschooling day? We all fall short of the glory of God, but are you allowing God to change you as He reveals those areas in your life that need to come under His Lordship? Like the lens of a microscope, what is God's Word revealing about the true state of your character?

Father, I humbly bow before You and confess my sin. Too many days I reflect my old nature rather than the new life in Christ You have given me. Increase the fruit of righteousness within my life that my character might reflect Your glory. In the name of Jesus, Amen.

Healing a Nation

May 3

"I exhort therefore, that, first of all, supplications, prayers, intercessions, and giving of thanks, be made for all men; For kings, and for all that are in authority" (1 Timothy 2:1-2a).

As a homeschooling parent, do you have a burden for your child's future as a United States citizen? As I watched the decay of morality in our nation during my short lifetime, my heart grieved for my children and what they would face during their adult years. Sin's influence has been accepted and legislated into laws that wreck havoc in families, business, and government. Soon, homeschoolers, as well as all Christians, will have the privilege to unite in prayer during the National Day of Prayer. Together, we can proclaim our faith in God and the need for prayer to bring our country back to "one nation under God."

Throughout the Old Testament, we read how God removed His hand of blessing when Israel failed to worship God as He commanded. Forgetting He was the source of their blessings when times were good, they repeatedly "did that which was right in his own eyes" (Judges 21:25b). Today, the world is not much different. Society makes its own rules for what is right and wrong, and the nation suffers as people put their trust in man rather than in God. God continues to call out as in days of old and says, "If my people, which are called by my name, shall humble themselves, and pray, and seek my face, and turn from their wicked ways; then will I hear from heaven, and will forgive their sin, and will heal their land" (2 Chronicles 7:14).

What about your family? Do you actively pray for those in authority in your city, state, and federal governments? If ever our country needed prayer, it's now! Won't you take a moment to pray as a homeschooling family again today? "This know also, that in the last days perilous times shall come. For men shall be lovers of their own selves, covetous, boasters, proud, blasphemers, disobedient to parents, unthankful, unholy, Without natural affection, trucebreakers, false accusers, incontinent, fierce, despisers of those that are good, Traitors, heady, highminded, lovers of pleasures more than lovers of God; Having a form of godliness, but denying the power thereof" (2 Timothy 3:1-5a).

Father, like the prophets of old, we cry for mercy and forgiveness for a nation that has forgotten You. Bring our country back to You in repentance and use our homeschooling family to intercede for those who have the power to make the changes that will glorify You.
In the name of Jesus, Amen.

Unlimited Power

May 4

"The effectual fervent prayer of a righteous man availeth much" (James 5:16b).

Amazing, isn't it? With all the technology available in the world, the most powerful tool we have as Christians is prayer. When we pray, God's power strengthens us. Teaching our children how to access this source of strength is paramount, for no other aspect of Christian living is as important as knowing how to talk and listen to God. However, some homeschool lessons are better caught rather than taught, and such is the case with prayer. The best curriculum for teaching prayer is simply praying out loud together with your child and allowing him to see and hear you talk to God.

Because praying was such a personal matter, I first shied away from letting my children hear my prayers. Sure, I let them hear me give praise and thanks for food and other blessings, but I knew communing with the Lord involved much more. My children also needed to hear me confess my sins and to intercede for others honestly and humbly. They needed to learn that prayer was more than vain repetitions (Matthew 6:7). I hoped as they listened, they would learn there's no limit to intimacy with the Creator of the universe. They could talk to God anytime about anything.

What about your prayer life? Would your children know how to pray after listening to you talk to God? If not, perhaps it's time to come to the Lord like the disciples and ask, "Lord, teach us to pray" (Luke 11:1b). Jesus knew the disciples would never survive without a powerful prayer life. Do you think your children are any different? "Therefore choose life, that both thou and thy seed may live: That thou mayest love the LORD thy God, and that thou mayest obey his voice, and that thou mayest cleave unto him: for he is thy life, and the length of thy days" (Deuteronomy 30:19b-20a).

Father, thank You for the power of prayer to find strength for every difficulty in life. Help me teach my children how to pray by bringing them into Your presence. In the name of Jesus, Amen.

Who Gets the Credit?

May 5

"A man's pride shall bring him low: but honour shall uphold the humble in spirit" (Proverbs 29:23).

Feeling pride in my son's accomplishment of graduating summa cum laude from a state university wasn't difficult. As a homeschooling parent, watching my son receive his degree in anthropology was the culmination of years of schooling. No parents could have been prouder, and we rejoiced in our son's outstanding achievement. The years of homeschooling had been worth the sacrifice, and my son's award proved again that a child could be successfully educated at home.

As I thought about the days, hours, and minutes involved in homeschooling my son, I realized God was the one who should receive the greatest award. Without His loving care, protection, and provision, we would have never survived homeschooling. God's loving guidance and wisdom taught countless lessons that were never recorded on my son's report card, and the many extracurricular opportunities my son enjoyed were divinely orchestrated by God's loving hand. God knew my son's hands-on learning and creative enthusiasm would have been stifled in public school. By convicting me to homeschool, God kept my son from joining the ranks of bored underachievers. "Yes, God should be taking the credit today," I thought to myself. "He kept every one of His promises and was everything we needed as we homeschooled."

During times of success and recognition, it's easy to forget God. The story of Herod in Acts 12:20-23 is a perfect example. Not only did he steal God's glory, Herod went one step further and took credit for being God. Allowing the people of Tyre and Sidon to praise and worship him, Herod did nothing when they began shouting, "It is the voice of a god, and not of a man" (vs. 22). Herod's haughtiness and pride led to a surprising, sudden death: "And immediately the angel of the Lord smote him, because he gave not God the glory: and he was eaten of worms, and gave up the ghost" (vs. 23).

Are you tempted to puff yourself up and take credit for your child's educational success? Even though you've invested time and effort, God is the one who is going before you. He gives creativity to your lesson plans, spiritual insights to apply His Word, and the resources and physical health to accomplish each day's tasks. Simply said, your homeschooling is nothing without God. "But he that glorieth, let him glory in the Lord" (2 Corinthians 10:17).

Father, forgive me when I steal Your glory. You alone deserve the praise for what our homeschooling family has become. Today, we lift our voices in thanksgiving for Your goodness and love. In Jesus' name, Amen.

 Share your thoughts about this devotional at aophomeschooling.com/125

Second Starts

May 6

"It is of the LORD's mercies that we are not consumed, because his compassions fail not. They are new every morning: great is thy faithfulness" (Lamentations 3:22-23).

Homeschooling was even harder during the 1980s than it is today. Starting out strong, I was determined to be the best homeschooling parent, but that was before I faced opposition. Some days, my relatives attacked with hurtful comments highlighting my inability to teach. Other days, public school officials sent threatening notes of truancy. Daily, strangers would challenge me with infamous questions like, "Why aren't your kids in school?" Without the benefit of experienced homeschoolers and organizations to help me through these confrontations, I vacillated in my homeschooling commitment. Succumbing to the pressure and ignoring God's call, I stopped teaching my children and said, "God, I can't do this. This is too hard!"

In Acts 12:25, John Mark started out strong, too, as he accompanied Paul and Barnabas on their first missionary journey. Near the city of Pamphylia, however, the pressures of the trip became too great, and he turned around and headed back home to Jerusalem (Acts 13:13). Perhaps it was the angry Jewish leaders trying to imprison the followers of Jesus, or the long days and short nights with little food and comfort. Whatever the reason, John Mark quit, and Paul had nothing good to say about him (Acts 15:37-38). When Barnabas wanted to take him on their second missionary journey, a conflict arose and Paul "thought not good to take him with them" (vs.38b).

Fortunately, God was gentler with me than Paul was with John Mark. Reminding me why I was homeschooling, He gave me another chance. As He confirmed the burden originally put on my heart, I went on in His strength to teach my children through high school. Like John Mark, I rejoiced in God's loving patience and the opportunity to start again.

What about you? If you've ever failed at homeschooling or living the Christian life, God is waiting to help you start over. Just pray right now and ask Him for the help you need. Whether it's strength to keep homeschooling or strength to find victory over a particular sin, God wants to show you grace, mercy, and love. He truly is the God of the second chance. "Like as a father pitieth his children, so the LORD pitieth them that fear him" (Psalm 103:13).

Father, thank You for Your great mercy. Please show me how to start again and to be obedient to what You've asked. In the name of Jesus, Amen.

 Share your thoughts about this devotional at **aophomeschooling.com**/126

Food for the Ages

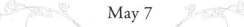

May 7

Since home cooking was quickly becoming a lost art, food preparation was an important part of our homeschooling. Although gourmet delights were appreciated, what our family enjoyed eating most were old-fashioned meals prepared with organic, farm-fresh meats, vegetables, and grains. Recipes for this type of cooking, however, weren't found in commercial cookbooks. Rather, these recipes came from the godly women who shared their culinary skills in the church cookbook. Gleaning from their expertise, we baked cakes, breads, and pies from scratch and learned the resourcefulness of using our garden's bounty for casseroles, soups, and salads.

In addition to helpful and healthy recipes, these wonderful cookbooks also held small nuggets of seasoned advice from gray-haired grandmas. Like Solomon's proverbs, these insightful sayings were sprinkled throughout the pages, giving my children and me food for thought as we cooked. Here are a few of my favorites:

"Church members are either pillars or caterpillars. The pillars hold up the church, the caterpillars just crawl in and out."

"If you want to be original, be yourself. God never made two people exactly alike."

"Love isn't blind; it just doesn't tell all it sees."

"A gossiper is like an old shoe—its tongue never stays in place."

"Food without seasoning is like talk without reasoning."

"Work is the yeast that raises the dough."

Whether it's cooking, cleaning, or homeschooling children, a younger woman needs the experienced knowledge an older woman provides. However, you have to be willing to share the recipes God has taught you. If you're a seasoned homeschool mom, is there someone whom you can bless with the many things the Lord has taught you? "The aged women likewise, that they be in behaviour as becometh holiness, not false accusers, not given to much wine, teachers of good things; That they may teach the young women to be sober, to love their husbands, to love their children" (Titus 2:3-4).

Lord, thank You for the women you've placed in my life to help me raise my family and care for my home. Use me now to be a blessing, so others might be encouraged to follow You as they homeschool. In the name of Jesus, Amen.

 Share your thoughts about this devotional at **aophomeschooling.com**/127

Quick Fixes

"Create in me a clean heart, O God; and renew a right spirit within me" (Psalms 51:10).

How could I say no? My children were asking for a day off from homeschooling to enjoy our favorite family activity—riding bikes. Since we had just moved to the country, we weren't aware of the problems that lay ahead. As we proceeded down the gravel road for our first outing, we traveled only a short way before three of our bikes started losing air in their tires. Stopping the other children, my husband examined the flat tires and found goatheads sticking into the tread. Apparently, the burrs that were ruining our day came from the puncture vine that grew easily in the ditches and roads near our new home.

Looking for a fast, inexpensive solution to the problem, we decided to purchase several tubes of "goo." However, we quickly discovered this sticky remedy was useless against the goathead's long, spiny ends. My husband's next idea involved purchasing an extra tire tube and cutting it in half to reinforce each bike tire with additional thickness. This idea also proved to be useless. After exhausting several other options, we finally bought what we should have purchased in the first place—expensive, solid tubes necessary for riding bikes on thorn-infested roads. After calculating the time, effort, and money spent, we realized how much our "quick fix" had cost.

Quick fixes usually have a way of costing more in spiritual matters, too. Like King David's sin with Bathsheba, we foolishly attempt to fix or cover up the sin in our life with short-term solutions. Bypassing prayer and the correction from God's Word, we waste time and energy thinking, "What's the easiest way to get out of this?" We refuse to listen to God's disciplining voice and trade confession and long-term Holy Spirit transformation for our man-made remedy.

What about you? Are you heading down life's road thinking you have everything under control? If you've been tempted to apply a quick fix to your sinful condition, you may find yourself with a flat tire or worse yet, headed for the ditch. Why not pull over now, and allow the solid truth of God's Word to bring about the change in your life that God desires? "For I will declare mine iniquity; I will be sorry for my sin" (Psalm 38:18).

Lord, I've been trying to fix this mess in my life for too long. I confess that what I've been doing is wrong. Please transform me into the person You want me to be. In the name of Jesus, Amen.

Asparagus Hunts

May 9

"And when she hath found it, she calleth her friends and her neighbours together, saying, Rejoice with me; for I have found the piece which I had lost" (Luke 15:9).

Hunting the roadside ditches for asparagus was a favorite spring-time activity for our homeschooling family. Every year, my oldest son was the first to ask, "When are we going to go looking for asparagus?" He loved eating this tasty vegetable. As if hunting for a treasure, he would map out our favorite wild asparagus locations on the county atlas. Harvesting asparagus appealed to his hunter-gatherer spirit that loved finding each spear hidden within the ditch grasses. Watching him walk down the ditch with paper bag in hand I said, "I'm not sure which you enjoy more, eating asparagus or hunting for it."

Smiling, he replied, "Oh, definitely hunting for it!"

As Christians, we should have the same intense desire to reach lost souls. Unfortunately, many of us turn away from such opportunities to spread the good news of Jesus Christ. Safe in our own little environment of believers, we fail to see the hurting hearts of the unlovely and unwanted. Isolated and protected, we remain in the salt shaker and fail to be the salt the Lord desires (Matthew 5:13). God challenges us to go looking for the lost. Like the parable of the lost sheep and the lost coin (Luke 15), we are to walk through life with eyes open to see the hearts of those needing the saving message of Christ's love and forgiveness.

When was the last time you shared the love of Jesus with someone in need of salvation? In the end, all that will matter are the lives of those who came to know Christ because of your witness. Will you seek the lost?

Father, please open my eyes to see those who are in need of Your saving grace. Grant me boldness to share the message of hope and forgiveness that they might find eternal life in Your name. In Jesus' name, Amen.

Share your thoughts about this devotional at **aophomeschooling.com**/129

The Consequences of Complacency

"Thou shalt love the Lord thy God with all thy heart, and with all thy soul, and with all thy strength, and with all thy mind" (Luke 10:27b).

Complacency was creeping into our homeschooling, and my son's attitude toward his math was growing more apathetic. Realizing he would never finish his entire curriculum by the end of the school year, he decided to face the problem with an "I don't care" outlook. Walking past his room one day I heard him say, "I'll be glad when school's done next week. Then I won't have to think about geometry anymore."

"Wrong," I thought to myself. "You're not getting off the hook that easily!" As Memorial Day approached, my son saw the green lights of summer flashing before his eyes. However, what he failed to notice was the "stop sign" in my hand called summer school. With workbook in hand, I informed him that school was still in session. Each day we would be completing two lessons in math until he had completed his work.

Complacent Christians are of no use to the Lord. Weighed down by sins or entangled in the affairs of the world, their effectiveness for Christ is nullified. Allowing Satan to lure them to sleep, they no longer have the passionate fire for serving Christ. Assured of salvation and wanting only enough of God to get by, they live life to please themselves rather than to serve God. In Revelation, God clearly states His feeling about "lukewarm" Christians: "I know thy works, that thou art neither cold nor hot: I would thou wert cold or hot. So then because thou art lukewarm, and neither cold nor hot, I will spue thee out of my mouth" (Revelation 3:15-16).

Has complacency wrapped its ugly fingers around your heart? If you haven't felt a burden for the lost, gone to church, or even spent time in prayer and Bible study for ages, chances are your fire is almost out. Before "I don't care" becomes a permanent part of your spiritual vocabulary, heed God's warning and let the Holy Spirit fill you anew. "That ye put off concerning the former conversation the old man, which is corrupt according to the deceitful lusts; And be renewed in the spirit of your mind" (Ephesians 4:22-23).

Lord, forgive me for letting the things of this world take precedence over my love and devotion to You. Rekindle my love and expose those things which have taken me away from You. In the name of Jesus, Amen.

Nothing More to Give

May 11

"It is God that girdeth me with strength, and maketh my way perfect" (Psalm 18:32).

Do you ever wake up and feel like you have nothing left to give as a homeschooling parent? During one quiet morning as I looked out the kitchen window, I felt exhausted physically, financially, and emotionally. I just wanted my house to be clean, but as I looked around the house, each task I had accomplished seemed to have been replaced by ten others. Laundry, dishes, and dirt seemed to be everywhere. Added to this overwhelming burden was a mountain of schoolwork waiting to be graded and lessons needing to be planned. I felt depleted to the point of despair and prayed, "Lord, I'm so tired. Will I ever finish all this work?"

The struggle to find strength for the battle is nothing new. We can quit homeschooling, but if countless other Christians have remained steadfast through their difficult times, we can too. Clearly, believing the old saying, "When life gets tough, the tough get going," isn't the answer. As Christian homeschooling parents, we already know we don't have the ability to conjure up strength on our own. The strength lies in our attitude toward God and acknowledging our dependency on Him. Like Paul, we must learn "for when I am weak, then am I strong" (2 Corinthians 12:10b). Like a little child strengthened by his parents to lift objects much too heavy for himself, we can rediscover God's strength to move mountains of housework, schoolwork, or whatever comes our way.

If you are experiencing homeschool burnout and finding yourself shutting down, God is waiting for you. Your all-powerful and loving heavenly Father has the strength you need to face today, tomorrow, and even eternity. Stop thinking about what you can't do. Start depending on God and find out what you can do through Him today. "I can do all things through Christ which strengtheneth me" (Philippians 4:13).

Lord, homeschooling is impossible without You. Show me how to cling to You and lift me above the weight of each day's tasks. In the name of Jesus, Amen.

Quiet Testimonies

May 12

"And be ready always to give an answer to every man that asketh you a reason of the hope that is in you with meekness and fear" (1 Peter 3:15b).

Homeschoolers have different ways of promoting the joys of homeschooling. Some share homeschooling's rewards on a grand scale, while others promote them by a quiet, willing testimony. When asked why we homeschooled, I offered explanations that included our belief in Deuteronomy 6:5-7 and the example of our everyday homeschooling experience. Those people truly interested would respond, "Boy, that's great! I wish I was able to do that!" Even my children's friends responded to a quiet testimony in a positive way. After coming over to play, they would leave saying, "I wish my parents would homeschool me!" The benefits of homeschooling were easily revealed as they heard and saw homeschooling for what it was—a better way to learn.

Although the Bible gives examples of great leaders whose witness changed the lives of thousands, it also shares stories of men and women whose testimonies only affected a few. Andrew brought his brother Peter to Jesus, Philip told the Ethiopian ruler how to be saved, and Ruth's faithful actions to her mother-in-law Naomi were a witness in themselves. Impacting the lives of just a few, their quiet testimonies had far-reaching effects and accomplished great things for God.

What about you? Do you ever feel your witness is insignificant? Don't doubt the power of your quiet testimony to make a difference in the lives of others. Although you may never be a talented speaker on a stage, your faithful words of love and encouragement can be the tool God uses to win a lost soul to Christ!

Father, thank You for every opportunity I have to tell others of Your amazing love. Use me today to encourage both my own family and others. In the name of Jesus, Amen.

Mother's Day Memories

May 13

"Her children arise up, and call her blessed" (Proverbs 31:28a).

Mother's Day was always special for me as a homeschooling mom. Each year, my children went the extra mile and demonstrated their love with thoughtful homemade cards and gifts. One Mother's Day, however, stands above the rest in my memory. That year, a well-known restaurant chain in our town sponsored a Mother's Day poetry contest for all the young writers in the community. Each contestant was required to submit a short poem sharing what their mother meant to them. After seeing the contest and prizes listed in the paper, my twelve-year-old daughter decided to enter and submitted her poem.

Several days later, a special envelope arrived in the mail from the restaurant. Upon opening the letter, my daughter discovered she had won the grand prize—one dozen red roses for her mother, a monetary gift of $25 for her, and a complimentary meal for our entire family at the restaurant. In addition, her poem was to be published in the local newspaper, and a special copy of the poem was to be printed and framed just for me. Enjoying the prizes was exciting, but even more wonderful was the message my daughter wrote in the poem. How blessed I was to read these words of love:

For My Mother
By JoAnna Tatman

Before even time began
My mother for me was planned.
She brought me unto the earth
Through the miracle of birth.

As a child in this world anew
She gave me guidance, wise and true.
She picked me up when I fell down
And kissed away my tears and frowns.

When I failed, she loved me anyway.
Her trueness lasts even to this day.
As a child and a mother
We will always have each other.

Even when life takes us apart
We from each other will not depart.
For she is the goodness inside my soul,
A strength on which I will forever grow.

Homeschool mom, do you know how deeply your children love you? Although you may not see their affections demonstrated every day, your children really do appreciate and love you for the sacrifices you make when homeschooling. You are the object of their affections, and if they haven't done so already, someday they too will rise up to call you blessed.

Lord, so many days I feel like my acts of love go unnoticed. Teach me to remember every kind word and deed is making a difference forever in the life of my child. In the name of Jesus, Amen.

 Share your thoughts about this devotional at **aophomeschooling.com**/133

You Want It When?

May 14

One reason parents choose to homeschool is the advantage children have in learning at their own pace. However, even homeschoolers must learn how to meet a deadline. Balancing these two approaches to learning required creativity as I prepared my lesson plans. Since I knew deadlines would teach my children to manage workloads, I assigned specific projects and assignments to complement their curriculum. Whether they expounded on a science concept by researching a hypothesis or wrote a lengthy paper for composition, they learned to gather the information and materials necessary to finish their assignment by a fixed date. Years later, they thanked me, as they saw the importance of meeting deadlines in the workplace.

The Bible also tells of a spiritual deadline for all mankind that is soon approaching. Some day Christ will return as Lord and King to judge the world. In Mark 13:32-33 Christ states, "But of that day and that hour knoweth no man, no, not the angels which are in heaven, neither the Son, but the Father. Take ye heed, watch and pray: for ye know not when the time is." Unlike deadlines in this life, God in His wisdom chooses not to reveal the specific time or hour of Christ's return. Jesus simply tells us to watch, pray, and to be ready. Unfortunately, many will miss the joys of heaven because they wait too long. By failing to heed Jesus' warning to respond now to the Gospel message, they will be lost for eternity and suffer eternal separation from God.

Are you telling others about God's final deadline? Although the message may not be popular, the promise of Christ's return is sure (2 Peter 3:8-10). Without a doubt, those who come to know Christ due to your witness will be sure to thank you one day as you stand together in the presence of the Lord. "Again, he limiteth a certain day, saying in David, To day after so long a time; as it is said, To day if ye will hear his voice, harden not your hearts" (Hebrews 4:7).

Lord, thank You for the promise of Your return. Please help me boldly share the message of Your love and forgiveness with as many people as possible before that final day. In Jesus' name, Amen.

Share your thoughts about this devotional at **aophomeschooling.com/134**

Upward Thoughts

May 15

"O how I love thy law! it is my meditation all the day" (Psalm 119:97).

Homeschooling families have incredible opportunities to train their children in righteousness. Without public mandates restricting our actions, we can enjoy daily devotions, prayer, and the Bible's wonderful truths. Just as exciting is the unlimited moments we have to direct our child's thoughts toward God. Throughout the entire school day, biblical applications can be interjected as they apply to our Christian curriculum or the problems of daily living. Growing in the Lord, our children's faith becomes vibrant and powerful as they learn to "think on these things" (Philippians 4:8b).

King David also learned the art of directing his thoughts toward God. Throughout the Psalms, he demonstrated how to daily mediate on God and His Word. Whether fighting giants, killing bears, herding sheep, or playing his harp, David focused his thinking toward God as he remembered His faithfulness and blessings. Even when running for his life from Saul, David trusted in God's protection and remained focused on what God could do rather than the hopelessness of the situation.

What about you? Is Satan bogging down your mind with homeschooling worries that cause you to forget God's blessings? If you're having trouble keeping your thoughts fixed on God, remember what He has already done. As you count your blessings every moment of the day, you'll find the strength to trust His promises for the future. "Finally, brethren, whatsoever things are true, whatsoever things are honest, whatsoever things are just, whatsoever things are pure, whatsoever things are lovely, whatsoever things are of good report; if there be any virtue, and if there be any praise, think on these things" (Philippians 4:8).

Father, thank You for the wonderful way You've blessed our family as we've homeschooled. Remind me of Your promises and strengthen me to hold fast to the joys of teaching my children at home. In the name of Jesus, Amen.

 Share your thoughts about this devotional at **aophomeschooling.com**/135

A Walk in the Park

"For the LORD taketh pleasure in his people: he will beautify the meek with salvation" (Psalm 149:4).

Are you too busy completing your curriculum to let your homeschooler play? During my first years of homeschooling, I foolishly lived under the pressure of completing our workbooks. I traded my children's playtime for finishing every problem and watched as they became more frustrated with this routine. Realizing something was wrong, I thought, "Why aren't they enjoying school anymore?" The next day as I struggled to finish math with my son, I saw we were getting nowhere. Finally, I stopped and said, "Why don't we just go for a walk and play in the park this afternoon?"

Immediately, my children's countenances changed as they excitedly responded, "Really, Mom? Yes, let's go!"

Leaving schoolwork behind, we packed the car and headed to the park. After playing only a few minutes, I saw my children's stress levels drop as they enjoyed the slides, merry-go-round, swings, and teeter-totter. Laughing and giggling, the smiles came back, and I knew the answer to my teaching problems. Homeschooling was more than just completing workbooks. It was also taking time for a walk in the park.

As Christians, we forget that God enjoys spending time with us, too. We get involved in "doing" things for God, when all He wants is for us to enjoy "being" with Him. Yes, serving the Lord is wonderful, but we must also take time to walk with God and experience the sweet joy of His loving presence. If you find yourself doing too much, perhaps it's time to take a break and enjoy a "Mary" moment at Jesus' feet.

Lord, thank You for Your love and the joy of being Your child. Teach me to relax in Your love and enjoy every moment with You. In the name of Jesus, Amen.

When God Says No

May 17

"In the day when I cried thou answeredst me" (Psalm 138:3a).

Our family was considered poor while we homeschooled. Living on one income left us with little money, and trips to the grocery store were made only for milk, flour, eggs, and other staples. We baked our own bread and supplemented our food budget with a bountiful garden. Thankfully, we always had something to eat, and my children never went to bed hungry. However, there were times during our homeschooling when I didn't understand why God allowed our financial situation. I longed for the convenience of prepackaged foods and thought, "It's not fair. Other homeschooling families don't have to cook from scratch, and they have so much more time for field trips and fun days."

My frustration continued until I taught my children the inspirational story of Amy Carmichael. Amy was a Christian missionary in India who founded an orphanage for thousands of children who otherwise would have suffered a bleak future. As a child, Amy prayed to have blue eyes instead of brown. When the color never changed, she was desperately disappointed that God hadn't answered her prayer. Amy's mother lovingly explained that "No" was an answer to prayer too, and years later, Amy discovered the reason for God's answer. To rescue the abused children in India, Amy had to disguise herself as a native. Dyeing her skin with coffee, Amy was able to keep from being recognized as a foreigner because her eyes were brown, not blue. After reading Amy's story to my family, I thought, "Maybe God has a reason for telling me "No," too."

As time went on and my children grew into adulthood, I finally understood God's reason for those hours spent cooking in the kitchen. Because our resources were limited, my children had enjoyed a healthy diet of homegrown, homemade food. They were fit and strong and had also learned how to be good cooks themselves. What I had considered a detriment to our homeschooling had actually been a huge blessing.

What do you do when God answers your prayer with "No"? Satan will tempt you to pout as you see greener grass on the other side of the fence, but don't believe him. God's perfect plan for your life will only be fulfilled as you learn to follow Him in obedience, including those times when He says, "No." "For I know the thoughts that I think toward you, saith the LORD, thoughts of peace, and not of evil, to give you an expected end" (Jeremiah 29:11).

Father, thank You for answering prayer. I confess that only You know what's best for my life. Like a child, help me to trust You when You say "No" and to realize that it's always for my good. In Jesus' name, Amen.

 Share your thoughts about this devotional at aophomeschooling.com/137

Spring Cleaning

May 18

"Ye have sinned against the LORD: and be sure your sin will find you out" (Numbers 32:23b).

Spring was here, and my children were wrapping up their schoolwork for the year one subject at a time. With fewer hours spent homeschooling, new projects were needed to direct my children's energy elsewhere. Since we had several dilapidated buildings on our farm that were shedding siding, shingles, nails, and small pieces of glass, I decided to "hire" my children to clean the mess. Giving them each a small bucket, I informed them that they could receive one cent for every nail and piece of glass they collected. Excited to earn their own money, they all agreed to do this new job.

Taking their new employment seriously, they reported to me daily with bucket in hand. Dumping the contents, I painstakingly counted each item and paid them accordingly. However, as the days went on, the contents of their buckets grew smaller as they became distracted by playing games and riding bikes. Not expecting much in my son's bucket, I was surprised the next day when he came to be paid. His bucket was almost full with broken pieces of glass, and he was expecting to make a lot of money. Smiling he said, "Let's count these right now, Mom!"

"OK honey," I replied. As we dumped the entire contents, I noticed something odd about the glass. Like the pieces of a puzzle, the edges all seemed to match one another. Suspiciously, I looked at my ten-year-old son and said, "Did you break a larger piece of glass into smaller pieces to earn more money?" Shocked that I had discovered his scheme, he looked at me and quietly admitted the truth. Inside, I laughed at his ingenuity, but outwardly we discussed the reasons why he wasn't getting paid that day.

As Christians, Satan tempts us into thinking there will be no repercussion for deceitfulness. When we fail to tell the store clerk that she's given the wrong change, use an outdated coupon, or try to return merchandise we've damaged saying it was a manufacturing flaw, God knows the truth. Like Achan in Joshua 7, your sin will find you out and God will reveal the truth. What about you? Is there some spring cleaning the Holy Spirit needs to do in your life?

Father, forgive me for those sins I excuse as "little white lies." Help me to say "No" to Satan's foolish temptations to get ahead and to deal honestly with others and You. In the name of Jesus, Amen.

Share your thoughts about this devotional at aophomeschooling.com/138

Birthday Surprises

May 19

"Lo, children are an heritage of the LORD: and the fruit of the womb is his reward" (Psalm 127:3).

My birthday present came early the year I turned twenty-five. The afternoon before my birthday, God gave me the gift of a new baby boy. Like all pregnancies that go past their due date, I worried about the new life inside me. However, when my son was finally born, there was no doubt he was healthy and strong. With a full head of red hair, a ruddy appearance, and weighing in at 9 pounds and 15 ounces, my bouncing baby boy looked like a tough outdoorsman as he greeted me with a smile.

Parenting this "easy keeper" was fun right from the start. My son slept, ate, and played exactly the way a mother would want. As he grew, he was ever the complacent child and never demanded or drew attention to himself. Humble in heart, he approached life with an inquisitive mind and sensitive spirit. As we homeschooled, my son was active, observant, and creative, and I knew his life was going to be different. John the Baptist was his biblical mentor, and like John, my son was happiest serving God while living in the great outdoors.

Twenty-five years later on my fiftieth birthday, my outdoorsy, archeologist son surprised me with another blessing. He bought me a new pair of durable, hiking sandals so I could accompany him on the mountain trail near his home. Crying, I read his words of love and the Bible verse he picked just for me: "How beautiful upon the mountains are the feet of him that bringeth good tidings, that publisheth peace; that bringeth good tidings of good, that publisheth salvation; that saith unto Zion, Thy God reigneth" (Isaiah 52:7)! Birthday surprises never cease! Praise God for His glorious gift of children!

Father, I lift my heart in praise to You for the wonderful blessing of children. Thank You for the privilege of being a parent and knowing the joys of a child's love. In the name of Jesus, Amen.

Why I Love Homeschooling

May 20

How do I love homeschooling? Let me count the ways:

• I love homeschooling because fixed hours aren't required to learn a subject. When I discovered God had given me a night owl who loved to sleep in, I simply adjusted and made a schedule that worked best for our family.

• I love homeschooling because there are so many fun things to learn. Not only are there great curriculums for covering the main subject areas, but there are also countless extracurricular topics and activities to explore. We once spent an entire week studying birds of prey when we found a wounded hawk in our yard after a severe wind storm.

• I love homeschooling because I have the flexibility to adjust our day depending on what God brings. If my child is grasping concepts quickly and wants to know more in language arts, great; I'll keep going and forget about doing history that day. If Dad has an impromptu meeting in another city, I can take advantage of the opportunity and schedule a family field trip.

• I love homeschooling because it gives me an opportunity to really know my children. As teacher and parent, I see both their heart and mind and have the blessed privilege to develop both in the Lord.

• I love homeschooling because I don't have to wait until school's out at 3:30 p.m. to receive a hug and a kiss. I have the joy of loving and being loved by my children throughout the entire day.

Why do you love homeschooling? Start your own list of reasons today and place it somewhere to remind yourself of homeschooling's many blessings. When Satan tries to steal your faith and discourage you, you'll be prepared to stand strong. Instead of saying, "Now, why was it that I wanted to homeschool?" you'll have answers that prove homeschooling is the best job in the world. "Above all, taking the shield of faith, wherewith ye shall be able to quench all the fiery darts of the wicked" (Ephesians 6:16).

Lord, thank You for giving me the opportunity to teach my children. Even though tough days will come, I know Your presence will guide us through. Help me appreciate the blessing of teaching my children each day. In the name of Jesus, Amen.

Unseen Sacrifices

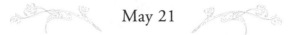

May 21

"But this man, after he had offered one sacrifice for sins for ever, sat down on the right hand of God" (Hebrews 10:12).

Homeschooling is so exciting because it provides spontaneous opportunities to learn. Such was the case the day my son worked on his Bible assignment. As he looked up Scripture passages on prayer, he noticed "The Praying Hands" plaque hanging on our wall and asked, "Whose hands are those?"

As we began researching, my son and I discovered an amazing story of sacrificial love. Albrecht Durer and his brother Albert both had a dream to become artists. However, living in a family of eighteen children, they knew their father could never afford to send both of them to art school. As they discussed the problem, they decided one brother would work in the mines to support the other while studying art. Then, when that brother had completed his studies, he would return the favor and work to support the other. Albrecht won the toss of the coin and went to school first, while Albert went to work in the mines.

Albrecht's talents were remarkable, and by the time he graduated, he was earning large fees for his commissioned works. Returning home a successful artist, he said to Albert, "Now it's your turn to go to school, dear brother."

With his body worn out from years of hard work in the mines, Albert replied, "No, it's too late for me. My fingers have all been smashed at least once and my arthritis is so bad I could never hold a pen or brush to a canvas. No, for me it's too late." As the tears streamed down Albert's face, Albrecht realized the great sacrifice his brother had made. Moved by this incredible gift of love, Albrecht painstakingly painted a portrait of the hands that had given him so much. Immortalizing his brother's hands, "The Praying Hands" became Albrecht's most well-known masterpiece!

After reading this remarkable story with my son, I was overcome with emotion. Thanking God for His divine guidance in teaching us a different lesson, I realized again that every sacrifice made to homeschool was worth the joy of seeing my children grow in their faith. What a privilege to give my all to help them achieve their best!

Lord, thank You for Your sacrificial death on the cross that offers eternal life and hope to all who believe. Please show me how to lay down my life daily to homeschool my children with the same sacrificial love. In Jesus' name, Amen.

 Share your thoughts about this devotional at **aophomeschooling.com/141**

Double-minded Homeschooling

"A double minded man is unstable in all his ways" (James 1:8).

How many times have you doubted your decision to homeschool—one, two, ten, more? I lost count on the number of times I failed to trust in God's provision and care. As a Christian parent, I knew we would never succeed if I continually allowed my emotions to be tossed around each time something went wrong. Doubt may be a natural human response, but either God had shown me to homeschool or He hadn't. Instead of looking at the waves of adversity, God asked me, "Will you walk by faith and trust in My leading?"

Like the man looking for help to heal his son in Mark 9:24b, I cried out to Jesus, "Lord, I believe; help thou mine unbelief."

Meeting me in my limited faith, the Lord gently showed Himself faithful as I sought His wisdom to homeschool each day. God first encouraged and empowered me with the truth of Deuteronomy 6:7 and other verses where God commands parents to "teach them (Scripture) diligently unto thy children, and shalt talk of them when thou sittest in thine house, and when thou walkest by the way, and when thou liest down, and when thou risest up." Next, He provided constant encouragement through several loving homeschooling families. Facing doubts of their own, we found strength together in prayer to fight unbelief (Matthew 18:20). Most of all, the supernatural answers to prayer and the Holy Spirit's guidance confirmed that our family was indeed walking where God desired.

If your doubts are outweighing your faith in homeschooling today, the Lord is waiting to show Himself mighty to you. Like Thomas, He doesn't want you to doubt any longer. Simply cry out and He'll show Himself to be Lord of your homeschooling. "But let him ask in faith, nothing wavering. For he that wavereth is like a wave of the sea driven with the wind and tossed" (James 1:6).

Father God, thank You for Your grace in leading our family on this homeschooling adventure. Please increase my faith and help me to see Your perfect plan for our family. In the name of Jesus, Amen.

Forgiving Failure

May 23

If you've ever felt guilty about past homeschooling failures, you're not alone. Many parents have known setbacks with over scheduling, under planning, and teaching unfamiliar courses. However, the worst failures experienced as homeschooling parents aren't related to academics or schedules. Our worst failures come when we fail to show the love of Christ. Losing our patience and becoming irritable with our children, we speak harshly and then suffer regret and remorse for foolish words and actions. Afterwards, even though we confess our sin, we fail to accept God's forgiveness and torture ourselves with our mistakes until we quit homeschooling altogether.

Until we understand that the Lord forgives and cleanses us from sin (1 John 1:9), we will continue to carry our guilt. Promising yourself that you'll do a better job homeschooling tomorrow or the next day only adds to your guilt. The forgiveness of sin isn't based on your performance. You've already proven that your performance isn't good enough. Your forgiveness is based on what Christ has done for you on the cross. When you acknowledge that He died in your place, He gives you a new thinking pattern guided by the Holy Spirit. In His power, you are able to set aside your selfish and fleshly desires that cause homeschooling failures.

What about you? Did you wake up this morning dragging around the guilt for your homeschooling failures from yesterday? You don't have to. You can find release from that bondage as you hand your past mistakes over to Christ. If you've confessed your sin, He's forgiven you, and there's no reason to feel guilty any longer. "He hath not dealt with us after our sins; nor rewarded us according to our iniquities. As far as the east is from the west, so far hath he removed our transgressions from us" (Psalm 103:10, 12).

Lord, help me to receive Your forgiveness and not to live in the shame of my failures. Give me wisdom to teach my children today and help me to trust in Your strength and not my own. In the name of Jesus, Amen.

Symbols of the Heart

May 24

Are there items in your house that have special meaning to your homeschooling family? Surprisingly, the object my adult children remember the most from our homeschooling days was our kitchen table. It was nothing special—just an old table beat up with scratches and scars, but it represented the heart of our family. As wide as it was long, this sturdy old table was big enough for everyone's schoolwork and craft projects. For twenty years, it supported the life and love of our homeschooling family as it brought us together to play, to eat, and to learn.

The Christian faith has many symbols, too, but the most meaningful certainly is the cross. Although this torturous tool was used to punish criminals, the cross of Christ stands in stark contrast. Pointing to the One who paid sin's penalty, the cross represents the heart of our Christian faith. With hope and forgiveness extended to all mankind, Jesus willingly sacrificed His life with arms opened wide to provide room for everyone who believes. Today, Christ asks all who believe in Him to do more than wear this symbol of faith around their neck. Each day, we are to declare His love to the world by taking up our cross and following Him (Luke 9:23). In fact, Christ says, "And he that taketh not his cross, and followeth after me, is not worthy of me" (Matthew 10:38).

Do you find it difficult to stand against the tide of anti-Christian sentiment that permeates today's society? As a homeschooling family, you don't need to be embarrassed that you teach your children with a Christian curriculum that teaches creation and the truth of the Scriptures. Take up your cross and be a witness about the heart of Christianity—the cross of Christ. "For the preaching of the cross is to them that perish foolishness; but unto us which are saved it is the power of God" (1 Corinthians 1:18).

Lord, help me to do more than wear the symbols of my faith in You. Show me how to boldly speak Your truth in love, so many more people will come to know the power of the cross. In the name of Jesus, Amen.

Influences for Good

The most important influence on your homeschooled child is the environment in which he grows. When parents demonstrate a healthy relationship between each other and with the Lord, a child's perspective about himself and his world is influenced for good. Parents who fear the Lord and live according to His Word have a far greater impact on homeschooling's success than parents who worry about having the best curriculum or the latest computer. Giving your child a Christian education, therefore, requires a homeschooling parent to be completely in line with God's will.

The life of Timothy in the New Testament is a wonderful example of a young person who benefited from the godly influence of his family. Timothy enjoyed a relationship with Jesus Christ because he first saw the fruits of a spiritual walk in the life of his mother and grandmother (2 Timothy 1:5). Through their sincere faith, Timothy learned the truth and became a Christian. Later, when meeting the Apostle Paul, Timothy proved himself to be a worthy disciple capable of enduring great hardships for the sake of the Gospel.

What kind of example are you setting for your child? In your day to day living and homeschooling, is your child seeing you seek God's strength, comfort, and wisdom? Are you serving in humility and incorporating the Scriptures into your decision making? If you want your child to be successful while homeschooling, make sure the example of your life leads him toward Christ instead of away from Him. Even as Paul exhorted young Timothy, "Be thou an example of the believers, in word, in conversation, in charity, in spirit, in faith, in purity" (1 Timothy 4:12b).

Lord, I stand in awe at the great responsibility You've given me to be a homeschooling parent. Let my life be a testimony of Your unending love and may my children grow to serve You with their whole hearts. In Jesus' name, Amen.

Nothing New

May 26

"There is no new thing under the sun" (Ecclesiastes 1:9b).

As I homeschooled my children, I was surprised to find myself reliving many of the same frustrations I experienced as a young student. One day, I watched as my daughter struggled to solve a story problem in algebra. As she tried to identify the unknown variables in the problem she cried, "Mom, I just don't get this!"

Remembering my own issues with story problems, I replied, "I know it's difficult to understand. Story problems were always hard for me, too. My junior high math teacher had to spend hours with me before I could finally figure them out."

"Really?" she asked. "I thought I was the only one who couldn't get these."

As Christians, Satan attempts to isolate and defeat us in our failures by convincing us that no one understands our problems. Although each person's experience may be slightly different, we all deal with the same basic sinful temptations mankind has experienced since the Garden of Eden (1 Corinthians 10:13a). Thinking we are alone in fighting our battles, we become discouraged in our Christian walk. We fall prey to Satan's age-old tactics of "the lust of the flesh, and the lust of the eyes, and the pride of life" (1 John 2:16b) and finally give up, thinking, "The victorious Christian life doesn't work for me."

What about you? Are you experiencing a personal struggle in your walk with the Lord today? Perhaps the stress of homeschooling is revealing character flaws that cause you to stumble. Don't despair. You're not alone. Others have experienced what you're going through and know how to help with encouragement and prayer. Best of all, you have a loving Savior who forgives and changes your life to "make all things new" (Revelation 21:5).

Father, I've failed so many times to live the way You want me to. Please lead me to godly friends who can help and give me strength to resist those temptations that would lead me away from You. In the name of Jesus, Amen.

Just Start!

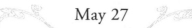
"When my spirit was overwhelmed within me, then thou knewest my path" (Psalm 142:3a).

My son was sitting at the kitchen table staring out the window with workbooks and other schoolwork scattered around him in a semi-circle two inches deep. I had given him multiple assignments for that week, and I also knew he had several long papers uncompleted from the week before. In addition, he needed to study for upcoming quizzes and tests. As I reminded him of everything that was due by Friday, I could see despair shutting down his mind. As he sat there looking forlorn, I gave him a hug and said, "Is there something I can help you with to get started?"

"No, Mom," he replied, "There's so much to do! How am I supposed to get this all done by Friday?"

Nehemiah must have felt like my son as he stood surveying the huge task ahead of him. Looking at the rubble of Jerusalem's walls that stretched on for miles, I'm sure he must have wondered where and how to start (Nehemiah 1-2). Fortunately, Nehemiah had prepared his work with prayer, and God answered by helping him begin. Moving King Artaxerxes to offer his support, Nehemiah left his cupbearer job in Shushan and returned to Jerusalem to rally the people. In addition, God also encouraged the hearts of the Jews who were living there to help repair each gate and rebuild every stone that had been torn down. In just fifty-two short days, Nehemiah and people repaired the walls that had been lying in waste for seventy years.

As a homeschooling parent, you may be facing too many "assignments" in your life. Cleaning, cooking, ministry, and homeschooling leave little time for spare moments. Every task seems important, so where do you begin? If you're feeling overwhelmed under the weight of your responsibilities, learn the lesson God taught Nehemiah and my son. Pray for strength and wisdom, pick your task, and just start working. You'll be amazed at what you can accomplish when the Lord is in it. My son certainly was when he finished every assignment that week, even with time to spare!

Lord, your Word says in Ephesians 1:19-20 that the same mighty power that raised Jesus from the dead is available to those who believe. Father, I claim Your promise and ask that You empower me today to accomplish every task You have given. In Jesus' name, Amen.

Memorial Day Memories

May 28

"So we thy people and sheep of thy pasture will give thee thanks for ever: we will shew forth thy praise to all generations" (Psalm 79:13).

Although Memorial Day (originally called Decoration Day) is a day for remembering those who have died in our nation's service, our homeschooling family observed this holiday like many other families. Visiting the gravesites of loved ones, my children decorated their headstones with a tribute of flowers. In many cases, my young children never knew the family members, and I would answer countless questions about their lives. I never tired of telling them about uncles, aunts, and great-grandparents and the special significance of their lives.

As Christian homeschooling parents, you also have the wonderful privilege of telling your children about the heritage of your faith. Sharing the story of Christ's death and resurrection, and what it means to you personally, will enable your children to learn more about their loving heavenly Father. Like a potter molding a piece of clay, you have the incredible opportunity to carve a lasting impression of God's goodness and love in their minds with every spiritual lesson you have learned.

Since life can change in a moment, make this Memorial Day count with your family. Don't just visit the cemetery and leave flowers. Talk about the people you loved, and more importantly, talk about the hope we have because Christ loves us. "Behold, I shew you a mystery; We shall not all sleep, but we shall all be changed, In a moment, in the twinkling of an eye, at the last trump: for the trumpet shall sound, and the dead shall be raised incorruptible, and we shall be changed" (1 Corinthians 15:51-52).

Lord, thank You for the loving memory of godly family members who have died and gone before us. We praise You for the hope of seeing them again and the sure promise of Your return. In Jesus' name, Amen.

Share your thoughts about this devotional at **aophomeschooling.com**/148

Broken Walls

"A brother offended is harder to be won than a strong city" (Proverbs 18:19a).

I'm not sure how the bad feelings began between my oldest and youngest child. Considering the fact they were both strong-willed, I suppose a conflict was inevitable. Whenever I needed my daughter's help in watching her brothers and sister, she was determined to make her little brother mind—no matter what. My young son, however, had other ideas. Resenting his sister's bulldog methods of control, he tested her authority every chance he got. Homeschooling became difficult, as I could never trust either of them together alone for any length of time. One day I finally asked my daughter, "Why don't you just talk nicely to your brother? Things get done so much easier when you speak with honey instead of vinegar."

"Oh, Mom," she cried. "He's just asking for it and I'm delivering." Years later, my oldest and youngest finally resolved their differences, but not until after many hurtful confrontations.

Left unchecked, bad feelings between siblings can last even a lifetime. Jacob and Esau were two such brothers who wasted twenty years in a broken relationship. Being more than an annoying little brother, Jacob actually stole Esau's birthright and then left town in fear of his brother's wrath. Years later, God commanded Jacob to return to the land of his father, but the huge obstacle of brotherly reconciliation stood in his way. When messengers reported seeing Esau and his band of 400 men coming toward them as they traveled, Jacob was sure his brother was coming to kill him and his family. Coming before the Lord in prayer, Jacob humbled himself and prayed, "Deliver me, I pray thee, from the hand of my brother, from the hand of Esau: for I fear him, lest he will come and smite me, and the mother with the children" (Genesis 32:11). God answered Jacob's prayer after a humbling all-night wrestling session (vs. 24-32), and when the two brothers met, they finally reconciled with an embrace and a kiss.

What about you? Do you have a poor relationship with your brother, sister, or some other family member? Have they been bulldogging you with negative remarks about homeschooling? If you're tempted to retaliate with a few hurtful remarks of your own, take heed and guard your words. Lifelong conflicts can be easily avoided if you respond in humble brotherly love. "A soft answer turneth away wrath: but grievous words stir up anger" (Proverbs 15:1).

Father, I know You desire the family to work as a unit, but I've allowed selfishness and pride to ruin my relationships with those closest to me. Show me how to live in forgiveness and to love my family when they're being unlovely. In Jesus' name, Amen.

Over My Head

"For without me ye can do nothing" (John 15:5b).

As I watched my daughter practice the piano, I knew I had made another mistake as a home-schooling parent. Assuming my limited experience with a few childhood piano lessons was enough to guide me, I began to teach my daughter how to play. However, the more we continued in my daughter's new interest, the more I realized my inadequacies as a proper piano instructor. Motivated by pride and a lack of finances to hire a qualified teacher, I continued teaching until my young daughter stopped playing and asked, "Mom, do you really know what I'm supposed to be doing?"

Surprised that she saw the problem more clearly than me, I humbly replied, "No honey, I think we're going to need extra help to learn how to play the piano correctly."

The seven sons of Sceva, a Jewish high priest, had a similar experience in Acts 19:11-17. As Jewish exorcists, they foolishly thought they could cast out demons by simply copying the work of the Apostle Paul. Without experiencing the transforming power of Christ in their own lives, they attempted to rebuke a demon living in a man saying, "We adjure you by Jesus whom Paul preacheth" (vs. 13b). Mocking their attempt to cast it out, the evil spirit replied, "Jesus I know, and Paul I know; but who are ye" (vs.15b)? Overpowering the Jewish exorcists, the man with the evil spirit beat them up and chased them out of the house.

If you're experiencing defeat in your teaching, chances are you may be in over your head. As a homeschooling parent, don't make the foolish assumption that you alone must teach everything to your children. Instead of hoping for the best or "faking it" as you teach in your own strength, ask your heavenly Father where to find the help you need. "Ask, and ye shall receive, that your [homeschooling] joy may be full" (John 16:24b).

Father, forgive me for thinking I can homeschool in my own strength. Show me when and where to get the help I need to raise my children in Your perfect will. In the precious name of Jesus, Amen.

Foolish Dreams

May 31

"Be content with such things as ye have" (Hebrews 13:5b).

For twenty-five years I have looked forward to uninterrupted nights, a house that stays neat longer than five minutes after I clean it, and a noise level below one decibel. As much as I loved my four children and teaching them at home, these were the things I longed for while we homeschooled. Now, years later, the very things that were so important are mine in abundance. However, the empty nights seem uninteresting, the house has no reason to be clean, as it sits empty all day, and the quiet is agonizingly loud. My foolish dreams of yesterday have come true, and I chastise myself for trading productive moments with my family for grumbling and complaining.

God gives us so much to be thankful for each day, but we choose to look past the blessings. Focusing our thoughts on illusive mirages of happiness, we think we know what will satisfy us best. We disregard God's provision and constant care and trade His blessings for future "if only's." Patiently, He waits for us to discover two important facts: He has already given us everything we need, and He only can satisfy the longings of the soul.

Do you ever long for the "good old days" before the demands of homeschooling? Dear one, please don't waste one more moment longing for "if only's." The homeschool blessings of today are far greater than any sacrifice you've laid at the Master's feet. "Delight thyself also in the LORD: and he shall give thee the desires of thine heart. Commit thy way unto the LORD; trust also in him; and he shall bring it to pass. And he shall bring forth thy righteousness as the light" (Psalm 37:4-6a).

Father, please forgive my ungrateful heart and help me see afresh all the blessings You so faithfully provide each day. Cause my heart to rejoice instead of complain and to serve You by serving my family. In the name of Jesus, Amen.

First-time Requests

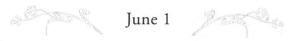

"Thou shalt hearken diligently unto the voice of the LORD thy God, to observe and to do all his commandments" (Deuteronomy 28:1b).

"I'm not going to tell you twice," I said to my daughter as she sat with her nose in a book. Frustrated, I thought to myself, "How many times do you have to ask your children to do something before they obey?" Expecting immediate obedience from my children seemed dogmatic, but our homeschooling was never going to survive without their willingness to obey when first asked. As I began to teach and maintain this new discipline, extra effort was required to reinforce my words. However, as my children learned to obey me, I knew they were also learning something even more important—how to obey God when He first asks.

The Bible has many examples of people who suffered the consequences of ignoring, questioning, or rebelling against God when He first spoke to their hearts. Moses was rebuked by God in Exodus 14:15 when he failed to lead the people through the Red Sea at the right time. Jonah suffered the hardships of a shipwreck and lived in the belly of a big fish before he finally went to Nineveh, and the entire nation of Israel wandered in the desert for 40 years before enjoying the Promised Land. Clearly, serving the Lord with immediate obedience is God's desire for His children.

Is there something God has been asking you to do? Perhaps He wants you to witness to a neighbor, teach in vacation Bible school, or restore a broken friendship. If you've been ignoring His voice, questioning His commands, or refusing to obey, He will reinforce His words. As a holy, loving Father, He's asking you to show your love by obeying—the first time He asks. "That thou mayest love the LORD thy God, and that thou mayest obey his voice, and that thou mayest cleave unto him: for he is thy life, and the length of thy days" (Deuteronomy 30:20a).

Father, I know You desire my obedience in all things. Forgive me when I drag my feet and fail to trust in Your Word. I love You. Please speak to my heart and show me again what You would have me do. In Jesus' name, Amen.

Wanted: Homeschool Teacher

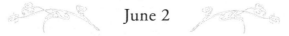

June 2

"Thy God hath commanded thy strength: strengthen, O God, that which thou hast wrought for us" (Psalm 68:28).

Have you ever thought about how an advertisement would read for a homeschool teacher? If truthfully stated, the ad would probably go something like this:

Now accepting applications—

Family seeking fun-loving, godly homeschool teacher. Applicant will be responsible for providing total educational development and daily personal care for children of multiple ages. Applicant will assume the following roles: cook, housemaid, nurse, taxi driver, administrative assistant, accountant, athletic coach, social director, computer technician, household and automotive repairman, gardener, course instructor in multiple subject areas and grade levels, and various other responsibilities. This is a full-time position—approximately 120 hours or more per week. Qualified candidates must be able to work well under pressure, multi-task, and prioritize work loads while maintaining a friendly, enthusiastic attitude. Quick thinking, good memory, and a varied background in extensive subject matter are a must. Promising candidates will be resourceful, adjust easily to distractions, and display creative, hard-working leadership abilities. Organizational and problem solving skills are a plus. Previous teaching experience and/or college preferred, but is not required. If you're interested in working in a fast-paced, ever-changing environment, this is the position for you! For more information on this exciting opportunity to earn fulfilling, one-of-a-kind rewards, please apply in person today.

After reading these qualifications, no wonder many parents walk away from this employment opportunity. Who can measure up to these standards? Praise God, you can! As you step out in faith and yield your weaknesses to God's strength, you'll not only get the job, you'll also successfully homeschool and discover the fantastic benefits of teaching your children at home. "Finally, my brethren, be strong in the Lord, and in the power of his might" (Ephesians 6:10).

Lord, homeschooling seems overwhelming, and there's so much to learn. Like the new guy on the job, teach me what I need to know to successfully homeschool with Your wisdom, strength, and power. In Jesus' name, Amen.

Summer School

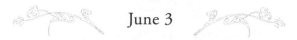

June 3

"But his delight is in the law of the LORD; and in his law doth he meditate day and night" (Psalm 1:2).

The first day of summer break was here, and my children were excited to enjoy a different homeschooling schedule for the next several months. Expecting a new routine, my children were surprised the first morning when we started our day with a Bible lesson and prayer. "Mom," my young son said. "I thought we weren't doing school during the summer months."

"Well, you're right," I replied, "but God commands us to daily stay in His Word, and there's no such thing as a summer vacation from the Bible."

Summertime can be a temptation for Christians to go on holiday from studying God's Word. With so many outdoor activities and vacations, we are distracted from our normal routine and forget the importance of feasting on God's Word. Like the nation of Israel, we must feed on our heavenly manna one day at a time to maintain our spiritual strength, even during those times when we travel to new and exciting places. Since the Bible is the spiritual food that nourishes our soul and keeps us from sin, we must maintain a disciplined study of its truths all year long.

What about your homeschooling family? Have you made lesson plans to continue teaching God's Word to your children this summer? Whether you dive into a particular book in the Bible or develop a topical study, school is never out for studying God's Word. "This book of the law shall not depart out of thy mouth; but thou shalt meditate therein day and night, that thou mayest observe to do according to all that is written therein: for then thou shalt make thy way prosperous, and then thou shalt have good success" (Joshua 1:8).

Father, thank You for Your holy Word that guides and strengthens. Forgive me for thinking I can live without studying and meditating on its truths each day, and please give me wisdom this summer to teach Your Word to my children. In Jesus' name, Amen.

Big Deals

June 4

"If we say that we have no sin, we deceive ourselves, and the truth is not in us" (1 John 1:8).

Just like other school children, homeschoolers also use excuses for not completing their schoolwork on time. As my children grew older, they learned several pat answers to justify their procrastination, including their favorite, "Don't worry. It's no big deal." Of all their excuses, this one probably annoyed me the most. Failing to acknowledge their wrongdoing and to take responsibility for their actions, this glib remark downplayed the importance of planning ahead and the significance of keeping a promise. I quickly realized if I didn't hold them accountable in small things, my children would also not be accountable in larger things later in life.

When dealing with the matter of sin, we also attempt to downplay its significance in our walk with God. Justifying ourselves, we consider character flaws and little white lies "No big deal." After all, who's going to notice or pay attention? In Psalm 5:4-5 we read the answer, "For thou art not a God that hath pleasure in wickedness: neither shall evil dwell with thee. The foolish shall not stand in thy sight: thou hatest all workers of iniquity." God is holy and the standards He sets for those who walk according to the light are measured by that holiness (1 Peter 1:15).

Obviously, God doesn't mess around with sin and neither should we. If you find yourself in opposition to God's Word and ignoring the Holy Spirit's promptings to abstain from an "insignificant" activity, be careful. You may think that it's no big deal, but it is to God. "But every man is tempted, when he is drawn away of his own lust, and enticed. Then when lust hath conceived, it bringeth forth sin: and sin, when it is finished, bringeth forth death" (James 1:14-15).

Father, I know there's no such thing as a small sin in Your eyes. Cleanse my heart today and help me to walk uprightly in the strength and power of Your love. In Jesus' name, Amen.

New Birth

June 5

"And he that winneth souls is wise" (Proverbs 11:30b).

As I tucked my two oldest children into their bunk beds, I felt the pull of my own bed calling me. Our homeschooling family had relocated near our mission organization's headquarters, so my husband and I could receive extensive child evangelism training. Late nights in preparing teaching visuals for our training lessons, studying biblical doctrine in-depth, and maintaining our homeschooling schedule had frazzled us both mentally and physically. Each night we were half asleep before we even laid our heads on the pillow, and tonight was no different. However, as I reached to turn out the light after reading a story to our oldest son and daughter, my daughter asked, "Mom, how can I get to heaven?" Smiling, I realized this was the moment I had been praying for since the day she was born. God was giving me the amazing gift of letting me be the one to guide my child through her second birth. Praying for extra physical strength and God's divine wisdom, I proceeded to share the message of salvation with both my daughter and my son that night. "How fitting," I thought as I rejoiced in their decision to accept Christ. "Christ taught me the Scripture I needed to know during our training in order to lead my own children to Him first."

Soul winners are not just born. They're taught, trained, and motivated by the indwelling power of the Holy Spirit. In fact, when Jesus was here on earth, He took three years to teach and train His disciples the art of soul winning. However, even with all the modern witnessing techniques of today, winning souls is still ineffective without the Holy Spirit's leading and conviction. Only God can illuminate the mind of unbelieving children or adults, convict their hearts of their sinful condition, and move their wills to respond in faith.

Are you prepared to share the hope that lies within you (1 Peter 3:15)? As a Christian homeschooling parent, God says you're part of a witnessing team (Acts 5:32). Yielded and obedient to the Holy Spirit, you have the amazing privilege of leading countless souls to the Savior of the world, starting with your own family. No matter what method you use, be prepared to share the Gospel and enjoy the greatest privilege of being a homeschooling parent—leading your child to Christ.

Father God, leading our children to a saving knowledge of You is one reason we homeschool. Please use me to teach them about You, and to invite them to receive You as Savior and Lord. In Jesus' saving name, Amen.

The Homeschooler's 23rd Psalm

June 6

"I am the good shepherd: the good shepherd giveth his life for the sheep" (John 10:11).

The Lord is my shepherd,

I shall not want.
He maketh me to live on less sleep:
He leadeth me through the noise of many voices.

He restoreth my soul: He leadeth me to teach
The right lessons each day, for His name's sake.

Yea, though I walk through the valley of undone
Laundry and kitchen messes, I will fear no evil:
For thou art with me, my teacher's guides and
Answer keys, they comfort me.

Thou preparest a table before me in the presence
Of threatening school officials and critical family members:
Thou anointest my head with heavenly wisdom, my cup runneth over.

Surely educated and godly children shall follow after me
All the days of my life: and I will dwell again one day
In a clean house with the Lord forevermore.

Praise God, we do have a good Shepherd who leads us through every homeschooling problem and provides for our every need. Best of all, our Shepherd knows us and promises never to desert us when the wolf comes seeking to destroy (John 10:11-13). As we listen to the Shepherd's voice and follow Him, we are sure to receive a great reward, as we reach the peaceful green pastures of Christ-like, educated children. "And when the chief Shepherd shall appear, ye shall receive a crown of glory that fadeth not away" (1 Peter 5:4).

Father, how I praise You for leading my children and me in the path of homeschooling. Without You, we surely would be confused and lost. We come to You again this day and pray for Your continued blessings as we follow You. In Jesus' name, Amen.

 Share your thoughts about this devotional at aophomeschooling.com/157

Playing with Money

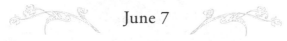

June 7

"The wicked borroweth, and payeth not again" (Psalm 37:21a).

Playing shopkeeper was one of my children's favorite math games while homeschooling. Frequently, we would set aside our math workbooks and set up our little store to learn money values, counting, and subtraction principles. Using miniature replicas of food items, a toy shopping cart, and a cash register, my children played for hours and never realized they were learning in the process. Substituting real money for play money made this educational game even more exciting and life-like. Playing frequently, my children progressed until they could easily add amounts mentally and count back change correctly. Due to their play, handling money became second nature. What's more, they also learned a life-long principle—no money, no purchase.

Unfortunately, the correct handling of money in real life is not as easy for some Christian families today. Although the Bible sets forth principles of being good stewards of God's blessings, many believers fail because they make purchases based on fleshly desires with the convenience of credit. Forgetting that these charges require an actual payment of real money, many Christians sink themselves and their families into large debts with no ability to pay. Interest rates accrue, and soon the debt load becomes so great that there is no hope of ever getting out of bondage. Breaking under the financial stress, some Christians lose friendships, ruin marriages, and perform foolish acts. The Scriptures speak to this problem when it says, "The borrower is servant to the lender," and "Be not thou one of them that strike hands, or of them that are sureties for debts" (Proverbs 22:7b, 26).

What about you? Are you being tempted to abuse credit as you face homeschooling on one income? Don't do it. Heed God's warnings in His Word and run to Him with your needs instead. If He has called you to homeschool your children, He will also provide; but He expects you to handle what He provides correctly.

Lord, forgive me for purchasing items I have no way of repaying. Help me to discipline my spending before I destroy the things in life I truly love. In Jesus' name, Amen.

Reaping the Reward

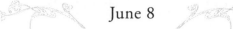

June 8

"Wait on the LORD: be of good courage, and he shall strengthen thine heart: wait, I say, on the LORD" (Psalm 27:14).

Homeschooling doesn't always produce immediate rewards. Sometimes many years go by before the fruitfulness of your faithfulness is revealed. Hours will be spent in loving and patient academic instruction of your children, as well as hours in training in righteousness before the benefits of homeschooling are seen. Personal spiritual battles will be fought against doubt, fear, and discouragement when they cause you to think, "This homeschool thing is just a waste of time." Most of all, God's promises will also need to be claimed, as you base your homeschooling on the truth of the Bible. Like all worthwhile endeavors, homeschooling will yield its fruit in due season, if you are willing to wait on God's timetable instead of your own.

Certainly, the life of Joseph in the Old Testament is one example we can set before us when homeschooling seems to be in its darkest hours. Although this young man started out as his father's favorite, his life quickly changed when jealousy got the best of his brothers. They threw Joseph into a pit, and then sold him as a slave. While in Egypt, Joseph continued to patiently live his life according to God's Word, even though he had to face false accusations and loneliness. However, many years later, Joseph finally experienced the rewards for maintaining a right heart attitude towards God and his brothers.

If you are in your first few years of homeschooling, don't despair and give up. Even though the bumps and bruises seem like too much, you will see the benefits of godly children who actually enjoy learning. In addition, your personal walk with the Lord will be rooted and strengthened, as you learn to trust in God's abilities and not in your own. Homeschooling works! Just keep trusting in God's Word when He says, "And let us not be weary in well doing: for in due season we shall reap, if we faint not" (Galatians 6:9).

Heavenly Father, thank You for blessing me with the task of teaching my children. Although some days seem difficult, I choose this day to keep my eyes on You. Please encourage me today and help me remain faithful, until I see the homeschooling blessings You have promised.
In Jesus' name, Amen.

 Share your thoughts about this devotional at aophomeschooling.com/159

No More Weeds

June 9

"If we confess our sins, he is faithful and just to forgive us our sins, and to cleanse us from all unrighteousness" (1 John 1:9).

Heading out the door to do morning chores before the heat of the day, my youngest daughter looked at me and implored, "Mom, do we have to pull weeds this morning? Can't we just go do something fun and play?"

Smiling, I replied, "No honey, every day we must work at removing the weeds, or they'll take over the yard and the garden. If we just do a little bit every day, it won't be such a big job later on."

Sighing, my daughter replied, "OK Mom, but sometimes I think homeschooling during the winter is more fun than not having school during summer. At least there aren't any weeds that grow then!"

In Old Testament days, ridding one's life of the "weeds" of sin was a painstaking and bloody process of offering after offering. Imagine having to live under all the Levitical laws to meet God's standard for forgiveness of sins. Even when all the requirements were met, it was still impossible for the blood of animals to take away sin. The sacrifices could only atone or cover the sins of man (Hebrews 10:3-4).

Praise God, when Christ came and died on the cross for the sins of the world, He fulfilled the law and offered one sacrifice for sin for all time (Hebrews 10:10-12). No longer do we have to offer sacrifices for sin. Christ has paid the penalty with His blood and cleanses all who receive His gift of eternal life. However, even though God sees us as forgiven through Christ's work on the cross, our flesh continues to pop up new "weeds" that quench and choke out the Holy Spirit's work in our lives. Like weeding a garden, if we come before the Lord's presence in prayer and confession each day, it's much easier to defeat Satan and sin.

Are there some weedy patches growing in your life? Don't wait until sin has you completely ensnared before you deal with it. Stop and take a moment right now and come before the Lord in prayer. Ask the Holy Spirit to give you strength to pull out those weeds, so your life might resemble a garden of Christ-like love.

Lord Jesus, thank You for paying the price for my sin. Like King David, I pray, "Create in me a clean heart, O God; and renew a right spirit within me" (Psalm 51:10). Show me those things in my life that need to be removed that I might glorify You with my life. In Your name I pray, Amen.

 Share your thoughts about this devotional at aophomeschooling.com/160

Choosing Wisely

June 10

"Thy testimonies also are my delight and my counsellors" (Psalm 119:24).

Choices are the very thing parents love about homeschooling, but they can also be very frustrating. After making the huge decision to homeschool, parents are immediately faced with a barrage of additional choices—which curriculum to use, what teaching method to follow, and countless other where, when, and how questions. With so many variables, new homeschoolers reach out to homeschooling experts for guidance. Unfortunately, God created every child and home uniquely, and what works for one family might not work for another. Although the experience of other homeschoolers can help guide us, ultimately only God can show us the perfect homeschooling plan He has designed for our family.

Trusting in the opinions of others can be helpful or disastrous, depending on the counselors you choose. King Solomon's son, Rehoboam, learned this lesson the hard way. After his father died and he became king, Rehoboam was faced with an intense rebellion of the people led by Jeroboam. Jeroboam and the people were insisting that Rehoboam be more lenient on the workforce than his father had been. After they voiced their complaints, they asked for a response. Telling them to come back in three days for his answer, Rehoboam first consulted with the elders who had served his father. Not liking their wise response of "speak good words to them, then they will be thy servants for ever," Rehoboam instead turned to the counsel of young men who grew up with him. Acting on their arrogant and prideful counsel, Rehoboam spoke harshly to the people and lost the following of almost the entire nation of Israel (1 Kings 12:1-17).

Are you overwhelmed by the myriad of homeschooling choices? Getting informed and familiarizing yourself with curriculums, techniques, and approaches is a great place to start. Be careful, however, when you actually make your decisions. Many opinions abound, but let the Lord's counsel be the one you trust most. In His wisdom, He'll continue to lead you as you, trust in His Word.

Lord, homeschooling seems so overwhelming, and I'm afraid of choosing the wrong things for my children. Please show me how and where to start and guide me as we start on this new journey together. In Jesus' name, Amen.

Going Under

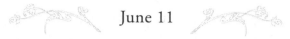
"The LORD is thy keeper" (Psalm 121:5a).

I'll never forget the day my son almost drowned. As I sat on the pool's edge after giving my son a swimming lesson, I watched as he played with his homeschooling friends. Since several lifeguards were on duty and the water was only waist-deep, I decided to close my weary eyes and rest for just a moment. Presuming my son was perfectly safe, even though he had only just started to learn how to swim, I allowed myself to drift off.

Suddenly, I heard someone shout in a panicked voice. Looking up and quickly scanning the water, I wasn't able to locate my son anywhere in the pool. Just as I stood up to look further, I saw an older boy pull my son from the pool's deep end. Coughing and choking, he was fighting to breathe. Minutes later, after we were sure he was all right, he told me the whole story: "Mom, I was just trying to practice my bouncing like you taught me. I guess I just bounced too hard and went right into the deep water." I'm not sure who was more frightened, my son or me, and for the next several days, I mentally punished myself as I considered what could have happened.

It's always tragic when young children are injured in an accident. Recorded in 2 Samuel 4:4 is the story of how Mephibosheth, the five-year-old son of Jonathan, was crippled in both his feet. In her hurry to flee after receiving the news of King Saul and Jonathan's death, Mephibosheth's nurse dropped him. Understandably, she was probably worried the child would be killed by the succeeding king, but her haste left this young boy lame for his entire life. However, God mercifully provided for Mephibosheth's needs years later when He moved King David to keep his covenant with his friend Jonathan (1 Samuel 20:15-17).

If you've had a tragedy in your home and struggle with forgiving yourself, God knows your pain. Being a homeschooling parent doesn't mean you can protect your child from every physical bump and bruise. Accidents happen, and many times there are no good reasons or answers to explain them. Only God knows what each day will bring, but praise the Lord, that even when bad things happen, He is still able to turn them around for good. "And we know that all things work together for good to them that love God, to them who are the called according to his purpose" (Romans 8:28).

Lord, I can't see the good in this situation right now, and I feel like it's all my fault. Please help me forgive myself and to trust that somehow, You will make sense of this problem. In Jesus' name, Amen.

Homeschooling in Reverse

June 12

"But as it is written, Eye hath not seen, nor ear heard, neither have entered into the heart of man, the things which God hath prepared for them that love him" (1 Corinthians 2:9).

As a homeschooling parent of young children, I couldn't imagine teaching my children through high school. My days were only focused on reading, writing, and arithmetic skills. Thinking about teaching college-prep courses was mind boggling. When talking with my husband about our children's future, the business manager in him said, "Why don't we start where we want our children to be educationally, spiritually, and emotionally in twelve years, and then work backwards from there."

"What do you mean?" I asked confused.

"If you wanted to make a cake, how would you go about it?" he asked. "You'd think of all the ingredients you'd need, how much time it would take to mix it together, and then you'd organize everything to bake it. Well, if we want to successfully teach the children everything they need to go to college someday, then we should start at that point and work backwards. Let's find out what subjects they will need to successfully complete and incorporate them into their studies over the next several years."

As Christians, we should also remember our final heavenly goal and work backwards as we live here on earth. With the Bible to guide us, we will find courses to successfully complete until the Lord's return. Living like Christ requires learning the fruit of the Spirit, so we can minister to the lost and hurting people God has placed in our lives. In fact, God has already prepared the good works He has planned for us to do. "For we are his workmanship, created in Christ Jesus unto good works, which God hath before ordained that we should walk in them" (Ephesians 2:10).

Are you walking with the Lord in light of His return? This earth is not your home and some-day soon, Christ will come back for those who love Him and bring us home to the place He has prepared for us (John 14:2-3). Are you prepared to meet Him and hear "Well done, thou good and faithful servant" (Matthew 25:21)?

Father, time is short and I know this life has only enough moments for me to accomplish Your will. Show me how to live each day for You and to share Your love with those around me. In the name of Jesus, Amen.

Share your thoughts about this devotional at **aophomeschooling.com**/163

Heavenly Ears

June 13

"Whither shall I go from thy spirit? or whither shall I flee from thy presence" (Psalm 139:7)?

I never understood the old saying, "Parents have eyes in the back of their heads," until I became a parent myself. After several messy disasters and naughty pranks played by my children, I learned to be in tune with the symphony of sound during our homeschooling. Even if I was in the kitchen preparing supper, I knew what each child was doing in other parts of the house by the noise involved. In fact, the only time I really worried was when there was no sound at all. Total quiet usually meant one of two things—all my children were reading a book, or they were into trouble.

In a far greater way, our heavenly Father also monitors the noise coming from His children. When we lift up our praises and prayers, He knows all is well within the hearts of His people. However, when we grow quiet and fail to come before His presence, He knows we're headed down a path that leads to trouble. Neglecting to talk to the Lord, we foolishly try to manage our lives on our own and find ourselves in the middle of problems. Lovingly, the Holy Spirit convicts us of our sin, and God waits for us to cry out so He can encourage us in our spiritual walk.

What about you? Have things been quiet at your house lately? If God hasn't heard your praise or prayers in a long time, right now is the best time to come before His throne. Take a moment to pray and praise the Lord for His loving care in your life. Even though He knows right where you are and what you need, He's waiting to hear from you today. "Hear my voice according unto thy lovingkindness: O LORD, quicken me according to thy judgment" (Psalm 119:149).

Father, please hear my prayer and forgive me for wandering away from You. Fill me today with Your power and wisdom, and lead me back to the place where my heart can commune with You. In the name of Jesus, Amen.

Old Glory

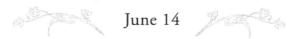

June 14

"His name shall endure for ever: his name shall be continued as long as the sun: and men shall be blessed in him: all nations shall call him blessed" (Psalm 72:17).

"Mom, it's my turn to hold the flag today, right?" asked my five-year-old son.

"Yes, honey," I replied. "But you can't be silly. If you want to hold the flag, you have to stand up straight and tall with your right hand on your heart."

As we started the day with the pledge of allegiance, holding the flag was considered an honor in our homeschool. My father was a World War II veteran who had passed on his love for country and flag to his children and grandchildren. Sharing heroic stories of combat and bravery, my father instilled a sense of pride and respect for the American flag, especially on June 14.

June 14 was first proclaimed Flag Day in 1916 by President Woodrow Wilson and officially became recognized as National Flag Day in 1949 when President Harry Truman signed the National Flag Day into law. Although June 14 is not declared an official federal holiday, it is a wonderful day for homeschoolers and all Americans to show respect for what our flag represents—one nation under God. With so many voices disputing that fact today, teaching our children to honor and handle the flag correctly is one way to develop a patriotic spirit and appreciation for those who died in protecting our flag.

Does your homeschooling family know how to honor the American flag? If not, June 14 would be a great day to start a short unit study on our nation's greatest symbol. As your children learn to honor those who have died to keep Old Glory waving, they'll also discover the Holy God who made our country great. "All the ends of the world shall remember and turn unto the LORD: and all the kindreds of the nations shall worship before thee. For the kingdom is the LORD's: and he is the governor among the nations" (Psalm 22:27-28).

Lord, help us to remember the blessings You gave this country because we trusted in You. Show me how to teach my children how to honor the flag that they might continue to keep this one nation under God. In Jesus' name, Amen.

On Target

"Where there is no vision, the people perish" (Proverbs 29:18a).

What plans have you made for your children this summer? During our first years of homeschooling, I made the mistake of failing to plan activities for our family. Tired of schedules and organizing throughout the school year, I wanted to take each day just as it came. Although this idealistic idea of allowing my children to play and explore on their own worked initially, I soon found them bored and looking for things to do. Coming to me for suggestions, I realized that even in summer, they needed a purpose and a plan for each day. Frittering away the summer was simply not going to do, and I needed to stay in tune with God's plan for their lives.

Wasting time is never wise in living the Christian life either. Nowhere in the Bible does it talk about sitting back and letting life pass you by. Rather, the Apostle Paul repeatedly addresses the need to discipline ourselves to achieve our utmost for God's highest. Buffeting our bodies and taking on the mind of Christ, we are to live each day wholly committed to doing the Lord's will. In fact, God commands us to present ourselves as living sacrifices that He might use us for His glory—no matter what time or day of the year (Romans 12:1).

What about you? Do you think you've earned time off from serving the Lord? Until the Lord returns, God expects you to be about His business each day using the gifts and talents He's given you. Don't be like the lazy slave in the parable of the talents who hid his talent in the ground (Matthew 25:14-30). Instead, come to the Lord each morning in prayer and discover God's purpose to keep your life hitting the mark. "I press toward the mark for the prize of the high calling of God in Christ Jesus" (Philippians 3:14).

Lord, forgive me for being lazy in my walk with You and ignoring Your plan. I recommit my life to You today to use for Your glory. In Jesus' name, Amen.

Fitting In

June 16

"Love not the world, neither the things that are in the world. If any man love the world, the love of the Father is not in him" (1 John 2:15).

The benefits of homeschooling are wonderful, but there are times when parents face difficult issues. As children grow into their teen years, they realize that homeschooling sets them apart from the mainstream. Wise parents will understand their teenager's need for acceptance during this transition into adulthood and provide an added sense of belonging. However, no matter how much affirmation you give your child, his true value and uniqueness will only be confirmed, as he realizes and understands his worth in God's eyes.

Dealing with the world's rejection is difficult for any Christian, no matter the age. God's Word tells us our true citizenship is in heaven (Philippians 3:20), and that we live as strangers in this world (1 Peter 2:11). Considering these facts, we too must understand that we will never fit into the world's scheme of things as we live for Christ. Not only does homeschooling set us apart, but being a Christian puts us on the world's "most hated" list. "If ye were of the world, the world would love his own: but because ye are not of the world, but I have chosen you out of the world, therefore the world hateth you" (John 15:19). Our worth and value, therefore, can only be based on what God thinks of us.

Do you ever feel ostracized as you homeschool your children? God sees all you're going through and promises to never leave you, nor forsake you (Hebrews 13:5b). Remember, you won't be a "stranger" forever. Some day, both you and your children will totally fit in, as you walk into the heavenly home God has prepared for you.

Lord, please show me how to encourage my teen as he struggles with the same acceptance issues as me. May we both be strengthened by Your unfailing love until You bring us home to heaven. In Jesus' name, Amen.

Thanks Dad

June 17

"My son, hear the instruction of thy father" (Proverbs 1:8a).

Moms have a tendency to think they are the "lone ranger" in homeschooling their children. Although we are often the sole instructor, dads equally contribute to a family's homeschooling success with their quiet and sometimes unnoticed acts of love and support. Father's Day is a wonderful time to recognize fathers for their important part in homeschooling for such things as the following:

• Providing the working capital to keep school from going in the red. Dad's hard-earned income enables us to buy fun educational material and curriculum, and to go on endless field trips.

• Being the substitute teacher who gives Mom a breather. Reading bedtime stories and practicing spelling words for Friday's test provide the extra support necessary to keep a 24/7 homeschooling mom from burning out. Even a simple physical education class of baseball or basketball helps make time for errands or personal R & R.

• Serving as the "principal of the school." The truth is, no one's child is perfect, and sometimes extra discipline is needed when homeschooling. Disruptive and disrespectful attitudes can be curtailed by the firm and loving correction only a father can provide.

• Providing practical know-how in carpentry, mechanics, plumbing and other daily-living skills. Children will love the money saved on future repair bills because their father taught them how to "fix" things on their own.

• Being the spiritual leader who guides the family into the most important truth they ever learn—God loves them and sent His Son, Jesus, to be their Savior.

What plans have you made to honor the homeschool dad in your house this Father's Day? Don't let your husband go unnoticed for all his acts of love and behind-the-scenes support. Show appreciation for all he does to make your homeschooling successful, and thank him for the love he communicates to your family. "Honor thy father and thy mother: that thy days may be long upon the land which the LORD thy God giveth thee" (Exodus 20:12).

Lord, thank You for the best teammate in the world and for the loving help He provides our homeschooling family. Help me to always appreciate and recognize what he does to keep our family strong and walking with You. In Jesus' name, Amen.

 Share your thoughts about this devotional at aophomeschooling.com/168

Toads, Turtles, and Tree Houses

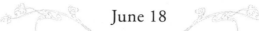

June 18

When summer months came to our homeschooling family, I had a hard time keeping up with the activities of my young sons. As they explored the farm, they frequently left their new discoveries on the kitchen counter to share with me. Unfortunately, these tremendous finds failed to provide the same enjoyment to a tired and skittish mother who was deathly afraid of reptiles, spiders, and creepy insects. I was never quite sure if I wanted to open their gifts of love or not!

However, there was one summer activity I always enjoyed doing with my sons. Hidden in the branches of the old box elder tree in the backyard, the boys' tree fort provided hours of welcome play and enjoyment. Sometimes we played board games. Other times we just enjoyed a cool glass of lemonade and cookies. Whatever the occasion, I was thankful to be considered "one of the guys" and always considered it a privilege when they invited me over to their "house."

As Christians, God also desires for us to share our homes with others. In Romans 12:13, God's Word tells us to be "given to hospitality" and to share what we have with the needs of the saints. With so many blessings God has provided at our disposal, our homes become the perfect place to minister to the hearts of the lonely and hurting within the body of Christ. However, not only are we to reach out to fellow homeschoolers and other Christians, God also exhorts us to go one step further: "Be not forgetful to entertain strangers" (Hebrews 13:2a). Inviting those who don't know Christ as Savior to eat at your table provides the loving and welcoming environment that opens hearts to the message of salvation.

Is your summer already scheduled to the limit and too busy to open your home to others? If so, maybe you can rearrange your activities and practice some old-fashioned hospitality. Whether it's an informal get together with church friends, a summer backyard Bible club, or a large community outreach block party, share the blessings God has given you and watch as others experience the joy of being loved. "Use hospitality one to another without grudging" (1 Peter 4:9).

Father, thank You for the delightful days of summer and the opportunities to minister to people with Your love. Show me how to bless others and use our home for Your glory. In Jesus' name, Amen.

Share your thoughts about this devotional at **aophomeschooling.com**/169

God's Gifts

"As every man hath received the gift, even so minister the same one to another, as good stewards of the manifold grace of God" (1 Peter 4:10).

My son was sitting at his desk with a contemplative look on his face, as he studied his lesson for school. With his Bible open to Romans 12, he was struggling with identifying his spiritual gift and how he might use it in Christian ministry. "Mom," he said. "I really don't know what gift God has given me. What do you think my spiritual gift is?"

"Well," I reflected. "I think one gift God has given you is the gift of service. I've seen how you love to help others both at church and at home. You never complain, and you seem to know what to do before someone even asks for help."

"Wow, you mean when I do that it's using my spiritual gift?" he asked.

"Yes," I replied. "You are using your gifts if you allow the Holy Spirit to show you when and where to help."

Every believer, including children, has at least one spiritual gift (1 Corinthians 12:7). Unfortunately, many Christians never identify their spiritual gifts and simply live life as a spectator rather than a participator. God desires his church to be active and growing with each believer playing an important part in its effective worship and work. Understanding your gifts, therefore, will help you find the best way to serve and eliminate frustrations over trying to do things like someone else. Not only will the church be strengthened and unified, but you'll also discover that spiritual gifts are really just Jesus working through your life as you carry on His ministry.

Do you know your spiritual gift(s) in the Lord? As you read Romans 12:3-9, ask God to reveal which gifts He wants to use through your life. Like my son, discover how much fun living the Christian life can be when serving the Lord with the gift He has given You!

Father, I want to glorify You with my life and discover the joy in serving You. Please reveal those gifts You've given me and empower me with the Holy Spirit to use them for Your glory. In Jesus' name, Amen.

Leading by Example

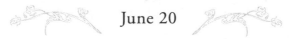

June 20

"For I have given you an example, that ye should do as I have done to you" (John 13:15).

When homeschooling your children, you often find yourself face to face with personal challenges to grow intellectually and spiritually. Relearning algebra and geometry in order to teach my children high school math was difficult, but memorizing their Scripture verses was even harder. Scripture memorization had been a discipline I failed to apply to my own life until my son asked one day, "Mom, do you know all these Scripture verses, too?" Admitting that I didn't, God convicted me to start hiding His Word in my heart right along with my children during their Bible lessons.

The best teachers and leaders in the Christian life are those who are willing to get their own hands dirty as they help others. Paul was such a man. Although he could have stayed in Jerusalem, he responded to God's call and went to the mission field. Willing to face shipwrecks, beatings, stonings, and other persecutions, God used him to lead thousands of people to the Lord. Even while he was ministering and establishing new churches, Paul supported himself by making tents in order not to be a financial burden on the church (Acts 20:33-35).

Are you willing to practice what you preach to your children, or do you take the easy road in your spiritual walk? Although no homeschooling parent is perfect, we can allow the Holy Spirit to change our lives for the better. If you want to make a lasting impression on your children's hearts as a godly homeschool parent, lead by example. "Nevertheless, whereto we have already attained, let us walk by the same rule, let us mind the same thing. Brethren, be followers together of me, and mark them which walk so as ye have us for an ensample" (Philippians 3:16-17).

Lord, I stand in awe at the responsibility You've given me in teaching my children. Let my life be an example of Your love and show me those areas that need to be strengthened to glorify You. In Jesus' name, Amen.

Share your thoughts about this devotional at **aophomeschooling.com/171**

Who's in the Middle of the Storm?

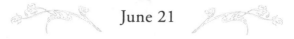

June 21

"I, even I, am he that comforteth you" (Isaiah 51:12a).

Summer storms were always a scary time for my young children. When the weather turned blustery on hot summer nights, I usually heard my two oldest children running down the hallway to my bedroom. Even though they had learned Bible stories of Jesus' power over storms and problems, their little hearts were simply too frightened by the strength of a threatening storm. Understanding their fears, I would let them crawl into my bed while the lightning cracked and the thunder boomed. After the storm passed, I would then carry their sleepy little bodies back to their own beds.

One night during a storm, I felt God's leading to teach my children an important spiritual lesson. Instead of allowing them to crawl into bed with me, I gently took them back to their room and tucked them into bed. As I sat with them, I taught a little song to comfort their fears while the storm raged outside. The words were simple enough for a four and five year old and talked about not being afraid since God is always with us.

As we sang the words together during the storm, my children experienced God's courage to face their fears. Although they didn't fall back to sleep right away, they were able to wait out the storm without terrified tears. More importantly, they learned whenever they were afraid in life, they could go to their heavenly Father for protection.

Are you in the middle of a storm right now in your life? Maybe you're facing the dark and painful moments of grief or loneliness. Whatever the problem, God promises in His Word that He will be with you (Hebrews 13:5b). Like a loving heavenly Father, He gently holds and comforts you when the darkness seems overwhelming or when the storm's power rages over you. Run to Him now, and you'll also discover He's in the middle of your dark storm. "Fear thou not; for I am with thee: be not dismayed; for I am thy God: I will strengthen thee; yea, I will help thee; yea, I will uphold thee with the right hand of my righteousness" (Isaiah 41:10).

Heavenly Father, I feel so scared right now, and like a child, I want to panic. I claim Your promise to never leave me, nor forsake me. Please hold me right now Father, and keep me safe. In Jesus' name, Amen.

 Share your thoughts about this devotional at **aophomeschooling.com/172**

False Assumptions

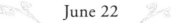

June 22

"Jesus answered and said unto them, Ye do err, not knowing the scriptures, nor the power of God" (Matthew 22:29).

Do your parents find knowing how to help when you homeschool difficult? Although my parents had raised seven children of their own, they always seemed hesitant to watch my children when I needed a helping hand. At first, I thought my children might be misbehaving during their stay, but my parents assured me that was not the case. However, after declining my request to watch them several times in a row, I finally asked, "Mom, why don't you want the kids to come over?"

Reluctantly she admitted, "Well, I just don't know how to help them do their schoolwork." Like a light bulb turning on in my head, I finally understood the problem. For months I had thought my parents didn't enjoy my children. In reality, they were feeling inadequate to supervise the homeschooling lessons I had prepared. From that day on, schoolwork was left at home. My children simply enjoyed being with their grandparents and helping with their daily chores. When time permitted, they played games and learned invaluable lessons in practical skills not found in a workbook.

Making incorrect assumptions can also get Christians into trouble in the body of Christ. Rather than interpreting Scripture with Scripture in the power of the Holy Spirit, many Christians make poor choices because they take God's Word out of context. Randomly picking isolated verses, they fail to clearly understand God's will and infer meanings the passage never intended. Even Christ faced this same temptation. When Satan misquoted Scripture in Luke 4:10-11, he challenged Jesus to prove He was the Son of God by throwing Himself down from the temple's pinnacle. Jesus refuted Satan's misinterpretation of Psalm 91:12 and quoted Deuteronomy 6:16 instead which states, "Ye shall not tempt the LORD your God."

Are you correctly handling the Word of God? Don't make false assumptions about the Scriptures that might jeopardize your homeschooling success. Read the entire Bible passage and remember to seek the Holy Spirit's guidance as you study God's Word. Heed the exhortation the Apostle Paul gave to a young believer in 2 Timothy 2:15: "Study to shew thyself approved unto God, a workman that needeth not to be ashamed, rightly dividing the word of truth."

Lord, without Your help, no one can understand the Bible. Please show me how to read and study Your Word that I might apply it and glorify You with my life. In the name of Jesus, Amen.

 Share your thoughts about this devotional at aophomeschooling.com/173

Swinging High

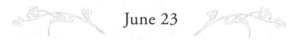

June 23

"I can swing higher than you," shouted my oldest daughter to the neighbor children who had come over to play.

"No you can't," they retorted. "We can swing just as high as you!"

As I washed the dishes and looked out the open kitchen window, I could hear their childish competitive banter and knew trouble was looming. Although taking a break from home-schooling during the summer provided more opportunities for my children's friends to visit, it also required more supervision of their activities. I watched as each child began to swing harder and higher. Just as I decided to dry my hands and walk outside to tell them to stop swinging so high, the entire swing set toppled over and crashed to the ground, along with the children. Fortunately, no one was seriously hurt, but the bumps and bruises taught each of them a valuable lesson in humility.

King Nebuchadnezzar also had to learn the hard lesson of humility before a holy God. After building a huge gold image of himself, he required everyone in the kingdom to bow down in worship. When three young Hebrew captives, Shadrach, Meshach, and Abed-nego, refused to worship this arrogant king's statue, God proved Himself mighty and delivered them from the fiery furnace and Nebuchadnezzar's wrath (Daniel 3:19-30). However, even after this humbling experience from God, Nebuchadnezzar again exalted himself by claiming credit for Babylon's glory (Daniel 4:30). For the next seven years, God punished Nebuchadnezzar's pride with insanity. He became like an animal, ate grass, and grew nails like bird's claws. At the end of that time, Nebuchadnezzar finally exclaimed, "Now I Nebuchadnezzar praise and extol and honor the King of heaven, all whose works are truth, and his ways judgment: and those that walk in pride he is able to abase" (Daniel 4:37).

What about you? Has selfish pride taken hold of your life? Even though you may think you have the answers to all of homeschooling's questions, you don't. Each child is a unique creation and gift from the Lord, and only He can guide you as you choose curriculum and lessons to successfully homeschool your child. Don't let your independent spirit cause you to stumble and fall. "Pride goeth before destruction, and an haughty spirit before a fall" (Proverbs 16:18).

Father, help me to remember You are in control of our homeschooling. Teach me to walk in Your ways and to rely on the Holy Spirit to guide me each day. In Jesus' name, Amen.

 Share your thoughts about this devotional at **aophomeschooling.com/**174

Unseen Worlds

"Be sober, be vigilant; because your adversary the devil, as a roaring lion, walketh about, seeking whom he may devour" (1 Peter 5:8).

Summer science was a part of our homeschool curriculum. One particular experiment my children enjoyed was discovering the minute world contained within a one square foot section of our lawn. After plotting and marking their sections, my children would lie on the grass for hours and take note of creatures and insects that would otherwise go unnoticed. Roly-poly bugs, ants, winged insects, beetles, and a host of other bugs, worms, and spiders comprised the intricately designed order of this small universe. Each new discovery brought an excited response of, "Mom, come and see this. Isn't this cool!" Like explorers in an unknown world, my children learned to see what most people miss in God's creation.

As Christians, we also face an unseen world that exists around us. Often, we are unaware of the angelic hosts and the spiritual battles they fight on our behalf, as we stand in prayer against the wiles of Satan. Like Elisha's servant in 2 Kings 6:17, our eyes need to be opened to God's power that defeats Satan and his lies. As we humble our hearts and lie at the Master's feet, He promises to give us everything we need to live a victorious life. However, we can never afford the luxury of growing comfortable in our Christianity. Unseen spiritual battles must be fought in the name of Jesus and the power of His blood. Although we may not see them with our physical eyes, they do exist. In fact, God's Word says, "For though we walk in the flesh, we do not war after the flesh: (For the weapons of our warfare are not carnal, but mighty through God to the pulling down of strong holds;)" (2 Corinthians 10:3-4).

Are life's problems pulling down your homeschool family? Although summer may seem like a time to relax, don't forget to stay alert and see each day through God's eyes. Allow Him to show you the unseen world of His mighty power and love that can handle any temptation Satan throws your way.

Father, please guide me today and keep me in the safety of Your love and protection. Help me to see Satan's temptations when they come and to stand against his lies in Your power. In Jesus' name, Amen.

Priceless Treasures

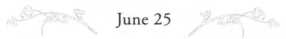

June 25

Attending local household and farm sales became a favorite activity for my son and me during our homeschooling summer break. We loved searching for new treasures, and my son learned the fine art of bidding on items as they were auctioned. As we arrived at one particular farm sale however, my spirit was saddened as we meandered through tables and boxes filled with antiques and old-fashioned keepsakes. An elderly widow who had lived alone for many years had passed away, and all that remained of her life was sitting before us. From homemade potholders and doilies to exquisite crystal and china, each item once treasured by this old woman was now up for sale. The value and memories they held meant nothing to the strangers purchasing them, and each item sold for next to nothing. "How sad," I said to my son. "These things should be selling for much more. They might as well be giving them away!"

Reflecting on the transactions before me, I saw the foolishness of my priorities in life. Someday, I too would return to dust like this old woman with all my possessions being rummaged through by a new generation of treasure seekers. The value of what I had owned would mean nothing, and my possessions would simply be sold at the cheapest price. As I thought more deeply, I realized Christ's words were true, "Lay not up for yourselves treasures upon earth, where moth and rust doth corrupt, and where thieves break through and steal; But lay up for yourselves treasures in heaven, where neither moth nor rust doth corrupt, and where thieves do not break through nor steal" (Matthew 6:19-20). Only the love I had shown to others while living for Christ would have any value, importance, and meaning.

What about you? Are you busy storing up treasures in heaven or are you just accumulating things? Whatever you possess in this life will mean nothing when you stand face to face with your Creator. After all, the only treasures you can bring to heaven are the lives of those who come to know Christ as a result of your witness.

Lord, forgive me when I value the wrong things in life. Teach me to know what's truly priceless in Your eyes, so Your will may be done in my life. In the name of Jesus, Amen.

Rod of Righteousness

June 26

"Wherefore let him that thinketh he standeth take heed lest he fall" (1 Corinthians 10:12).

Do you find disciplining your homeschooler difficult? I did for several different reasons. First, I hated being the "policeman" and the temporary conflict it caused when teaching my children. Being esteemed as their "hero" with all the answers was much more fun. Second, administering fair justice for the offense wasn't always easy to determine. Many times, what appeared to be misbehavior in one child was actually caused by the deliberate aggravation by another child. Most of all, I found disciplining my children difficult because I knew my own failings to meet God's righteous standards. More often than not, I usually found myself committing a similar offense within a few days of disciplining them for the very same thing.

The Bible tells us "There is none righteous, no, not one" (Romans 3:10b). Everyone has sinned and turned to his own way in one thing or another. Whether it's lies, cursing, or bitterness, we all have feet that are quick to run to evil. Christ says that even thinking about such deeds is the same as committing the acts of sin (Matthew 5:28). Therefore, we must learn to deal gently and mercifully with other believers when they sin. In Christian love, we must hold a balance of loving forgiveness and accountability that takes into account our own sinful nature.

If patience has run thin and you find yourself disciplining your homeschooler too severely, remember God's patient forgiveness towards you. He is the One who is able to give you the wisdom you need to give your child the "right" training in righteousness. "Brethren, if a man be overtaken in a fault, ye which are spiritual, restore such an one in the spirit of meekness; considering thyself, lest thou also be tempted" (Galatians 6:1).

Heavenly Father, help me to see the faults in myself just as easily as I see them in my children. Show me how to lovingly correct their errors and to teach them of Your forgiveness and unconditional love. In the name of Jesus, Amen.

Sacrifice or Blessing?

June 27

"For when I am weak, then am I strong" (2 Corinthians 12:10b).

God allowed me the privilege of teaching my children many things in 25 years of home-schooling. However, during those same years, my children also taught me several important lessons. First, I learned to savor the joy of life's moments. Reading a story or having time to talk was far more important than keeping the house perfectly organized and clean. Second, I learned to experience the wonder of God's creation through a child's excited eyes. Everything is fresh and new to a little one, and God desires me to experience each new day in the same way. Perhaps the most important lesson my children taught me was to have an unquestioning faith in God. Even when homeschooling cut the family budget in half, my children's faith challenged me to trust God for every need. Undoubtedly, I was the one who received the better education in our family's homeschool.

God's Word declares that if we choose to follow Christ in this life, we must be prepared to suffer (1 Peter 4:1). Showing the love of God to others isn't easy, and many times we may think God is asking too much of us. However, the blessings God imparts to those who desire to live godly in Christ Jesus far outweigh the sacrificial obedience required in learning lessons in God's schoolroom. Not only does the Holy Spirit intercede for us on our behalf (Romans 8:26), but He also guides and fills us for each day's tasks (John 16:13). The more we deny ourselves and give in serving the Lord, the more we experience the sweetness of His fellowship.

Have you experienced God's sustaining power and love in your homeschooling? When the days seem long and you feel like you've given everything you have to give, let the Lord show you a better way. As you allow Him to guide you, you'll discover His promises are true and His blessings are far greater than any sacrifice made by you. "My grace is sufficient for thee: for my strength is made perfect in weakness. Most gladly therefore will I rather glory in my infirmities, that the power of Christ may rest upon me" (2 Corinthians 12:9b).

Father, I praise You for the great privilege of being Your servant. There's no way I can out give You, and I thank You for Your abundant love that never ceases to encourage me through life's problems. In Jesus' name, Amen.

Handing over the Reins

June 28

"Likewise, ye wives, be in subjection to your own husbands" (1 Peter 3:1a).

Our homeschooling day had been long and filled with interruptions. My toddlers had been cranky, and phone calls about organizing activities at church had put us behind schedule in our schoolwork. Herding my children from one subject to the next as quickly as possible, I felt like a trail boss blazing through our schoolwork. However, as the sun began to set, I realized we weren't going to finish our lessons for the day. Finding the best stopping point in our studies, I told my children to quickly put their workbooks away. My husband would soon be home from work, and it was time to pull out the "chuck wagon" to feed all my hungry hands.

Delegating kitchen responsibilities to my older children, we began to prepare supper. A short time later, my husband arrived and he also helped in the preparations by setting the table. As he completed the chore, I continued to give more instructions to him and the children with the same "trail boss" attitude I had been using all day. Although my husband gladly helped with the assignments, I sensed a problem in his response to my commands. Forgetting to hand over the reins to our home, I realized I had been bossing my husband just like my children.

Although homeschooling husbands and wives work as a team, husbands must be allowed the opportunity to assume the leadership role in the family. Unfortunately, after being in charge of the home and the children all day, many homeschooling moms have difficulty in transferring that responsibility. In fact, our independent spirit and self-sufficient ways tend to leave Dad out of the homeschooling picture altogether. If you find yourself making the same mistake as me and not allowing your husband to lead, perhaps it's time to remember God's exhortation in Ephesians 5:22-23a: "Wives, submit yourselves unto your own husbands, as unto the Lord. For the husband is the head of the wife, even as Christ is the head of the church."

Lord, I know You've designed the home to work according to Your plan. Please show me how to work together with my husband when homeschooling and to transfer the leadership of our family to him once he is home. In Jesus' name, Amen.

Share your thoughts about this devotional at **aophomeschooling.com**/179

Poor, Pitiful Me

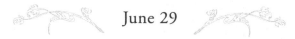

June 29

"O give thanks unto the LORD; for he is good: because his mercy endureth for ever" (Psalm 118:1).

Standing in the basement doing laundry, I wondered, "How much of your life do you sacrifice before there's nothing more to give?" I was missing a beautiful summer day outside and feeling frustrated that there was so little time for the things I enjoyed. I dreamed of relaxing in the sun with an ice cold glass of lemonade and a good book or riding my horse into the open pastures near our ranch. Homeschooling seemed to be consuming my entire life, and each day I felt a little more drained. If I wasn't teaching my children, I was cleaning their messes. Would there ever be time again for me?

Self-pity is a destructive force in a person's life because it fails to acknowledge God's goodness with a grateful heart. The Hebrew nation's constant grumbling is a prime example (Psalm 106:25). For over 470 years, they cried out to God for a deliverer to rescue them from bondage in Egypt. When deliverance finally came and Moses led them to the Promised Land, they continued to complain, even to the point of longing to go back to Egypt. Although God had proven Himself mighty with miracles and provisions, they failed to be thankful for His loving hand of protection.

What about you? If the demands of homeschooling have got you down, stop your personal pity party and think again about what the Lord has done. Yes, your days might be busy, but God has blessed you with incredible opportunities to change the world through your children's lives. Let praise and thankfulness replace your "poor me's" and watch as God blesses your faithfulness in serving Him as a homeschooling parent. "I will bless the LORD at all times: his praise shall continually be in my mouth" (Psalm 34:1).

Father, forgive my selfishness when I fail to appreciate all You have given to our family. Lift my heart today and help me to focus on those things in life that are truly important. In Jesus' name, Amen.

Share your thoughts about this devotional at aophomeschooling.com/180

Unfulfilled Days

June 30

Do homeschooling parents ever admit that life is anything but one blissful moment after another with their children? If they're honest, they will. As much as we would like to proclaim homeschooling's benefits and see our children's lives through "rose-colored glasses," we must also attest to our children's sinful behavior that causes disruption in the home and unproductive homeschooling days. Children easily demonstrate sinful actions of selfishness, greed, jealousy, and other undesirable characteristics that require daily correction and training in righteousness. Like management in the workplace, wise homeschooling parents must allow for down times in academic productivity to address the more important issue of character building in their child.

Amazingly, there are many similarities between our relationship with our children and God's relationship with us. As His children, we demonstrate actions that disrupt God's family of believers. With selfishness, pride, and rebellion, we fail to be productive in accomplishing God's will. Daily, God must discipline us and provide the instruction in righteousness that will develop Christ-like character. Patiently, He continues to perfect the work which He has begun in us, so our lives will bear much fruit for His name's sake (Philippians 1:6).

Are the frustrations of homeschooling tempting you to give up teaching your children? Do you find yourself taking one step forward and two steps backwards? Just as God gently corrects and teaches you in your spiritual walk, allow the Lord to help you show that same patience towards your children. Although your days may seem unfulfilling, you are giving your child the exact education he needs. "Therefore, my beloved brethren, be ye stedfast, unmovable, always abounding in the work of the Lord, forasmuch as ye know that your labour is not in vain in the Lord" (1 Corinthians 15:58).

Lord, how difficult it is to stay on track in our homeschooling! Remind me that we are learning more than just academics and show me how to deal with my children's true needs. In Jesus' name, Amen.

To Please or Not to Please

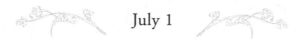

July 1

"That ye might walk worthy of the Lord unto all pleasing, being fruitful in every good work, and increasing in the knowledge of God" (Colossians 1:10).

I loved homeschooling my children when they were four, five, and six years old because it was so easy to teach them. Curious and loving, my children were as anxious to please as they were to learn. Mom and Dad's approval meant the world to them as they attempted to master new skills, and any words of encouragement and affirmation from us were soaked up like a sponge. Granted, at this age my children loved learning for learning's sake, but in large part, they also studied hard, so we would be proud of their educational accomplishments.

As Christians, God also desires that we would come before His presence and live to please Him. He has so much to teach us and knows we'll be happiest if we understand His will and obey His plan for our life. However, many of us ignore God's desire and waste years seeking the approval and affirmation of others, including our own family. As we attempt to please everyone but the One who loves us most, we eventually find ourselves frustrated and burned out.

How about you? Are you so busy trying to please everyone that you've forgotten about pleasing God? If you struggle in keeping Christ your first love, consider the One who loves you so much that He sent His Son to die for your sins. With so great a love, doesn't He deserve to be number one on your "to please" list? "By him therefore let us offer the sacrifice of praise to God continually, that is, the fruit of our lips giving thanks to his name. But to do good and to communicate forget not: for with such sacrifices God is well pleased" (Hebrews 13:15-16).

Heavenly Father, every breath and every moment I experience here on earth is from You. Teach me to worship and please You with all that I am. All glory to You for being such a loving and wonderful God. In Jesus' name, Amen.

A Hannah Heartache

July 2

"Lo, children are an heritage of the LORD: and the fruit of the womb is his reward" (Psalm 127:3).

When you are facing mountains of laundry or dealing with childhood squabbles, it's hard to imagine the heartache of couples who long for children. Two of our dearest friends experienced such heartache. For ten years they tried without success to start their own family. Realizing that God had chosen a different path for their marriage, they decided to "adopt" our children and actively help us when homeschooling. Whenever they came to visit, my children would squeal with delighted anticipation and run to the door to greet them. Natural-born teachers at heart, they usually brought a new educational gift to entertain our children or would spend countless hours reading their favorite stories. Even though bitterness in not having children of their own could have ruled their hearts, they chose instead to share their lives with unselfish love.

The story of Hannah in 1 Samuel also tells of the heartache of a childless woman. Crying out in despair before the Lord in the temple, Hannah knew the anguish of being barren. As she prayed silently for a little one to fill her arms, Eli the priest mistook her prayers for a drunken stupor. Hannah bravely told him her story and asked for God's blessing on her life. Eli assured her that God had indeed heard her prayer and told her to go home. The following year, Hannah's prayer was answered and Samuel was born. For several years she experienced the privilege of mothering this young boy and then fulfilled her vow to bring him to the temple to serve the Lord (1 Samuel 1:11).

Every child is a miracle and a precious gift from God. Whether our own or someone else's child, we have the unique opportunity to be an influence for God's good in the hearts and minds of little ones. Our dear friends discovered that fact many years later. After the lengthy and expensive process of adoption, God finally gave them their heart's desire. Together we cried tears of joy for two precious baby girls. God had answered their prayers, and we praised Him for His most wonderful blessing in life—children. "He maketh the barren woman to keep house, and to be a joyful mother of children. Praise ye the LORD" (Psalm 113:9).

Lord, how wonderful it is to be a parent! Thank You for the privilege of loving children and teaching them Your truths. Even when the days are long and hard, help me to always treasure this most precious blessing. In Jesus' name, Amen.

The Homeschooling Fight

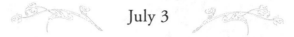

July 3

"I have fought a good fight, I have finished my course, I have kept the faith" (2 Timothy 4:7).

Christian education is a spiritual battle that must be fought by every homeschooling parent. The desire to see our children raised according to the standards of God's Word requires more than wishful thinking. We must ever be alert to Satan's schemes and the world's ways to suck our children into the mainstream of ungodly learning. We must be willing to risk popularity and acceptance to lead our children down an educational path that declares God is at the center of all things and the beginning of all creation. Most of all, we must declare our own love for Christ and be willing to crucify the flesh and its selfish desires in order to win our children's hearts to the Lord.

The great men and women of faith mentioned in Hebrews 11 are listed as our inspiration to hold fast to God's truths. Like Abraham, we must be willing to follow the Lord wherever He leads. Like Moses, we must be willing to give up the pleasures of life to serve a higher purpose. Like Rahab, we must have faith to believe what the Lord says is true. Like Noah, we must face opposition daily, even if it takes years to complete the task God has given. Like countless others who never saw the results of their faith, we must cling courageously to the future promise that God will bless the work of our hands in the lives of generations to come (Psalm 112:2).

Are you feeling the temptation to give up on homeschooling? Sending your children to public school next fall may seem appealing, but it's simply taking the easy way out. If the Lord has led you to teach your children, pray for the courage and wisdom you need to stand firm and fight. Raising your children in the Lord is as much a spiritual battle as resisting temptations for yourself. Don't give in to the lies and harassment of those around you. Fight for the hearts and minds of your children and for the work God can do through their lives in winning countless souls to Christ.

Lord, renew Your passion within me today to homeschool and teach my children Your truths. Guide us as we prepare for schooling in the fall and show me how to hold fast when taking an easier road seems much more appealing. In Jesus' name, Amen.

More Than a Celebration

July 4

"Freedom is never free." -Author Unknown

Memorizing historical documents was an important part of our homeschooling history lessons. Unfortunately, my children were less than enthusiastic about this particular assignment. Often, they would forget the value of the words they recited and either speak as quickly as possible or in slow, monotone voices. One day, as my son recited the beginning of the Declaration of Independence at the speed of light, I stopped him mid-sentence and asked, "Have you ever considered the price that was paid when those men signed the words you're now reciting?"

"No, not really," he answered nonchalantly.

"Well, maybe we should stop here and do a little study to find out," I replied. As we sidetracked our original lesson plans, my son discovered an amazing fact. When each of the 56 men signed their name to the declaration on July 4, 1776, they did indeed pledge their lives, their fortunes, and their sacred honor. King George III and Great Britain pursued each name on the document with a vengeance and were determined to eradicate this rebellious group of colonists who declared, "No king but King Jesus!"

"Wow, Mom, I never knew they gave up so much just so we could be free!" exclaimed my son. "I guess the Fourth of July is more than just fireworks and hotdogs."

As Christians, we also take for granted the privileges we enjoy in Christ. The Bible tells us that God did not spare His Son, but He delivered Him up for us all (Romans 8:32a). Through the shedding of Christ's blood (Hebrews 9:22), we are able to defeat Satan and sin. Do you value the price that was paid for your salvation, as well as your country? Let this Fourth of July be a double blessing in your life, as you consider not only the privilege of being an American, but also the privilege of being called a child of the King. "Forasmuch as ye know that ye were not redeemed with corruptible things, as silver and gold, from your vain conversation received by tradition from your fathers; But with the precious blood of Christ, as of a lamb without blemish and without spot" (1 Peter 1:18-19).

Lord, thank You for giving me the opportunity to live in a country that was founded by godly men who loved You. Teach me to value their sacrifice and to continue proclaiming Your great name to all generations. In Jesus' name, Amen.

 Share your thoughts about this devotional at aophomeschooling.com/185

How Big Is God?

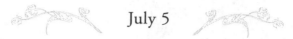

July 5

"But my God shall supply all your need according to his riches in glory by Christ Jesus" (Philippians 4:19).

When homeschooling limits your finances, do you trust God to provide for your every need? As I sat in the doctor's office and listened to him confirm my fourth pregnancy, I had no idea how God was going to help us afford the medical bills. Homeschooling and daily living expenses involved with raising three children had consumed my husband's total income. I knew we had no way to repay the costs for prenatal care, and I was forced to inform my doctor of our situation as he attempted to schedule my next appointment. Compassionately, he replied, "OK, let's just go ahead and schedule your next visits anyway. If God provides the money, you can pay me. If not, we'll just forget about the bill."

Reluctantly, my husband and I accepted our doctor's proposal, and I proceeded with my monthly visits throughout the summer months. Then, as we began our regular homeschooling schedule in August, the most amazing thing happened. A local business called and offered me a part-time accounting job writing dividend checks. I could perform the work at home during the evening hours, and if I finished the project before October, I could earn an hourly rate that was far above the current minimum wage. For the next two months, I worked long hours to homeschool during the day and complete my work at night for my new job. Exactly one week before I delivered our fourth child, I finished the project and earned not only enough money to pay our doctor, but also enough money to cover the entire hospital bill. God in His goodness had proven Himself faithful to provide for our every need.

Are you facing a financial crisis in your family because you have chosen to homeschool? God is big enough to meet even the most challenging situations. There is no problem too great that He cannot solve and no need so large that He cannot provide. Simply lay your burden before the Lord in prayer, and you'll be amazed at what He can do! "I have been young, and now am old; yet have I not seen the righteous forsaken, nor his seed begging bread. He is ever merciful, and lendeth; and his seed is blessed" (Psalm 37:25-26).

Lord, we praise You for Your abundant and timely provisions that reaffirm Your loving hand on our lives. Thank You for being big enough to meet every homeschooling need we have and using our family for Your glory. In Jesus' name, Amen.

Pruning Pains

July 6

"Every branch in me that beareth not fruit he taketh away: and every branch that beareth fruit, he purgeth it, that it may bring forth more fruit" (John 15:2).

As we walked through the garden one morning during our summer break from homeschooling, my daughter watched as I began to pinch off the tops of several tomato plants. With a shocked look on her face, she cried, "Mom, what are you doing? We've been trying to get these plants to grow for weeks and now you're destroying them!"

"No," I gently responded. "These plants have grown tall enough. If I don't cut them back now, they'll only grow more vines instead of tomatoes. We need to break off the top so the energy of the plant goes toward bearing fruit."

"OK," she replied hesitantly in disbelief. "But I sure hope you know what you're doing."

The process of pruning can also seem shocking in our spiritual lives. When God allows circumstances that outwardly appear to destroy our hopes and dreams, we may humanly react like my young daughter in the garden. Not understanding the purpose behind the pain, we are tempted to believe that God doesn't know what He is doing or that He doesn't love us. However, if we learn to come to the Lord in humility and total dependence during these trying times, He will carefully shape our character into the image of His Son. In the end, the fruit of righteousness that God desires in all His children, will be produced from His careful and loving pruning.

Do you feel like your life is in the pruning process? If circumstances seem to be robbing your joy and causing you to doubt God's love, don't let your pain cause you to run from the Lord. Instead, run into the arms of your loving Father and allow the Holy Spirit to comfort you, as God continues to perfect the good work He has begun in you. "My brethren, count it all joy when ye fall into divers temptations; Knowing this, that the trying of your faith worketh patience. But let patience have her perfect work, that ye may be perfect and entire, wanting nothing" (James 1:2-4).

Father God, my heart aches from the problems in my life, but I choose to reach out in faith and believe You are in control. Please show me Your loving grace and help me to understand the work You're doing in my life. In Jesus' name, Amen.

Share your thoughts about this devotional at **aophomeschooling.com**/187

Making Your Mark

July 7

Bird watching (ornithology) was a favorite hobby of our homeschooling family in the summer. In fact, it became such a favorite pastime that we purchased a beautiful official field guide on North American birds just to identify unfamiliar species. Each time a family member identified a new bird, we made a mark next to the bird's picture in the book. At first, my children were reluctant to write anything in the pages of a "resource" book. Past experience in studying other subjects had taught them this was unacceptable. However, as we logged more and more sightings, they became comfortable using the guide and grew more interested in identifying every species contained within its pages.

Learning to mark Bible passages during insightful times in your spiritual walk is also difficult for most Christians. Writing in the margins and underlining verses may seem uncomfortable at first. However, the more you apply the Word of God to your current circumstances, the more comfortable you become in noting those verses speaking to your heart. As you highlight verses and passages that bring encouragement, comfort, and hope, you'll leave a trail of the Holy Spirit's work in your life through the wonderful promises of God. Since the Word of God is living and active (Hebrews 4:12), you'll even discover new lessons from the same passages as you continue to grow in Christ.

Is the Bible the most read and the most marked book on your shelf? If not, consider using the Word of God as your worktext for daily living. The thoughts and wisdom God imparts as you study His Word are worth noting—not only to remind yourself of what God has done for you, but also to teach others the same lesson when they face similar difficulties in life. After all, what greater legacy can you leave than the recorded history of your spiritual walk with God in the pages of your own Bible? "For the word of God is quick, and powerful, and sharper than any twoedged sword, piercing even to the dividing asunder of soul and spirit, and of the joints and marrow, and is a discerner of the thoughts and intents of the heart" (Hebrews 4:12).

Lord, thank You for Your written Word that leads me into truth. Help me to treasure those insights You choose to reveal as I apply Your Word to my life, and to record them as a testimony of Your unfailing love. In the name of Jesus, Amen.

Share your thoughts about this devotional at **aophomeschooling.com/188**

No Worthless Thing

"The light of the body is the eye: if therefore thine eye be single, thy whole body shall be full of light" (Matthew 6:22).

The best decision we made after choosing to homeschool was choosing to remove the television from our home. Since both my husband and I had been raised with Saturday morning cartoons, public television, and after-school programs, we found it difficult to let go of the comfortable familiarity of television programming. However, God's conviction was sure as He made us aware of the time we were wasting watching unproductive entertainment. In addition, we both had seen the deterioration of programming and advertising content which included blatant disregard for life, the Lord, and sexual decency. Fortunately, we finally turned off the tube and obeyed the Holy Spirit's promptings before our children became caught in the same trap.

Many New Testament believers faced a similar problem in leaving past loves as they began to grow in Christ. In the Apostle Paul's letters to the Ephesians, he repeatedly exhorted this early church to refrain from the practices and lusts in which they had participated before coming to a saving knowledge of Christ. His call to purity and holiness in daily living included removing those former things that were not only a distraction, but also a temptation that would return them to a sinful lifestyle. Paul didn't mince any words when he said, "If so be that ye have heard him, and have been taught by him, as the truth is in Jesus: That ye put off concerning the former conversation the old man, which is corrupt according to the deceitful lusts; And be renewed in the spirit of your mind; And that ye put on the new man, which after God is created in righteousness and true holiness" (Ephesians 4:21-24).

Although following the Lord's leading was difficult, our homeschooling family began to realize multiple blessings after removing our television. Communication and heart-felt times of sharing developed, intellectual knowledge was stimulated through reading inspiring literature, exercise and preparation time for healthy meals increased, creativity was enhanced, and family fun and laughter filled our home. With so many benefits waiting to be experienced, what is keeping your homeschooling family from pulling the plug on your TV? "I will behave myself wisely in a perfect way. O when wilt thou come unto me? I will walk within my house with a perfect heart. I will set no wicked thing before mine eyes" (Psalm 101:2-3a).

Father, every day is a challenge to avoid the distractions and temptations that keep my heart and mind from following You. Please show me how to discipline my life that I might glorify You in all that I do. In the name of Jesus, Amen.

 Share your thoughts about this devotional at aophomeschooling.com/189

God's Provisions

July 9

"Therefore I will look unto the LORD; I will wait for the God of my salvation: my God will hear me" (Micah 7:7).

Preparing for the new school year started early in our home. Lesson plans needed to be made for each child, and boxes of new and used curriculum needed to be sorted. As I began to look ahead into my son's ninth grade science, I realized we were missing a very important component to a successful year—a quality microscope. For the past several years, we had managed with an inexpensive model, but a serious study in biology required something better. However, with my homeschooling budget already spent on curriculum, I had no idea how we could afford this additional expense.

Throughout the remainder of the summer, I continued to worry over the situation. On several occasions, I attempted to lay the burden at my Lord's feet and leave it there, but then the waves of anxiety would creep over me again. Soon, only a week remained before our scheduled start date for school, and I more or less gave up on the dream of having a new microscope. Even my idea of sharing a microscope between several homeschooling families was turned down by my friends.

That weekend, however, God took me to His schoolroom to teach me a valuable lesson about His timetable and provision. My brother, who was a medical doctor, called unexpectedly, and somehow we got onto the topic of science during our conversation. By chance (I don't think so), he mentioned he had a microscope left over from his pre-med days in college, and he promised to send it to my son. Thinking it was probably somewhat similar to what we had now, both my son and I were amazed when we opened my brother's package on the first day of school. There, in all its glory, sat a high-tech, state-of-the-art scientific microscope complete with glass slides and other lab paraphernalia. My eyes filled with tears as I realized again God's unfailing blessings on our homeschool. Yes, if we learn to wait on the Lord, He is never early nor late in sending us exactly what we need. "For since the beginning of the world men have not heard, nor perceived by the ear, neither hath the eye seen, O God, beside thee, what he hath prepared for him that waiteth for him" (Isaiah 64:4).

Lord, your loving faithfulness is too high to comprehend and too wonderful to understand! Thank You for guiding our family while we homeschool and always sending what we need, when we need it. In the name of Jesus, Amen.

Second Guesses

July 10

"Call unto me, and I will answer thee, and shew thee great and mighty things, which thou knowest not" (Jeremiah 33:3).

What was I thinking? In a few short weeks, I was going to be teaching my two oldest children at home. As I opened the boxes of curriculum that had just come in the mail, I reflected on my commitment. Already, the negative feedback from family and friends had caused me to second guess my decision, and I wondered if it was too late to get out. Sure, I had taught my children their alphabet and numbers, but teaching them to read and learn mathematics was a whole new ballgame. Could I really do this? What if I really made a mess of things or couldn't stand the pressure of being home 24/7? As I struggled with these thoughts and others, I took my fears to the Lord and asked, "Am I really supposed to be homeschooling my children, or did I just imagine all this in a weak emotional moment?"

The story of Gideon became a comfort to me as I wrestled with the answer to this question. Like me, Gideon was unsure of God's leading and prayed, "If thou wilt save Israel by mine hand, as thou hast said, Behold, I will put a fleece of wool in the floor; and if the dew be on the fleece only, and it be dry upon all the earth beside, then shall I know that thou wilt save Israel by mine hand, as thou hast said" (Judges 6:36b-37). God graciously answered Gideon's prayer and went one step further when Gideon asked for the reverse scenario to take place with the fleece the following day.

Encouraged by Gideon's story, I placed my own fleece on the ground to confirm God's desire for me to homeschool my children. Asking for specific encouragement, God first led me to His Word in Deuteronomy 6:6-7. Feeling empowered by its truth and the Holy Spirit, my final confirmation came that evening as I tucked my children into bed. Grabbing me tightly around the neck and placing a big kiss on my cheek, each of my children said, "Thanks for teaching us Mommy. We're going to have so much fun!" And guess what happened—for the next twenty-five years, we did!

Lord Jesus, thank You for being a loving God who answers me when I pray. Please strengthen me now to homeschool and to always come to You when life makes me confused and uncertain. In Jesus' name, Amen.

 Share your thoughts about this devotional at aophomeschooling.com/191

Lessons from an Aspen

July 11

"But now are they many members, yet but one body" (1 Corinthians 12:20).

Summer vacation was a great learning adventure for our homeschooling family. As we took trips to the mountains, my children experienced lessons from nature that made both science and Scripture come alive. One lesson in particular came from a large stand of beautiful aspen trees. As we hiked past their white trunks, my son shared a fact he had learned from his schoolwork. "Mom, my science worktext says that aspen trees grow from one common root. Is that true?"

"Yes," I replied. "Every one of the individual trees you think you see is actually one big tree."

Excitedly, he ran from one tree to the next and cried, "Mom, look! This one tree must be over two miles long!"

Talking further, we discussed the similarity between the aspen tree and the body of Christ. "Each believer is like the individual aspen tree and plays a unique role in God's family," I said. "However, we all grow from one common root, Jesus Christ, and we must work together in the body."

Smiling, my son replied, "Yeah, I get it Mom. If we all do what we're supposed to as Christians, we'll show God's beauty like this bunch of trees . . . I mean tree," he laughed as he quickly corrected himself.

Do you know where God has placed you in the body of Christ? Although some gifts may seem more important than others, they're not (1 Corinthians 12:23-24). Each believer contributes to the well-being of the body by faithfully using the gifts God has given. Whether your spiritual gift is teaching, serving, or showing mercy, you can bloom where you're planted and give God the glory as you depend on the life-giving root of Christ's forgiveness and love. "Rooted and built up in him, and stablished in the faith, as ye have been taught, abounding therein with thanksgiving" (Colossians 2:7).

Father, thank You for my place in the body of Christ. Use our homeschooling family for Your glory and let us praise You with lives fully committed to Your purpose and plans. In Jesus' name, Amen.

 Share your thoughts about this devotional at **aophomeschooling.com/192**

Fueling the Flame

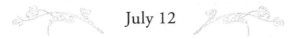

July 12

"Restore unto me the joy of thy salvation; and uphold me with thy free spirit" (Psalm 51:12).

Sadly, a homeschooler's passion to teach his child sometimes begins to fade. The daily demands of caring for a household and the intense effort required in homeschooling drains even the most dedicated parent. When the homeschooling fire begins to die out, many may choose a half-hearted approach or adapt a martyr, make-it-through-the-day mentality. Others may stop homeschooling altogether and send their child back into a traditional school setting. The wise homeschooling parent, however, will see the coals growing dim and find the fuel necessary to rekindle the flame of passion first given by God. But how does one go about finding that fuel?

To reignite the vision of his child's education, the best thing a worn-out homeschooling parent can do is ask the Holy Spirit to come and control him anew. As a parent deals with his own personal walk before the Lord, the time spent in self-examination and repentance will show areas in our character that need strengthening. Prideful attitudes are adjusted and total dependence on God's guidance is reestablished, allowing Him the right to reign over the entire homeschooling process. Most of all, the Holy Spirit is able to clearly reveal Satan's discouragement and remind us what was happening when the passion was last burning brightly.

Have trials and discouragement stolen your first love of homeschooling? The fiery conviction you once felt for your child's education will die if you don't find the right fuel source to keep it on fire. Stay faithful to the call God has given and let the Holy Spirit lead and strengthen you today. As you read your Bible, memorize God's Word, and pray for the Holy Spirit's wisdom, you'll be amazed as God provides everything you need to keep the home fires burning! "Meditate upon these things; give thyself wholly to them; that thy profiting may appear to all. Take heed unto thyself, and unto the doctrine; continue in them" (1 Timothy 4:15-16a).

Lord, please rekindle the love of homeschooling in my heart. Remind me of the many blessings we have already experienced as a family and strengthen me to remain faithful as we face the upcoming school year. May You be praised in all we do. In Jesus' name, Amen.

You Be the Judge

July 13

Let's face it. When you live together 24/7, a homeschooling family is bound to have disagreements and disputes. Our family was no exception. Daily, I found myself settling conflicts between my children over insignificant issues. While they were young, I realized my direct involvement was necessary in helping my children talk out their differences. However, as they grew older, I encouraged my children to resolve more and more of their own conflicts. Instead of me listening to their complaints and acting as a judge and jury, they learned to take responsibility for their actions and resolve their hurts and disagreements in Christ-like love. As my role became less, my children learned a valuable lesson—judging their actions honestly before God usually eliminated others from having to do so.

As Christians, the Bible also commands us to judge ourselves. To judge ourselves rightly, we must lose the total self-life that seeks only to please itself. Judging our actions and thoughts in light of God's Word, we become Christ-conscious, not self-conscious. Just as importantly, we become Christ-controlled rather than self-controlled. All that is self is laid at the feet of Jesus as we recognize that in our self "dwelleth no good thing" (Romans 7:18). Judging ourselves also involves valuing others as better than ourselves (Philippians 2:3) and becoming selfless instead of practicing self-esteem.

What about you? Do you have trouble with your fleshly nature that cries out to please itself? Homeschooling can bring out the worst in our character as we face the daily pressures of raising a family and teaching them at home. If you find yourself demanding that everything go according to your plans in order to make life easier for yourself, you may want to follow some good advice: "For if we would judge ourselves, we should not be judged" (1 Corinthians 11:31).

Lord, examine my selfish heart and reveal those things that fail to honor You. Please forgive me when I fail to act like Your servant and show me again how I can consider the members of my own family as more important than myself. In Jesus' name, Amen.

World's Worst Critic

July 14

Homeschooling parents can be their own worst critic. Because the "teacher" inside strives for truth and accuracy, most have a tendency to judge themselves too harshly. Whenever I failed to teach a lesson perfectly or didn't have an immediate answer to my children's questions, I felt like a failure. After all, wasn't a teacher expected to know everything about every subject and have all the answers right at his fingertips? Thinking back, I now laugh at my foolish, unrealistic expectations of myself during those first years of homeschooling. Surprisingly, the hardest lesson learned in our homeschooling family was learned by me—no one's perfect, so learn from your mistakes and move on.

As Christians, we also have a tendency to be too hard on ourselves. We should seek holiness in our daily lives and strive to crucify the flesh's desire to sin, but we must also realize a very important fact—only Christ is perfect and we are frail and but dust (Psalm 103:14). Since we inherit a sinful nature (Romans 3:23) and are susceptible to temptation, Christ knows us better than we know ourselves and challenges us to "Watch and pray, that ye enter not into temptation: the spirit indeed is willing, but the flesh is weak" (Matthew 26:41). Although God knows how to "deliver the godly out of temptations" (2 Peter 2:9a), and provides a way of escape (1 Corinthians 10:13b), He also forgives us when we make mistakes and fail to listen to Him. As we come in repentance, Christ chooses not to deal with us according to our sins, but instead, His compassion removes our sin as far as the east is from the west (Psalm 103:10-13).

How about you? Are you beating yourself up over a past sin which you've already confessed to God? Dear child of God, you no longer have to be under Satan's false bondage of guilt. If you've confessed and repented, Christ has forgiven you. Learn from your mistake and then smile again knowing you're a child of God. Claim for yourself one of the greatest promises in the Bible: "There is therefore now no condemnation to them which are in Christ Jesus, who walk not after the flesh, but after the Spirit" (Romans 8:1).

Father, thank You for giving me new hope whenever I fail to follow You completely. Thank You for Your mercy and lovingkindness that always encourage my heart to try again. In Jesus' name, Amen.

 Share your thoughts about this devotional at aophomeschooling.com/195

Dear Diary

July 15

"And these things write we unto you, that your joy may be full" (1 John 1:4).

As I sat reading my thoughts from my prayer journal, I realized just how much my life had changed from the year before. Our first year of homeschooling had stretched me to the limit, and God's Word had encouraged me time and again. Favorite Bible passages and verses were written in entries on difficult days and the tear-stained pages reminded me of emotional and financial frustrations. However, also recorded were countless moments of joy and discovery in watching my children grow and learn. Looking back, I saw how God had kept His promises and faithfully led me through the exciting and difficult task of homeschooling. Although some prayers were still yet to be answered, my written chronicle was an encouragement to continue trusting the Lord for the next school year.

Maintaining a written record of God's miracles and blessings is an important aspect of any Christian's faith. As you document particular times of growth and blessing, you begin to understand God's purpose and plan for your life. Like seeing the bigger picture on a big screen TV, you become more aware of the specific details and events God is using to shape your life. Not only that, any homeschooling parent can also tell you the very act of writing down information aids in memory retention. Each time you write, God's spiritual lessons become cemented in your mind to increase and strengthen your personal faith.

With summer almost over and the new school year quickly approaching, why not try the best advice I ever received from a seasoned homeschooler? Purchase a personal diary for this year's homeschooling adventure, and let your thoughts and reflections take you to a new appreciation for homeschooling and the wonderful Lord you serve! "He will regard the prayer of the destitute, and not despise their prayer. This shall be written for the generation to come: and the people which shall be created shall praise the LORD" (Psalm 102:17-18).

Heavenly Father, what a joy to read and remember Your faithful presence as You upheld and provided for all our homeschooling needs! How great and good You are! Please show me how to lead my children to You, so they can learn the same incredible lessons You've taught me. In Jesus' name, Amen.

Wonderful Words of Life

July 16

Sometimes it's not the words you say, but how you say them that can encourage or dishearten your children. Proverbs 12:18 says, "There is that speaketh like the piercings of a sword: but the tongue of the wise is health." We as parents must guard the words we choose to say as we homeschool our children. Phrases like "good job" or "I really like the way you did that!" are great motivating tools to use with your children.

Unfortunately, we get lazy in our attitudes and think we can say whatever we want to our children and not affect them. My son brought this to my attention one day while I was speaking to a friend on the phone. I overheard him say to his sister, "I wish Mom would use her telephone voice when she is talking to us!" Ouch, that hurt! I realized my son noticed a difference in the choice of words I used and the kindness inflected in the tone of my voice when talking with someone other than him.

I learned a valuable lesson that day. If our families are the ones we love the most, we need to talk with the loving words that will bless instead of discourage them. When our children do not understand a new concept being taught, correction needs to be done in a gentle and loving manner. Using words that make them feel inferior or slow is something we must avoid at all costs. Allow them the dignity to be wrong.

Don't ruin the atmosphere in your home with thoughtless remarks. Nothing will destroy your success in homeschooling quicker than phrases like "Are you still working on that?" or "I don't know why you do not understand this. Your brother learned this right away." Ask for God's grace each day to fill your speech with His words and to show the love that will help your child be successful in their studies. Proverbs 16:24 says, "Pleasant words are as a honeycomb, sweet to the soul, and health to the bones."

Lord, help me choose my words today as if I was speaking to You. Show me how to encourage my children during our homeschooling day in all I say and do. In Jesus' name, Amen.

 Share your thoughts about this devotional at aophomeschooling.com/197

Ingredients for Success

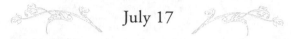

July 17

As a young girl growing up, there were two influences from my parents that forever shaped me and gave me the confidence to make a difference in this world. They also were the two things that molded me into the homeschooling mom I am today.

One was the unspoken words in my mother's unconditional love even for a rebellious, disrespectful daughter. Repeatedly, I broke her heart with all of the foolish choices I made as a teenager. She, however, demonstrated the love of Christ with her patient prayers and knew that somehow God would change my life.

The other influence came one day when I was in the tenth grade. I remember handing my report card to my father and seeing the look of pride in his eyes. When he saw the straight "A's" on the paper in his hand, he told me I had the ability to be anything I wanted. I felt so empowered with that blessing. Knowing my earthly father thought I was capable of so much gave me the confidence to face whatever came into my life.

God the Father loves us in much the same way. He gives us unconditional love and significance. As the "apple of His eye" (Psalms 17:8), He tells us we "can do all things through Christ which strengtheneth us" (Phil. 4:13) and blesses us with "Every good gift and every perfect gift" (James 1:17). We are His treasured children, and He invites us to call Him "Abba, Father" (Romans 8:15). We have been grafted into His family if we receive the forgiveness He offers through the blood of His Son Jesus. He has a purpose and a plan for us to succeed, even as homeschool parents.

Father God, thank You for taking my broken life and giving it meaning. Thank You for Your Son's saving grace and the joy of knowing I am loved. Help me give what was given to me. Help me love my children unconditionally and lead them to the purpose You have planned for their lives. In Jesus' name, Amen.

 Share your thoughts about this devotional at **aophomeschooling.com/198**

Too Hot to Trot

July 18

It was day seven of a two-week, 95 degree and above heat wave. I was thinking our home-schooling family had done fairly well in not losing our tempers. As I walked outside to do the evening chores, however, I noticed several jobs left undone by my children. Frustrated with their poor performance, I continued to the barn to feed the horses when I noticed my daughter riding her horse bareback in the arena. Dripping wet, the horse appeared to be sweating pro-fusely. Angrily, I barked, "Don't you know you shouldn't be riding that horse when it's this hot outside? Cool that animal down right now and get those chores done like I asked!"

As my daughter cowered and walked past me, I saw the hurt expression on her face. My angry outburst had wounded her spirit, and I knew I needed to make short order of asking forgiveness. Walking up to her, I said, "I'm sorry, honey. I shouldn't have yelled at you like that."

"That's OK, Mom," she replied, "I forgive you. I'm sorry I didn't get the chores done like you asked. I was just waiting for it to cool down before working outside and the reason my horse looked wet wasn't from sweat, it was actually from the water I used to cool her off. I was just riding her from the pasture to the barn to put her inside in the shade."

Humbled by her loving response to my false accusations of irresponsibility, I asked forgive-ness again and said, "I'm so sorry. How foolish I was to get so angry without even asking you a few simple questions!"

Anger may be a real human emotion, but like any other emotion, it should never be dictated or con-trolled by the flesh, no matter what the temperature is outside. Galatians 5:20 tells us that the Lord views wrath as a work of the flesh and James 1:20 says, "the wrath of man worketh not the righteous-ness of God." God's remedy for controlling anger's destructive outbursts includes bridling the tongue (James 3:5-6) and allowing the Holy Spirit to help us be "swift to hear, slow to speak" (James 1:19). If homeschooling and the summer heat are getting to you, take a step back, count to ten, and pray for God's help to see and hear the problems for what they are: opportunities to display His grace instead of your anger. "He that is slow to wrath is of great understanding" (Proverbs 14:29a).

Father, forgive me when I allow anger to control my emotions and to destroy my relationships. Help me to be controlled instead by the Holy Spirit and to remember that true love is always patient, kind, and long-suffering. In Jesus' name, Amen.

 Share your thoughts about this devotional at **aophomeschooling.com/**199

Home of Contented Homeschoolers

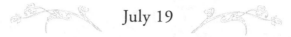

July 19

"And be content with such things as ye have: for he hath said, I will never leave thee, nor forsake thee" (Hebrews 13:5b).

Because you are a homeschooling parent, chances are your family has given up the "two-income" dream. You've probably done without in many areas including new clothes, vacations, and eating out. Have you been noticing how everyone else seems to have much nicer homes and cars than you? Have you been thinking you are being left behind?

If so, don't allow your focus to be blurred. Stand firm against the evil one and his lies. Satan comes to us in our weak moments of frustration and fatigue and tries to convince us that everyone else has it better. Maybe if you just got a "regular" job and went back to work, you could get out from under the financial burdens you have. Matthew 6:25 says, "Therefore I say unto you, Take no thought for your life, what ye shall eat, or what ye shall drink; nor yet for your body, what ye shall put on. Is not the life more than meat, and the body than raiment?"

Trusting God for all your needs to homeschool involves a faith that will continue to be stretched. The extra expenses involved in buying curriculum and school supplies will even add more to that strain. Knowing God will meet those needs but not always the wants is the balance homeschool parents must find. God always provides, even if it is only macaroni and hot dogs. If we don't have the latest in fashion or the best house on the block, we still can enjoy life and the wonderful privilege of teaching our children. May we be like the Apostle Paul when he said in Philippians 4:11, "For I have learned, in whatsoever state I am, therewith to be content."

Lord, help me to look to You today for all I need, and make me thankful for the many blessings You've already given. Thank You that in Christ, I have all things. In Jesus' name. Amen.

Share your thoughts about this devotional at **aophomeschooling.com/200**

Aren't You Being Selfish?

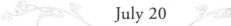

July 20

"Keep thy heart with all diligence; for out of it are the issues of life" (Proverbs 4:23).

The words were still echoing in my mind. "If every Christian homeschools his child, what will happen to the public schools?" asked a Christian friend as we chatted over the phone. "Doesn't God tell us to be salt and light in the world?"

Although I didn't have a good answer then, I thought about my friend's exhortation and logic. Examining our reasons for homeschooling, I considered the negative effect of continually exposing my child's heart to humanistic and ungodly teaching. Most elementary-aged children lack the reasoning skills to discern truth from conflicting messages, so how then would a young child be able to debate with a teacher who didn't value the truths of Christ? After all, didn't recent statistics also prove that even highschoolers had difficulty in maintaining their faith throughout college? Clearly, expecting my young daughter to be the salvation for the evils of the public school seemed like a gross burden to place on her shoulders. Was I being selfish in caring about my child's needs before those of society? I didn't think so.

God has given parents the priority of first teaching and training their own children. Yes, Jesus wants our children to influence the world, but they can hardly do so until they are prepared. God's Word tells us to keep the heart with all diligence and that a child must be trained in the way he should go (Proverbs 22:6). Therefore, before a young person can influence for good without being influenced by evil, they must have a plumb line of truth based on God's Word. Unfortunately, homeschooling families are accused of brainwashing their children with religious nonsense and being intolerant to different ideas and beliefs.

As a homeschooling parent, have you been asked the "What about the kids left behind in public school" question? You know your child's heart. Don't let the world's "salt and light" argument deter you from following God's mandate for raising your child.

Father, thank You for giving me the responsibility to teach my children. Show me how and when to guide them into the world with the Gospel message of love and forgiveness.
In Jesus' name, Amen.

 Share your thoughts about this devotional at aophomeschooling.com/201

Treasures on the Mirror

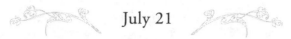

July 21

Every week when I cleaned the bedroom, I would always run into them. The time and effort needed to move them out of the way to dust became longer and longer. To anyone else, these items probably looked like a lot of clutter, but to me they were treasures from the heart.

What do you do with all those special treasures your children bring to you each day to say they love you? Trinkets like braided bracelets, love poems, bugs, rocks, dandelions, and pencil sketches begin to grow into quite a collection of items, especially since I had more than one child. My solution needed to reflect sensitivity and show how much I valued and appreciated their affection.

My refrigerator door and bedroom mirror became the favorite collecting points for most of the items. Every morning and night I was reminded of my children's love through these thoughtful tokens. I recall hearing one of our children ask their father one day, "Does Mom really like all the things we bring to her?" His wise reply was, "Just go look at Mom's mirror; what do you see?" These treasures of love framed my reflected image each time I looked into the mirror. They represented who and what I was as a homeschooling parent. I was surrounded by a family I loved and who loved me. What greater joy could any parent have?

God has given you special treasures, too, that reflect His love each day. The beauty of His creation in a sunset, the assurance of His Holy Spirit when troubled by fears, the comfort of His promises in the Word, and the joy of His salvation are the trinkets He places on the mirror of your heart. "Behold, what manner of love the Father hath bestowed upon us, that we should be called the sons of God" (1 John 3:1a). You are surrounded by a great and awesome God who loves you so much. What greater joy could you have?

Father, thank You for all these reminders of love from my children. Help me treasure each one as I treasure the daily reminders of Your love for me. May we all continue to draw closer together as a family and to You. In Jesus' name. Amen.

Quantity Is Quality Time

July 22

Many years ago, parental experts were advocating that "quality time" was all that was necessary for your children instead of quantity time. This belief possibly began to appease the consciences of some women who chose careers over their children and didn't want to deal with the feelings of abandoning their child to the day care center.

However, my personal experience with organized "quality time" was quite different. I found that you could not experience quality unless there was also the dimension of quantity time involved with your children. After all, they were not little robots who turned on and off affections and responses when the convenience of the moment fit into my schedule. They came to me at inopportune times and opened their hearts when I least expected.

The favorite "talk time" for one of my teenage daughters was 11:00 p.m. Being a morning person, I could feel the lure of the pillow on my bed at 8:30 or 9:00 p.m. at the latest. Staying up later in the evening to spend time with her was always a challenge. Some nights we would just hang out together and play games or watch TV. Other nights we would have deep theological debates about God, life, and boyfriends. I never knew when those bonding moments would take place, but I knew that unless I made myself available, she would never share her heart.

I learned later that part of the reason for my daughter's responses were a result of her particular love language. She felt the most loved when someone wanted to be with her. Giving gifts, acts of service, words of endearment, and physical touch were important, but having someone who wanted to be with her communicated the most love.

Homeschoolers have a unique environment to provide both the quantity and quality time their children need. Deuteronomy 6:7 states, "And thou shalt teach them diligently unto thy children, and shalt talk of them when thou sittest in thine house, and when thou walkest by the way, and when thou liest down, and when thou risest up." This verse is speaking in regard to instructing our children in God's Word and shows the importance of taking advantage of all times during the day to interact.

Are you spending real quality time with your children? Just because you are homeschooling doesn't mean you are connecting with your child's heart. Allow those quantity times to turn into quality times by being available and looking for opportunities to share meaningful experiences.

Lord, thank You for all the special moments of love You provide each day. Help me see the real needs of my children and continually reach out with a heart of love. In Jesus' name. Amen.

 Share your thoughts about this devotional at **aophomeschooling.com/203**

Shifting Shadows

July 23

"Behold, I am the LORD, the God of all flesh: is there any thing too hard for me" (Jeremiah 32:27)?

Anyone in our homeschool family can tell you that I got the short end of the stick when it comes to artistic abilities. In fact, the only artistic talent I had was drawing stick people! So when two of my children began to demonstrate drawing skills with their doodling, I knew their graphic artist father was the one to teach this subject. Since Dad was at work more than ten hours a day though, I needed to supplement his teaching time with some instruction of my own. Deciding to teach the concepts and leave the technique to Dad, I looked for inexpensive ideas to illustrate my lessons. As we returned home from our afternoon walk one evening, as the sun was beginning to set and cast shadows of our figures against the farm buildings. The perfect illustration for teaching drawing perspective, I used our shadows to explain the concept to my young son and daughter.

However, my children weren't the only ones who learned a lesson that day. As I thought about perspective, I realized I also needed to apply it to my life. Being the emotional person I was, I had a tendency to blow things way out of proportion. My over exaggerated perceptions of a problem had caused difficulty in my family's lives many times. Convicted by the Holy Spirit, I understood that God desired me to see things through His eyes.

What about you? Do you have a tendency to make mountains out of molehills? Don't let your fears and worries cause you to make rash decisions and judgments. Come to the Lord in prayer, and let Him show you a new perspective on things. Trust me, you'll be glad you did, and so will your family! "The LORD looketh from heaven; he beholdeth all the sons of men. From the place of his habitation he looketh upon all the inhabitants of the earth. He fashioneth their hearts alike; he considereth all their works" (Psalm 33:13-15).

Father, thank You that nothing touches my life without Your knowledge. Help me find Your peace today in the midst of my problems and remember that You have everything under control. In Jesus' name, Amen.

Caught Red Handed

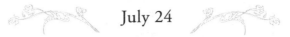

July 24

The red flags were all there. As a homeschooling parent, you would have thought I would have seen the little signs much sooner—struggling in daily work, but getting straight "A's" on quizzes and tests; erased answers on tests; the desire to correct their own work; and teacher keys in the wrong place on the shelf. My trust in my children blinded me to the fact that they ever would succumb to the temptation to take the easy way out and cheat. It was a sad day when I found out the truth.

"Wherefore let him that thinketh he standeth take heed lest he fall" (1 Corinthians 10:12). God tempered my discipline of my child that day with the knowledge that I, too, take the easy way out in many areas of my life. I think my secret little sins of laziness, procrastination, and overeating will not find me out, and I can continue ignoring God in the areas of my life He wants to discipline.

How about you? Are you cheating on preparing your lesson plans, your devotion time with the Lord, or some personal habit that is robbing God of His glory? "For in that he himself hath suffered being tempted, he is able to succour them that are tempted" (Hebrews 2:18). Christ understands what you are going through. He suffered the same types of temptations when He was here on earth. Praise God He has provided a way for us to win over temptations: "There hath no temptation taken you but such as is common to man: but God is faithful, who will not suffer you to be tempted above that ye are able; but will with the temptation also make a way to escape, that ye may be able to bear it" (1 Corinthians 10:13). Look for the way of escape today. Make no provision for the flesh.

Lord, don't let me cheat You out of all You desire for me. Show me those areas of my life that I need to bring under Your Lordship. Thank You for Your forgiveness each time I fail. Help me to see the way of escape and take the strength You provide to be obedient to You and Your Word. In Jesus' name. Amen.

Measuring by Messes

July 25

Somewhere in the middle of my homeschooling experience, I made the mistake of measuring what activities we would or wouldn't do by the mess involved. I had lost the spontaneous joy of having fun on a child's level and saw those messy learning times as one big chore. Perhaps I lost the joy because I was so tired physically or maybe because I was lazy. Either case, I deprived my children of many enjoyable experiences simply because I didn't want to make a mess.

Keeping our lives neat and orderly is a good thing, but we must also be willing to get our hands dirty. Jesus was willing to grab the towel that washed the feet of His disciples. He also touched and healed the sick and the diseased in body, as well as the sinful, dirty hearts of lost people. He was never afraid to get involved and to be in the middle of a mess. Zaccheus, the Samaritan woman at the well, and the thankful leper must have been so grateful for the cleansing joy of His love. "If I then, your Lord and Master, have washed your feet; ye also ought to wash one another's feet. For I have given you an example, that ye should do as I have done to you. Verily, verily, I say unto you, The servant is not greater than his lord; neither he that is sent greater than he that sent him" (John 13:14-16).

Father, forgive me for only wanting to serve You in the comfortable tasks that are nice and neat. Help me to remember You're strong enough to clean up any mess from life's dirty problems. Use me today to be a blessing to the hurting and helpless. In Jesus' name, Amen.

Nothing to Wear

July 26

Teaching our young children to dress themselves in the morning takes patience. We painstakingly wait as they learn to manipulate buttons, zippers, and shoelaces. But by far the most agonizing aspect of the morning ritual of getting dressed is the statement, "I can't find anything to wear." As mothers we realize this statement doesn't mean there is nothing in the drawers and closets, nor does it mean your child has not looked hard enough. What they really are saying is they think the clothes available to them are not good enough for them to wear.

We as adults dress ourselves in the same fashion. We waste our time manipulating the outward appearance because we worry about what other people will think. What about going to the closet of God's Word and choosing to dress ourselves according to His wardrobe as in Colossians 3:12-14: "Put on therefore, as the elect of God, holy and beloved, bowels of mercies, kindness, humbleness of mind, meekness, longsuffering; Forbearing one another, and forgiving one another, if any man have a quarrel against any: even as Christ forgave you, so also do ye. And above all these things put on charity, which is the bond of perfectness." Do we desire to dress in the "clothes" God has given us, or do we continue to "not find anything to wear?"

Becoming more Christ-like is the ultimate goal for us as homeschooling parents. The Lord does not look on the outward appearance of man, but at the heart, as when Samuel was led by the Lord to anoint David to be king. Choosing to dress ourselves with compassion, kindness, humility, gentleness, patience, and love is what He can use the most to influence our children and teach them how to live godly lives.

So what will you put on to wear this morning? Look to His Word and find the clothes that fit and reflect God's character to your family and your world. All the academics you teach will not have as lasting of a value as modeling the love of Jesus Christ in your words and actions. "But put ye on the Lord Jesus Christ, and make not provision for the flesh, to fulfil the lusts thereof" (Romans 13:14).

Father, thank You for giving me the opportunity to dress in the character of Christ. Show me those areas in which I have forgotten to put on the "clothes" You have provided. Help me to reflect Your Son in all I do and say this day. In Jesus' name, Amen.

Share your thoughts about this devotional at aophomeschooling.com/207

In the Limelight

Did you imagine your role as a homeschooling mother to be quiet and obscure? Did you picture yourself being behind the scenes and working as a support person only? Nothing could be further from the truth! Every time someone asks, "Where do your children go to school?" you are immediately thrust into the spotlight and find yourself facing an endless barrage of questions.

Many great women of the Bible also faced the same challenge. They had to stand up or speak up for the cause God had placed in their lives. Abigail was led by God to save her family by going ahead of her husband's foolishness and providing a meal for King David and his men. Ruth braved danger in gleaning the wheat from Boaz's field in order to save Naomi and herself. Rahab believed in the God of Israel and put out a scarlet rope to save her family from Joshua and his army. Deborah the prophetess went to battle because Barak didn't have faith to fight without her.

Take courage and know that the God of the universe is with you. Just as He went before Israel as a cloud by day and a pillar of fire by night, He will go before you and give you the words to say when you are confronted. Matthew 10:19b-20 says, "Take no thought how or what ye shall speak: for it shall be given you in that same hour what ye shall speak. For it is not ye that speak, but the Spirit of your Father which speaketh in you." Trust the Holy Spirit to lead you and be not ashamed of the wonderful opportunity God has given you to home-school your children.

Lord, make me courageous today and not afraid. Give me the words to say to represent You to a lost and dying world. Lead me today so I can guide the children You have given me. In Jesus' name, Amen.

Mr. Stop

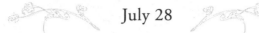

July 28

It was just a little thing, really. I mean, who would have ever thought a little bird could make such a difference in all our lives? But he did.

He was a red-wing black bird that always greeted us sitting on the same stop sign whenever we drove to town. Because of the brilliant, red plumage on his wings and the location of his unusual home, we began to refer to this new friend as Mr. Stop. The joyful song he sang encouraged our family each time we passed his home, but it was the simple faithfulness of his presence that left a profound impression on the minds of my young children. Mr. Stop was always there protecting his nest and gathering food for his wife and family.

Every year in the spring, the pattern would repeat itself, and again Mr. Stop would return and come into our lives for the summer months. An unforgettable lesson of faithfulness was being forged into our family's life. We didn't realize how much the consistency of this little bird's presence meant to all of us until we moved away to homeschool in another state.

Do you know the faithfulness of God's presence is surrounding you today in a far greater way than you may think? Psalm 139:7-10 says, "Whither shall I go from thy spirit? or whither shall I flee from thy presence? If I ascend up into heaven, thou art there: if I make my bed in hell, behold, thou art there. If I take the wings of the morning, and dwell in the uttermost parts of the sea; Even there shall thy hand lead me, and thy right hand shall hold me." The God of the universe securely watches over you no matter where you are and faithfully protects and provides all you need to homeschool your children. Take a moment now to stop and enjoy the sweetness of His presence.

Heavenly Father, thank You for always being with me and guiding our family as we homeschool today. I trust Your Word, and know I am not alone. In Jesus' name, Amen.

Principle of Multiplication

July 29

In 1934, Dawson Trotman founded The Navigator's ministry to sailors during World War II with the belief that everyone who is born into God's family is to multiply. Being saved himself from a life of drunkenness and corruption, Dawson believed if a person would lead someone to Christ and then disciple him until he led another person to Christ, every six months within fifteen years, over two billion people would be living for the Lord. Billy Graham preached at his funeral in 1956, and stated, "I think Dawson Trotman has personally touched more lives [for Christ's sake] than anybody I have ever known." Quite a statement coming from a man whose gospel message of salvation has since been preached to millions!

As a young, homeschooling mother, I felt my life was quite insignificant for many years. I couldn't see God's big picture for my life and the importance of being faithful in teaching and discipling my children in the Lord. But then I read the story of Dawson Trotman and his thoughts of the multiplication principle. I realized more people would be reached by entrusting the truths of God to my children than if I went out and ministered on my own. My first mission field was sitting right in front of me!

How well do you know your multiplication facts? Do you know that your homeschooling will not only reap rewards now, but also in the future? Teaching your children spiritual as well as academic truths will forever change the lives of many people because of the godly influence your children will have on them. II Timothy 2:2 says, "And the things that thou hast heard of me among many witnesses, the same commit thou to faithful men, who shall be able to teach others also."

Lord, help me multiply the number of those who will hear the message of Your love, forgiveness, and salvation by investing all my efforts in teaching the children You have given me. Thank You that what I am doing has lasting value in Your eyes and for the harvest of souls You have prepared. In Jesus' name, Amen.

At a Loss for Words

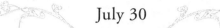

July 30

One day I found my son sobbing in a tree in our back yard. He had just experienced a heart-breaking loss, and there were no words to comfort him. Twenty of his twenty-five chickens had been killed by our outside farm dog. Only eight short weeks ago, we had brought them home as a school project. Faithfully, he had raised them from small, fluffy yellow chicks to the young, white-feathered chickens that loved to sit in his arms. He had made a roost and a special feeder for them and was just beginning to enjoy gathering one or two eggs per day.

However, that all changed in a moment when our dog broke into the chicken coop. Going on a rampage, our dog killed all but five of his clucking children. Although living on a farm and seeing other animals die had toughened my son's outlook toward death, I knew only God could help him in his loss as he asked, "Why?"

As homeschooling moms and dads, the Holy Spirit offers us the same comfort when we struggle with the "whys" of life. So many days we feel heartbroken by the worries and pain of the world and don't know how to pray. May you find comfort in knowing that His Spirit is lifting you up before the Father even now, while you can't find the words to express your heart. "Likewise the Spirit also helpeth our infirmities: for we know not what we should pray for as we ought: but the Spirit itself maketh intercession for us with groanings which cannot be uttered" (Romans 8:26).

Father, thank You for the Holy Spirit who understands my weaknesses. Please intercede for me today because I don't know how to pray. In the name of Jesus, Amen.

Lost Car—Found Faith

July 31

"A man's heart deviseth his way: but the LORD directeth his steps" (Proverbs 16:9).

My six-year-old son came running up to me with crocodile tears in his eyes and cried, "Mommy, I can't find my favorite car! Can you please help me?" Walking with him into the living room, we proceeded to look for his favorite toy race car that he had just received for his birthday. Our efforts were to no avail—it was not to be found anywhere. I saw the anxious look on his face and knew we had to do something. Taking him by the hand, we sat down together on the couch and prayed.

"Let's ask God where it is. I'm sure He knows," I said.

After we finished our prayer, we returned to our morning homeschool routine. Little did I know, God had already prepared an invaluable lesson for both me and my young son. As we sat back down on the couch to read my son's science lesson, his lost car popped up from between the cushions. Excitedly, we thanked the Lord for showing us the car's location and the answered prayer was forever cemented in my son's mind.

The lesson my son learned was that an all-knowing God was big enough to handle any problem he might have in life. God's lesson for me was that He was the better teacher. He had a syllabus of truths for my children to learn each day. My job as a homeschooling parent was to be sensitive to those Holy Spirit subject areas, so my children wouldn't miss the most important lessons in life.

How about you? Are you so structured in your homeschool day that you cannot allow for any deviations for God's instruction? If so, pray for God's wisdom and will to be revealed. Don't lose the opportunities for you or your children to find the greatest truths in the world. "Trust in the LORD with all thine heart; and lean not unto thine own understanding. In all thy ways acknowledge him, and he shall direct thy paths" (Proverbs 3:5-6).

Father, thank You that You know what my children need to learn each day. Help me to listen to Your voice and allow You to instruct our family in righteousness and truth. In Jesus' name, Amen.

Cup of Water

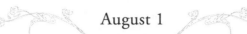

August 1

"Why would you want to stay at home with your kids? Are you NUTS?" Have you ever heard these questions when you told someone you decided to homeschool your children? Most homeschooling parents have at one time or another. We are a different breed who receive little or no recognition from the world for our efforts. Expecting applause or appreciation for teaching our own children are dreams we have long since given up, along with paychecks and promotions. So how does a homeschooling parent cope with the lack of support and affirmation he needs to continue educating his children at home?

God's Word gives us the answer in Matthew 10:42: "And whosoever shall give to drink unto one of these little ones a cup of cold water only in the name of a disciple, verily I say unto you, he shall in no wise lose his reward." Although the world does not value a homeschooling parent, God says that even giving a drink to a thirsty child has a reward. How much more for us parents who have chosen to sacrifice our dreams for our children's future?

Knowing that our heavenly Father sees and cares is enough to encourage us to remain faithful. Even though no one else understands, we can choose to respond to His promise: "And whatsoever ye do, do it heartily, as to the Lord, and not unto men; Knowing that of the Lord ye shall receive the reward of the inheritance: for ye serve the Lord Christ" (Colossians 3:23-24). Let the Lord's love be enough for you today as you start another year of homeschooling. Someday you will receive a full reward for all you have done. "Humble yourselves therefore under the mighty hand of God, that he may exalt you in due time" (1 Peter 5:6).

Father, forgive me when I feel sorry for myself or complain that no one appreciates me. I know You love me and value my obedience in homeschooling our children. Help me remain faithful and humble to give You the glory in all that we do. In Your Son's name. Amen.

Starting Over

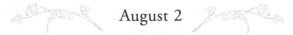

August 2

"Jesus Christ the same yesterday, and to day, and for ever" (Hebrews 13:8).

Almost three years ago, I watched as my youngest son left for college. He was the last of four children, and my homeschooling years had come to a close, or so I thought. The heartbreak I felt in the symbolic finality of his saying good-bye was immense. Sure, I would see my adult children and share wonderful moments together in the future, but our family would never be the same. Added to my overwhelming feeling of loss was the apprehension of a fifty-plus retired homeschooling parent's future. "What now?" was the question that continued to reverberate in my mind.

I didn't have to wait long for God's answer to my question. Moving back to my hometown to care for my aging mother, God took me to a whole new homeschooling experience. Miraculously, He orchestrated an employment opportunity where I could write about the lessons I learned from Him during our homeschooling years. Here I am today, writing to you and praying that my words will help you hold fast through the hard times to discover your own homeschooling blessings. What an opportunity—God is so good! Each day I feel like I'm starting over as He takes me back through the memory banks of my mind to recall moments of success and failure. I see the faces of my children throughout our homeschooling years and remember my past to give you a hope and a vision for your future.

Amazingly, I also still fight many of the same spiritual battles I faced as a young homeschooling parent: battles of laziness, procrastination, worry, doubt, and pride. Even at my age, God continues to mold me into the likeness of His Son, and I claim the Apostle Paul's words, "Being confident of this very thing, that he which hath begun a good work in you will perform it until the day of Jesus Christ" (Philippians 1:6). Most of all, I've come to realize that no matter if you're a brand new homeschooling parent at the age of twenty-six or an old-time retiree, Jesus is the same wonderful, loving protector and provider "Who comforteth us in all our tribulation, that we may be able to comfort them which are in any trouble, by the comfort wherewith we ourselves are comforted of God" (2 Corinthians 1:4).

Lord, thank You for the incredible adventure of homeschooling and giving me the strength to see the end rewards and blessings. Please encourage those who are homeschooling today to remain faithful so they too may reap the fruit of their years of sacrifice and love. In Jesus' name, Amen.

 Share your thoughts about this devotional at **aophomeschooling.com/214**

One Day at a Time

August 3

"Therefore, my beloved brethren, be ye stedfast, unmovable, always abounding in the work of the Lord, forasmuch as ye know that your labour is not in vain in the Lord" (1 Corinthians 15:58).

As a homeschooling parent, do you ever wake up in the morning and want to run away and hide from your responsibilities? Last night's dishes, last week's laundry, and yesterday's school work all clamor for your attention. Your baby's cry reminds you of yet another need, and your young toddlers seek your affection and time for play. On top of that, your church is having difficulty finding help with Sunday school and the nursery, and you know you should offer your assistance. Exhausted before the day has even begun, you throw the covers back over your head and think, "Why would God give me all this responsibility? Doesn't He know I can't take care of everything? Where can I go to get away from all of this work?"

When the pressure of obeying God's call seems too much, it's tempting to look for the easy way out. Just ask Jonah. God had given him the task of prophesying to the wicked city of Nineveh, but Jonah decided it was too big a responsibility. Hopping a boat to Joppa, Jonah worked just as hard at running away and hiding from God's call as he would have worked if he obeyed. Fortunately, God gave this reluctant prophet another chance to accept the job He had given. After being thrown overboard and spending three days in the belly of a big fish, Jonah decided that being a preacher wasn't that bad, even if it was to a wicked city like Nineveh.

If the responsibility of facing another year of homeschooling is causing you to run and hide, be encouraged. Although you can't see the way through the work right now, the Lord promises to uphold you with His wisdom and strength when you need them (Isaiah 41:10). As you obediently follow His will in homeschooling today, He continues to guide you with the next step tomorrow. Step by step, day by day, you will get through the work and accomplish all He has planned for your homeschooling family. "I will instruct thee and teach thee in the way which thou shalt go: I will guide thee with mine eye" (Psalm 32:8).

Heavenly Father, the responsibility of homeschooling is weighing me down. Please give me the courage I need to face the new year, and show me how to lead the precious children You've given me. In Jesus' name, Amen.

The Writing on the Wall

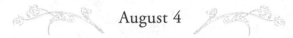

August 4

My daughter's feet pounded on every step as she went up to her room. I should have known it was going to be "one of those days" when I saw the mood she was in the very moment she woke up. Everything had been a test—eating breakfast, getting dressed, school work. "Why can't kids just do as they are told?" I thought to myself.

Ephesians 6:4 states, "And, ye fathers [and mothers], provoke not your children to wrath: but bring them up in the nurture and admonition of the Lord." Even though I knew this verse to be true, I went into a private pity party instead. Wouldn't my life be easier if I sent my daughter to public school and avoided all these confrontations? I could be a mom who stayed at home and did her nails instead of a mom who checked schoolwork in the bathroom, gave spelling tests while cooking supper, and folded piles of laundry at midnight. Why was I the bad guy here?

Suddenly, the quietness in my daughter's bedroom shattered my thoughts. I decided to go upstairs and see what was happening and talk to my daughter about her behavior. Expecting her to be on the bed crying in repentance, what I found was quite the opposite. As I opened the door, there was a mural in black crayon drawn across the yellow-flowered wall paper in her room. The anger and frustration I had used in disciplining my daughter moments ago was now communicated in her scribbles and marks before me. I knew I had pushed her too far. I saw the writing on the wall.

I wasn't quite sure who was being disciplined that day. Certainly, my actions had been far from righteous when I had sent my daughter to her room in anger. Truly, the greater lesson had been learned by me. My anger was not the tool to be used in disciplining my children.

What about you? Do you intimidate your children with your size and "authority?" Stop and think: "For the wrath of [Mom] worketh not the righteousness of God" (James 1:20).

Holy Father, forgive me when I discipline my children in the flesh instead of according to Your Word. Thank You for Your mercy in my mistakes and help me show that same mercy to my children as we homeschool each day. In Jesus' name, Amen.

Love's Compassion

August 5

"That the Lord is very pitiful, and of tender mercy" (James 5:11b).

Parents who teach their children at home have a tendency to sacrifice the fruit of gentleness on the altar of homeschooling. Ever the exacting teachers, we sometimes forget our role as merciful comforters when educating our children. My foolish insensitivity to my children's needs was revealed one day when my daughter came running into the house. Whimpering, she cried out, "Mom, an ant bit me!"

Knowing her aversion to insects and assuming she was trying to avoid her schoolwork, I ignored the tears and replied, "Oh my, it was just a little ant. It couldn't have hurt that badly!" As unfeeling as a robot, I hugged her quickly, told her to stop crying, and sent her on her way to finish her studies.

Several days later, I reaped the humbling consequences for my apathy to my daughter's pleas. Sitting in the sandbox near our new home, I warmed my toes in the sand and watched as my children built towering castles. Suddenly, a sharp pain in my foot made me yell, "Ouch!" I was sure I had been stung by a bee or a wasp, but when I looked down, I only saw an ant. What I didn't know, however, was that this was no ordinary ant. Native to the area, it was a red harvester ant whose bite was as painful as any bee sting. Showing the true compassion I should have shown her, my young daughter came to me with a genuine hug and said, "It's okay, Mommy, I'll help you!"

Have you become so busy or dogmatic in your homeschooling routine that you fail to show compassionate love? Staying on task and accomplishing educational goals is never more important than expressing gentle, heartfelt concern to your children. Whether it's an emotional hurt on the inside or a painful wound outside, let love's compassion be your guide in all your actions. "He shall feed his flock like a shepherd: he shall gather the lambs with his arm, and carry them in his bosom, and shall gently lead those that are with young" (Isaiah 40:11).

Father, your tender love encourages me so much each day. Please keep my heart soft, so I can express that same love and teach the most important lesson my children can learn—compassion. In Jesus' name, Amen.

 Share your thoughts about this devotional at **aophomeschooling.com/217**

Wayward Children

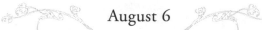

August 6

Nothing breaks a parent's heart more than living with a disobedient child. After investing so much time teaching godly values as well as academics, homeschooling parents are especially discouraged when their children refuse to live according to God's Word.

The life of Samson is a prime example of a disobedient child in the Old Testament. Although his parents had raised him according to the Levitical laws of a Nazirite—a life that was to be holy and pure—Samson's life was far from righteous. Following a path of sinful pleasures that led him far from God and his parents, Samson suffered blindness and slavery as a consequence of his sin. Eventually, Samson did repent, and God renewed his strength to destroy the Philistines who had tried to destroy him (Judges 13-16).

Is your house in turmoil because one of your children has chosen the wrong path? Do you lie awake at night and pray that God will honor Proverbs 22:6, "Train up a child in the way he should go: and when he is old, he will not depart from it?" If so, don't stop praying for his heart to come back to the Lord. Your intercessory prayers do make a difference against the evil that would destroy him. Intercede for your child's soul in the powerful name of Jesus and the blood He gave on the cross. "Brethren, if any of you do err from the truth, and one convert him; Let him know, that he which converteth the sinner from the error of his way shall save a soul from death, and shall hide a multitude of sins" (James 5:19-20).

Jesus, I don't know what to do for my disobedient child. All I can see today is the pain he is causing our family. Open my eyes to see the battle for his soul, and use me to intercede in prayer. Thank You for the victory only You can give. In Your precious name, Amen.

Signs of the Time

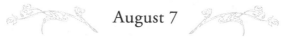

August 7

"So likewise ye, when ye see these things come to pass, know ye that the kingdom of God is nigh at hand" (Luke 21:31).

When taking nature hikes for science, one homeschooling activity my children especially loved was looking for animal tracks in the soft mud or snow. Identifying creatures from their tracks became a favorite game, and my oldest son especially took to the challenge. With a field guide in hand, not only did he learn to identify the shapes of particular animal prints, he learned to read other signs as well. Bruised or broken vegetation, hairs snagged on branches, feathers, opened nuts, and scratches in tree bark all provided additional signs in determining an animal's trail.

As he grew older, my son became more proficient in his tracking abilities and could easily locate my whereabouts on our family farm. Many times after I had walked to a quiet spot to read a book or be alone, my son would sneak up and scare me in fun. Laughing, I would say, "I don't ever have to worry about getting lost because I know you'll be able to find me."

When Jesus was alive on earth, He also told His disciples about signs that would mark the time before His return. In Matthew 24, Christ's list of signs included wars and rumor of wars (vs. 6), famines and earthquakes (vs. 7), false prophets (vs. 11), and an increase in lawlessness (vs.12). Jesus also told His disciples that His return would be as evident as the lightning in the sky (vs. 27) and that He would return in the clouds with power and great glory (vs.30). Although no one knows the exact hour or day of Christ's return (Mark 13:32), the signs will clearly mark the trail before that time.

Have you been watching for the signs of the Lord's return? Are you earnestly anticipating seeing your loving Savior face to face? Don't let Christ's return surprise you and catch you unprepared. Live your life today in such a way that you're prepared to see Him this very moment! "But the day of the Lord will come as a thief in the night; in the which the heavens shall pass away with a great noise, and the elements shall melt with fervent heat, the earth also and the works that are therein shall be burned up. Seeing then that all these things shall be dissolved, what manner of persons ought ye to be in all holy conversation and godliness, Looking for and hasting unto the coming of the day of God" (2 Peter 3:10-12a).

Father, thank You for the joyous promise of Your Son's return. Open my eyes to see the signs of Your faithfulness and love that guide me each homeschooling day, and help me to live in hopeful expectation until I see Jesus. In His name, Amen.

 Share your thoughts about this devotional at **aophomeschooling.com/**219

First Words

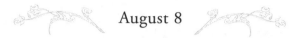

"When I was a child, I spake as a child, I understood as a child, I thought as a child: but when I became a man, I put away childish things" (1 Corinthians 13:11).

If you homeschool young children, chances are you constantly correct their pronunciation of many words and verb tenses. Correcting their speech becomes a daily task and one that should be taken seriously in order to instruct them in proper grammar usage. "Hangaber" and "Sgetti" were our children's first words for hamburger and spaghetti. Although the correct words were eventually learned, our children continued to pronounce these words as they had first said them. Unfortunately, they remain a part of our family's vocabulary even today.

As Christians, we also have a tendency to retain childish things in our walk with the Lord. However, God wants us to grow into spiritual maturity and do away with childish things. We are to move from speaking, thinking, and reasoning as a child to trusting in the Lord with a mature faith. No longer should we speak impulsively, take offenses easily, or pout when life doesn't go our way.

What about you? Are you still acting like a child in Christ? If so, now is the time to start growing. "Brethren, be not children in understanding: howbeit in malice be ye children, but in understanding be men" (1 Corinthians 14:20).

Father, forgive me for acting like a child in my faith. I know You want me to grow into the fullness of Your love and blessings. Please show me how. In Jesus' name, Amen.

Subject to Change

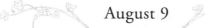

August 9

"A man's heart deviseth his way: but the LORD directeth his steps" (Proverbs 16:9).

If there's one thing you can count on as a homeschooling parent, it's change. Like the weather, no two days are ever exactly the same. More times than I can remember, my best-made lesson plans and organized activities were altered by the day's events. Whether my children became absorbed in a particular topic and spent more time studying or an untimely interruption caused a delay in teaching a lesson, it was necessary to make adjustments without becoming anxious. Whatever failed to be taught one day was usually made up within the next few days, and I learned not to worry about the setback, as long as we continued to move forward with our studies.

As time went on, I determined to let God order our daily events. Committing the day to Him each morning, I found peace in yielding to His Lordship and control to follow His perfect plan. The "Serenity Prayer" hung on my kitchen wall as a constant reminder to let the Lord guide our homeschooling.

What about you? Do you stress over the changes that come your way throughout your homeschooling day? Relax, if you've given God control over your homeschooling day, He will help you accomplish everything that needs to be done. Besides, God has a few lesson plans of His own for you and your children to learn. "The preparations of the heart in man, and the answer of the tongue, is from the LORD. Commit thy works unto the LORD, and thy thoughts shall be established" (Proverbs 16:1, 3).

Father, thank You for guiding us each day while we homeschool. Show me how to rest in Your wisdom and love to teach my children what You want them to know. In Jesus' name, Amen.

 Share your thoughts about this devotional at **aophomeschooling.com/221**

Nearsighted Homeschooling

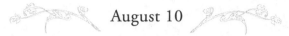

August 10

"A man's pride shall bring him low: but honour shall uphold the humble in spirit" (Proverbs 29:23).

As I drove home from our back-to-school shopping spree, I felt confident I had finally purchased everything we needed for a successful school year. My schoolroom was ready, the curriculum had been ordered, and now these additional school supplies would complete my preparations for starting our year off right. Smiling smugly to myself, I thought I had everything under control.

As I relaxed and looked out the window, I noticed a majestic hawk soaring overhead and brought it to my children's attention. Frustrated, my oldest daughter kept peering into the sky, but couldn't locate the bird at which we were pointing. Stopping the car, I asked her to read the words on the sign up ahead, but she couldn't see them. Slowly, I drove closer and closer until she could finally make out the letters. What a revelation of my foolishness! "I sure had everything under control," I thought to myself. "My daughter was nearsighted, and I hadn't even realized it until just now!"

As Christians, we also have a tendency to be short-sighted when life is going well. Living in the success of "now," we think our current blessings are the result of our own hands. Like the Old Testament nation of Israel, we fail to acknowledge God's hand of divine intervention in our lives. Unfortunately, many times we must experience painful or humbling reminders in order to correct our vision to see the true picture—God is in control, not us.

If you're starting your new school year depending on your own abilities, be careful. Only the Lord can show you those things that will make your homeschooling truly successful. As you depend on the Holy Spirit, you will not only discover wisdom to teach, but you'll have your eyes opened to see all God desires for your family. "Unto thee lift I up mine eyes, O thou that dwellest in the heavens. Behold, as the eyes of servants look unto the hand of their masters, and as the eyes of a maiden unto the hand of her mistress; so our eyes wait upon the LORD our God" (Psalm 123:1-2a).

Lord, forgive me for my foolish pride that fails to acknowledge You as Lord. Open my eyes to see Your plans for our family and teach me to constantly depend on You. In Jesus' name, Amen.

 Share your thoughts about this devotional at **aophomeschooling.com/222**

Foolish Mothers

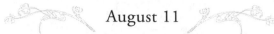

August 11

"Every wise woman buildeth her house: but the foolish plucketh it down with her hands" (Proverbs 14:1).

As homeschooling mothers, we hold within our hands the power to create a wonderful school day or a horrible one. Our attitude can dictate a day filled with joy or one filled with tense anxiety. In Proverbs 6:19, the Lord states that strife is one of the seven things He hates. Strife can develop from many situations, including heated debates and unresolved arguments with your husband. Left unchecked, marital strife causes you to be abrupt and short with your children. Seeds of anger, bitterness, and hate are planted in your children that ultimately destroy your home.

God's answer to our selfish, "I'm not wrong, so I don't need to say I'm sorry" attitude is found in Ephesians 4:26-27: "Be ye angry, and sin not: let not the sun go down upon your wrath: Neither give place to the devil." God has more than one reason for you not to be at odds with your husband—your relationship to God Himself is broken, your relationship to your husband is hindered, and your relationship to your children is damaged.

Is there strife in your home today? Are you the one allowing it to perpetuate? Don't give place to the devil whose goal is to destroy your homeschool and your family. Be reconciled before the sun goes down tonight and seek forgiveness from the Lord and your mate. Don't be like the woman who tears down her own house!

Lord, forgive me for allowing bad feelings to continue between my husband and me. I know You hate strife, and only in Your strength can I forgive. I want to start again today to build our home Your way. In Jesus' name, Amen.

 Share your thoughts about this devotional at **aophomeschooling.com/223**

Mission Impossible

August 12

Have you been weighing the pros and cons of homeschooling and trying to decide what to do this year for your children's education? Although the idea of schooling your children at home seems like a daunting task, you can successfully teach them. Planning schedules, purchasing curriculum, and making lesson plans may sound foreign to you right now, but God will help you if you will simply pray and ask for His leading. Not only will He send the encouragement and support you need from homeschooling families, but He'll also show you where to get the ideas, resources, and supplies you need to complete the task.

Abraham's servant in Genesis 24 also knew about facing a huge undertaking. Under oath, he was sent out by his master Abraham to search for the perfect wife for his son Isaac. Just imagine that task, trying to find a woman who would be willing to return with a complete stranger from a foreign land to marry a man she had never met. In today's world, that would be considered "mission impossible!" Abraham's servant was no fool and knew the obstacles facing him. Knowing he could never succeed without God's divine intervention, this servant prayed for success and started out in faith on the long journey. Fortunately, his mission had a happy ending when Rebekah proved to be the answer to his prayers and just the woman for Isaac.

God is waiting to give you success in homeschooling, too, but you must first obey His call and step out in faith. Even if you don't receive the answer to every homeschooling question you have right now, God will prove Himself mighty and guide you each day, one step at a time. As you see the Lord's divine leading and specific answers to prayer, you'll praise God like Abraham's servant. Most of all, you'll be thankful you didn't allow your doubts to cause you to self destruct before seeing homeschooling's many blessings. "But without faith it is impossible to please him: for he that cometh to God must believe that he is, and that he is a rewarder of them that diligently seek him" (Hebrews 11:6).

Father, my faith is weak, and I'm fearful about committing myself to teaching our children. Please show me how to homeschool, and lead me to those people who can help me get started. In Jesus' name, Amen.

Over the Edge

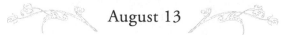

August 13

All of us start homeschooling for a particular reason—some defining catalyst that throws us over the homeschooling fence. Some homeschoolers make the decision to teach their children due to a negative experience with public school. Prompted into action by their children's negative attitudes and personality shifts, these parents are concerned about meager instruction, the absence of godly curriculum, or a threat to their child's safety.

Other homeschoolers, like me, began teaching because of a deep conviction that God had a different plan for their family. I firmly believed in Christian education, but cost factors, doctrinal differences, and maintaining family closeness eliminated a Christian school option. Homeschooling was our best choice. I knew God wanted me to teach academics and spiritual truths according to His Word. What I discovered was the thrill of learning right along with my children. Math, history, science, geography, language, and other subjects all took on a new dimension when the Lord was in the lesson.

If you feel the Lord leading you to homeschool, stop sitting on the fence. Homeschooling is a rewarding career. Homeschool websites, curriculum fairs, and support groups are just waiting to help you get started. May the words in Joshua 24:15 guide you in your choice: "But as for me and my house, we will serve the LORD."

Lord, I accept Your leading to homeschool and ask You to send the help I need. Please clearly show me how to prepare our children to live a life that will glorify You. In Jesus' name. Amen.

Great Aspirations

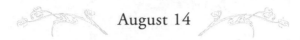

August 14

"Faithful is he that calleth you, who also will do it" (1 Thessalonians 5:24).

Have you ever wanted to do something great for God? You know, something great like being a gifted Bible teacher, a talented Christian singer, or an inspirational evangelist? I did, but as a young mother living in a remote rural area with two small children and one on the way, I couldn't imagine how. I wanted my life to count for God, but for the most part, no one knew I even existed. Our single income left our family with one vehicle for my husband's use in getting to work. I was isolated and made irregular trips into town for groceries, library books, and church activities. Most of my days were consumed with simply homeschooling, cleaning house, and caring for my family. "Not much opportunity to do great things for God," I thought to myself, as I prepared for another homeschooling day after my morning devotions.

As the years went on and I studied the Scriptures more in-depth, I noticed an amazing fact. More often than not, God used the ordinary lives of men and women to accomplish His will. Mary, the mother of Jesus, was just an average, obedient teenager. Ruth, the great-grandmother of David, was a hardworking daughter-in-law, and Gideon, one of Israel's greatest judges, was the least in his father's house. Even several of the disciples were simple fishermen with humble beginnings. Like mine, all these lives were insignificant and obscure, but God used them in miraculous ways to do great things.

Are you wondering if your life would have more meaning if you gave up homeschooling to pursue something more worthy for the Lord? Don't let Satan deceive you with his lies. Although you may feel like your life is mundane and serving no purpose, God is giving you the greatest opportunity to impact the world right where you are! As you faithfully homeschool your children, not only will their lives be forever changed by the truths of God's Word, great things will happen as countless others come to know the Lord through their future witness. "Humble yourselves therefore under the mighty hand of God, that he may exalt you in due time" (1 Peter 5:6).

Father, only You can take the ordinary and make it extraordinary. Take my life and our homeschooling, and use them however they will give You the most glory. In Jesus' name, Amen.

Share your thoughts about this devotional at **aophomeschooling.com/226**

Security Blankets

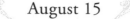

August 15

"For thou, LORD, only makest me dwell in safety" (Psalm 4:8b).

What makes you feel safe—a clean bill of health from the doctor? a well-stocked pantry in the kitchen? or how about a large balance in a checking account? We all have things that make us feel protected, but life can throw you a curve. In just a moment, everything can change.

Homeschooling in the early 1980's was a challenging experience. When our family chose to venture into this unconventional form of education, we faced many adversaries. Accusing us of truancy and threatening to take our children away, our local public school superintendent was our worst enemy. Foolishly, we had thought we were safe to teach our children at home because so many hard-fought homeschooling laws had been passed. However, since the language in these laws was unclear, we found ourselves between the proverbial "rock and a hard place." We were forced to our knees in prayer.

In the midst of the turmoil, God reminded us He was our security blanket. As Moses was allowed to see the glory of God pass by in the cleft of the rock (Exodus 33:21-22), God proved Himself mighty and showed us His glory by providing a way to homeschool. One of two schools registered in our state to have homeschool satellite programs accepted our children into their program. This provision was our "Red Sea" experience and the beginning of a journey to the Promised Land of four successfully educated children.

What about you? Are you facing a personal challenge in your life that seems insurmountable—a lack of money, a broken relationship, a wayward child? Are there voices and circumstances surrounding you causing you to fear? God is your refuge. Run to Him and be safe. "The name of the LORD is a strong tower: the righteous runneth into it, and is safe" (Proverbs 18:10).

Father, I'm scared. I don't know how this problem is going to be resolved. Please keep me safe and wrap Your loving arms around me. Show me Your deliverance, and give me the faith to trust You for the answer. In Jesus' name, Amen.

Share your thoughts about this devotional at aophomeschooling.com/227

Less Than the Best

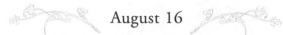

When your children turn in assignments that reflect less than their best effort, what do you do as a homeschooling parent? I can recall a specific instance when my teenage son had, once again, turned in less than his best. Although I could have graded his paper accordingly, his half-hearted efforts were simply not acceptable this time. Scanning his poorly written essay, I asked, "Do you really think this is your best effort?"

"Yeah, I suppose so," he responded quickly, trying to avoid any further discussion.

Not letting him off the hook, I replied, "You've had plenty of time to prepare, and I think we both know you can do better. I want you to study Leviticus 22:17-33 and then rewrite this assignment by tomorrow."

Shuffling out the door, I heard him sigh and mumble, "Okay."

My children aren't the only ones who suffered from the temptation to give less than their best. During Old Testament times, God's people also succumbed to the temptation to offer blemished animals for their sacrifices (Malachi 1:14). God's requirement to bring a spotless sheep, cow, or goat as an offering for sin was being ignored. Accepting an animal that was less than perfect was not permitted by the Lord (Leviticus 22:20). Today, God's requirement of giving our best is still the same. He isn't interested in our half-hearted efforts, and His holiness demands the best we have as we worship and offer ourselves as a living sacrifice.

What about you? Are you giving the Lord the best part of your day in prayer and Bible study, or do you say a few quick "thank-you's" before you fall asleep at the end of a busy homeschooling day? Do you trade sleeping-in and watching TV evangelists for the effort required to become involved in a local church on Sunday morning? Do you give what's left of your paycheck instead of tithing from the top? Like my teenage son, it's time to write a new story with your life and start giving the Lord your best! "I beseech you therefore, brethren, by the mercies of God, that ye present your bodies a living sacrifice, holy, acceptable unto God, which is your reasonable service" (Romans 12:1).

Father, you are holy, and I humbly bow before You today. Forgive me for offering my "seconds" and still expecting You to bless my life. Take me and change my heart, so it is wholly committed to You in all I do. In the name of Jesus, Amen.

Homeschool Stereotypes

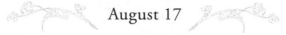

August 17

"Be not overcome of evil, but overcome evil with good" (Romans 12:21).

As a homeschooling parent, have you ever known the frustration of being stereotyped? Unfairly, mainstream America has deemed us unfashionable, overly protective, dogmatically religious, and socially backwards. Like other stereotypes that develop from negative assumptions, homeschooling parents suffer from unjust labels with unfounded perceptions of their true character. Added to this misconception is the fact that homeschooled children are also stereotyped.

Breaking loose from these hurtful stereotypes is difficult, but as Christian homeschooling families, we can change how the world views us. Instead of becoming defensive and argumentative when homeschooling adversaries slander our name, we can show God's love through our Christ-like character and actions. Whether we're shopping at the mall, attending a community event, or eating at a restaurant, we can erase incorrect images with courtesy, respect, and genuine concern for others. In addition, godly homeschoolers can best illustrate one reason for teaching our own children by displaying a servant's heart that looks for ways to help others in need. Christ Himself said it best in the Sermon on the Mount: "Bless them that curse you, do good to them that hate you, and pray for them which despitefully use you, and persecute you" (Matthew 5:44b).

Do you struggle with vengeful thoughts when others look down on you for homeschooling? Don't let the homeschool stereotype discourage you. Prove those labels wrong, and respond to the negative remarks with the love of Christ. After all, isn't that the most important message we're trying to teach our children as we homeschool? "For consider him that endured such contradiction of sinners against himself, lest ye be wearied and faint in your minds" (Hebrews 12:3).

Lord, forgive my anger when others make fun of us for homeschooling. Help me to tell them of homeschooling's blessings and to show the same love You did when mankind mocked and ridiculed You. In Jesus' name, Amen.

Too Many Loads

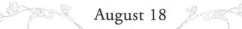
"Cast thy burden upon the Lord, and he shall sustain thee: he shall never suffer the righteous to be moved" (Psalm 55:22).

Does your burden seem heavy today? Too many loads of laundry, too many ungraded papers, half-finished art projects, or birthday cards left unwritten? Sometimes we are overwhelmed with all that has to be done as a homeschooling parent.

God sees and knows your burdens. He cares and will provide the strength you need to face each day's tasks. Matthew 11:28 tells us, "Come unto me, all ye that labour and are heavy laden, and I will give you rest." Just when you think you can't do another thing, trust God to send help in the most unexpected way. Homeschooling forces us parents into knowing that it is not by might, nor by power, but by His Spirit that we are able to love and teach the children He has given us. Take heart and know that He will never leave you nor forsake you. After all, these are His children, and He will keep His promise to lift every burden you have.

Lord, I feel so tired. Please fill me with Your strength to make it through today. Thank You for Your promises and not giving me more than what I can bear. Please send the help I need to face all the tasks before me. In Jesus' name, Amen.

Young Love

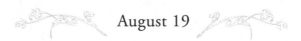

August 19

"Whoso findeth a wife findeth a good thing, and obtaineth favour of the LORD" (Proverbs 18:22).

I'll never forget the day my son declared his future marriage intentions. As we sat in church Sunday morning waiting for the service to begin, a new family filed in and sat in the pew opposite ours. For the next several minutes, I watched as my son observed the youngest female member of their family—a vibrant, freckle-faced redhead with a smile that went from ear to ear. Just as the pastor stood up to announce the first hymn, my son pulled on my sleeve and nodded towards the crimson-haired beauty. With all the earnestness a six-year-old could muster, he proclaimed, "Mommy, someday I'm going to marry a girl just like that!"

Although my young son's innocence made me smile, I was convicted that day to begin praying for my children's future spouses. With the world's philosophy quickly redefining marriage, I realized fewer young people were willing to honor the spiritual truths of Hebrews 13:4a, "Marriage is honourable in all, and the bed undefiled." If marriage was God's will for my children's future, I needed to be on my knees in prayer for them. Like Abraham's concern for Isaac, I knew God desired my children to be yoked equally to another believer (2 Corinthians 6:14).

As a Christian homeschooling parent, what are you teaching your children about marriage? Are you displaying a godly role model and encouraging them to follow the Lord, as they wait on His will and timing for a future mate? Six-year-old boys and girls grow up, and they'll be looking to you for guidance and wisdom. Teach them what God says about true love in His Word, so they can make the right decision that lasts a lifetime. "Charity never faileth" (1 Corinthians 13:8a).

Father, as I homeschool my children today, their marriage and future adult responsibilities seem so far away. Help me to prepare them for life, not only with academics, but also with a clear understanding of Your truths and will for their lives. In Jesus' name, Amen.

Peaceful Sleep

August 20

"Casting all your care upon him; for he careth for you" (1 Peter 5:7).

The human body's need for sleep has always amazed me. God has designed us to literally "turn off" like a machine for eight hours or more each night. Science tells us sleep is something our bodies need to do. It is not an option. During our sleeping hours, some parts of the brain actually increase their activity dramatically, and certain hormones are produced by many of the body's major organs and regulatory systems that continue to work.

Unfortunately, as a young homeschooling mom, I was missing out on my much needed sleep. I struggled with daily worries and anxious thoughts like "Will my children turn out okay if I homeschool? How can I teach a subject I don't even know? How will we pay the bills if I homeschool?" Household chores were also keeping me up late into the night, and I was exhausted as I tried to do too much.

Then one night, I read a promise God seemed to write just to me: "It is vain for you to rise up early, to sit up late, to eat the bread of sorrows: for so he giveth his beloved sleep" (Psalm 127:2). What an eye-opener! God only had so much for me to do each day, and what was left undone was not important. All He asked of me was to pray for wisdom to accomplish His perfect will each day. His provision to meet my unfinished tasks would come by sending extra help, inspiring new ways to organize, or miraculously providing whatever I needed.

After that day, my life changed. I was able to lay my head on my pillow each night and not worry about the basket of laundry waiting to be folded or the unfinished lesson plans for tomorrow's schoolwork.

When was the last time you had a good night's sleep? Do you struggle with trying to do more than God intended? Bringing your homeschooling worries to the Lord means trusting Him for wisdom and provision for all your needs. Will you rest in Him tonight and experience the peaceful sleep He intended? "Take therefore no thought for the morrow: for the morrow shall take thought for the things of itself" (Matthew 6:34a).

Father, forgive me for not getting the rest I need. Help me to trust You with homeschooling my children, so we accomplish what needs to be done each day. In Jesus' name, Amen.

Following Traditions

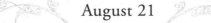

August 21

"Beware lest any man spoil you through philosophy and vain deceit, after the tradition of men, after the rudiments of the world, and not after Christ" (Colossians 2:8).

I hate to admit it, but the first years I homeschooled, I tried to make our homeschooling a carbon copy of what I experienced in traditional school. Following the same regimented routine I remembered, I attempted to convert our home and teach my children with standards and techniques meant for a classroom of twenty-five children. Thankfully, God helped me to discover a more robust way to teach our school lessons, and my children became happier in their studies.

Following the traditions he had learned, the Apostle Paul also had to change his thinking toward the new believers of the early church. As a devout Hebrew and learned scholar of the law, he saw Christians as a threat to the foundations of his faith. Believing he was preserving the true worship of God, Paul zealously pursued these new believers to eradicate them. Hundreds of men, women, and children died as a result of his actions until he saw the light and encountered Jesus on the road to Damascus. Years later, Paul confessed his mistake in 1 Timothy 1:12-13 when he said, "And I thank Christ Jesus our Lord, who hath enabled me, for that he counted me faithful, putting me into the ministry; Who was before a blasphemer, and a persecutor, and injurious: but I obtained mercy, because I did it ignorantly in unbelief."

What about you? Is your faith in Jesus Christ based simply on following the empty traditions you learned as a child, or do you truly know the One who uniquely created you? Jesus loves you and wants to have an intimate, dynamic relationship, so you can experience not only forgiveness of sin, but also the abundant life He has promised (John 10:10). Why not ask the Holy Spirit to touch your heart today, and let Him show you a whole new way to love the Lord?

Father, forgive me for coming to You with empty acts of worship. Take my life and use me for Your glory. Teach me from Your Word and guide me with the Holy Spirit that I might serve You with a heart that is passionate and alive. In Jesus' name, Amen.

Share your thoughts about this devotional at aophomeschooling.com/233

Letting Go

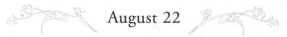

It happened today. I knew it was going to come someday, but I wasn't quite ready. My five-year-old son and I were walking back from the barn after doing the evening chores. As we headed toward the house, I felt my hand reach for his to walk back together. In just that instant, my son's hand pulled away instead, and I knew. I knew he was growing up and letting go.

As homeschool parents, we have even a greater temptation to hang on to our children when they begin to let go. Instead of looking for opportunities to launch our children into the world, our loving and protective nature wants to shelter them from all the hurts and injustices that will come their way. Instead of holding on so tightly, we must let go and allow them to place their hand into the hand of God. Psalm 37:24 says, "Though he fall, he shall not be utterly cast down: for the LORD upholdeth him with his hand."

Are you struggling with letting go? Maybe you feel like Mary, the mother of Jesus, when after she had spent three days looking for her lost twelve-year-old son, she heard Him say, "How is it that ye sought me? wist ye not that I must be about my Father's business" (Luke 2:41-51)? You can trust God to take care of your child, even when you are not there to hold his hand. God knows his needs and will help your child just like He has done for you. "But I trusted in thee, O LORD: I said, Thou art my God. My times are in thy hand" (Psalm 31:14-15a).

God, help me to place my child's future in Your hands. Remind me of all You have done for me, so I may believe in Your loving care for him. In Jesus' name, Amen.

Back-to-School Tools

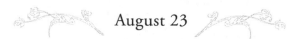

August 23

Would you like to know the best back-to-school item to have for a profitable year of homeschooling? No, it's not a new computer, and it's not a new microscope, math manipulative, or the latest educational game. In fact, you may be surprised to learn that the most effective tool you have is simply the positive words you use to encourage your child. No high-tech gadget or apparatus can ever leave as profound an effect on your child's education as saying things like, "Wow, you did a great job on that test!" and "How did you learn that so quickly?" Though it seems too good to be true, affirming your child with words of praise is the quickest way to motivate him to higher academic achievement.

As Christians, God also knows how encouraging words will help us achieve success in our spiritual walk. Repeatedly, His Word provides the words we need to hear to encourage us through life's hardest lessons. Read His promises to those who are in Christ Jesus:

"Nay, in all these things we are more than conquerors through him that loved us" (Romans 8:37).

"Ye are of God, little children, and have overcome them: because greater is he that is in you, than he that is in the world" (1 John 4:4).

"But thanks be to God, which giveth us the victory through our Lord Jesus Christ" (1 Corinthians 15:57).

Do you find yourself apprehensive as you face a new homeschooling year? Don't despair. The tool that will help your children achieve academic success is the same tool God uses to help you. The King of the Universe loves you and will encourage you to achieve even more than you dreamed possible. "But the Comforter, which is the Holy Ghost, whom the Father will send in my name, he shall teach you all things, and bring all things to your remembrance, whatsoever I have said unto you" (John 14:26).

Lord, thank You for Your encouraging words that fill me with hope and joy. Please help me to seek You each day as we homeschool to achieve all You have planned for our family. In the name of Jesus, Amen.

Truth or Consequences

August 24

"The fear of the LORD is the beginning of knowledge" (Proverbs 1:7a).

Until I became a homeschooling parent, I never knew how obvious a young child looks when telling a lie. Living together 24/7 gives you a distinct advantage in reading your child's body language and facial expressions, and my children knew I could tell instantly when a lie was coming from their lips. In addition, my children's respect for our house rules also helped to curtail lies. Knowing they would receive a lessened punishment for telling the truth, they were quick to tell on themselves and confess their wrong doing.

Having a healthy respect and fear of God will also help a Christian resist Satan's temptations. When our flesh is strong and urging us to sin, walking away and saying no is easier when we consider our accountability to Almighty God. Like our children, our fear of God's discipline should prevent evil actions from taking place in our lives. As we come to revere God and hate sin as He does, we will seek to live our lives in such a way that pleases Him.

What about you? Are you living in some deception today? God already sees and knows the lie you're living. Don't stay in your sin and wait to be caught like Achan (Joshua 7). Come to your Heavenly Father now, confess your sin, and let His loving discipline correct the error of your ways. "And ye have forgotten the exhortation which speaketh unto you as unto children, My son, despise not thou the chastening of the Lord, nor faint when thou art rebuked of him: For whom the Lord loveth he chasteneth, and scourgeth every son whom he receiveth" (Hebrews 12:5-6).

Lord, forgive me for lying and foolishly trying to hide my sin from You. I confess that what I have done is wrong and ask You to cleanse me from my unrighteousness. In Jesus' name, Amen.

Call the Yellow Bus

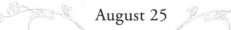

August 25

"Well, I guess you'd better quit. Just call the school and have them send the little yellow bus to pick up your kids tomorrow," I said sarcastically to my friend who was discouraged after a long week of homeschooling. These were certainly not the most encouraging words to say to a fellow homeschooler, but it was effective. Responding with a renewed commitment to homeschool, she sought the Lord's guidance and changed her curriculum to better fit her daughters' learning styles.

As homeschoolers, we've all been at the place of wanting to "throw in the towel." Satan provides numerous temptations and reasons for us to quit homeschooling our children. However, God's Word says, "No man, having put his hand to the plough, and looking back, is fit for the kingdom of God" (Luke 9:62b). We need to be steadfast and not give up when our children complain, other people slander, and daily chores become too much. Looking back takes our eyes off the One who can lead us through a difficult time, and we simply need to ask God to make a way through the problems: "For your Father knoweth what things ye have need of, before ye ask him" (Matthew 6:8b).

My friend still remembers that turning point in her homeschooling. Hopefully, you'll be gentler than me as you encourage other homeschoolers. There is a promise waiting to be received for instructing our children at home—godly children and godly parents! "Cast not away therefore your confidence, which hath great recompence of reward. For ye have need of patience, that, after ye have done the will of God, ye might receive the promise" (Hebrews 10:35-36).

Jesus, my strength to homeschool is in You alone. Only Your wisdom can help me teach Your children what they need to learn. Provide the encouragement I need today, and help me hold fast to the promises You give in Your Word, Amen.

If I Had Known

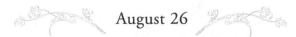

August 26

Looking back over your homeschooling experiences, what would you do differently? Enjoy these reflections gleaned from other homeschooling parents just like you:

• If I had known that teaching my children would be so much fun, I would have started homeschooling sooner.

• If I had known my children were going to grow as fast as older women said they would, I would have treasured our time together even more.

• If I had known my son was going to become an archeologist and dig in the dirt for a profession, I would have never worried about removing the stains when washing his jeans.

• If I had known all my children would go on to receive college degrees, I would have never second guessed my curriculum choices and teaching abilities.

• If I had known how unimportant it was to keep a spotless house, I would have gone to bed on time, instead of spending countless hours cleaning, organizing, and tidying up for the next day.

• If I had known how living on one income would build a solid faith in God, I would have gladly lived with less without all the complaining.

• If I could only experience the thrill of one job to last an entire lifetime, I would homeschool my children all over again.

Whatever lessons you've learned from homeschooling so far, you're incredibly blessed to teach your children. Praise God for the wonderful opportunity to be both your child's parent and teacher! "For I know the thoughts that I think toward you, saith the LORD, thoughts of peace, and not of evil, to give you an expected end" (Jeremiah 29:11).

Lord, I lift up a grateful heart of praise and thank You for all my homeschooling joys. As we begin a new school year, please help me appreciate the benefits of homeschooling even more. In Jesus' name, Amen.

Hang up the Phone

August 27

Distractions—they can eat up a day of schooling faster than you know, and there seems to always be plenty to choose from. Many days I've wondered, "Where did the time go?" The time I lost was usually spent on things that seemed beneficial or constructive. One of these was the temptation to answer the phone. After all, it may be an emergency, right?

A ringing phone for me was like a piece of candy to a child—not to be resisted. Besides, who can stand listening to a ringing phone? Being on the phone seemed innocent enough, until my children needed me. Oftentimes, they would have to wait to have their questions answered until I was done talking to a friend. "Just let it ring" became my children's motto.

Do you feel like you are always behind and homeschooling is becoming a burden? Pray to ask God to show you what activities need to be eliminated from your daily schedule. Homeschooling is too important to your children's future to not give it your best effort. Get rid of those distractions that may be worthwhile in themselves, but eat too much of your time each day. "Wherefore seeing we also are compassed about with so great a cloud of witnesses, let us lay aside every weight, and the sin which doth so easily beset us, and let us run with patience the race that is set before us" (Hebrews 12:1).

Lord, help me to prioritize my schedule today and not be taken in by those things that distract me. My children are depending on me to teach them, and I need Your wisdom to know what is valuable and what isn't. In Jesus' name, Amen.

Fresh Starts

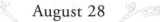

August 28

Every August, our homeschooling year started the same way. After the brown delivery truck left our driveway, four excited children would eagerly tear open the boxes of curriculum. Workbooks and teacher's guides would be laid on the floor and quickly checked against the packing slip. Then, like openings gifts on Christmas morning, my children would delightfully spend the rest of the day thumbing through the pages of their new curriculum. Inevitably, the fresh, colorful workbooks caused everyone to become so motivated, we would begin homeschooling the very same day.

Fresh starts are even more exciting in the Christian life. Helping someone come to an understanding of sin and to knowing the joy of God's forgiveness, is by far the greatest blessing you can experience. The eager anticipation and thirst for God in a new believer is contagious. Wanting to grow and know God more deeply through His Word, these new Christians pass their enthusiasm to older saints and challenge them to grow in their faith as well.

When was the last time you told someone about the saving love of Jesus? If your walk with God seems dry and worn out, today's the day to give yourself and someone else a fresh start in Christ. "Therefore if any man be in Christ, he is a new creature: old things are passed away; behold, all things are become new" (2 Corinthians 5:17).

Lord, thank You for the exciting message of Your forgiveness and love! Help me to share it anew today with someone who desperately needs to experience Your grace. In Jesus' name, Amen.

Obedient Love

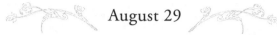

Homeschool disciplining would be easier if, like new clothes, our children came with a label. Directions would clearly state whether to use hot (spanking), warm (time out), or cold (grounded) water and when to line dry (take away privileges) or tumble dry (extra chores—community service). Unfortunately, our children don't come with wash and wear tags. We must rely on the Lord's wisdom to guide us when correcting and instructing our children in obedience.

Since all have sinned and come short of the glory of God (Romans 3:23), teaching our children to be obedient is a big part of a homeschooling parent's day. Training in righteousness falls on us, and we must teach our children to embrace the truth of Ephesians 6:1: "Children, obey your parents in the Lord: for this is right." However, building this godly character trait takes time. As homeschooling parents persist in their disciplining efforts, children eventually learn to be obedient both to parents and the Lord.

Christian parents must also learn to be obedient to the Lord. We may say we love the Lord, but often we fail to prove this love with our actions. Like a rebellious child, we pout, talk back, and demand our own way. God gives us the example of obedience in His Son: "Though he were a Son, yet learned he obedience by the things which he suffered" (Hebrews 5:8). Will you seek to show your true love for the Lord by obeying and doing what He asks? "He that hath my commandments, and keepeth them, he it is that loveth me: and he that loveth me shall be loved of my Father, and I will love him, and will manifest myself to him" (John 14:21).

Lord, like a parent, You lovingly remind me to obey You each day because You wish to bless me. Help me discover the depth of Your love and thoughts of Your heart by honoring You and doing what You've asked. In Your name, Amen.

One Step Back

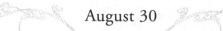

"Be still, and know that I am God: I will be exalted among the heathen, I will be exalted in the earth" (Psalm 46:10).

Have you ever started your day sensing something was wrong with your homeschooling? As I crawled out from under the covers, I knew we needed to set the academics aside and let the day just happen. Our family relationships had been growing distant, the stress level had been building, and our homeschooling was feeling more like a chore than a blessing. Our family needed to experience the joy of being together again. Phonics rules, spelling words, and algebraic equations could wait. Today, I simply wanted to enjoy my precious children and play.

Our relationship with God can also get misconstrued as we grow in Christ. We forget that God is more concerned about being with us than our concern of doing things for Him. We hurry from one worthwhile ministry to the next and fill our lives with noble schedules for winning the lost or discipling new believers. However, even as Mary chose to worship and sit at the Master's feet, we also must step back and rediscover the simple joy of being with Jesus. No schedules, no events, no projects—just quietly loving our Lord and relishing His presence.

Can you remember the last time you relaxed and enjoyed the day for what it was—a chance to breathe and live as you take in the goodness of God's creation and love? Today's the day to take one step back, turn off the noise, and listen to the silence. Drink in the beauty of your Creator and rejoice as God speaks to your heart! "In thy presence is fulness of joy; at thy right hand there are pleasures for evermore" (Psalm 16:11b).

Lord, I love You so much. I bow before You in worship and praise You for Your loving goodness. Hallelujah, I give You this day and rejoice in Your presence! In Jesus' name, Amen.

No Fear

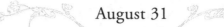

"Be of good courage, and he shall strengthen your heart, all ye that hope in the LORD" (Psalm 31:24).

Let's face the facts. There are some people who shouldn't homeschool their children. For whatever reason, they lack the resources or ability to teach, and their children would do better in a conventional school setting. However, there is another side to the coin. Many parents who should be schooling their children at home, aren't. Responding in fearful apprehension, they use the excuse, "It's great others can homeschool, but I could never do that!" The status quo or their own inhibitions have convinced them of failure, while God waits for them to believe in His wisdom and guidance for success.

Many great leaders in the Bible faced similar initial fears. Moses, Joshua, and Gideon all experienced anxiety and thought, "This job is too big for me." Afraid to try and wanting to quit before they even started, God challenged them to reach out and trust Him for courage and strength. God graciously gave Moses a spokesperson in Aaron, Joshua was given encouragement at Jericho by God's holy messenger, and Gideon received confirmation of his call through a fleece that was both wet and dry. Stepping out from behind their fearful excuses, they were used greatly by God to accomplish His will.

What task has God set before you that you're afraid to attempt? In addition to homeschooling, is He asking you to work with the church youth group, serve in a short-term mission, or start a Bible study in your home? Whatever His leading might be, don't let fear stop you from stepping out in faith. God is mighty, and He will go before you and help you accomplish great things for His glory. "Call unto me, and I will answer thee, and shew thee great and mighty things, which thou knowest not" (Jeremiah 33:3).

Lord, forgive me for being afraid to follow You. Sometimes what You ask seems too big for me to accomplish. Use me for Your glory and strengthen me now to follow You in obedience. In Jesus' name, Amen.

Homeschool "Firsts"

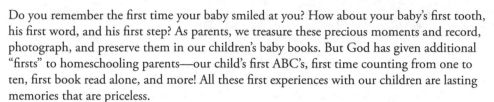

September 1

Do you remember the first time your baby smiled at you? How about your baby's first tooth, his first word, and his first step? As parents, we treasure these precious moments and record, photograph, and preserve them in our children's baby books. But God has given additional "firsts" to homeschooling parents—our child's first ABC's, first time counting from one to ten, first book read alone, and more! All these first experiences with our children are lasting memories that are priceless.

Jesus enjoys us, too, as His first fruits: "Of his own will begat he us with the word of truth, that we should be a kind of firstfruits of his creatures" (James 1:18). The blood He gave when dying on the cross was for you. He even recorded your name in His Book of Life when you repented and received His forgiveness of sin. Now and for eternity, you can experience His presence. He looks forward to each new "first" in your growing faith and treasures you as His precious child. Hallelujah!

Lord God, thank You for Your wonderful love for me! I can hardly begin to fathom Your thoughts toward me as Your child. I lift my heart in praise to You, Almighty One! In Your Son's name, Amen.

One More

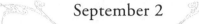

September 2

"For I acknowledge my transgressions: and my sin is ever before me" (Psalm 51:3).

As a homeschooling family, does it seem like your laundry is an endless assignment that never gets completed? As my son and I finished the last load one morning before starting school, my daughter walked in with yet another basket of dirty clothes. With his sense of accomplishment deflated once again, my son turned to me and said, "I think taking care of dirty laundry is like fighting against sin. There's always one more waiting to be cleaned."

My son's analogy may have seemed trite, but the more I thought, I realized he was correct. Until Christ returns, we will continue to fight temptation as we live in sinful, fallen bodies. Although the Holy Spirit dwells in every believer, the dirty ugliness of sin is constantly being revealed in our lives. Like another basket full of unclean clothes, our sins must be confessed daily and cleansed before the Lord (1 John 1:9).

Is it time to start another load of wash in your spiritual life this morning? Even though the battle may seem to never end, take heart. One day we will receive glorified bodies and stand before the Lord washed in the blood of the Lamb. Praise God, there will be an end to sin and the dirty mess it causes! "So when this corruptible shall have put on incorruption, and this mortal shall have put on immortality, then shall be brought to pass the saying that is written, Death is swallowed up in victory. O death, where is thy sting? O grave, where is thy victory? The sting of death is sin; and the strength of sin is the law. But thanks be to God, which giveth us the victory through our Lord Jesus Christ" (1 Corinthians 15:54-57).

Father God, how I look forward to the day when sin and death are forever defeated! Today I cry out once again like David, "Wash me throughly from mine iniquity, and cleanse me from my sin" (Psalm 51:2). In the name of Jesus, Amen.

 Share your thoughts about this devotional at aophomeschooling.com/245

Escape Routes

September 3

"The Lord knoweth how to deliver the godly out of temptations" (2 Peter 2:9a).

From the time my children were old enough to understand, fire drills were part of our homeschool safety lessons. Sounding the smoke alarm, I instructed each child how to escape in the event of a house fire. My children always thought it was great fun to climb out their bedroom window and meet outside at our flag pole. In fact, they each learned their escape routes so well, it only took a matter of seconds to vacate the house.

As my children grew into their teens, I realized they faced another danger as hazardous as fire – peer pressure. Knowing they needed an escape route to walk away from ungodly temptations, I said, "Whenever you find yourself in a bad situation and you need to get out, you can use me for an excuse. Don't let others lead you into sin or just sit there and get burned. Get out as soon as you smell the smoke and say, 'I have to go home early tonight,' or 'My parents need help at home.'"

God also provides an escape route when Satan tempts His children. Knowing we are not able to say "No" in our own strength, God makes a way for us to run from evil before it consumes us. Whether we struggle with procrastination, discouragement, or impure thoughts, 1 Corinthians 10:13 says, "There hath no temptation taken you but such as is common to man: but God is faithful, who will not suffer you to be tempted above that ye are able; but will with the temptation also make a way to escape, that ye may be able to bear it." Let the Lord reveal your personal escape route from the temptation you're facing today, and then get out as fast as you can!

Father, my flesh is weak and sin's desires seem so appealing. Help me walk in obedience to Your Word and show me the way to escape the temptations that are causing me to sin against You. In the mighty name of Jesus, Amen.

Share your thoughts about this devotional at aophomeschooling.com/246

Connecting the Dots

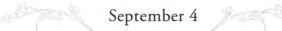

September 4

"So teach us to number our days, that we may apply our hearts unto wisdom" (Psalm 90:12).

"Dot-to-Dots" were one of my children's favorite math worksheets. Each time we used this method to review counting in our homeschool math lesson, my children excitedly followed the dots and guessed what the picture would be when they were done. However, in their excitement to finish, sometimes they would hurry too fast. They would count incorrectly, miss a number, and the result would be a distorted picture. Forced to start over, they would begin again and count more carefully until they finally exclaimed, "Look at what I made!"

Like the "Dot-to-Dots" in my children's lessons, God also gives us wisdom and guidance one step at a time. Teaching us to number our days and to live by faith, He slowly reveals the perfect picture for our lives. As we seek His face each morning and walk in His understanding, He provides what we need to recognize the next step. Even when Satan tempts us to hurry and make life work out on our own, God gently corrects us as a master teacher and gently leads us back where we need to be. Lovingly, He teaches us to follow His pattern to proclaim, "Look what God has made out of my life!"

How about you? Are you counting on your own strength to see you through homeschooling this year, or are you obediently seeking God's wisdom for each day's lessons? Don't let your homeschooling family get off track. Count on the One who has counted every hair on your head (Matthew 10:30) and star in the sky (Psalm 147:4) and let Him guide you in the perfect path. "Doth not he see my ways, and count all my steps" (Job 31:4)?

Lord, sometimes homeschooling seems like a maze, and I don't know where to go next. Please lead me and show me how to teach with Your guidance, power, and wisdom. In Jesus' name, Amen.

 Share your thoughts about this devotional at aophomeschooling.com/247

No Other Gods

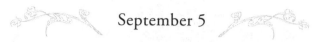

September 5

"Thou shalt have no other gods before me. Thou shalt not make unto thee any graven image" (Exodus 20:3-4a).

Somewhere in my homeschooling experience, my children became the focus of not only my day, but also my entire life. I found myself thinking of their needs constantly and became self-absorbed in making their lives happy and successful. Although a measure of this devotion and attention was appropriate, there was a surplus of affection that was being misdirected. My children had become my idols who I worshiped with all my energy and time.

Lovingly, God set a course of events to correct me of my mistake. The lesson culminated when I read the story of Abraham and Isaac in Genesis 22. Abraham's willingness to sacrifice his son on an altar in worship to the Lord convicted me. I knew I loved my four children too much to let them go. The thought of losing them at a young age was more than I could bear. Somehow I knew God was asking me to lay them, my greatest treasures, at His feet. Living for the Lord first and serving my family second was the correct order of priorities.

Have your children become your idols? You may not think so, but evaluate your thought life, your daily schedule, and your heart. Who is the object of your worship and devotion—Jesus or your family? Don't rob God of the devotion due to Him. "Thou shalt not bow down thyself to them, nor serve them: for I the LORD thy God am a jealous God" (Exodus 20:5a).

Heavenly Father, forgive me for putting my children before You. All I have is from You, including my family. Today, I'm making You the first priority in my life. In Jesus' name, Amen.

Homeschooling's Price

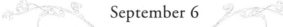

September 6

"I am crucified with Christ: nevertheless I live; yet not I, but Christ liveth in me" (Galatians 2:20a).

I'm feeling selfish today. I look at the schoolwork waiting to be corrected and this week's lesson plans still waiting to be finished, and I want to escape somewhere. My life seems like it's not my own, and I resent the fact that I can't do what I want, when I want. Homeschooling requires me to be so disciplined, and I'm starting to feel trapped. I want to take a break from housework, diapers, schedules, and endless questions, but I'm the one in charge. I feel like a huge burden is on my back.

Does the above scenario describe you today? Do you wish you could experience the wonderful benefits of homeschooling and escape the responsibilities? Sorry, but it doesn't work that way. If you want your children to achieve academic, as well as spiritual success, you have to give yourself 100% and commit to homeschooling. Like the man who calculated the cost in building a tower or the king who assessed his army before he went to war (Luke 14:27-33), following the Lord's call to homeschool your children requires giving your all. Yes, God knows when you need to rest and will show you how to catch your breath, but He also asks His disciples to carry their cross. So who will you follow today, yourself or the Lord? "If any man will come after me, let him deny himself, and take up his cross daily, and follow me" (Luke 9:23b).

Lord, forgive my attitude and help me refocus on the call You gave to homeschool. Teach me again that Your will and Your way is better than any life I can conceive. I love You and thank You for my family. In Jesus' name, Amen.

Transitions

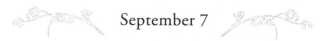

September 7

"And an highway shall be there, and a way, and it shall be called The way of holiness" (Isaiah 35:8a).

After the initial excitement wears off, the first year of homeschooling can seem quite challenging. Parents and children adjust to new routines, and things don't always go as smoothly as planned. Gears grind as schedules get interrupted, children misbehave, and new disciplines are learned. During this crucial transition period, many homeschoolers feel overwhelmed and think they made a mistake. Some even give up and say, "Homeschooling is too hard, and it's not for me."

Shifting gears to homeschooling doesn't have to be difficult if God is in control. Like an automatic transmission smoothly brings a car up to speed, God's presence and power provides the finely-tuned peace and patience that keeps your homeschooling successfully cruising down the road. Whether you're facing bad attitudes, deprogramming your children from public education, or simply learning how to use your curriculum effectively, God's wisdom will guide you if you ask for it (James 1:5).

What's the status of your homeschooling today? Is your patience blown like a steaming radiator? Is your engine running rough as you power through the day in your own strength? Don't call the tow truck to send your homeschooling to the salvage yard just yet. Give God the wheel and let the Holy Spirit overhaul your homeschooling to start enjoying the ride of your life! "Call unto me, and I will answer thee, and shew thee great and mighty things, which thou knowest not" (Jeremiah 33:3).

Father, please guide me today as our family travels down the homeschooling highway. Empower me with the Holy Spirit and fill me with Your presence to keep going when the road gets bumpy. In Jesus' name, Amen.

Holding Grudges

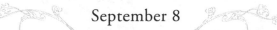

September 8

For several days, I had been watching my oldest son and daughter interact. Like a pending thunderstorm, something was definitely brewing between them. The conflict began when my exuberant son ruined his sister's art project by running excitedly through the room. Although the damage was unintentional, my son's less-than-sincere apology awakened a vengeful spirit in my daughter's heart. The conflict culminated the following day when my son again raced through the room and ruined another project of my daughter's. Exasperated, my daughter responded by intentionally destroying her brother's history project.

Forgiving others can be difficult for many people, especially when a close friend or family member has wronged you. Are you the type of person who silently waits for an opportunity to get even or relishes the idea of paybacks? "Recompense to no man evil for evil. Provide things honest in the sight of all men. If it be possible, as much as lieth in you, live peaceably with all men. Dearly beloved, avenge not yourselves, but rather give place unto wrath: for it is written, Vengeance is mine; I will repay, saith the Lord" (Romans 12:17-19).

God sees the wrongs you experience in life. Jesus suffered the greatest injustices when He was on earth and showed us how to respond to them. "Who, when he was reviled, reviled not again; when he suffered, he threatened not; but committed himself to him that judgeth righteously" (1 Peter 2:23). Can you commit the injustice you are now facing to the Lord? Will you let go of the grudge you are holding and forgive? "For if ye forgive men their trespasses, your heavenly Father will also forgive you" (Matthew 6:14).

Lord, I know I should forgive the wrong done to me, but something within me wants to hold on to this pain. I realize that keeping this hurt will only make this situation worse. Help me follow Your example and release this pain by forgiving. In Jesus' name, Amen.

Who Speaks for God?

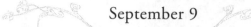

September 9

"And my tongue shall speak of thy righteousness and of thy praise all the day long" (Psalm 35:28).

During the early 1980s, there were few voices that publicly championed the cause of homeschooling. Fortunately, the men and women who did speak out were effective, powerful, and passionate communicators who left a lasting impact on my life. As a young parent with two preschool-aged children, I paid attention to their knowledgeable research, books, and advice against traditional schooling. Willing to go against the flow, they set the precedent for today's modern homeschooling movement and inspired thousands of homeschooling families just like mine to do the same.

After Christ's ascension to heaven, perhaps no other man furthered the cause of Christ during Bible times more than the Apostle Paul. Being willing to go to the Gentiles, he too set a new precedent when sharing the Gospel message. The Jewish leaders were upset as Paul established new churches with thousands of Gentile believers who came to a saving knowledge of Jesus Christ. As these new believers suffered for their faith, they also boldly spoke the truth of Christ crucified, and the world was forever changed.

How about you? Are you willing to speak for God in today's world? Although you may be tempted to succumb to the world's intimidation, you have an opportunity to use your voice to speak out for Jesus. As you homeschool, know your Bible and boldly share its truths. Then watch as God uses you to make a difference in the lives of your children, as well as countless others. May we all be like Paul when he declared, "That therein I may speak boldly, as I ought to speak" (Ephesians 6:20b).

Lord, give me courage to declare You as Lord, and let me be as the early believers when they prayed, "Grant unto thy servants, that with all boldness they may speak thy word" (Acts 4:29). In Jesus' name, Amen.

Second Chances

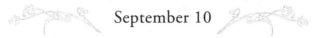

September 10

"For the mountains shall depart, and the hills be removed; but my kindness shall not depart from thee, neither shall the covenant of my peace be removed, saith the LORD that hath mercy on thee" (Isaiah 54:10).

How many times in your life have you wished to go back in time and do something over? Maybe you wouldn't have bought that expensive car, chosen that college, or passed up an opportunity to tell someone about Jesus. All of us would like a "do over" in something.

Praise God, He is a God of second chances. He forgave David of his sin with Bathsheba and continued to use him as king over Israel. After Moses tried to deliver God's people his way, God brought Moses back to Egypt to lead His people to the Promised Land. Jonah reached the sinful city of Ninevah with the message of repentance after first disobeying and running away from God.

If you feel like a homeschooling failure, this message is for you! Don't give up! Pray and ask the Lord to show you how to homeschool. Try a different curriculum or change your daily schedule. Homeschooling is flexible. Start over and find a routine that works for your family. God will help you again. "It is of the LORD's mercies that we are not consumed, because his compassions fail not. They are new every morning: great is thy faithfulness" (Lamentations 3:22-23).

Jesus, my heart cries out to You today. I've been homeschooling on my own for too long. Show me again the right way to teach my children. In Your name, Amen.

Tragic Memories

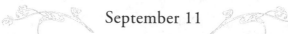

September 11

There are certain moments in time that people vividly remember in connection with a certain date in history. My mother can recall exactly where and what she was doing when Pearl Harbor was attacked in World War II. I can recall where and what I was doing when John F. Kennedy was shot. My daughter now recalls where and what she was doing the day the World Trade Center twin towers burned and crashed to the ground. For three days, homeschooling stopped, and we, along with millions of others, watched the awful events of those days. Her thoughts are forever recorded below in her poem written shortly after that tragic day:

September 11, 2001
By JoAnna Tatman

Out of the clear blue sky
I saw thousands die.
I saw people jump to their death.
I saw America hold its breath.

I saw the sadness of the world.
I saw the flag at half staff furled.
I saw the grief of a President.
I saw America lose its innocence.

I see the towers fall in my mind.
I think I've seen it a hundred times.
I saw America cry and pray.
I will never forget that horrible day.

I saw acts of the most evil kind.
I know we can never turn back time.
I'll remember those who fight to save
Freedom, in the land of the brave.

Even in our darkest moments in time, we can know God is with us. "Who shall separate us from the love of Christ? shall tribulation, or distress, or persecution, or famine, or nakedness, or peril, or sword? For I am persuaded, that neither death, nor life, nor angels, nor principalities, nor powers, nor things present, nor things to come, Nor height, nor depth, nor any other creature, shall be able to separate us from the love of God, which is in Christ Jesus our Lord" (Romans 8:35, 38-39).

Dear God, thank you that even in tragic times when the world is falling down around us, we are conquerors through Him who loved us!

Share your thoughts about this devotional at **aophomeschooling.com/254**

Glory Days

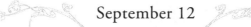

"I'm bored," complained my oldest son. "I don't have anything to do." Normally, those words created images of countless tasks to give my son during our homeschool day. However, today I sensed the Lord asking me to teach a lesson from His Word instead.

"Mountaintop experiences don't happen every day," I said. "You'll find that life is usually 80% ordinary and 20% extraordinary. Most of your life will involve being faithful in the normal everyday routine, but when God chooses, He will give something that changes your life forever."

Exciting experiences can be bought in this life, but the life-changing moments that give true satisfaction and fulfillment come only through the power of the Holy Spirit. Think of Mary, the mother of Jesus, who faithfully lived a quiet life until the angel Gabriel told her she would give birth to the Savior. Joseph became ruler over Egypt after years of suffering and separation from family. Moses met God through a burning bush after forty years of isolated living as a shepherd.

Looking back on your life, how many extraordinary moments have you had? Faithfully serving God in the ordinary makes you a candidate to serve God in the extraordinary. "His lord said unto him, Well done, thou good and faithful servant: thou hast been faithful over a few things, I will make thee ruler over many things: enter thou into the joy of thy lord" (Matthew 25:21).

Father, help me remember that You have a special plan and purpose for my life. May I be found faithful in the everyday things, so I am ready for the extraordinary when they come.
In Jesus' name, Amen.

By Their Fruits

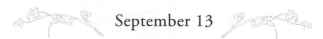

September 13

How long do you need to teach your children at home before you "officially" become a homeschool family? Like the tests that evaluate a child's academic performance, you can assume homeschooling has arrived at your house when the following are true:

You have more books in your house than groceries.

Your children show up for school in their pajamas.

Your house décor consists of time lines, maps, assorted craft projects, and half-finished science experiments.

Your trips to the library require a laundry basket to hold all the books.

Your refrigerator is perpetually covered in art projects and completed assignments.

Your children think reading history is best achieved while lying on your bed with the family cats.

Your kitchen pantry holds more school supplies than cooking supplies.

Your child's favorite classmates are his siblings.

Christians, too, have distinct marks that help us gauge whether we are growing more Christlike. In Galatians 5:22 we read of fruits that should be displayed if we are truly following the Lord—love, joy, peace, longsuffering, gentleness, goodness, faith, meekness, and temperance. As these fruits become more evident in our lives, we can trust the Holy Spirit is working to conform us to the image of Christ (Romans 8:29). What about your life? Is there fruit that proves you're a follower of Jesus? "Ye shall know them by their fruits" (Matthew 7:16a).

Lord, thank You for the transforming power of the Holy Spirit. Let my actions demonstrate Your love not only to my family, but also to the world. In Jesus' name, Amen.

Homeschool Complaints

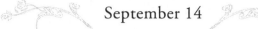

September 14

"Do all things without murmurings and disputings" (Philippians 2:14).

Is your homeschool infected with the whining disease? Like the early stages of most health problems, you may not recognize its symptoms at first. When assigning schoolwork, especially in your child's least favorite subject, this dreaded disease usually starts with an exasperated sigh. Next, it spreads into a short question such as, "Do I have to do this assignment?" If not diagnosed and treated early, the whining disease finally takes over your homeschool completely until you hear things like, "Why do I always have so much schoolwork to do? I don't want to do this!"

Whining, grumbling, murmuring, and complaining all stem from the same, sinful problem—rebellion. In Numbers 12, God reveals His attitude towards this deadly disease when dealing with the murmuring of Miriam and Aaron. Thinking they knew better than their brother, Miriam and Aaron spoke against Moses and said, "Hath the LORD indeed spoken only by Moses? hath he not spoken also by us" (Numbers 12:2b)? God heard their whining and quickly applied His cure. Calling all three to the tent of meeting, He defended Moses' leadership and struck Miriam with leprosy for seven days.

Are you allowing a whining, rebellious spirit in your homeschool? Unfortunately, children are not the only ones who can become infected with this disease. Parents, too, can find themselves easily complaining to God about the sacrifice and work responsibilities involved with homeschooling. Don't allow a negative spirit to destroy your homeschool family. Like Aaron, confess your foolish complaints. Pray for the joy of homeschooling to be restored in your home.

Father, forgive me for murmuring against Your plan for our family. Teach me to treasure each day with my children and give me a thankful heart for both the blessings and responsibilities of homeschooling. In Jesus' name, Amen.

It's Mine!

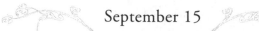

September 15

"That they do good, that they be rich in good works, ready to distribute, willing to communicate" (1 Timothy 6:18).

The yelling echoed off the walls of our schoolroom for the last time that day. All three of my homeschool students were being sent to different corners for another timeout. I shook my head as I walked away and wondered, "Why is sharing so difficult for young children? They are always worried about getting their 'fair share' of everything!" The new art supplies we had purchased were an enticement to selfishness, but certainly not worth the name-calling and fighting I had been hearing. Today was another opportunity to help my children understand that God gives us everything we need. We can afford to share with others.

Christ is our best example in teaching sharing. Philippians 2:3-8 says, "Let nothing be done through strife or vainglory; but in lowliness of mind let each esteem other better than themselves. Look not every man on his own things, but every man also on the things of others. Let this mind be in you, which was also in Christ Jesus: Who, being in the form of God, thought it not robbery to be equal with God: But made himself of no reputation, and took upon him the form of a servant, and was made in the likeness of men: And being found in fashion as a man, he humbled himself, and became obedient unto death, even the death of the cross." Christ gave up everything to come to earth to suffer and take your place for the punishment of your sins. He is the One who willingly shared His life so you could receive forgiveness of sin and eternal life. According to Hebrews 12:10, we even can share in His holiness because of the sacrifice He gave in dying on the cross.

Has your house been experiencing the "It's mine" syndrome? Don't allow this attitude to take root in the heart of your child or yourself. Remember, everything we have has been given to us by the Lord. "Every good gift and every perfect gift is from above, and cometh down from the Father of lights" (James 1:17a).

Father, I know how selfish I can be. You are the One who has blessed me with everything, and I am not my own. Help me acknowledge my dependence on You and share all that I am with others today. In Jesus' name, Amen.

 Share your thoughts about this devotional at **aophomeschooling.com/258**

Secondhand Lessons

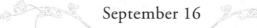

September 16

"Except ye be converted, and become as little children, ye shall not enter into the kingdom of heaven" (Matthew 18:3b).

Much like the rural, one-room schoolhouse of years ago, homeschooling families enjoy the unique benefits of learning academics together. After practicing our multiplication tables one morning, I quizzed my daughter and asked, "What is four times five?" Expecting her to answer, I was totally surprised when my four-year-old son replied nonchalantly, "Twenty." Sitting on the floor quietly playing with his toy cars, I didn't realize how much he had over-heard during our math lesson. Without even knowing it, my young son had learned the same information by hearing me teach his older sister.

Academics weren't the only lessons shared in our home. Dealing with toddler and preteen issues and bringing them under God's lordship were eye-openers for all ages. Not only did my younger children glean biblical wisdom from their idolized, older siblings, my older children also understood God's design involved in rearing a family and the responsibilities of setting a godly example. In addition, the faith of my little ones taught me incredible spiritual lessons of God's love and forgiveness. Truthfully, I know I wouldn't be the Christian I am today without having learned just as much from my children as they did from me.

What lesson is God trying to teach you through your children today? You may think you are the teacher, but as you learn, love, and live together as a Christian homeschool family, God has a few secondhand lessons for you to learn as well. "Whosoever therefore shall humble himself as this little child, the same is greatest in the kingdom of heaven" (Matthew 18:4).

Heavenly Father, thank You for the wonderful opportunities You've given to learn from each other as we homeschool. Help me to hear You speak through my children's hearts and to know You're guiding us in Your wisdom each day. In the name of Jesus, Amen.

 Share your thoughts about this devotional at **aophomeschooling.com/259**

Old Mother Hubbard (Part 1)

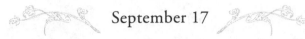

"But seek first the kingdom of God and his righteousness; and all these things shall be added unto you" (Matthew 6:33).

I felt like Old Mother Hubbard as I went to the kitchen cupboards that morning. I don't know why I even bothered to look. I knew there was nothing in them to make a meal for my four young children. The situation looked rather bleak for a cook who could make a meal out of just flour, eggs, and milk, but today I didn't even have those ingredients. I looked out the window at the winter snow that covered my garden—no vegetables to be found there. What was I going to do?

My husband was on a short-term mission in Africa, and I was all alone, homeschooling our children in the middle of winter. I had no money, no food, and no way to even get out from the blizzard that had blocked our long driveway to our country home. I began to think about how we had prayed and asked the Lord for opportunities to serve Him in missions. God had assured us through His Word that He would keep His promises to take care of us—but now I had four pairs of hungry eyes wondering what their mother was going to do.

I don't know what came over me that morning. I opened every cupboard door and the refrigerator. I sat the children down in the middle of the kitchen, and we began to pray. I almost shouted at God when I spoke and reminded Him that He had promised to take care of us. Right now we had nothing—nothing to eat, no one to help, and no escape. Just the night before I had read in Psalm 37:25, "I have been young, and now am old; yet I have not seen the righteous forsaken nor his seed begging bread." I prayed that God would keep His promises, but things didn't look too good.

To be continued in tomorrow's Daily Focus.

Father God, I'm afraid and cry out to You like David, "What time I am afraid, I will trust in thee" (Psalm 56:3). Show me the way and give me the strength to walk in Your will. In Jesus' name, Amen.

Old Mother Hubbard (Part 2)

September 18

(Continued from yesterday's Daily Focus.)

"And it shall come to pass, that before they call, I will answer; and while they are yet speaking, I will hear" (Isaiah 65:24).

When we were done praying, my children and I got up and started our day. Not even thirty minutes had passed when I heard a pick-up truck coming up our driveway. Unbelievably, our pastor from a town 15 miles away walked up to the door and handed me an envelope. The pastor said someone at church had given the envelope to him on Sunday, but he didn't know what was in it. He just "happened to be going" to the town near our home and had decided to drop off the envelope. Then, just that quickly, he was gone.

I stood there with the envelope in my hand and opened it. The hundred dollar bill inside may as well have been a thousand dollars to me. I knew the money was God's answer to our prayers. I quickly bundled all the children in their coats and drove to town, following the path our pastor's truck had made in our driveway. God was going to fill up all those empty cupboards!

I never knew who our benefactor was, but I did learn a valuable lesson I have never forgotten. God is able to show Himself the mightiest when we are the weakest. "But as it is written, Eye hath not seen, nor ear heard, neither have entered into the heart of man, the things which God hath prepared for them that love him" (1 Corinthians 2:9).

Lord, what a great and mighty God You are! Never let me forget that my very breath is in Your hands. Thank You for always keeping Your promises and providing what I need. I worship You alone. In Jesus' name, Amen.

 Share your thoughts about this devotional at aophomeschooling.com/261

Broken Promises

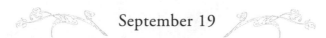

September 19

"Again, ye have heard that it hath been said by them of old time, Thou shalt not forswear thyself, but shalt perform unto the Lord thine oaths" (Matthew 5:33).

"But you promised," whimpered my ten-year-old daughter. "You said we could go swimming if we finished all our schoolwork." Although the words were softly spoken, they echoed in my ears as she left the room.

"Only a little disappointment," I justified to myself, "she'll get over it." Little did I know this broken promise also broke my daughter's faith in her mother's word.

While homeschooling our children, we sometimes make promises we don't keep. Each day we may attempt to motivate or discipline with words we don't really mean. Unkept promises disillusion our children, and unmeant threats instill fear and doubt. Not following through on phrases like, "If you work hard on your math, I'll give you . . ." or "When your father gets home, he's going to . . ." leaves children wondering if they can trust their parent's word. What can we do as homeschooling parents to guard our mouths from these foolish utterances?

God's Word in James 5:12 says, "But above all things, my brethren, swear not, neither by heaven, neither by the earth, neither by any other oath: but let your yea be yea; and your nay, nay; lest ye fall into condemnation." God says not to make promises or threats with your words, especially when you have no intention of keeping them. Your children need to know that you mean what you say. Before you speak idle words again today, stop and consider the price—the broken heart of your child. "But I say unto you, That every idle word that men shall speak, they shall give account thereof in the day of judgment" (Matthew 12:36).

Lord, forgive me when I say things to get a quick fix to a problem at home with my children. Help me weigh my words and remember to honor all of my commitments—no matter how small. In Your Son's name, Amen.

Share your thoughts about this devotional at **aophomeschooling.com/262**

As Close as it Gets

September 20

"Seek ye the LORD while he may be found, call ye upon him while he is near" (Isaiah 55:6).

As I read the statistic on the Internet, all I could say was, "Wow, praise God!" According to the National Home Education Research Institute's website, approximately 1.9 to 2.4 million children were educated at home in the United States during 2005 and 2006. What a difference from when I started homeschooling in the early 1980's! At that time, there were only an estimated 50,000 children being educated at home each year. As I considered the figures and did the math, I realized that since 1985, homeschooling has grown over 4,700%!

The incredible growth of homeschooling in America can be attributed to many factors. However, I think the greatest factor is that parents are rediscovering God's original design for the family. Children and parents were never meant to be separated for days (sometimes weeks) with overloaded schedules that keep them passing in the night. How can any family be expected to have loving relationships with that routine? Homeschooling continues to grow because it provides a unique, nurturing environment where families can communicate throughout the day. Loving bonds are formed, and mutual respect is cultivated between siblings and parents. With God as the head, the family functions as He intended, and we reap the rich blessings of family togetherness.

Like our homeschooling families, God never intended for us to live apart from Him. Daily, we must come to Him in prayer and Bible study to continue to grow spiritually. Without the loving and nurturing guidance from the Holy Spirit throughout the day, we will lose the intimacy God desires with His children. How about you? Can you remember the last time you had a heart-to-heart talk with Him? If not, "Draw nigh to God, and he will draw nigh to you" (James 4:8a).

Lord, forgive me for letting other things pull me away from the most important relationship in my life—You! Help me to hear Your voice right now and to always stay close to Your heart and will for my life. In Jesus' name I pray, Amen.

Share your thoughts about this devotional at **aophomeschooling.com**/263

Quiet Encouragement

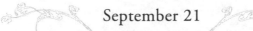

September 21

"But when thou doest alms, let not thy left hand know what thy right hand doeth: That thine alms may be in secret: and thy Father which seeth in secret himself shall reward thee openly" (Matthew 6:3-4).

Children love secrets, and one joy I experienced as a homeschooling parent was teaching my children the thrill of being secret gift-givers. Following Christ's illustration in Matthew 6, I encouraged them to ask God's guidance to think of ways to bless their family, friends, and neighbors. At first, this task was difficult, since little ones like to tell everything they know. However, as my children grew older, not only did they become thoughtful and generous givers, they also became quite adept in disguising any connection with the gift. Countless times, I found myself humbled and encouraged when receiving a gift at day's end without knowing who had laid the treasure on my pillow.

What about your homeschooling family? In a world where most people are trying to take and get ahead, teaching your children to give secret gifts from God can seem quite contrary. Like Christ Jesus who died for us while we were yet sinners (Romans 5:8), help them bless another homeschool family, church family, or unsaved neighbor near you today. Let your children discover the exciting truth of Acts 20:35b: "It is more blessed to give than to receive."

Father, every good and perfect gift is from You, and we can only give away what You have already given to us. Use our family to be a secret blessing to someone today, and may You receive all the glory and praise. In Jesus' name, Amen.

Where Is God?

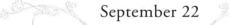
"Wherefore if they shall say unto you, Behold, he is in the desert; go not forth: behold, he is in the secret chambers; believe it not. For as the lightning cometh out of the east, and shineth even unto the west; so shall also the coming of the Son of man be" (Matthew 24:26-27).

My son was only six when our family invested in a quality telescope for star gazing. Star charts and nightly excursions to see the planets and stars became part of our homeschool curriculum. My young son's strong interest in this subject amazed me, especially one night when he asked, "When are we going to see God?" I realized then that he had been expecting to see God in the heavenly night sky through the telescope's lens.

Although my son's idea of finding God in the sky by looking through a telescope was slightly incorrect, the Bible does tell us that Christ's return will be evident to all the world. "Immediately after the tribulation of those days shall the sun be darkened, and the moon shall not give her light, and the stars shall fall from heaven, and the powers of the heavens shall be shaken: And then shall appear the sign of the Son of man in heaven: and then shall all the tribes of the earth mourn, and they shall see the Son of man coming in the clouds of heaven with power and great glory" (Matthew 24:29-30). Even the angels announced to the disciples that Christ would return in the same way he left earth—in the clouds (Acts 1:11).

Christ is returning to earth someday. Although no one knows when that time will come, we need to live expectantly for that moment. "The Lord is not slack concerning his promise, as some men count slackness; but is longsuffering to us-ward, not willing that any should perish, but that all should come to repentance" (2 Peter 3:9). Are you ready for His return? Have you given your life to the Lord? Now is the time to accept Jesus as your Savior! "That if thou shalt confess with thy mouth the Lord Jesus, and shalt believe in thine heart that God hath raised him from the dead, thou shalt be saved" (Romans 10:9).

Lord Jesus, you are a great and holy Lord. I believe the promise of Your return is real. I repent of my sins and accept You as my Savior. In Your name I pray, Amen.

Shortcuts

"Till we all come in the unity of the faith, and of the knowledge of the Son of God, unto a perfect man, unto the measure of the stature of the fulness of Christ" (Ephesians 4:13).

Life is full of shortcuts. High-priced technology has changed the way we live and made shopping so easy we can get what we want with a simple click or a wave of a debit card. Although technological advances have also made homeschooling easier, there is one aspect to teaching our children at home that can't be fast forwarded—your children's spiritual growth. Developing biblical values and godly character requires a daily, concentrated effort in building God's truths precept upon precept. Money simply cannot buy "instant access" to Christianity or purchase short cuts in learning God's lessons in humility, obedience, and submission.

Trying to "fast track" Christianity has been a problem since the Lord returned to heaven. In Acts 8:13-24, Simon, the ex-magician, thought he could bypass the disciplines of being trained in righteousness. Wanting to impress the crowds and perform miracles like Peter, Simon offered money to find a shortcut to the Holy Spirit's power. Rebuking him for his fleshly attempts to control God, Peter said, "Thy money perish with thee, because thou hast thought that the gift of God may be purchased with money. Thou hast neither part nor lot in this matter: for thy heart is not right in the sight of God" (Acts 8:20b-21).

What about you? Are you guilty of looking for shortcuts in your spiritual growth? Quick prayers and short devotionals are not enough. Spend time alone with the Lord today in prayer and Bible study and let the Holy Spirit reveal those changes that need to take place in your life. "Therefore leaving the principles of the doctrine of Christ, let us go on unto perfection" (Hebrews 6:1a).

Lord, forgive me for being like a child and looking for the easy way out of Your lessons. Help me to walk with You today and not to run ahead of the disciplines that teach me Your truths. In Jesus' name, Amen.

Saving Sammy

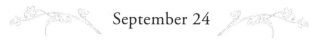

September 24

"Quench not the Spirit" (1 Thessalonians 5:19).

Have you ever had those moments in time when you saw something about to happen, but felt helpless to stop it? I was having one of those moments as I watched my son's black lab take notice of a car coming over the hill over a mile away from our home. In that instant, I could see and sense what was about to happen in my mind.

For several months, we had included dog obedience training in my son's homeschool curriculum. Both my son and I had become frustrated with his black lab, Sammy. We had taught him many things, but the one thing we couldn't teach him was to give up chasing cars. Even though we had a long driveway and lived in the country, our space wasn't enough for him. We had even resorted to tying him up, but today we had let him loose to play as we worked outside.

Before I could grab the collar on this fifty-pound fireball, Sammy started running toward the car he had seen. Both my son and I ran after him, screaming for him to stop. Everything went into slow motion, as I saw that the dog and the car were on a collision course. We did all we could, but Sammy would not obey and stop. He was broadsided by the car at 50 mph.

The disobedience of Sammy provided a significant spiritual lesson for my son. Although Sammy had learned to do many things right, his death was caused by the one vice he refused to give up: wanting his own way. He literally ran headlong into trouble, and met death at the end.

God grieves over your sinful disobedience each day, too. You let the Holy Spirit teach you the Word, but then refuse to be disciplined in the areas you are weakest. Because you do not see an immediate consequence, you run headlong into your vices of laziness, selfishness, or criticizing, and think they will never hurt you. But you are always on a collision course when you remain in known sin. The Holy Spirit is quenched by your defiance, and soon you are unable to hear His voice calling you back. Don't wait for a wreck to turn you around. Stop and yield your life to the Lord, today! "I beseech you therefore, brethren, by the mercies of God, that ye present your bodies a living sacrifice, holy, acceptable unto God, which is your reasonable service" (Romans 12:1).

Jesus, I can't hear You right now, and it seems like Your voice has been quiet for a long time. Forgive me for allowing sins to remain in my life after You have taught me the truth. I repent today and ask You to fill me anew with the Holy Spirit. In Your precious name, Amen.

 Share your thoughts about this devotional at **aophomeschooling.com/267**

Pillow Talk

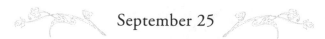

September 25

"But God hath revealed them unto us by his Spirit: for the Spirit searcheth all things, yea, the deep things of God" (1 Corinthians 2:10).

Sunlight was just beginning to filter through my bedroom windows as I opened my eyes to another homeschooling day. Realizing I had slept through the alarm, I quickly threw back the covers to jump out of bed and start breakfast. However, as I did, I was surprised to find my two youngest children snuggled in my blankets. Quietly waiting for me to wake up, they were holding a book and eager to continue reading the story we had only half finished the day before. Smiling, I said, "Okay, let's just start school right now." Tucking each child in the blankets on either side of me, I opened their book, and we began to read together. For the next thirty minutes, we all enjoyed our unconventional classroom, and I thanked God again for the spontaneous joys of homeschooling.

Like the unexpected learning moments that occur in homeschooling, we never know when the Holy Spirit is going to speak to our hearts. As God impresses His Word upon our minds in Bible study or miraculously chooses to answer a specific request when on our knees in prayer, we experience a special touch of God's goodness and mercy. As we are snuggled in the warmth of our Father's love, the Holy Spirit teaches us the truth (John 16:13a) and gives us a taste of our future home in heaven (Ephesians 1:14). Even when we're weakest and God seems far away, the Holy Spirit intercedes for us "with groanings which cannot be uttered" (Romans 8:26b). What a wonderful God we serve! Praise Him as He touches your life today with special moments of understanding and love. "That the God of our Lord Jesus Christ, the Father of glory, may give unto you the spirit of wisdom and revelation in the knowledge of him: The eyes of your understanding being enlightened; that ye may know what is the hope of his calling, and what the riches of the glory of his inheritance in the saints" (Ephesians 1:17-18).

Heavenly Father, thank You for the presence of the Holy Spirit in my life. I praise You for the power and divine wisdom that comes from above and for revealing Your will in my life each day. All praise and glory to You! In Jesus' name, Amen.

 Share your thoughts about this devotional at **aophomeschooling.com/268**

The Great Pretender

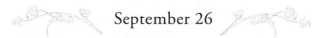

September 26

"Neither is there any creature that is not manifest in his sight: but all things are naked and opened unto the eyes of him with whom we have to do" (Hebrews 4:13).

Someone has once said that children can see right through you. If you doubt, watch as you attempt to teach your children or a class of young people. If you are nervous, scared, or unprepared, they will quickly take advantage of your weakness.

Your credibility as a homeschool teacher will also be compromised when you pretend you know the answers to all the questions your children ask. Admitting you don't know and saying, "Let's find the answer together," will hold "more stock" than pretending.

God knows when you are pretending with Him as well. You may try to hide behind righteous actions, but He can see the condition of your heart. Christ had much to say about the Pharisee hypocrites of His day when He was here on earth. He rebuked them by saying, "Woe to you!" and called them "white sepulchres" who were clean on the outside but not on the inside. He condemned them for their pretending.

What about you? Are you pretending today? Do you change your speech or actions depending on whom you are with? God can see right through you. He knows your heart and what you really think. What He desires is your broken heart instead of your false worship. "The sacrifices of God are a broken spirit: a broken and a contrite heart, O God, thou wilt not despise" (Psalm 51:17).

Heavenly Father, forgive me for thinking I am righteous because of my actions. I know You paid the price on the cross for my sins, and without Your forgiveness, all my deeds are as filthy rags. Help me to be real today and truly worship You. In Jesus' name, Amen.

Share your thoughts about this devotional at **aophomeschooling.com/269**

Divine Guidance

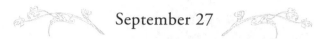

September 27

"In the hidden part thou shalt make me to know wisdom" (Psalm 51:6b).

If ever a parent needed the wisdom of Solomon to resolve disputes, it's a homeschooling parent. Since we live with our families 24/7, we face more instances of sibling conflict than other families. Unfortunately, homeschooled children are no different than any other children and will fight over the most trivial things. Like Solomon, many times you're forced to stand in judgment as you physically separate two children who are arguing. Worst of all, there's no teacher's guide or answer key to give you the helpful information you need to resolve problems. Applying the right discipline to correct your child's behavior requires discernment from the Holy Spirit and wisdom from God's perfect curriculum—the Bible.

Wisdom isn't only needed for resolving disputes while homeschooling. It's also necessary in every aspect of the Christian life. Daily, we face problems, issues, and temptations that require divine knowledge in making the right decision or response. How do we know when we're relying on our own "smarts" or actually following God's divine wisdom? James 3:17 tells us the answer: "But the wisdom that is from above is first pure, then peaceable, gentle, and easy to be intreated, full of mercy and good fruits, without partiality, and without hypocrisy."

Does self-ambition or jealousy control your decision-making, or have you discovered God's true wisdom for making godly choices? Whether you are giving your homeschoolers guidance or seeking help for yourself, God's wisdom will always take you in the right direction. Best of all, His wisdom is readily available to anyone who will humble himself to ask for it. "If any of you lack wisdom, let him ask of God, that giveth to all men liberally" (James 1:5).

Father, forgive me for trusting in my own intelligence when facing life's problems. Please give me Your wisdom today for all the decisions I need to make. In Jesus' name, Amen.

 Share your thoughts about this devotional at **aophomeschooling.com/**270

The Ongoing Battle

Is homeschooling here to stay? According to recent statistics, over two million children are homeschooled in the United States. Organized state associations, local support groups, and Internet forums, blogs, and websites give homeschoolers a sense of security that the public accepts home education as a viable educational alternative. Even Justice Clarence Thomas of the U.S. Supreme Court listed homeschooling as a viable educational option in a ruling in Morse v. Frederick.

However, those who oppose homeschooling are still alive and well. Like Tobiah and Sanballat's opposition to Nehemiah's rebuilding of Jerusalem's wall (Nehemiah 6), there are those who war daily against homeschooling and its philosophy. In case you doubt this fact, let me share some comments I've recently read on blogs about homeschooling:

• The education of our country's children is too important to be left in the hands of their parents.

• The idea that only the parent can teach the child and abandon the public education system is normally the sign of a deeply threatened, controlling personality.

• There are more kids doing this homeschooling stuff than ever before. How can they ever compete in the modern world when they grow up with strict brainwashing and medieval attitudes?

• All homeschooling will do is guarantee your kids are as stupid as you are.

Christians, too, must realize our war with Satan never ceases. Until Christ returns, we will face daily battles against evil. We may think that once we've received Jesus as our Savior, we'll never deal with adversity again. However, nothing is further from the truth. In 1 Peter 5:8, we are warned to "Be sober, be vigilant; because your adversary the devil, as a roaring lion, walketh about, seeking whom he may devour."

Although Christ has already defeated sin and death, we must earnestly stand against the wiles of the devil to remain victorious in our Christian life. Like the opponents of homeschooling, we must be aware that Satan is ever out to destroy us. Only as we stand strong in God's truths and the Holy Spirit's power will we be able to overcome evil with good. "Finally, my brethren, be strong in the Lord, and in the power of his might. Put on the whole armour of God, that ye may be able to stand against the wiles of the devil" (Ephesians 6:10-11).

Lord, thank You for the victory won on the cross. Teach me to walk in Your truth and power that I might stand against Satan and his lies. In the mighty name of Jesus, Amen.

Dry Times

September 29

Have you ever experienced those moments during your homeschooling year when creativity seems to have shriveled? You know your lessons, but the inspiration on how to make them fun has dried up. Your children have already done the suggested activities in your teacher manuals, and they need something new. You try to think of what to do, but the ideas are just not there.

The only way to find that creativity again is to go the "Creator." Jesus has the market on creative genius! "For by him were all things created, that are in heaven, and that are in earth, visible and invisible, whether they be thrones, or dominions, or principalities, or powers: all things were created by him, and for him" (Colossians 1:16).

The Holy Spirit can also help you tap into the "juices" that will make your homeschooling day exciting again—divine inspiration custom-made for your children and you. "But the Comforter, which is the Holy Ghost, whom the Father will send in my name, he shall teach you all things" (John 14:26a).

Lord, thank You for being such a loving, creative God. I humbly come to You today and ask for Your help with homeschooling. Show me what to do and how to teach, so my children will learn what they need to know. In Jesus' name, Amen.

 Share your thoughts about this devotional at **aophomeschooling.com/272**

Playing Hookie

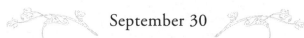

September 30

Does staying under the warm sheets sound appealing to you this morning? Would you like to sleep in and then take the day off to get caught up with all the housework? After all, chores would get done a lot faster with four pairs of little hands to help.

I Corinthians 15:58 says, "Therefore, my beloved brethren, be ye stedfast, unmoveable, always abounding in the work of the Lord, forasmuch as ye know that your labour is not in vain in the Lord." As a homeschool mom, some days you just don't feel like having school. Being super mom lost its novelty a long time ago, and you would just like to have your house be cleaned, organized, and feeling like a "home" again instead of a cluttered schoolroom.

God calls us to obedience in all areas of our life, including homeschooling. As much as you want to check homeschooling off your list today, don't. Your children's future depends on your daily discipline of placing homeschooling as a priority. Dirt and clutter will always return, but not the opportunities to teach your children. God is waiting for you to get up and get going. Be steadfast and throw those covers off. "And whatsoever ye do, do it heartily, as to the Lord, and not unto men" (Colossians 3:23).

Lord, forgive me for not staying focused on what I should do today. Strengthen me to resist Satan's temptation of doing other tasks before our homeschooling. In Jesus' name, Amen.

Share your thoughts about this devotional at aophomeschooling.com/273

I Quit!

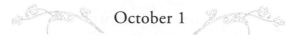

Now that you have homeschooled for a few months, are you finding difficulty in staying motivated? Is homeschooling not quite what you expected—too much work? Giving up is not the answer; giving in to the Lord is. "Knowing this, that the trying of your faith worketh patience. But let patience have her perfect work, that ye may be perfect and entire, wanting nothing" (James 1:3-4).

Homeschool parents don't always realize they are attending classes each day just like their children. God's assignments may not be on a computer on in a workbook, but they are just as real and challenging. The basic courses of Patience for Parents, Forgiveness Forever, Endurance 101, and Sacrificial Servanthood cause us to grow more Christlike in our actions. We study the Scriptures and look for answers to new questions we face each day. We pray at test time, hoping to pass. We pray for God to grade on a curve, or at least to allow a retake.

God knows what He is doing. Both you and your children are being "schooled" at home. Together you will learn all the lessons of life He has prepared for you. Hang in there—it's always too soon to quit! "But let patience have her perfect work, that ye may be perfect and entire, wanting nothing" (vs. 4).

Father, I don't know if I have what it takes to keep homeschooling. Stretch me Lord! Help me see those areas in my life that are slowing me down and causing me to stumble. Thank You for all You've done for me on the cross. Give me the strength and wisdom to keep going.
In Jesus' name, Amen.

Speed Kills

Timed reading tests for comprehension were a killer for my homeschooled children. They really disliked this part of their curriculum. No matter how hard they tried, they always seemed to miss one or two questions because they were not able to read the entire story within the allotted time. My children found timed reading tests quite frustrating because they wanted to get every question correct.

Teaching our children to speed read and retain information quickly is a necessity in our fast-paced lifestyles. Society seems to be in a hurry. We hurry to eat at fast-food restaurants, speed in our cars to work and activities, and quickly surf through scores of Internet information or television programs.

There is one thing in life, however, you cannot hurry—a mature faith in the Lord. Spiritual growth cannot be sped up by the wants of any person. God simply grows us at His own rate, watered and nurtured by the Holy Spirit and His Word. No amount of practice or preparation can cause the process to go any faster. His utmost concern is for us to be rooted and grounded to withstand the storms of life when they come. "As ye have therefore received Christ Jesus the Lord, so walk ye in him: Rooted and built up in him, and stablished in the faith" (Colossians 2:6-7a).

Are you in a hurry right now? Is this quick devotional the only time you have planned to spend with the Lord? If so, slow down! Enjoy God's presence. Let the Holy Spirit fill you and teach you from the Word so you can get the answers right on the tests you will face today.

Jesus, forgive me for hurrying from one thing to the next. I know I need to spend more time with You. Slow me down, Lord, so I discover the strength and wisdom You have to give.
In Your name, Amen.

Two Are Better Than One

The majority of the teaching in homeschooling falls on the mother. She is the one who usually stays home and oversees the schoolwork. But what about dads? What is their responsibility in the homeschool process? How involved do they need to be, really? What most homeschooling moms long for is a team teacher in their husband. Teaching at least one or two subject areas or even helping with daily chores, such as washing clothes or making supper is a big help.

Homeschooling is much more effective when husbands team up with their wives to share in the responsibilities. The Bible says, "Two are better than one; because they have a good reward for their labour" (Ecclesiastes 4:9). Both parents are helped by this team-teaching approach to homeschooling. The children, too, enjoy the diversity of more than one teacher to make learning fun!

There is strength to be found in marriage and life with the team approach, too. In fact, God goes on to tell us in Ecclesiastes 4:10-12 that if either of them falls, the one will lift up his companion. Two are able to resist, and a cord of three strands is not quickly torn apart. With God, you, and your husband, you will not only succeed at homeschooling, but also at facing the responsibilities of life.

Father, thank You for the power You provide in working together. Show us how to pull together as husband and wife to make homeschooling the best it can be for our family. In Jesus' name, Amen.

Homeschool Tattletales

October 4

"Hatred stirreth up strifes: but love covereth all sins" (Proverbs 10:12).

My son could hardly wait to talk to me one day during our school time. I could tell he had something important to say and was anxiously waiting to share the news. As soon as the words came out of his mouth, I knew where the conversation was headed. Midway through his first sentence, I interrupted, and a surprised look crossed his face. I asked, "Are you telling on your sister for a particular reason? No one likes a tattletale."

Homeschool children are no different from other children about wanting to "spill the beans" about someone else. By nature, they have a strong sense of right and wrong but often misuse this sense by tattling to make their siblings look bad. Parents must teach their children to confess their own sins as easily and learn to help others in their mistakes instead of condemning them. "And above all things have fervent charity among yourselves: for charity shall cover the multitude of sins" (1 Peter 4:8).

Romans 13:10 says, "Love worketh no ill to his neighbour." Do you find keeping a "juicy" piece of news to yourself difficult? Do you think your responsibility is to expose the failings of others in order to make things better for yourself? Here are two questions you can ask yourself to gauge your actions to see if you are telling or tattling: Do I need to share this information to keep someone from being hurt physically? Am I sharing this news to get someone into trouble or out of trouble?

Remember, love covers a multitude of sins. Ask God for wisdom to know how to help a brother rather than condemn him.

Father, show me how to be full of grace today toward someone who has made a mistake. Convict me of any self-righteousness and use me to lead this person back to You. In Jesus' name, Amen.

Share your thoughts about this devotional at **aophomeschooling.com/277**

Let's Play

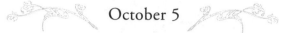

"The LORD thy God in the midst of thee is mighty; he will save, he will rejoice over thee with joy; he will rest in his love, he will joy over thee with singing" (Zephaniah 3:17).

The favorite words of every young girl or boy are "Do you want to go play?" What home-schooled child can resist an enthusiastic mother or father who wants to ride bike, hide in tree houses, or dig in sand boxes? Our children love leaving the academic schoolwork behind and spending time together just having fun!

Can you let go of adult responsibilities to have a moment's fun on your child's level? Let your children push you until you're dizzy on a merry-go-round, skip stones on the edge of a lake, play dolls or cowboys, or make tents together out of blankets and the living room chairs on a rainy afternoon. Leave the dirty dishes and unmade beds and go play a board game, work a puzzle, walk outside, throw a frisbee, or swing on the swings. There is still a child in all of us who knows how to play!

God in heaven wants us to have fun being His child, too. Although we need to reverence our Holy God, serious and somber-faced Christians sometimes lose the joy and excitement of living for Jesus. Psalm 17:8 says we are the apple of God's eye and He delights in us. When was the last time you really had fun being a Christian? Let the message of God's love and salvation in Christ cause you to rejoice again and sing praises today! "O come, let us sing unto the LORD: let us make a joyful noise to the rock of our salvation. Let us come before his presence with thanksgiving, and make a joyful noise unto him with psalms. For the LORD is a great God, and a great King above all gods" (Psalm 95:1-3).

Jesus, thank You for reaching down in Your greatness to love and forgive me. The joy of knowing I am loved by You fills me with such happiness. Living for You is so much fun! In Your name I pray, Amen.

Totally Lost

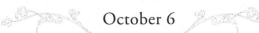

October 6

Some days, even the best homeschool teacher has trouble communicating a lesson. Whether you're teaching equations in algebra or diagramming sentences in grammar, a change begins to occur in your child when he does not comprehend the information you are covering. You've seen the look—a blank stare, a squint, eyebrows up in the form of a question mark. The body begins to fidget and unintelligible utterances come from his mouth. He doesn't have a clue what you are talking about and is totally lost. What are you going to do?

When I was new to homeschooling, I walked away in frustration or assumed my child was not paying attention. I tried repeating the same information or using a louder voice. With infinite variations, the battle went on until I realized the problem was not with my child; it was with me. I was the teacher, and I had failed to teach. I needed to try again and approach the information from a different angle—a new learning style or additional visual aids.

Thankfully, God doesn't lose His temper or walk away from us when teaching life's lessons. When we begin our fussing routine or get that lost look, He gently wraps His arms around us and takes us back to where we last understood. Lovingly, He leads us to godly counsel from Christian friends or words of wisdom from the Scriptures. The Holy Spirit customizes each particular lesson until we grow "in the grace and knowledge of our Lord and Saviour Jesus Christ" (2 Peter 3:18).

Do you feel lost today? Let the Lord guide you back to where you should be. "Trust in the LORD with all thine heart; and lean not unto thine own understanding. In all thy ways acknowledge him, and he shall direct thy paths" (Proverbs 3:5-6).

Jesus, thank You for always knowing where to find me. Without You, I am totally lost in teaching my children. Show our family where we need to be and how to keep our eyes on You. In Your name, Amen.

Share your thoughts about this devotional at aophomeschooling.com/279

Mrs. Clean

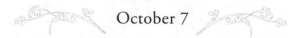

October 7

"I can do all things through Christ which strengtheneth me" (Philippians 4:13).

Inside the house, the kitchen sink was full of dishes, and the laundry baskets were piled high with dirty clothes. The floors were full of crumbs, and the windows had enough fingerprints to fill the files of the FBI. Outside, the lawn looked like a herd of horses needed to chew it down, and the children's toys were scattered from one end of the farm to the other. Company was scheduled to arrive for supper, and the meal was not yet prepared. I laughed to myself, wondering which of these tasks I would actually accomplish in addition to our homeschooling day.

Thinking about all the work made me tired and unable to even know where to start. Looking to God, I felt Him gently urge me to begin. I did and somehow a miracle began. The day became supernatural, and I literally felt like angels were working with me to get every job accomplished. There were no interruptions, no accidents, no fights, nothing was lost, and nothing broke. I flew from one chore to the next, while keeping an enthusiastic smile and teaching my children their lessons. I couldn't believe the amount of work I accomplished that day, and I've never had another one quite like it.

Sometimes the numerous issues in our spiritual walk also seem daunting. We wonder how a family member will ever be saved, why we keep falling into the same old sins, and if we can ever forgive our mother-in-law's thoughtless remarks. Temptations and trials attempt to render us impotent. We become discouraged and give up in despair before we ever begin to live for the Lord. You don't need to live under the weight of sin and pain. God sent His son Jesus to deliver us from a defeated life. Jesus arose and left an empty grave as proof that we to have access to the same mighty power that raised Him from the dead (Ephesians 1:19). All your burdens can be lifted by the miracle of His grace. Is life too heavy to bear right now? Jesus says, "Come unto me, all ye that labour and are heavy laden, and I will give you rest" (Matthew 11:28).

Father, some days I wonder if I can take one more problem. Thank You for giving me the strength to bear the weight of my discouraging difficulties. Help me begin to fight the spiritual battles around me in the power of Your name. In Jesus' name, Amen.

I Am Not Ashamed

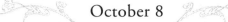

October 8

"Whosoever therefore shall confess me before men, him will I confess also before my Father which is in heaven. But whosoever shall deny me before men, him will I also deny before my Father which is in heaven" (Matthew 10:32-33).

Most parents—homeschooling or not—have experienced a time when their children were embarrassed to be with them. The sting of this rejection can hurt our feelings, but if we are to succeed as homeschooling parents, we must move beyond our feelings. We must address the issue of why our child is embarrassed and not become defensive or retaliatory in our response.

The apostle Peter had to suffer the consequences of a broken heart and a guilty conscience when he feared to be associated with Christ. Three times he blatantly rejected the accusations that he was one of Christ's disciples. The roaster's crow echoed in his ears as he ran away in shame after cursing and swearing, saying, "I know not this man of whom ye speak" (Mark 14:71).

How about you? Are you embarrassed and afraid to say you are a child of God in certain groups of people? Do you sheepishly keep silent when you should speak up for Christ? Do you fearfully restrain from sharing the gospel message that may bring salvation to someone who is lost? Don't let Satan deceive you into denying Christ because of embarrassment or fear. The light of Christ needs to be shining brightly in your life and not dimmed by denying your Lord. May you be as bold as the apostle Paul who proclaimed, "For I am not ashamed of the gospel of Christ: for it is the power of God unto salvation to every one that believeth" (Romans 1:16a).

Heavenly Father, forgive me for letting Satan rob me of the greatest privilege I have—saying I am Your child. Help me today to stand up for You and Your Word. I love You Lord, and let me live today boldly proclaiming You as my Lord and Savior. In Your Son's name, Amen.

Share your thoughts about this devotional at **aophomeschooling.com/281**

In the Distance

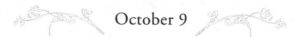

Today was especially difficult as a homeschooling mom. I was beginning to believe my three-year-old daughter would be wearing diapers until she was twenty-one. I was also frustrated with my son's lack of understanding fractions. I was ready to give up and let him learn to measure in whole numbers for the rest of his life. My life seemed stuck in the "forever" of this time. My children would never move beyond this point in their education, and I would never do anything different as a woman. Each day would be a repeat of the last with home-schooling, laundry, cooking, and church responsibilities. Would there ever be an end to this seemingly endless repetition?

As I loaded the children into the car for another trip to the grocery store, God spoke to my heart in a simple, but powerful way. Looking into the side mirrors for traffic, I suddenly noticed the words written on the glass: "Objects in mirror are closer than they appear!" God was showing me that the end to this homeschooling period of my life was closer than it appeared!

As time went on, I discovered that life was a series of transitions—chapters that are opened, read, and then closed for the next to begin. What chapter of your life are you in as a home-schooling parent—babies, toddlers, teenagers, empty nest? Things will not always remain the same. Enjoy the moment you are in now to the fullest. God is with you and knows exactly what you should be doing. "To every thing there is a season, and a time to every purpose under the heaven" (Ecclesiastes 3:1).

Father, thank You for life and each experience You provide. Help me take today and make this time a blessing to my family. Show me how to faithfully continue homeschooling and look forward to every opportunity to teach my children. In Jesus' name, Amen.

Teacher or Mom

October 10

As much as I enjoyed homeschooling my children, there were days when I longed to be only a mother. Moms have the fun job of displaying tenderness by kissing away hurts and telling their children they are wonderful, but God had an additional task for me. He also wanted me to be my children's school teacher. I had to take out the red pen and correct their papers to challenge them to study harder. Finding loving ways to critique their work and push them was not always easy. My children were forced to respect and relate to me both as mother and teacher.

I feared this dual role would create an emotional distance between my children and me. As the homeschooling years went on, I realized those fears were unfounded. The relationship I had with my children as mother gave me opportunities to minister to their personal issues and concerns. The relationship I had as their teacher provided moments for counseling college and career choices, editing job resumes, and more. I became the resource my children went to first when they needed help, and we grew even closer.

God's multiple roles in our Christian walk amaze me, too. He is our loving Abba Father, Savior, best friend, and Holy God. He commands our fear, devotion, love, and respect—all the while teaching us to grow closer to Him. He is the first person we should run to for our needs. He is both a gentle Shepherd and a jealous God who loves us with passionate, unconditional love. Praise Him today for being your heavenly Father and all you need!

Heavenly Father, thank You for the many ways You bless me each day! I worship You as my Holy God, adore You as my Father, thank You for being my Savior, and treasure You as my friend. Help me to enjoy Your love today and walk in the blessings You provide. In Jesus' name, Amen.

All Alone

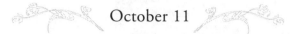

"Turn thee unto me, and have mercy upon me; for I am desolate and afflicted" (Psalm 25:16).

Is the feeling of loneliness hovering over you like a cloud today? Has homeschooling taken so much of your time that you haven't seen your friends for days? Do the piles of housework, schoolwork, and unfinished projects feel like a wall separating you from the rest of the world? Do you and your husband pass each day like two ships in the night? Do you wonder if anybody cares or even knows you are alive? Again, here you are facing another day of home-schooling all alone.

Oh, precious one, do you know how much you are loved by the Lord of the universe? He sees you right now where you are and is waiting for you to look at Him. He holds out His hands in love and says, "Stop crying, my child. I am here for you." He has bottled up your tears (Psalm 56:8) and desires to breathe strength into your heart. He wants you to crawl on His lap and wait for wisdom as He holds you in His arms of love (Isaiah 40:11).

Christ is no stranger to loneliness. Many times in the Scriptures He left His disciples to go pray in a place described as lonely or a desert (Luke 4:42). He knows what you are feeling today and wants to take your loneliness away. Don't allow loneliness to overwhelm you. Instead, let it push you into the arms of your loving Father. He is waiting to bless you and fill you with the drive to homeschool again.

Jesus, here I am—empty and nothing without You. Reveal Your mighty presence to me Lord, so I may walk in the strength of Your love. Drive the loneliness I feel away and let me rejoice in Your goodness. In Your name I pray, Amen.

Under the Bed

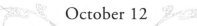

October 12

I'm sure I wasn't the first mother who had to deal with her child's deception while homeschooling. One day I found toys that were supposed to have been picked up and put away correctly pushed under my son's bed. I sat down on the bed and wished I could escape the correction that needed to take place in my child's life. The mess under the bed would be much easier to ignore than dealing with my child. Thankfully, at least this deception could be fixed, even though the time needed to discipline would rob teaching time from our homeschooling day.

Many years ago, Jacob's deception couldn't be fixed when he fooled his father Isaac into blessing him instead of his brother Esau. At his mother's prompting, Jacob went the full length in deceiving his father by feeling, smelling, sounding, and acting like Esau as he prepared his father's favorite meal. Jacob walked away, stealing the blessing of his father and the firstborn birthright intended for Esau (Genesis 27). Esau anguished in his heart that no blessing was left for him (Hebrews 12:16-17).

However, it was many years before that blessing was enjoyed. In fear of his brother's wrath, Jacob fled to another country and was alienated from his family. After working seven long years for his wife, Jacob experienced Laban's deception when he substituted his daughter Leah for Rachel at the wedding. He suffered an additional seven years of working for his father-in-law before he was allowed to marry Rachel, the woman he loved.

Deception always works that way. What seems to be an immediate reward turns out to be an on-going burden. Are you trying to make your life easier by hiding things "under the bed?" Do you think no one sees the deceptive patterns you've allowed to take over your life, such as little white lies, taking advantage of the goodness of others, or making others look bad so you can get ahead? Unlike Isaac, God sees and knows what you are doing—He isn't fooled. Will you confess and repent today and let God discipline you to fix the mess you have made? He's the only One who can.

Lord, search my heart and reveal those things that are dishonoring to You. Forgive me for allowing deception into my life. Help me recognize the temptation when it comes and stand in the power of Your name to fight this form of lying. In Jesus' name, Amen.

Sick Days

Because of sickness, the winter of 1988 was the worst interruption to our homeschooling days. Chicken pox hit our family hard, and for one long month homeschooling was set aside as I worked to nurse my four children back to health. Every two weeks, one after another, my children fell ill and laid on the couch to recover. Every day was consumed with making healthy recipes, wiping runny noses, and finding activities for my children to occupy themselves while healing from the red, itching sores. Quarantined, I wondered, "Will I ever see the outside world again?"

In Leviticus 13, isolation was a remedy for leprosy for God's people. A priest would look for signs on the skin of people or on their articles of clothing that showed them to be unclean. Upon the priest's pronouncement, a person would be removed from the rest of the community until that person's body was healed (Leviticus 13:46).

Isolation can also bring healing as you face the sickness of sin in your life. Alone and free of distractions, you can hear the Holy Spirit gently nudging you to make changes that are necessary in your life. Healing and forgiveness from Christ renew your soul and restore a healthy relationship between you and the Lord. You are able to face the world again living a Christ-honoring life. "If a man therefore purge himself from these, he shall be a vessel unto honour, sanctified, and meet for the master's use, and prepared unto every good work" (2 Timothy 2:21).

Has the sin of self-pity, impatience, or greed spotted your walk with the Lord and made you sick? If so, isolate yourself immediately and go to your healing high priest—Jesus. He has promised to wash us and cleanse us if we come to him in repentance. "If we confess our sins, he is faithful and just to forgive us our sins, and to cleanse us from all unrighteousness" (1 John 1:9).

Heavenly Father, forgive me for the things I have allowed to dirty my life. Wash me today that I might be a vessel fit for Your service, which will bring honor to Your name. In Jesus' name, Amen.

Best Friends

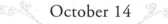
"A friend loveth at all times" (Proverbs 17:17a).

Have you ever watched young girls interact? They can be the best of friends one moment and dire enemies the next. Because of petty differences and easily hurt feelings, young girls are notorious for having a new "best friend" each week. My homeschooled daughter found it difficult to keep up with these fluctuations in her friends. What she wanted most was an "Anne of Green Gables" kindred spirit in whom she could confide (Philippians 2:20).

The Bible gives us a great example of true friendship—Jonathan and David. Willing to lay down their lives for each other, they displayed a standard for us to follow. The example of their loyal friendship shows what is needed to be a friend and keep a friend. "And Jonathan said to David, Go in peace, forasmuch as we have sworn both of us in the name of the LORD, saying, The LORD be between me and thee, and between my seed and thy seed for ever" (1 Samuel 20:42a).

Are you faithful to your friends? Do you work at making and keeping relationships alive even during your busy homeschooling days? Don't forsake the treasure of a true friend! Schedule time into your homeschool day this week to bless the friends God has so graciously given you. Remember, too, to schedule time for your best friend—the One who sticketh closer than a brother—Jesus! "A man that hath friends must shew himself friendly: and there is a friend that sticketh closer than a brother" (Proverbs 18:24).

Jesus, thank You for all the wonderful people You have brought into my life. Help me to treat each one as a special gift from You. Thank You for being my "best friend" and giving me the Holy Spirit to remember all You have said. In Your name, Amen.

Four-legged Classmates

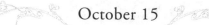

"A righteous man regardeth the life of his beast" (Proverbs 12:10a).

Is there anything sadder than watching a dog say goodbye to his favorite boy or girl as he or she goes off to school? Every day countless pets are separated from their young masters as they leave for school, but not so with homeschoolers. We are the fortunate ones who enjoy the privilege of having four-legged classmates to comfort us and make us laugh.

Since pets have always been a part of our family, making them a part of our homeschool was only natural. Morning and evening chores that involved our pets were incorporated into our children's daily schedule. To make up for any work involved with their care, they experienced the advantages of sharing a good book with a warm kitty or playing together with an effervescent puppy. Only during the winter, did our children complain as they faced the cold weather to care for their furry friends.

Animals are not only special to us, but they are important to God as well. The pleasure of naming each of God's creatures was given to Adam (Genesis 2:19-20). After the flood, God made the covenant of the rainbow as a sign to both man and His creatures (Genesis 9:9-13). God also used His creatures to accomplish His specific will—a donkey talked to Balaam, ravens fed Elijah, and a great fish rerouted the rebellious prophet, Jonah.

Do you set a good example for your children in taking care of your family's pets? They need more than food and water—daily grooming, exercise, and love are essential to their well being. God values all of His creation, including animals. He requires good stewardship of these creatures and has entrusted their care to you. Keep your four-legged students attending class with your children. Remember, "a righteous man regardeth the life of his beast" (Proverbs 12:10)!

Lord, thank You for the animals You bring into our lives that give so much entertainment and joy. You are such a creative and loving God to think of so many different creatures! Challenge us today to be responsible and not neglect the care of our pets. In Jesus' name, Amen.

Compared to What?

October 16

My youngest son's discouraged face told me there was more to his frustration in receiving a "C" on his spelling test. I saw there was deep emotion waiting to be expressed. I offered a listening ear and a patient hug and he began to share, "I'm not as smart as everyone else in this family." He "knew" he wasn't as good as his siblings, and he wanted to be an "A" student, too. His broken heart reflected my own childhood experience with insensitive teachers comparing my performance in school to high-achieving, older siblings.

Comparing your children can be dangerous: "But they measuring themselves by themselves, and comparing themselves among themselves, are not wise" (2 Corinthians 10:12b). God has uniquely gifted each of your homeschooled children and values each one. Encourage them to find their place in the family and then in the world. A sense of self-worth is developed as your children find areas in which God created them to excel. My son's niche was finally found in math, music, and fishing. Hands down, neither his brother nor his sisters could top him in those areas.

How many times a day do you compare yourself to others? Do you wish you looked like someone else, had her home or money, or were as smart as she? God knew this was a problem for all mankind when He gave His commandment, "Thou shalt not covet thy neighbor's house, thou shalt not covet thy neighbor's wife, nor his manservant, nor his maidservant, nor his ox, nor his ass, nor any thing that is thy neighbor's" (Exodus 20:17). Compared to Christ, we all fall short of the glory of God. Let Him lead you into His perfect will for your life and find the joyful niche He has created just for you. There is no better place to be for now and eternity!

Lord, thank You for giving me significance in this life. Help me remember I have value because of the great price that was paid for me on the cross. I choose to look at You today instead of comparing myself to others. In Jesus' name, Amen.

 Share your thoughts about this devotional at aophomeschooling.com/289

Wisdom from Above

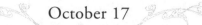

October 17

"The fear of the LORD is the beginning of wisdom: a good understanding have all they that do his commandments: his praise endureth for ever" (Psalms 111:10).

We had just spent another day going over the practice questions that might be used in the ACT college entrance tests. My son was getting tired of the extra school work required to prepare for this important test, but I ignored his grumblings. After all, didn't he know that he had to be the smartest child there? I had high expectations to say the least.

All homeschooling parents desire their child to excel in intelligence. We constantly worry and second guess whether they are learning what they should. We compare our children to the children of fellow homeschoolers and those taught in a school. We may even go to the extent of having our children take regular achievement tests—all in the desire to prove our children are learning. All this comparing and testing may prove our children are smart, but does this testing show they are wise?

King Solomon in the Old Testament is described as "wiser than all men" in 1 Kings 4:31. He spoke over 3,000 proverbs and 1,000 songs. People from all nations came to hear his wisdom, and his discernment was like the sand on the seashore (1 Kings 4:29-34). Even the Queen of Sheba was amazed at Solomon's wisdom and said how blessed his men and servants were who heard him speak. God's Word tells us in 1 Kings 3:5-15 that Solomon's great wisdom was given as a gift from God. The Lord blessed Solomon because of his humility and desire to lead God's people. Solomon learned that "The fear of the Lord is the beginning of wisdom," which is true intelligence.

Do you think you're smart and you know all the answers? Do you figure out problems on your own and think your way is always the best way? Look up and be truly wise! God's wisdom is not according to this world. "Where is the wise? where is the scribe? where is the disputer of this world? hath not God made foolish the wisdom of this world? But God hath chosen the foolish things of the world to confound the wise; and God hath chosen the weak things of the world to confound the things which are mighty" (1 Corinthians 1:20, 27). Live in humble obedience to God and receive the true wisdom from above to pass the tests in life.

Lord, forgive me when I think I'm so smart. Your wisdom is what I need, not an earthly intelligence. Humble my heart today and teach me what I need to know. In Jesus' name, Amen.

Daily Reminders

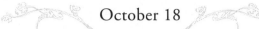

October 18

Brush your teeth, pick up your room, make your bed, do your chores, wash your hands, practice your piano, and take out the trash. The list of reminders we give our children each day goes on and on. Every day we remind our children to do things they should already know to do.

Homeschooling moms have the added task of spending countless hours reviewing rules and facts and reminding our children what they have already learned in school. Our children may attempt to fly through review lessons, thinking they "know it all," when in reality, they have forgotten the material learned. Many times they want to move on to new things and forget about the effort needed to review, review, review.

The Apostle Peter knew he needed to remind the new believers in Christ of the truths they had learned in 2 Peter 1:12: "Wherefore I will not be negligent to put you always in remembrance of these things, though ye know them, and be established in the present truth." Peter knew they needed to practice the truths they had learned and be reminded daily to be faithful to the One who had saved them—Jesus. Moral excellence and holiness were at stake, and he wanted these new believers to apply diligence in their faith. Peter was a great teacher and stirred them up by way of reminder (2 Peter 1:13).

What spiritual truths need to be stirred up today in your life? Have you forgotten to spend time with your first love—Jesus? Have you forgotten the power of praise to defeat a negative thought life? Do you remember to witness to the lost who need the Lord? Are you living expectantly, waiting for Christ's return? Open the Word of God today and let the Holy Spirit stir your heart to remember Christ's great love for you. "But the Comforter, which is the Holy Ghost, whom the Father will send in my name, he shall teach you all things, and bring all things to your remembrance, whatsoever I have said unto you" (John 14:26).

Lord, I confess my memory is not what it should be. Help me remember today the many blessings You have provided in the past and the truths that will keep my heart close to You. Thank You for being such a wonderful Savior! In Jesus' name, Amen.

Share your thoughts about this devotional at aophomeschooling.com/291

Out of Control

"The LORD is in his holy temple, the LORD's throne is in heaven: his eyes behold, his eyelids try, the children of men. The LORD trieth the righteous" (Psalm 11:4-5a).

Learning to drive in our "homeschool" driver's education class looked much different than the normal driving class most young people attended. Dad's job was to teach our children the laws and rules for operating a vehicle, but what he truly enjoyed was instructing them in driving safety. During his driver's education instruction, he showed our children how to steer back onto the road if one wheel slipped onto the shoulder, how to stop in an emergency without locking the brakes (this was before anti-lock brakes), and his favorite—driving in icy conditions.

Since our state had long winters, he especially focused on driving on icy roads. He took our children to a huge, abandoned parking lot and put the car into a spin (this resembled the effect of hitting a patch of ice on the road while driving). The panicked look that appeared at first on each of our children's faces was slowly erased as he showed them how to gently steer into the skid to correct the car's out-of-control path. Over and over they would practice this skill until it was mastered. Many years later, my oldest son's life was saved from a serious accident because of his father's thorough instruction.

Our heavenly Father's teaching methods in learning how to live safely in His care also involves repeated lessons. His Word says that He tests and tries us to refine us like gold (Proverbs 17:3). When our poor choices cause self-induced problems, our lives go into a skid. Gently, He shows us how to turn back to His Word to find the answers we need to straighten the out-of-control path we are on. Whether we have allowed ourselves to overspend, overeat, overwork, or participate in ungodly activities, God is able to teach us how to depend on the Holy Spirit to guide us safely back to Him. God's ultimate goal for us is to pass His "driver's course" and enjoy the freedom and safety of living in Jesus.

Is your life out of control? Are you off the "straight and narrow path" and headed for the ditch? If so, let the Lord take the wheel and gently steer you back to where you should be—your very life may depend on it. "Furthermore we have had fathers of our flesh which corrected us, and we gave them reverence: shall we not much rather be in subjection unto the Father of spirits, and live" (Hebrews 12:9)?

Father, forgive me for making so many choices that have put me on this path of destruction. Take my life and straighten me out before I cause more pain to You, myself, and others. In Jesus' name, Amen.

 Share your thoughts about this devotional at **aophomeschooling.com/292**

The Last Thing I Need

October 20

Learning not to give unsolicited advice to my homeschooled children was difficult as they were growing older. I usually went overboard in my explanations in case something would go wrong. I wanted to save them from failure, expense, and pain. However, I learned that some of the most amazing lessons are taught to our children when we wait to rescue them. As they struggle to find the correct answer or make the right decision, they are being prepared for a life led by the Lord.

Both Mary and Martha were looking for answers in their grief. Their brother Lazarus had died because Jesus had not arrived in time. Jesus could have gotten to Bethany much quicker than He did, but He chose to wait two extra days (John 11:6). Martha responded by telling the Lord that if He had been there, He could have saved her brother (John 11:21). When Christ said to roll away the stone of Lazarus' grave, Martha offered advice the Lord didn't need to hear a second time when she said, "Lord, by this time he stinketh: for he hath been dead four days" (John 11:39b). Martha's limited faith was being challenged to become an unlimited faith in Jesus. Christ proved He not only could heal the sick, but He was also able to raise someone from the dead.

Does your faith limit God in what He can or cannot do in your life? Are you willing to be still and know that He is God (Psalm 46:10)? God knows what He is doing, and the last thing He needs is your advice. He is waiting to see if you will trust and believe in Him for the impossible, instead of telling Him what to do. Will you trust Him today for the answers you need?

Lord, you are a great and mighty God who doesn't need my help or advice. Forgive me for telling You what to do and limiting what You want to do in my life. Help me today to trust in Your way and Your will. In Jesus' name, Amen.

Time for Church

October 21

"Not forsaking the assembling of ourselves together, as the manner of some is" (Hebrews 10:25).

On Sunday morning when you say, "It's time for church," what response do you get from your homeschooled children? Depending on the age of your children, those words bring a variety of responses. Teenagers roll over and want to sleep another two hours, elementary-age children would rather play and dislike getting ready, and toddlers are too young to care, but require extra effort in preparing diaper bags.

The Lord told the children of Israel to remember to set aside a day to worship when He gave His people the Ten Commandments in Exodus 20:8-11. One day of the week was to be set apart to keep it holy. Throughout church history, this practice has continued. But today you would not recognize Sunday as being any different from any other day of the week.

What does Sunday look like at your house? Do you find yourself skipping church regularly? Do you take advantage of "half-sick" children and use them for an excuse to stay home? Is getting everyone to church on Sunday mornings too big a fight? Don't give in and take the easy way out! There is a special blessing waiting for you today as a corporate group of believers: "For where two or three are gathered together in my name, there am I in the midst of them" (Matthew 18:20). God is waiting to meet with you and delights in your praises and worship. Don't use this day for shopping or getting caught up on chores. Both you and your children need to learn to discipline your lives. "I was glad when they said unto me, Let us go into the house of the LORD" (Psalm 122:1).

Lord, forgive me for being lazy. Getting my family to church is so difficult at times. Help me organize this Saturday and prepare to meet You this Sunday with my children. In Jesus' name, Amen.

Divine Lessons

October 22

"Beloved, believe not every spirit, but try the spirits whether they are of God" (1 John 4:1a).

Homeschooling that is led and guided by the Holy Spirit proves to be the most successful. Prayerfully choosing curriculum, daily schedules, lesson plans, field trips, extra-curricular activities, or even books used for reading or literature class allows God to influence your children's education. God is the best at customizing our children's education because He knows the future plans for each of their lives (Jeremiah 29:11).

God is also the best at customizing your daily spiritual lessons. He wants you to succeed in your walk with Him, as well as homeschooling. In order to make sure you are listening to the right advice, He tells you to "test" the spirits to find out whether or not they are of God. Anything that does not confess Jesus Christ is not from God (1 John 4:2-3). God will never lead you to do something or teach something contrary to the Word of God. He uses other mature Christians to guide and instruct you, as well as circumstances, to help point you in the right direction.

God's divine lessons are waiting for you today: "But the Comforter, which is the Holy Ghost, whom the Father will send in my name, he shall teach you all things" (John 14:26a). The Lord is looking for those whose heart is completely His (2 Chronicles 16:9a), so He can use them to bring glory to His name. Do you desire a deeper walk with God? Then start obeying His Word. In obedience, He will show you more of Himself to give you the most exciting life you could ever imagine. "He that hath my commandments, and keepeth them, he it is that loveth me: and he that loveth me shall be loved of my Father, and I will love him, and will manifest myself to him" (John 14:21).

Father, thank You for sending the Holy Spirit to guide me. Speak to me today and fill me with Your Spirit. Show me how to live a life that will glorify Your name. In Jesus' name, Amen.

Share your thoughts about this devotional at **aophomeschooling.com/295**

Paralyzed by Fear

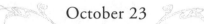

October 23

"For God hath not given us the spirit of fear; but of power, and of love, and of a sound mind" (2 Timothy 1:7).

"I'm never going back to the mountains again until we have a better car," I stated resolutely to my husband. This trip was the last time I would risk getting stranded because of car problems. Our homeschool field trips to isolated mountain areas in Colorado would just have to wait until we could afford a new vehicle.

Many months went by before the urge to see God's wilderness drove us to try again. With the same car, our family ventured out with a picnic lunch, hoping for a wonderful day of hiking in the woods. As we headed west of Denver, I noticed the engine beginning to sputter. Cars were flying past us as we slowed to almost a crawl on the busy interstate. Both my husband and I wanted to cry as we pulled over again to the side of the road.

Together we said a quick prayer and tried to reassure our four children that all would be well. Opening the hood, my divinely-inspired husband removed the air cleaner from the top of the engine and plugged the hole with a handkerchief to prevent dirt from being sucked into the engine. Restarting the car and pulling back into traffic, we unbelievably regained normal speed. For the remainder of the trip, we had no problems. The easy fix to our car's high-altitude problem mocked me as I thought of all the trips I had forfeited because of fear.

What blessings from God are you missing today because of fear? Are you afraid to fellowship in large crowds, travel to see your family by car, plane, or boat, or enjoy new experiences because of the unknown? God promises in Proverbs 3:25-26, "Be not afraid of sudden fear, neither of the desolation of the wicked, when it cometh. For the LORD shall be thy confidence, and shall keep thy foot from being taken." God is in control and you do not need to be afraid. As Christ calmed the storm for the disciples in the boat, He is more than able to protect you from unknown problems. Will you give your fears to Him today and receive His blessings?

Lord, so many times I miss Your best because I am afraid. Please walk with me through these fears and help me see You in every situation. In Jesus' name, Amen.

Gray Areas

October 24

The quiet time I was experiencing with the Lord before my homeschooling day overwhelmed me with conviction. I watched as the morning sun's rays attempted to burn off the gray cloud of fog that had settled as a blanket over our farm. The cool night air had met the warmth of the earth, and the resulting fog was locked in a battle with the sun's rays. As the strength of the sun's light grew more brilliant, the lesson God was teaching me also became clearer.

The heat from the problems of homeschooling during the last few days had met with the coldness of my disobedient, spiritual heart. Thankfulness had been replaced with grumbling and complaining about all the work I had to do. "Gray areas" of not knowing God's will had formed like a cloud and I was confused. I attempted to justify my sinful actions to God based on the world's standards. In the valley of ungratefulness, the foggy cloud was encompassing more of my life. I was beginning to feel completely lost. Then God's rays of truth in Philippians 2:13-14 burned away the cloud, "For it is God which worketh in you both to will and to do of his good pleasure. Do all things without murmurings and disputings."

Do you see gray clouds forming on the horizon of your life? God's Word is the light that will clear up those foggy areas. "Thy word is a lamp unto my feet, and a light unto my path" (Psalm 119:105). As you read His Word, you will discover that God is light, and in Him there is no darkness at all (1 John 1:5).

Lord, your Word is such a blessing for finding my way! Thank You for gently showing me Your truth and exposing those areas of sin that cloud my life. Help me stay close to the light of Your love today. In the name of Jesus, Amen.

Grandma Goodbyes

October 25

As Grandpa and Grandma drove out our yard to return to their home nine hours away, my daughter sat looking out the living room window with tears in her eyes. Each time they came to visit, I dreaded the day they were scheduled to leave. The emotional heartache my young daughter experienced made concentrating on homeschooling for the next several days difficult.

The disciples knew such a heartache when Christ was arrested in the garden, put on trial, and crucified. Peter and John, along with the others, wept bitterly when the One they had loved and followed was gone. Even though He had told them He would rise on the third day, they thought Jesus was no longer in their life. They wondered if they would ever see Him again.

Do you ever feel like God has left you, especially in your homeschooling? Do you think everyone has abandoned you to figure out how to teach on your own. Don't let Satan's lies fool you! Jesus has promised, "For he hath said, I will never leave thee, nor forsake thee" (Hebrews 13:5b). God is lovingly watching and interceding in your life. He knows what you need to teach your children each day and will provide all you need to do it. Keep trusting in Him. Someday He will even be coming back for you, too. "Let not your heart be troubled: ye believe in God, believe also in me. In my Father's house are many mansions: if it were not so, I would have told you. I go to prepare a place for you. And if I go and prepare a place for you, I will come again, and receive you unto myself; that where I am, there ye may be also" (John 14:1-3).

Jesus, thank You for not leaving me to homeschool alone. Help me to remember You are as close as my next prayer. I look for Your help today and hope in the promise of Your future return. In Your name, Amen.

Share your thoughts about this devotional at **aophomeschooling.com/298**

Dressed to Kill

October 26

What did you look like this morning as you began homeschooling your children? Were you still dressed in your pajamas or sweats? Did you prepare yourself as if you were working at an 8 to 5 job, or did you skip the time-consuming effort until later? Busy homeschooling mothers don't always have time to put their best foot forward each day, especially with their appearance. We cheat by putting our hair in a ponytail again and wearing disheveled clothing as we stand instructing our children in their schoolwork.

Can you picture yourself going to school where the teachers looked like they were fit to kill instead of "dressed to kill?" Wouldn't learning be less attractive and somewhat discouraging to see someone stand before you day after day, not caring about what he looked like? Probably so. So why do we as homeschooling mothers think we can skip the attention to detail in our appearance before our homeschooled children?

God desires that we do our work to the best of our ability: "And whatsoever ye do, do it heartily, as to the Lord, and not unto men" (Colossians 3:23). Our job as homeschoolers should be done "heartily" and not half-heartedly. We need to present both ourselves and the academics we teach in a professional manner that will give glory to God and encourage our children to give their best as well.

Do you know what you are going to wear to your homeschool class tomorrow? Your outfit doesn't have to be the latest fashion, but is it clean, ironed, and honoring to the Lord? Why not take the time to look your best each day to make learning more attractive for you and your child?

Father, help me prepare each day to give homeschooling my best effort. I realize that sloppiness on the outside is a reflection of my attitude on the inside. Remind me to honor You in my appearance each day as I teach my children. In Jesus' name, Amen.

Left Behind

I saw the expression on my youngest son's face as the last of his older siblings packed to leave for college. Saying goodbye to his sister was going to be very difficult. As the remaining two children left at home in our homeschooling family, they had shared so much together. But our family was transitioning once again. My son was starting to realize that with all his classmates gone, he would have to homeschool alone.

Being the last child to leave a homeschool family is probably more difficult than being the first. Although the benefits of receiving one-on-one instruction, more curriculum, and additional extra-curricular options seems desirable, the last child also assumes the negative aspects of homeschooling alone—all the chores, the experienced, watchful eye of parents, and the lack of the "family fan club" at games and activities in which they are involved. Separation from homeschool siblings can add to a sense of isolation and loneliness, or it can propel the youngest child to grow in his walk with the Lord.

David was the youngest brother in his family. He, too, probably watched as each of his three older brothers left to fight in the war against the Philistines. He probably felt the family transitioning pains and bore more responsibility as he cared for his father's flocks of sheep. Fortunately, the years of being schooled by God alone would help prepare him on his path to becoming king, as David faced the dangers of lions, bears, and a cursing giant (1 Samuel 17).

Whom do you run to when life gets tough and you need help? Although spouses, parents, and extended family are a great resource to find encouragement and strength, the first place we should turn is into the arms of our loving God. With His perspective, strength, and guidance, we can face whatever comes into our life and accomplish His perfect will. After all, life changes in a blink, and sometimes the family we love and depend on will not be there. Go to prayer in God's school and let Him teach you lessons on following Him and discipleship. "He that loveth father or mother more than me is not worthy of me: and he that loveth son or daughter more than me is not worthy of me. And he that taketh not his cross, and followeth after me, is not worthy of me" (Matthew 10:37-38).

Jesus, I know I've been depending too much on my family for the help and answers I should be seeking from You. Today, I come to You in prayer to seek Your perfect will for the decisions I need to make. Help me to follow You alone. In Your name, Amen.

The Call

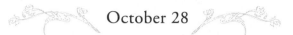
"As for me, I will call upon God; and the LORD shall save me" (Psalm 55:16).

Receiving "the call" late at night is the dread of every parent—homeschooling or not. Our call came around 12:45 a.m. one Friday night. The officer on the other end of the line told us our son was being held at the police station. As we drove to town, I was thankful our son wasn't dead or injured in a car accident. However, I knew that the discipline his father and I were planning may make him wish he was dead.

Someday there will be another call that will bring dread into the heart of every person who doesn't know Jesus Christ as Savior. Christ will come with His angels and call all the nations to come before Him in judgment (Matthew 25:31-46). Many will claim they knew Christ, but He will say, "Depart from me, ye cursed, into everlasting fire" (vs. 41). All opportunity to call upon the name of the Lord and be saved (Romans 13:10) will be gone, and they will be separated from God forever (2 Thessalonians 1:8-9).

Such a horrific moment should motivate everyone to tell others about the saving knowledge of Jesus Christ. The idea of anyone being lost for all eternity is heartbreaking. Let the Lord use you and your homeschool to reach as many as possible before that awesome and terrible day of the Lord. "How then shall they call on him in whom they have not believed? and how shall they believe in him of whom they have not heard? and how shall they hear without a preacher" (Romans 10:14)?

Heavenly Father, move my heart to be the one who "brings the tidings of good news" to the lost, so they can hear of Your saving love. Give me a burden for those who are caught in the darkness of sin. Teach me how to have "beautiful feet" to go where you want me. In Jesus' name, Amen.

No Brainer

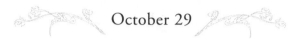

October 29

"Foolishness is bound in the heart of a child" (Proverbs 22:15a).

What seems an obvious choice to us as homeschooling parents is not so easy for our children. When we say "What were you thinking?" to our children for making foolish decisions, we forget that we, too, found ourselves in difficult situations when we were young. Many times, the only thing that separates our choices from our children's, is a few years of wisdom from having been there and done that. What is even worse is when we as homeschooling parents make foolish choices, even when we know the right thing to do.

Saul is an example of this foolishness in the Old Testament. God had chosen him to be king of Israel, and following the Lord seemed like a "no brainer." However, Saul made a bad choice for the last time when he chose to assume the role of a priest. Instead of waiting for Samuel to come and offer the sacrifice to the Lord, he panicked when his army began to disband for fear of the Philistines, and he offered the sacrifice himself. This foolishness and desecration of God's holiness brought the end to his reign as king (1 Samuel 13:8-14).

Foolishness usually seems more obvious in others than in our own lives. Even though we know what we should do, we allow circumstances to force us into making decisions that are wrong. We listen to the voice of everyone but God, and wonder how we ended up in debt, in court, or on our backs looking up at the One we should have followed in the first place.

What about you? Have your foolish actions led you down a road you never intended? Do you wish you could turn around and get back to where you started? Just as the prodigal son finally came to his senses in the pig pen after living a foolish life that wasted his inheritance and broke his father's heart, you can come to your heavenly Father and seek His forgiveness, too. He is waiting with outstretched arms to welcome you back. Don't wait, turn around and come back to Him today!

Lord, forgive the foolish choices I have made because of fear and pride. I submit my life to You in humble obedience. Help me to live according to Your Word. In Jesus' name, Amen.

 Share your thoughts about this devotional at aophomeschooling.com/302

Snakes in a Sandbox

October 30

Homeschooling while living in our "little house on the prairie" in western Nebraska was both exciting and dangerous. We lived with sand burs, relentless wind, prairie dogs, harvester ants, coyotes, scorpions, and worst of all, rattlesnakes.

Since you never knew if rattlesnakes would be hiding in the long grass, under a rock, or even in the flower beds, we had to teach our young children to be on a constant lookout during the summer. What made things even more complicated was the fact that "good" bullsnakes looked exactly like "bad" rattlesnakes except for the shape of their heads and the "rattles" on the tail. Our cowboy neighbors tried several times to teach me and our children the difference. I refused to learn this lesson. To me, the only good snake was a dead snake!

Fortunately, my oldest son paid better attention to these identifying marks. When a four-foot "rattler" was hiding in my children's sandbox one day, my son killed it with a garden hoe. After I recovered from the shock of my son's bravery, we became the typical homeschool family and took advantage of this opportunity. We skinned the snake to examine the anatomy of a reptile for biology, tanned the hide to make jewelry for art class, and studied what living in the West was like during the 1800's for history.

We face many "snakes" in our spiritual lives, too, and you never know where they may be hiding. Satan's temptations are cleverly hidden and disguised, but we can recognize them and have the courage to say "no" if we claim God's power from the Bible. I Peter 5:8-9 tells us to resist the serpent of old because he prowls around like a lion seeking someone to devour. When Satan tempts you as a homeschooling parent to become discouraged and feel sorry for yourself, claim the promises in God's Word to defeat this enemy of God. "For though we walk in the flesh, we do not war after the flesh: For the weapons of our warfare are not carnal, but mighty through God to the pulling down of strong holds" (2 Corinthians 10:3-4).

Father, thank You for showing me the truth from Your Word to win over Satan's temptations. Help me stay alert to defeat him through Your power so my life will glorify You. In Jesus' name, Amen.

 Share your thoughts about this devotional at aophomeschooling.com/303

I'm Sorry

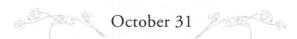

October 31

"Now I rejoice, not that ye were made sorry, but that ye sorrowed to repentance" (2 Corinthians 7:9a).

I stood in front of the mirror in the bathroom with my makeup case in my hands. There seemed to be a sense of irony in the fact that I was putting on a "pretty face" for the rest of the world to see, but inside I was an angry and ugly homeschooling mother. The morning had gone from bad to worse with my husband's car that wouldn't start, a broken washing machine, and my mother's "helpful" advice. I should have talked to the Lord when I felt the tremors coming, but instead, my pent up emotions erupted onto my ten-year-old son like a violent volcano when he failed to complete his math assignment. I had quickly said, "I'm sorry," for my outburst, but my son's expression told me I had hurt his loving heart.

As I looked into the mirror, God showed me the truth of what was happening. Between feeling like a failure because we lacked the finances to maintain our appliances and the rejection by my family for homeschooling, I was angry at Him. I had looked for the encouragement and approval I needed in the wrong place and was disappointed when I didn't find it. Taking my frustration out on my son's failure had simply transferred the same feeling to him.

As I opened my make-up case, I prayed the rest of the day would go better. To my surprise, I saw little pieces of paper folded on top of the different colors of eye shadow. Opening each piece of paper, I found the words, "I LOVE YOU, MOM!" written by my son. Humbled, I knew I should have been the one seeking to restore our relationship. I started to cry and realized I would never get my makeup on that morning. I walked into my son's room and started over. This time I truly said, "I'm sorry."

Lord, too many times I've said I'm sorry without really meaning it. Help me realize what others are feeling when I have hurt them. Place a repentant heart of compassion in me to restore these broken relationships. In Jesus' name, Amen.

 Share your thoughts about this devotional at aophomeschooling.com/304

The Perfect Homeschool World

November 1

• In a perfect homeschool world, your children would greet you with a smile each morning and help prepare breakfast and clean up afterwards.

• In a perfect homeschool world, there would be no sibling fighting, lost workbooks, or unprepared students.

• In a perfect homeschool world, your children would learn their lessons the first time, eliminating any review.

• In a perfect homeschool world, you would have brilliant applications and visual aids prepared for every subject area you are teaching each day.

• In a perfect homeschool world, the laundry would clean and fold itself, so you could enjoy the evenings with your spouse.

• In a perfect homeschool world, there would be enough money to buy all the curriculum you wanted.

• In a perfect homeschool world, you would find encouraging notes from your children thanking you for being such a wonderful parent and teacher.

•In a perfect homeschool world, you would always have the right answer to every one of your children's questions.

Unfortunately, this world is not perfect. We live in a fallen and sinful world that tempts us (1 Corinthians 10:13). Every day I must go to the One who is perfect for strength, wisdom, and guidance to live my life as a shining example of His love to my family and to the world. I am not perfect, but He is (Hebrews 7:25-26)! I rejoice that although my homeschool world is not perfect, I know the One who is. He goes before me each day and prepares the path in which I will walk. Today, I trust Him again to take everything I experience as a homeschooling parent and cause it to work together for good (Romans 8:28).

Lord, I know that I fall short each day in living a perfect holy life. Help me be patient and loving toward my family and others when they fall short as well. None of us is perfect, except You. Thank You for being a holy God who loves me in spite of my shortcomings. In Jesus' name, Amen.

 Share your thoughts about this devotional at **aophomeschooling.com/305**

A New Perspective

November 2

Imagine going to a job each morning where you can set your own schedule. You arrive when you want, take breaks whenever you want, and leave for an extended lunch hour without anyone breathing down your neck. Answering your phone calls and emails is regulated to a minimum each day, and the work responsibilities and goals you have are varied. There is no dress code or security passes to wear around your neck, and no one cares if you eat at your desk or play your favorite radio station. Your boss is off site, and you can manage your work load however best suits your needs. Your work is rewarding and exciting, and you usually see immediate results from your efforts. Wouldn't we all love to have a job that fits this description? YOU DO, as a homeschooling parent!

Many homeschooling parents get caught up in the fact that they never receive a paycheck like their working counterparts. However, if you look at the God-given task of teaching your children at home from a new perspective, you begin to see what a blessing the career choice of homeschooling is for you. So many drawbacks of the "typical" job do not relate to your world. You have the freedom to pursue your position in ways many working parents never do.

Too many times in my years as a homeschooling mother, I failed to see the bigger picture of what God was doing in my life and in the lives of my children. I needed to have my eyes opened like Elisha's servant who saw the whole army of heaven around him (2 Kings 6:17). From God's perspective, what you are doing as a homeschooling parent has long-lasting and eternal value.

So, go to work tomorrow morning, and picture yourself at the best job you could ever have. The grass is greener on this side of the fence, and your regular paycheck of "hugs and kisses" from your family is more rewarding than what a company can pay you. Enjoy the freedom you have as a homeschooling parent and be the successful teacher God intended you to be! "And whatsoever ye do, do it heartily, as to the Lord, and not unto men; Knowing that of the Lord ye shall receive the reward of the inheritance: for ye serve the Lord Christ" (Colossians 3:23-24).

Jesus, what a wonderful opportunity You have given me! Not only do I get the blessing of being a parent, but You have also blessed me with an awesome career of being a teacher! Help me keep my eyes on You today as I homeschool. In Your name, Amen.

Who's Responsible?

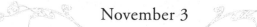

November 3

Our monthly homeschool meeting was over, and we were cleaning the house after everyone had left. The young children of several couples had played together with our four children for most of the evening, and there was a trail of toys throughout the house. Walking to my son's room with my hands full of toys, I stopped short as I went through the doorway. I couldn't believe my eyes as I stared at his broken bed. The scene told me that the bed had been converted into a trampoline, and from the look of things, whoever had bounced on it had a good time.

Lining my children up for an interrogation didn't take long. One by one I drilled them with questions, trying to find out who was responsible. My anger at this senseless destruction probably prompted each one to claim innocence in the matter. After fifteen minutes of explanations, I realized that "nobody" was at fault. You know, "nobody" is that invisible person who lives at everyone's home—the one who gets the blame when bad things happen.

Our children are not the only ones who avoid taking the blame. We do, too, don't we? Who likes to admit their mistakes or suffer the consequences for their actions? We are all quick to let the blame fall on someone else, especially if there are so many people involved that the obvious offender cannot be found. The sin of Achan in Joshua 7 is a prime example. Not until God literally lined up the entire nation of Israel tribe by tribe, did Achan finally confess his sin of stealing gold, silver, and a beautiful garment from the city of Ai. Caught in his deception, Achan and his family, as well as all of his belongings, were destroyed for violating God's holiness.

What about you? Do you weasel out of your mistakes by letting others take the blame for your actions? Do you have enough integrity to stand up and say, "It was my fault. I was responsible?" Whether the issue is big or little, don't wait until someone has to back you up against the wall before you admit you've done wrong. "Confess your faults one to another, and pray one for another, that ye may be healed" (James 5:16a).

Father, forgive me for staying silent and letting others suffer the consequences of my wrongs. Help me admit when I have made a mistake and not lie by trying to cover up the problem. In Jesus' name, Amen.

Share your thoughts about this devotional at **aophomeschooling.com/307**

What's Cooking?

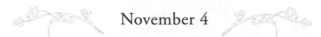

November 4

What type of food do you serve at your homeschool cafeteria? My children's favorite benefit of homeschooling was the fresh and delicious meals we made together as a family. No canned or prepackaged entrees were allowed. Learning how to cook was a mandatory lesson we incorporated into each child's curriculum. All the family appreciated the tasty A+ lessons of lasagna, stir-fry, oven-baked pot roast, fresh pies, cakes, breads, salads, and others.

However, teaching your children how to cook also means making messes. Peeling potatoes, mixing batter for cookies, and measuring spices and ingredients lead to many "accidents." Learning how to wipe up a spill, clean flour off containers, and wash the extra baking dishes were skills that also needed to be learned before enjoying the benefits. Of course, these skills were never quite as fun as the process of preparing the food. Our children wanted the fun of cooking without the hassle of cleaning up.

Our Christian walk is much the same. We want to sit at God's table and enjoy the benefits of the Holy Spirit without going through the disciplines of living a holy life. We make a mess of devotions and prayer times and wonder why God is not using us more. We use "canned" approaches in witnessing and fail to seek God first in prayer.

Is there an area of your life that needs disciplining—reading magazines and books that honor the Lord, making time for devotions and prayer, or maintaining a pure thought life? Share your area of struggle with a trusted friend and make yourself accountable. Find the help you need to stay disciplined and close to the Lord. "And every man that striveth for the mastery is temperate in all things. Now they do it to obtain a corruptible crown; but we an incorruptible. I therefore so run, not as uncertainly; so fight I, not as one that beateth the air: But I keep under my body, and bring it into subjection: lest that by any means, when I have preached to others, I myself should be a castaway" (1 Corinthians 9:25-27).

Lord, show me the areas in my life that fail to honor You. Please lead me to a Christian friend who will help me stay disciplined in those areas, so my life will glorify You. Thank You for loving me so much and always forgiving me when I fail. In Jesus' name, Amen.

The Diagram of Life

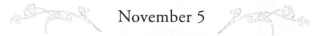

November 5

Learning how to diagram sentences was emphasized in our homeschool. We always began by diagramming the verb first, the subject next, and then the remainder of the words in the sentence. The constant review of this technique caused my daughter to tell me one day, "Mom, I can't even read a sentence anymore without seeing it diagrammed in my mind!"

If we could diagram success into our lives, we would also have to begin with the verb "saves." When asking, "Who or what saves?" we would locate "Jesus" as the subject. Without this simple beginning, the remainder of our lives will be broken and disjointed. If we accept the subject, Jesus, and the verb of what He can do for us, save, we will find our lives communicating love to the world and glory to our Heavenly Father. "Believe on the Lord Jesus Christ, and thou shalt be saved" (Acts 16:31).

Father, thank You for sending Jesus to die for my sins. I confess that I have sinned and accept Your free gift of eternal life today. Take my life and use it to glorify You. In the wonderful name of Jesus, Amen.

Good Intentions

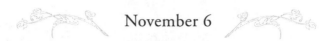

November 6

"Love not sleep, lest thou come to poverty; open thine eyes, and thou shalt be satisfied with bread" (Proverbs 20:13).

Another morning was getting away from me. I knew I should have gotten up early when I heard the alarm clock, but the covers felt so good on this crisp, fall morning. Certainly God wouldn't mind if I prayed to Him while lying down under the blankets. As I began my prayers, I felt my body start to drift. Shaking off the sleep, I started once again but the sleepiness came back. An entire hour later, I was still in bed. I was late to start homeschooling my children and knew I would be playing "catch up" for the rest of the day without God's strength or guidance.

Peter, James, and John lost the same battle of sleep when Jesus asked them to pray in the Garden of Gethsemane. Three times the Lord asked them to pray, and three times they fell asleep and heard His words, "What, could ye not watch with me one hour? Watch and pray, that ye enter not into temptation: the spirit indeed is willing, but the flesh is weak" (Matthew 26:40b-41). Falling asleep when Jesus needed them most, the disciples certainly failed.

Do you have good intentions to have a quiet time with the Lord each morning? Good intentions are not enough! Satan loves to tempt us to listen to the desires of our flesh and miss our devotions. Without the Holy Spirit's empowering, we, too, will fail in our attempts to walk with the Lord, as well as in our efforts to homeschool. Don't be like the disciples or the foolish virgins in Matthew 25:1-13 who fell asleep waiting for the bridegroom. Stay alert and offer the prayers and worship to the Lord that is due Him. "Yet a little sleep, a little slumber, a little folding of the hands to sleep: So shall thy poverty come as one that travelleth; and thy want as an armed man" (Proverbs 24:33-34).

Jesus, forgive me for being lazy in my efforts to come to You each day. I recognize the importance of Your sweet fellowship and recommit my life to You today. In Your name, Amen.

Showing Off

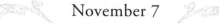

November 7

"A man's pride shall bring him low: but honour shall uphold the humble in spirit" (Proverbs 29:23).

My son and daughter had finished their schoolwork early and were heading out the door to go on a long bike ride for the remainder of the afternoon. I was looking forward to the additional free time from our homeschooling day to work in my flower garden. I waved and smiled as they left the yard and said, "Have a nice time." Little did I know, the plans for the afternoon were soon to change.

I watched as my son decided to show his sister that he could ride a bike without using his hands. Showing off, he continued riding until he reached a patch of loose gravel on our road. In an instant, he was airborne like some cartoon character and landed with a thud in the middle of the road. Unfortunately, he didn't bounce back. I ran to pick up his bleeding body and checked for broken bones.

Showing off usually leads to some type of catastrophe. King Hezekiah made such a mistake when he decided to show his possessions to the king of Babylon (2 Kings 20:12-13). Isaiah the prophet rebuked him for being so foolish and prophesied, "Behold, the days come, that all that is in thine house, and that which thy fathers have laid up in store unto this day, shall be carried into Babylon: nothing shall be left, saith the LORD" (vs.17). The king of Babylon knew a good thing when he saw it. He conquered Jerusalem many years later and carried away every one of those treasures.

Do you struggle with wanting to impress others? Do you flaunt your possessions or achievements so other people will think highly of you? Do you doubt your worth in the Lord's eyes, so much that you puff yourself up to find value? Don't be like a child and show off. Humble yourself before you are humiliated by your actions. God's Word says, "Likewise, ye younger, submit yourselves unto the elder. Yea, all of you be subject one to another, and be clothed with humility: for God resisteth the proud, and giveth grace to the humble. Humble yourselves therefore under the mighty hand of God, that he may exalt you in due time" (1 Peter 5:5-6).

Lord, forgive me for robbing You of Your glory when I show off in front of others. Everything I have and am is because of You. May You receive all glory and praise. In Jesus' name, Amen.

 Share your thoughts about this devotional at **aophomeschooling.com/311**

Great Expectations

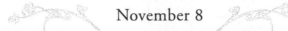

November 8

Countless times during the day, homeschooling parents are approached by their children with a request. Expectantly, they come for advice, for help with a problem, or for words of encouragement and love. The thought that you might not have the answer, the time, or the ability to help never crosses their minds. Most homeschool parents gladly respond by doing all they can to meet these "great expectations."

If you are a child of the King, you also have the same ability to come before your heavenly Father with your requests. Hebrews 4:16 tells us, "Let us therefore come boldly unto the throne of grace, that we may obtain mercy, and find grace to help in time of need." Unlike the limitations you face when meeting your child's request, Jesus has the ability to give you everything you need and waits to show you the "exceeding riches of His grace" (Ephesians 2:7). He never gets tired when you ask Him countless questions or even the same question over and over. Christ even loves you with an "everlasting love" and seeks to draw you unto Himself (Jeremiah 31:3b).

Is there a question on your mind that you would like to talk about with Jesus? Are you wondering how to pay your bills on one income, how to find time during the day for yourself, or how to seek forgiveness from your children for losing your patience? Because Christ shed His blood on the cross, you can come "boldly" before God's throne of grace. Come now. You don't even have to wait your turn! God is capable of multi-tasking. He can meet more than one need at a time. All you have to do is come, ask, and receive. "And this is the confidence that we have in him, that, if we ask any thing according to his will, he heareth us: And if we know that he hear us, whatsoever we ask, we know that we have the petitions that we desired of him" (1 John 5:14-15).

Lord, thank You for being such a great God who can meet all my needs. I rejoice that I can come to You each day and find the help, advice, love, and encouragement I need to homeschool. I worship You today! In Jesus' name, Amen.

It's Too Hard!

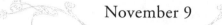

November 9

"Behold, I am the LORD, the God of all flesh: is there any thing too hard for me" (Jeremiah 32:27)?

Motivating our homeschooled children to learn can seem like a daunting task. Many times we hear them say, "It's too hard," and we are tempted to put off teaching difficult lessons. Whether you are attempting to teach your child how to research material for a term paper or the proper steps for long division, step back and teach in smaller increments to keep him on track. Help your child learn the lesson one step at a time, and this will bring him more success in learning the information.

Joshua had a hard task facing him when he and the nation of Israel finally crossed into the Promised Land God had given them. They had to drive out the nations that were already living there—a very hard task and a very large task, especially since some of the people were giants! City by city and tribe by tribe, God told Joshua what to do, and He gave the people victory in conquering the land.

Sometimes the problems homeschool parents face seem larger than life, too. We tell God, "It's too hard!" and are tempted to give up. Maybe you are faced with teaching your child high school subjects or you have a special needs child who requires extra attention. Ask God to help you break down the problem into smaller parts and show you the solutions you need to find success. You don't have the wisdom to know how to work things out, but God does. He will help you teach those difficult high school subjects or your special needs child. Don't despair—nothing is too difficult for God!

Lord, you are a great and mighty God. I know that teaching our children is Your will. Please show me how to solve the giant problems that have come because we chose to homeschool. In Jesus' name, Amen.

Share your thoughts about this devotional at **aophomeschooling.com/313**

Homeschool Hunger

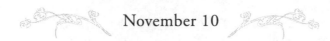

November 10

The book I was hungry to read had been sitting on my desk for over two months. Stacked neatly in a pile with other half-read books, I wondered if I would ever get to read it. I wanted to be a successful homeschooling parent who remained teachable, but my limited time prevented me from indulging in every subject I loved. Instead, I challenged my intellect by thoroughly researching the subjects I taught my children.

There is another type of hunger, however, that homeschool parents must feed—a hunger for righteousness. We must come to the Lord expectantly each day to learn and digest what He desires to teach us from His Word. "Teach me thy way, O LORD; I will walk in thy truth: unite my heart to fear thy name" (Psalm 86:11). Unlike other books, we cannot afford to leave our Bibles unread and stacked on our desks.

So, isn't it time to become a student again and learn something new about God and His Word? How well do you know your Bible? Have you ever read through it entirely? Do you know how to cross reference Scripture, memorize verses, use a concordance, read maps, or find the Greek and Hebrew meaning of the words used in the verses? There is so much to learn. Don't stop with what you know. Grow! "Blessed are they which do hunger and thirst after righteousness: for they shall be filled" (Matthew 5:6).

Father, there is so much I have to learn about You! Restore to me the joy of discovering what an awesome and loving God You are! Teach me something new today and help me to hunger for more and more of Your wisdom. In Jesus' name, Amen.

Sowing and Reaping

November 11

Learning to read and enjoying good literature were seeds we consciously planted into our homeschooled children. We cultivated in them a desire to read by first reading to our children when they were young. As they grew older, they mastered phonics rules and eventually became avid readers themselves.

To feed their insatiable appetites for books, the library became our second home. Books were literally hauled to and from the library each week in a large tub. The librarians dreaded our coming and going because of the time involved to process our books. However, taking advantage of this public resource enabled us to nurture a love of literature while subsidizing our homeschool curriculum expenses. Years later, I wasn't surprised when my children reaped the benefits of being good readers by getting their first part-time jobs as librarians.

The law of sowing and reaping applies to our spiritual lives, too. Whether we are children or adults, we plant seeds of righteousness that glorify the Lord (Proverbs 11:18) or seeds that will reap pain, suffering, or death (Proverbs 22:8). Many times, we make choices based on the moment, and we forget that someday there will be a harvest of our actions, now and for eternity.

What are you sowing in your life? Are you making choices that produce a harvest of righteousness, or do the seeds of sin seem to be taking over? Maybe it's time to step back and let the Holy Spirit pull out those "weeds" that have begun to choke your spiritual life. "For whatsoever a man soweth, that shall he also reap. For he that soweth to his flesh shall of the flesh reap corruption; but he that soweth to the Spirit shall of the Spirit reap life everlasting" (Galatians 6:7b-8).

Lord, help me plant those things in my life that will glorify You and weed out those things that don't. I claim Your strength again today to stop and pray before I make each decision. In Jesus' name, Amen.

Matters of the Heart

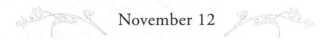

November 12

"For I know the thoughts that I think toward you, saith the LORD, thoughts of peace, and not of evil" (Jeremiah 29:11a).

Is there anything more agonizing to homeschooling parents than watching their child struggle when taking a test? Whenever my children went through contortions trying to remember facts hiding in their memory banks, I wanted to run to their rescue. Sometimes, I even went so far as to drop a few "hints" to help them succeed in their efforts. Surprisingly, my children perceived just the opposite about my feelings. Thinking I enjoyed using my red pen, they didn't understand the ache in my heart when I corrected their wrong answers. As their parent, I didn't want them to fail. I wanted them to triumph in their tests.

What's even more surprising is the misconception many Christians have of their Heavenly Father. Picturing God as holy and just, they forget that God is also merciful and loving. God doesn't look forward to punishing us for what we've done wrong. In fact, just the opposite is true. He wants us to succeed in our Christian walk and discover all the blessings He has waiting for us. Every day when "tests" come and we can't remember the right answers from His Word, He helps us succeed by sending encouraging "hints." Whether a godly friend reminds us of His love or the Holy Spirit gives us wisdom to discern a problem, we can rest assured that "If God be for us, who can be against us" (Romans 8:31b)?

Have you been getting a few problems wrong in the tests of your life? Take heart, dear friend in Christ. The Lord isn't waiting to condemn you (Romans 8:1). He loves you and wants to help you find victory in the power of His mighty name. "How precious also are thy thoughts unto me, O God! how great is the sum of them! If I should count them, they are more in number than the sand" (Psalm 139:17-18a).

Lord, thank You for being a God who loves me more than I can imagine. Lift me today and remind me again of all You've given me as Your child. In the name of Your dear Son, Amen.

Signs of Christ

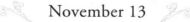

November 13

If your homeschooling family is like most, there are probably many symbols of your faith located in your home. We had several crosses throughout the house that the children made during art class, and our refrigerator was plastered with new Sunday school papers each week. We had the word "Jesus" made with barbed wire and hung on the wall in the kitchen. We even had a screen-saver on our computer's desktop with changing pictures and Scripture passages.

The most unique signs we had of our faith were the computer-generated Scripture plaques my son made for art class. Printed, laminated, and located in strategic places throughout our home, we had God's Word to see and memorize everywhere we went. Scripture passages were on the bathroom mirror, on the bed headboard, on the kitchen windows above the sink, and even by the speedometer in the car. These wonderful symbols of God's written promises encouraged us and proclaimed our faith to all who entered our home.

More important than the symbols we have on the outside of our lives, is the symbol and seal of the Holy Spirit that we receive on the inside when we become a child of God (Ephesians 1:13). The indwelling Holy Spirit is a reminder of the future inheritance we have in Christ (Ephesians 1:14). We see the power of God as we yield our lives to His control, and He even displays His fruit in us for others to see (Galatians 5:22-23).

How do you display your faith for others to see? What does that cross stand for on the bumper of your car, the front door of your house, or around your neck? Is it just another decoration? If you identify with the One who died upon it for your sins, let His forgiveness change your life. Become a symbol of His unconditional love for the whole world to see! "For the preaching of the cross is to them that perish foolishness; but unto us which are saved it is the power of God" (1 Corinthians 1:18).

Lord Jesus, thank You for the cross and Your willingness to suffer and die for my sins. I thank You again today for the Holy Spirit's presence in my life. Let both my home and my life symbolize Your love so others will see the way to eternal life. In Your blessed name, Amen.

 Share your thoughts about this devotional at **aophomeschooling.com/317**

Pouting Pains

November 14

Rebellion has many faces, and the big pout on my daughter's face was definitely one of them. With three other children in our homeschool classroom, she didn't like being the one who had to wait for help with her questions. Watching her body language, I realized there was a much bigger problem waiting to be dealt with than the one in her math lesson.

My daughter's actions brought back memories of the beginnings of my own rebellious days. What had started as simple, little pouting episodes to get my own way had turned into all-out, get-in-your-face rebellion toward my parents as a teenager. Being the last of seven children, my parents were usually too busy to put out the flames of my sinful rebellion when they erupted. Because these seemingly small pouting sessions were left unchecked, they burned a hole in my character and my life. Many years of pain from "getting my own way" passed before my heart was humbled before a mighty God.

Have you bought into the world's lie that you deserve what you want, when you want it? Dear one, don't go down that path of destruction! Although there may be joy for the moment, pain and suffering will meet you at the end. "An evil man seeketh only rebellion: therefore a cruel messenger shall be sent against him" (Proverbs 17:11). Jesus loves you too much to let your pouting spoil things. Trust Him to meet every need you have, and you'll never get burned again by the world's empty promises. "For all that is in the world, the lust of the flesh, and the lust of the eyes, and the pride of life, is not of the Father, but is of the world. And the world passeth away, and the lust thereof: but he that doeth the will of God abideth for ever" (1 John 2:16-17).

Jesus, I submit my life to You again this day. Forgive me when I try to take control and fail to trust You. Help me fight off the fiery darts of the devil that tempt me to rebel against Your will. In Your name, Amen.

Give Praise When Due

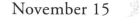

November 15

"Withhold not good from them to whom it is due, when it is in the power of thine hand to do it" (Proverbs 3:27).

Do you think praising your homeschooled children will cause conceit and pride in their character? Since I received few compliments as a child from my stoic Dutch and German parents, I wondered if my praise would lead to an over-inflated ego in my children. I struggled with this question and searched the Scriptures for an answer until one day I read, "Wherefore comfort yourselves together, and edify one another, even as also ye do" (1 Thessalonians 5:11).

My children would probably say I was tough on them as a homeschool parent. I didn't grade on a curve, and 96% and above was considered an "A." I used the dreaded "red pen" liberally in language arts lessons and compositions, and I rarely "fudged" when playing a board game to let them win. However, even though I was tough, I learned to lavish my children with large amounts of praise. I complimented them whenever they did an excellent job on a paper or whenever they showed initiative and creativity in completing a project. I looked for ways each day to tell them how proud I was of them personally and academically. A few encouraging words made such a difference in their lives!

God created us to give praise—first to Him and then to others. He loves to hear our prayers that proclaim His goodness and our songs of highest praise. God even wants us to bring a sacrifice of praise to Him when life brings difficult times. Are you discouraged today? Is praising the Lord the last thing you feel like doing? Move past your feelings to obedience and bring the sacrifice of praise unto the Lord. God is in control of your life. Whatever the circumstances, He deserves our worship as a holy God. "O let not the oppressed return ashamed: let the poor and needy praise thy name" (Psalm 74:21).

Father, when I look at the problems in my life, I find it so difficult to praise You. Help me turn my eyes upon You now and sing glorious praise to You, my King. I worship You my great and holy God! In your Son's name, Amen.

Share your thoughts about this devotional at aophomeschooling.com/319

My Incredible Journey

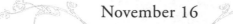

November 16

The story of God's people, Israel, in the Old Testament draws a striking parallel to my journey as a homeschooling parent. For years, I had been caught in the bondage of believing that public school was the only way to educate my child. Miraculously, we experienced God leading our family out of this "slavery" and through our "Red Sea" when He provided a path to teach our children through a homeschool satellite program. Chased by the Pharaoh of the school system with threats of truancy, we walked though our difficulty on dry land and watched as the waves crashed over top of those who worked so diligently to keep us from teaching our children at home.

Like Israel, we sang praises to God for His deliverance and began our journey to the Promised Land of four successfully educated children. We, too, complained about the lack of familiar food and water because finances were short. We tasted the bitter waters of Marah when we attempted to teach our children in our own strength. We slowly learned to look to our cloud by day and pillar of fire by night and felt God's protection from the heat of well-meaning, but critical family members and the cold rejection of an uninformed community.

We would have died from the serpent bites of laziness and anger, but looking to the cross saved us, as we saw God's forgiveness for each mistake. We saw parents give up, claiming that homeschooling was too hard, and we watched as their families became swallowed up again by the public school like the rebellion at Korah.

We even doubted God's presence on many occasions and set up a golden calf of making our school look exactly like the public school. But our Moses was Jesus, and each day He faithfully led us back to where we needed to go. He gave us the Ten Commandments of His Word, and we experienced His loving presence as we obeyed its truths.

Looking back on the journey, I see Jesus' loving hands lifted over our family. I praise Him for the incredible journey we experienced in teaching our children at home. Don't give up on your homeschooling journey. The Promised Land is all that God said it would be!

Father, I pray for the many homeschooling families who are on the adventure of teaching their children at home. Bless them this day and provide the same guidance You gave to us. Show them that You are mighty and able to take care of every homeschooling need. In Jesus' name, Amen.

 Share your thoughts about this devotional at aophomeschooling.com/320

You Can Do It

November 17

"Faithful is he that calleth you, who also will do it" (1 Thessalonians 5:24).

Have you been experiencing setbacks lately while homeschooling? Are your children rebelling or acting bored? Do friends continue to harass you about your decision and worry that your children will be socially inept by the time they graduate? Is all the hard work of balancing time for your spouse, your children, and yourself just too much? Are the unpaid bills or unfinished chores keeping you awake at night? Maybe God never really wanted you to homeschool in the first place? After all, if He did, things wouldn't be so hard, right?

Those are the experiences and thoughts I felt homeschooling four children. Second guessing myself, I was ready to walk away and experience the "good life" of corporate reward and fulfillment. Anything had to be better than the frustration I was going through now. But each time I determined to give up and send my children to school, a wonderful day of homeschooling blessings would encourage me again. My spiritual and homeschooling journeys became intertwined, and I learned that any success I had when teaching my children was dependent on my closeness to God's heart.

My days of looking for a way out eventually ended when God gave me my own homeschooling life verse, "Therefore I endure all things for the elect's sakes, that they may also obtain the salvation which is in Christ Jesus with eternal glory" (2 Timothy 2:10). I knew I could endure any homeschooling negatives for the sake of my children's salvation and growth in Christ. I was ashamed and humbled before God with my foolish fears and doubts. Even though I had been faithless and ready to quit to avoid suffering, God had remained faithful and encouraged me when I needed encouragement most (2 Timothy 2:13a).

God is waiting to encourage you today, too. He wants to meet you right where you are and give you the strength you need to be a faithful teacher. Learn from His sacrificial and loving example to faithfully teach you. "Looking unto Jesus the author and finisher of our faith; who for the joy that was set before him endured the cross, despising the shame, and is set down at the right hand of the throne of God. For consider him that endured such contradiction of sinners against himself, lest ye be wearied and faint in your minds" (Hebrews 12:2-3).

Jesus, your love for me amazes me every day. My life is not my own, and I recommit my family and homeschooling to You today. Use me to be a blessing to these wonderful children. Help me stand against the temptation to feel sorry for myself. In Your precious name, Amen.

 Share your thoughts about this devotional at aophomeschooling.com/321

Author Unknown

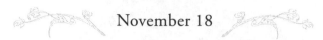

As I stood in front of the formidable shelves of books in our local library, I wondered where to begin. Finding thought-provoking books with godly and moral values shouldn't have been so difficult, but it was. Frustrated, I prayed and asked God to help me in my search for wholesome literature for my children. The thought, "consider the source" came to my mind. I realized God was prompting me to first study the authors, and then I would find the right books.

No matter how objective an author attempts to be, his beliefs and attitudes are reflected in the words and content he chooses to write about. Studying the author's life before reading his book saves hours of wasting time reading nonsense and foolishness. I learned you couldn't always "judge a book by its glitzy cover" and that it was better to flip to the back panel and read the author's biography first.

Praise God, we don't have to worry about trusting the authors' words of the greatest book written—the Bible. Although God used the personalities of thirty-five different men to pen the words, they only wrote as God moved them: "But holy men of God spake as they were moved by the Holy Ghost" (2 Peter 1:21b). God is the author of every inspired word contained within the sixty-six books of the Bible (II Timothy 3:16).

God is not only the author of the Bible, but He is also the author of our faith (Hebrews 12:2). He is also the author of love, and we love Him because He first loved us (1 John 4:19). He is the author of forgiveness who died for us while we were yet sinners (Romans 5:8). God even authored the saving work He began in us and will perform it until Christ returns (Philippians 1:6).

Is God the author who has influenced you the most in your life? If not, go again to the Bible and rediscover the wonder and holiness of the mighty One who wrote it. His promises are sure, and His words will guide you throughout your entire life. Not only is He the author of our beginning, but He will also be the author of the end. "I am Alpha and Omega, the beginning and the end, the first and the last" (Revelation 22:13).

Father, you knew me before I was even born, and I thank You for being the author of my life. Reveal more of Yourself to me through Your holy Word and continue to show me how to live for You until You bring me home. In Jesus' name, Amen.

 Share your thoughts about this devotional at **aophomeschooling.com/322**

The Done Box

November 19

Sitting in the corner of our kitchen like a trophy on a mantle was the "done" box. Each homeschooling year was begun with a new box to collect each of our children's completed worksheets and lessons. Originally designed to provide documentation of our children's schoolwork to state authorities, the done box came to represent something different as the homeschooling years went on.

The done box became a physical representation of my children's diligence, hard work, and determination to complete their studies. When we became discouraged and thought we had not achieved much in our homeschooling, the piles of paper in the done box became a reminder of our productivity. Seeing what we had completed motivated us to continue working hard to finish our homeschool year.

Many times, we wonder if God is really leading us in our spiritual walk. Like David in Psalms, we need to remember where we have been and how God has led us (Psalm 42:6). Looking back on all God had done for him as king, David could only sing praises to God and look forward to the next step in God's plan.

Do you need to be encouraged in your homeschooling today? Take a look back and see what you have accomplished with your children. Have your children become good readers? Do you see godly character qualities reflected in their behavior? Is your family emotionally close and strong? Thank God today for what He has strengthened you to do, and continue looking forward to the next homeschooling step. "Brethren, I count not myself to have apprehended: but this one thing I do, forgetting those things which are behind, and reaching forth unto those things which are before, I press toward the mark for the prize of the high calling of God in Christ Jesus" (Philippians 3:13-14).

Jesus, I give You the glory for the homeschool blessings You have given to our family. Thank You for all the past victories and encourage me to trust You for our homeschooling future. In Your precious name, Amen.

Another Day at the Sink

November 20

"Let us therefore come boldly unto the throne of grace, that we may obtain mercy, and find grace to help in time of need" (Hebrews 4:16).

If homeschool parents had lecture podiums like school teachers, mine would have definitely been the kitchen sink. From this central location, I was able to deliver endless hours of instruction in spelling words, poem memorization, and multiplication facts. Multi-tasking from this "lectern" proved to be the only way I could complete daily lesson plans and my chores of washing dishes, preparing meals, and cleaning messes.

However, more than academics were taught from this "homeschooling hub." The kitchen sink was also the center of holiday activities, political and theological debates, and personal counseling sessions while washing and drying dishes. Although I felt chained to it at times, I realized later that the kitchen sink was the center of our family's home. My children's fondest homeschool memories were seeing their mother happily working in the kitchen and knowing she was available to help answer any question they might have.

God wants to be the center of your life, too. His podium is not a kitchen sink, but a great, white throne (Revelation 20:11). From it, He is able to answer your prayers, and He loves to instruct you each day in how to live your life for Him. You can come boldly to this throne of grace anytime you are afraid or unsure about what to do. If homeschooling is starting to make you feel chained down, find the secret of success by keeping God in the center of your life. Go to the center of the Bible, Psalm 118:8, and rediscover how you can be in the center of God's will today.

Jesus, I invite You to be the center of my life and home. Thank You for being such a loving God who answers all of my prayers. The strength of Your holy presence brings joy to my soul and peace to my anxious heart. In Your name, Amen.

Anger Management

November 21

You never mean to use anger to discipline your children, but sometimes it becomes part of your homeschooling day. Perhaps you're too tired to get up again to reinforce your correction for the millionth time, or maybe you subconsciously model the parenting you received when you were a child. Whatever the reason, you find yourself caught in the deadly trap of yelling at your children to make them obey.

I'm sure my yelling must have made God cringe as He heard me destroying my children's tender hearts. Unfortunately, when they ignored the rough words, I felt like I was losing control, so I used even tougher words. I justified myself in the name of discipline, but I knew this wasn't the right way to correct a child. I knew I needed help. My anger was beginning to control more than my children. It was beginning to control me!

Finally, conviction came to me one day when I "lost it" with my young son. I still remember the day on the stairsteps up to his room. Time stopped as I saw my son's frightened eyes in response to my anger. How could someone so small and innocent be blamed for bringing out the huge ugliness inside of me? I never thought that pressure from situations beyond my control would push me to such actions, but God certainly revealed the worst inside my black heart. I needed to learn some anger management, fast!

James 1:19-20 brought me to my senses, "Wherefore, my beloved brethren, let every man be swift to hear, slow to speak, slow to wrath: For the wrath of man worketh not the righteousness of God." On January 5, 1983, I realized my anger for what it was. I found the gentle forgiveness of God's correction and earnestly applied this same forgiveness to my children for the rest of their homeschooling days. Disciplining my children remained, but my anger no longer had a place in it. Instead, house rules and accompanying consequences for violations were decided upon as a family and posted on the refrigerator.

Does anger play a role in disciplining at your house? If so, do not give the devil an opportunity to cause you to sin any longer (Ephesians 4:27). Let Christ's love fill your heart and your home and "Let all bitterness, and wrath, and anger, and clamour, and evil speaking, be put away from you, with all malice: And be ye kind one to another, tenderhearted, forgiving one another, even as God for Christ's sake hath forgiven you" (Ephesians 4:31-32).

Father, forgive me today for using my anger when disciplining my children. Convict me of this sin and help me to always discipline in love. In Jesus' name, Amen.

 Share your thoughts about this devotional at **aophomeschooling.com/325**

White Dog—Black Dog

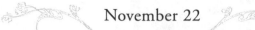
"I will offer to thee the sacrifice of thanksgiving, and will call upon the name of the LORD" (Psalm 116:17).

A new day to homeschool waits in front of you, but already your restless mind is walking you through the countless problems and chores left over from yesterday. You feel the negativity crawling up your back like an impending viral cold. Once again, you face the choice of feeding the white dog of hopeful expectations and thankfulness or the black dog of despair and complaining. Which dog will you choose to feed with your thoughts?

To feed the white dog of thankfulness is really a choice each of us makes. After all, doesn't everyone have issues to deal with in life? Maybe the issues involve wayward children, a lack of finances, hurt feelings, or the loss of a loved one. Whatever the problem, God asks us to continue to look to Him and express a heart of thankfulness. "In every thing give thanks: for this is the will of God in Christ Jesus concerning you" (1 Thessalonians 5:18).

There were ten lepers in Luke 17:13 who needed healing and cried out, "Jesus, Master, have mercy on us!" But why was there only one who came back to thank Christ when He healed them of their dreaded disease? Apparently nine of them hadn't yet learned the lesson of feeding the white dog of thankfulness. Selfishly, they went on their way enjoying their good fortune. But one leper understood like Job that it was God who gives us everything we have or have not: "The LORD gave, and the LORD hath taken away; blessed be the name of the LORD" (Job 1:21b).

How about you? Which dog is barking at you the loudest today? Will you choose to feed the white dog with thankful thoughts for your children, home, and other blessings, or will you feed the black dog with your thoughts of frustration, failure, and anxieties over what you do not have? Both dogs want to grow stronger in your life. Which will you feed?

Jesus, forgive me when I feed the black dog of my old sinful, selfish nature that says: "Life isn't fair!" Forgive me for whining like a little puppy, and help me express a heart full of thankfulness in praise to You today! In Jesus' name, Amen.

Five Kernels

November 23

"I will greatly praise the LORD with my mouth; yea, I will praise him among the multitude" (Psalm 109:30).

My children loved studying the heroic story about the Pilgrims in our homeschool history class. The Mayflower voyage, Squanto's corn planting and hunting lessons, and the first Thanksgiving all captured my children's deepest interest. But the one story of the Pilgrims that most affected my family was the story about "The Starving Time" during the spring of 1623.

Imagine going through the cold, New England winter living off a slim, summer corn crop and a few fish. Every person suffered daily from hunger and watched as the food supplies continued to dwindle. Tradition states that eventually, all that was left for this band of Pilgrims to eat each day was five kernels of parched corn. Certainly, this is a stark contrast to the Thanksgiving most of us experience!

Because my children's compassionate hearts were touched by this story, we began placing five corn kernels by each of our plates for our Thanksgiving Day meal. We used this tradition to remember the Pilgrims' sacrifice and to reflect on the many blessings God had given us. One by one, we would each take our five kernels and offer thanks for five blessings. This ceremony came to be the most meaningful time of our Thanksgiving Day meal.

What are you thankful for this Thanksgiving? God has blessed you with so much—salvation, health, children, and a home. Perhaps you can encourage your own children to be thankful this Thanksgiving. Count the kernels and count the blessings from our loving Father. "Every good gift and every perfect gift is from above, and cometh down from the Father of lights" (James 1:17a).

Gracious Father, what a loving God You are! I praise You for all the good things You have given me. When I get discouraged, help me to remember Your goodness every day of the year, as I count my many blessings. In Jesus' name, Amen.

 Share your thoughts about this devotional at aophomeschooling.com/327

In High Places

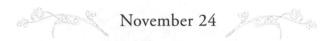

November 24

"For there is no power but of God: the powers that be are ordained of God" (Romans 13:1b).

Standing in the rotunda of our state capitol, I knew this homeschool field trip was going to be a memorable day for my children and me. We could feel the history of past generations all around us as we visited our state senator, a long-time family friend. We had come to see the compelling process of how a bill becomes law, and we weren't disappointed.

Sitting on the floor of the legislature, our senator taught my children many things that day. He showed them how bills are introduced on the floor, how they are voted upon, and how bills get pigeon-holed because of amendments or filibusters. But the most important lesson he taught them came when he humbly shared his faith in God and said, "All these honored congressmen and women are just ordinary people put in high places by God."

Jesus chose twelve men to represent Him to the world before He left this earth. These disciples started out as simple, ordinary fishermen, tax collectors, and laborers, but Christ gave them all power and authority to be His witnesses (Mark 3:13-15). Although they didn't work in capitol buildings making laws, they were able to change the world through their faithful testimonies and God's mighty power.

Maybe you're feeling unimportant and insignificant today as a homeschool parent. Are you wondering if what you're doing will really make any difference? Although you may never stand before legislators or kings, God has given you an audience He values very much— your children. These precious gifts have been given to you to teach, and He wants you to lead them into a personal, godly relationship with Him. Besides, who knows what great and mighty things will be accomplished through their simple, ordinary lives?

Father, thank You for using the ordinary people in this world. Strengthen me to be faithful in the place You have given me to be Your witness—my home. Show me how to teach my children to follow Your leadership, so You can use them mightily. In Jesus' name, Amen.

The Pit Hours

November 25

"Cast thy burden upon the LORD, and he shall sustain thee: he shall never suffer the righteous to be moved" (Psalm 55:22).

The toughest time of the day for homeschool moms of young children has to be from 6:30 p.m. to 8:30 p.m. For some reason, God chooses to give children a second wind after supper, but forgets to include the moms. We have to collect the pieces of a long homeschooling day that lie strewn throughout the house and also give baths, read nighttime stories, and put the children to bed. With our energy levels already running on empty, all of this work seems like a formidable, medieval castle. Where are our knights in shining armor to rescue us?

Praise God, my knight was my wonderful husband. He developed a system that knocked down these chores with one swift blow. While I cleaned the kitchen after supper, he managed the bath time, pajamas, and book reading. Together, we would both be finished in time to tuck each child into bed with prayers and kisses. Without my husband's loving help, I'm sure the dragons of homeschool discouragement would have eaten me alive.

Are you facing the nighttime dragons of homeschool despair? If so, ask God to send you the help you need. If your husband isn't available to help, perhaps there is another family member who can help you face this time of the day with courage—grandparents, older children, others? God knows you need extra strength. He will redeem you from the pit and send the knight you need. "Fear thou not; for I am with thee: be not dismayed; for I am thy God: I will strengthen thee; yea, I will help thee; yea, I will uphold thee with the right hand of my righteousness" (Isaiah 41:10).

Jesus, I'm so tired! Please help me find the strength I need to finish all that needs to be done. I trust You for the provision I need today. In Your name, Amen.

 Share your thoughts about this devotional at **aophomeschooling.com/329**

Fleshy Teaching

November 26

Do you remember the day you decided to homeschool? You knew you needed to make a change in your child's education, but you had no clue how to get started. You felt helpless and utterly dependent on God's guidance and waited on His leading to know where to go and whom to talk to for advice.

Now that a few years have passed, your dependence on the Lord has begun to wane. You're homeschooling more each day in your own fleshy effort, and have forgotten about your total dependence on the Lord. Left unchecked, your homeschooling efforts are headed for a major failure without God's strength and wisdom for each day. "Thus saith the LORD; Cursed be the man that trusteth in man, and maketh flesh his arm, and whose heart departeth from the LORD" (Jeremiah 17:5).

How would you rate yourself as a homeschool parent today? James 3:1 reminds us that teaching our children is a great and awesome responsibility: "My brethren, be not many masters, knowing that we shall receive the greater condemnation." The judgment that will fall on us as teachers is stricter than if we choose not to teach. Christ illustrated this point well to the disciples in Matthew 18:6, "But whoso shall offend one of these little ones which believe in me, it were better for him that a millstone were hanged about his neck, and that he were drowned in the depth of the sea."

What you teach each day influences and shapes your little ones. Be careful not to teach in your own efforts. Go to the Lord and ask for the Holy Spirit to give you the confidence of being in His will, instead of controlling things yourself. "Not by might, nor by power, but by my spirit, saith the LORD of hosts" (Zechariah 4:6).

Father, forgive me for homeschooling in my own strength. You have a perfect lesson plan for my children each day. Help me seek Your face every morning in prayer, so I am teaching my children what they need to know. In Jesus' name, Amen.

Tough Teaching

November 27

"But, Mom," my son cried. "I know I already did these math problems! I don't want to do them over again. My paper has to be somewhere!"

"I'm sorry," I replied. "You may have done them, but they're not here now. We've spent fifteen minutes looking for your math worksheet, and it's nowhere to be found. You'll have to do them over."

Frustration crossed my son's face, but I resisted the temptation to let this missing assignment go unaddressed. Another precedent was being set and my son needed to realize he was responsible for maintaining and organizing his work. My actions seemed tough, but I was considering the future. No college professor or employer would tolerate an excuse of, "I had it somewhere, but I can't find it now."

Sometimes God has to be a tough teacher to us as well. King David's attempt to bring the ark of the covenant back to Jerusalem in 2 Samuel 6 is a prime example. Although the Bible doesn't explain the reason, David neglected to transport the ark according to God's holy laws—on poles carried on the shoulders of the high priests (Exodus 25:14). Instead, David placed the ark on a cart, and Uzzah suffered death when he reached out to steady the ark when the oxen nearly upset it. David had done the right thing, but not in the right way. His irreverence for God's commands and holiness brought about God's response of tough correction.

How about you? Are you in the middle of the consequences of your selfish sin and God's tough love? Quit trying to fix things your own way. Let yourself be trained by His righteousness. You may have to suffer for awhile, but even though you've failed, God's unconditional love will still guide you to the next step. "Now no chastening for the present seemeth to be joyous, but grievous: nevertheless afterward it yieldeth the peaceable fruit of righteousness unto them which are exercised thereby. Wherefore lift up the hands which hang down, and the feeble knees; And make straight paths for your feet, lest that which is lame be turned out of the way; but let it rather be healed" (Hebrews 12:11-13).

God, forgive me for trying to fix my mess on my own. Strengthen me to learn from this mistake by Your firm but loving hand of correction. In Jesus' name, Amen.

 Share your thoughts about this devotional at aophomeschooling.com/331

The Real Deal

"Brethren, pray for us" (1 Thessalonians 5:25).

Seated with my children in the living room, we had just begun our homeschooling day with devotions. The morning had been hectic like usual, and I wasn't in the best of moods. No matter how hard I tried, the starting time for school seemed to be getting later each day. Feeling incompetent as a teacher and trying to make up for lost time, I quickly asked my children, "Is there anything we need to pray about?" Several needs were expressed by each of my young children, which I hurriedly wrote down. But as I started to pray, my son interrupted and asked, "Mom, what about you? Is there something you need prayer for today?"

As usual, his little emotional monitors had seen right through me and perceived my anxiousness and lack of sincerity. Nobody has time for a fake, especially children. Now was the time to admit the truth about what I was really feeling. "Yes, honey," I answered. "I need God to help me slow down and enjoy the day with you."

Exposing our hearts can be a struggle. Homeschooling parents think they have to be spiritually strong for the family and forget that sometimes the best prayer warriors in the family can be their own children. Although we must be careful to share appropriate prayer requests with younger children, their simple, trusting prayers might be the ones that encourage and bless us the most.

Living behind perfectly painted smiles and "I'm fine" responses, isolates us from the love of others, including our children. Don't deny them the privilege of interceding in prayer for your needs. "Confess your faults one to another, and pray one for another, that ye may be healed. The effectual fervent prayer of a righteous 'child' availeth much" (James 5:16).

Heavenly Father, I humbly come before You and thank You again for giving me such wonderful children. I truly am blessed to be loved by them and by You. Help me appropriately share my weaknesses and find strength today from their caring prayers. In Jesus' name, Amen.

Hiding Out

November 29

Do you feel empty today? Is the idea of homeschooling your children overwhelming? Some days, you just don't feel like being profound and inspirational. You would rather hide in bed under the covers or lock yourself away in the bathroom for several hours. The last thing you have is your act together, and you don't feel like disciplining yourself to keep going. Saying yes to your selfish feelings and jumping into irresponsibility would be so much easier.

Wait. Stop and think about those who are depending on you. Just as you expect your children to fight off feelings of laziness and complacency, you, too, must reach up to the One whose purpose and plans are so much higher than yours. God has put you in this place of leadership for a reason. To be the leader of your children's education, you must ask God for the strength you need to make homeschooling decisions.

Saul was no different in accepting his leadership role in the Old Testament. Instead of assuming and looking forward to being the first king of Israel, he was found hiding himself by the baggage (1 Samuel 10:21-22). Samuel had already anointed him privately as king (1 Samuel 10:1), but when time came for Saul to be made king publicly, Samuel had to bring all the tribes of Israel forward to find him. Saul, too, wanted to escape his responsibilities and hide out.

So, will you jump into the arms of God today or into the arms of irresponsibility? My prayer is that you will find the courage you need to continue being faithful in your homeschooling. May you believe the same promise God gave Joshua when he faced his responsibilities of leading God's people into the Promised Land: "Have not I commanded thee? Be strong and of a good courage; be not afraid, neither be thou dismayed: for the LORD thy God is with thee whithersoever thou goest" (Joshua 1:9).

Heavenly Father, my homeschooling responsibilities are weighing me down today. Please lift me up and give me the courage I need to keep going. Please fill me with the Holy Spirit and show me how to lead the precious children You have given me. In Jesus' name, Amen.

Share your thoughts about this devotional at aophomeschooling.com/333

What's Next?

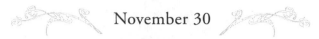
"But let him ask in faith, nothing wavering" (James 1:6a).

One technique I commonly used to motivate my children when homeschooling was the "cliff hanger." I would entice my children's appetite to learn by only presenting enough information to get them excited. Reading only to a climatic part in a story, I would stop and say, "If you want to find out what happens, you'll have to read the rest for yourself!" This tactic was a great motivator, especially for my oldest daughter who couldn't stand not knowing the ending.

As adults, not knowing the ending can be frustrating, too. Who doesn't want to know what is going to happen next? If we had our way, we'd love to have God spell out the answers and endings to life's problems. But like the men and women of faith listed in Hebrews 11, we must learn how to live trusting God. Tucked away in this great chapter is the secret that will enable us to keep going when we don't know what we should do—diligence. Hebrews 11:6 says, "But without faith it is impossible to please him: for he that cometh to God must believe that he is, and that he is a rewarder of them that diligently seek him." We sacrifice faith's reward too easily!

Do you believe God will show you what to do when you need an answer? Are you diligently seeking Him each day believing that He exists and hears every one of your prayers? Read far enough into His Word today until you find a promise just for your problem, and then trust His Word to light your path (Psalm 119:105)! You may not know the answer or see the ending to the problem you are facing right now, but like the men and women of faith who have gone before you, you know the One who is leading you. He will reward you with understanding and wisdom to face every cliff hanger you may have.

Father, thank You for not abandoning me. Some days I have no idea what to do to handle the day's homeschooling problems. Please hear my prayer of faith today and reveal the answers I need. In Jesus' name, Amen.

Big Sky, Big God

December 1

"Thou makest the outgoings of the morning and evening to rejoice" (Psalm 65:8b).

Living in western Nebraska where the sky is bigger than the ground, our homeschooling family developed a particular love of studying the clouds and the sky. On countless occasions, one of my children would come running into the house and say, "Mom, you've got to come and see this!" Walking outside together, we would stand and watch as God painted a breathtaking scene just for us on the canvas of His sky. Each inspiring sunrise or sunset seemed to make all the homeschooling problems of the day fade away into insignificance.

For the next several years, I learned the "art" of enjoying God's beauty. Each time I felt the four walls closing in on my homeschooling day, I would walk outside to view God's multicolored and intricately patterned sky. The kaleidoscope of colors that surrounded me in the vastness of His sky reminded me of my smallness and God's greatness. I realized I was totally dependent on my infinite Creator for all things, including the courage and creativity that I needed to face another homeschooling day.

Are the pressures of homeschooling squeezing the life out of you today? If so, step outside, look up to the sky, and drink in His beauty. God is waiting to revive you today with the glory of His presence and the wonder of His magnificent creation in the heavens. "O LORD, our Lord, how excellent is thy name in all the earth! who hast set thy glory above the heavens. When I consider thy heavens, the work of thy fingers, the moon and the stars, which thou hast ordained; What is man, that thou art mindful of him? and the son of man, that thou visitest him" (Psalm 8:1, 3-4)?

Lord, how great You are! I give You the glory today for being such an awesome God! I praise You for the beauty of Your creation and reminding me that I am in Your constant care. In Jesus' name, Amen.

Are You Listening?

December 2

Like many homeschooling mothers, I sat working at the kitchen table as my children worked on their schoolwork. Although I was supposed to be teaching, I was also doing several other jobs at the same time—washing clothes, cooking supper, and grading papers. As I snipped fresh green beans from our garden for our evening meal, my son asked me a question about his math. He was having difficulty with factoring numbers and needed my help.

"Mom," he said. "Are you listening to me?"

"Yes, I'm listening," I replied not looking up from my work.

"But Mom, would you please listen to me with your eyes?" he quickly responded.

Looking up, I understood what he was really saying. He wanted my undivided attention.

Many times we, too, fail to give God our undivided attention. How many times do you coordinate the noon meal and the following day's activities in your mind while listening to the Sunday morning sermon? What about when you are praying together with people in a Bible study group—does your mind wander to work and worries, or do you actually pray with the person who is speaking? Not focusing our thoughts on the sermon or the prayer requests causes us to wander from being a part of God's will.

Are the day's responsibilities distracting you from hearing God's voice today? Do your prayers seem to get stuck on the ceiling? Do you find yourself rereading what you just read in the Bible and not getting anything from the passage? Stop and look up. Focus your eyes on the One who loves you most. He is waiting for your undivided attention, so He can teach you great and marvelous things. "For the eyes of the LORD run to and fro throughout the whole earth, to show himself strong in the behalf of them whose heart is perfect toward him" (2 Chronicles 16:9a).

Lord, forgive me for my half-hearted attempts at prayer and devotions. Teach me to honor You by diligently seeking You with all I am, so I walk in Your perfect will today. In Jesus' name, Amen.

What Should I Do?

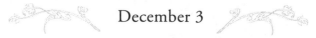

"A man's heart deviseth his way: but the LORD directeth his steps" (Proverbs 16:9).

Do you ever wish you could wake up in the morning and let someone else figure out how your homeschool day is supposed to go? My indecisiveness in homeschooling was usually generated by the fear of making the wrong decisions. What if we were using the wrong curriculum? What if my children weren't getting enough social interaction? What if my children weren't learning what they needed to know to be successful in college? Wasn't there someplace I could go to find all the answers, so I didn't have to second guess myself anymore?

Gideon had a problem with deciding what to do when God called him to defeat the enemies of Israel, the Midianites. He wasn't so sure he saw the warrior in himself that God claimed him to be in Judges 6:12. How could he fight against these men trained in war when all he had known was farming? But Gideon learned the secret to defeating indecision. He simply brought the problems of fighting the battle to the Lord and left the choices up to Him. He only needed to obey and do what God showed him. Even when his faith was small and he had to ask for God's guidance a second time, God lovingly answered with the fleece of faith that was first wet, and then dry.

Are you wringing your hands with indecision and wondering if you have what it takes to be an effective homeschooling parent? Remember the story of Gideon. You may not be a "certified" teacher, but you know the Lord is mighty. If He has called you to homeschool, He will tell you the answers to every question you have about how to teach. He will make you a mighty warrior in the education of your children, and perform amazing miracles of provision when you need them most. You can leave all the decisions to God, and He will show you the way. "And thine ears shall hear a word behind thee, saying, This is the way, walk ye in it, when ye turn to the right hand, and when ye turn to the left" (Isaiah 30:21).

Father, I really need Your help to know what to do today when homeschooling my children. Show me what lessons to focus on and what lessons to leave for another day. Guide me with Your Word and bring those circumstances into our lives that reveal Your divine hand of guidance. In the name of Jesus, Amen.

Treasures in Heaven

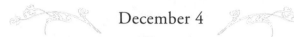

December 4

"For where your treasure is, there will your heart be also" (Luke 12:34).

My twelve-year-old son's favorite pastime after our homeschooling day was looking for hidden items in the ground with his metal detector. Searching for money, old bullet shells, jewelry, and other items consumed hours of his time. At first, I loved seeing his excited face as he came running into the house with each latest "treasure." But then I noticed a change in his attitude. Like a gambler placing his next bet, he seemed to be driven to find the next treasure that might be worth hundreds of dollars. Greed had taken over, and we needed to bring his hobby under Christ's lordship.

As Christians, we spend hours looking for purpose and meaning in the treasures of this world, too. Sadly, these treasures begin to lose their value and we start to look for bigger and better cars, homes, cameras, clothes, and pleasurable items. Like the foolish man in Luke 12:16-21, whose life was cut short, we may find someone else enjoying the very treasures we were storing for ourselves. "But God said unto him, Thou fool, this night thy soul shall be required of thee: then whose shall those things be, which thou hast provided" (Luke 12:20)?

What about you? Is your treasure in heaven or are you building bigger barns for more treasures on earth? Heed God's warning today and think about making yourself rich toward God, instead of pleasing yourself. "Lay not up for yourselves treasures upon earth, where moth and rust doth corrupt, and where thieves break through and steal: But lay up for yourselves treasures in heaven, where neither moth nor rust doth corrupt, and where thieves do not break through nor steal" (Matthew 6:19-20).

Father, every day I feel bombarded by the temptation to want more. Help me to concentrate on the things on this earth that are truly important and to search the Scriptures for the treasures of Your promises. In the name of Your son, Jesus. Amen.

"My Life's a . . ."

I tried to listen to the deeper message my high school daughter was communicating as she went on about all the terrible things in her life. Her list continued to lengthen until she stopped mid-sentence and said, "My life's just a pain." Most of her issues involved trusting God for future provisions and the challenge of waiting on Him for these unknowns. I could see her faith being stretched, but I was bothered by her ungrateful response to what God had already given her. Couldn't she see all the blessings around her? Didn't she know and appreciate how much we had sacrificed to give her the best education at home?

Just as I started to have a pity party, God stopped me and spoke to my heart. "Dear one," He said. "Don't you know that you complain to me every day? I gave you everything I had when I sacrificed my life on the cross to save you, yet you grumble about this and that and forget the price I paid to call you my child." Wow, God doesn't pull any punches. He was absolutely right! Many times throughout our homeschool years my actions and words had failed to communicate a loving trust in His provision. Perhaps my own daughter's struggle was simply reflecting my own failings in trusting God. I was doubly convicted of my ungrateful heart.

Together, my daughter and I turned to God's Word. We let the anxious thoughts go as we laid our problems before the Lord. Instead of whining and complaining, we brought our petitions before God with thanksgiving for what He had already given us (Philippians 4:6). God had already blessed us with so much, and He opened our eyes to trust Him for the unknowns that lay ahead.

Are you struggling with the future and where life is headed? Do you feel like you'll never reach any of your dreams? Turn around and look at every blessing He has given you in the past, and you'll be amazed! God has done so much. Can't He do even more? Trust Him to meet your needs today. "Thou wilt keep him in perfect peace, whose mind is stayed on thee: because he trusteth in thee" (Isaiah 26:3).

Father, forgive me for doubting Your loving care for me. I know You have everything under control and will reveal Your will to me at the proper time. Help me to defeat the discouraging doubts when they come and to cling to You for all I need. In Jesus' name, Amen.

Down, but Not Out

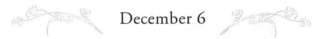

December 6

You know your homeschooling day hasn't gone well when your husband comes home from work and finds you crying. Some days being a Christian and a homeschooling mom puts you into situations that tear you down and bring you to tears. The rejection by others overwhelms, frightens, angers, and discourages you into giving up. The world does all it can do to convince you that you are a fool for following Christ and His call to educate your children.

But opposition to following God's plans is nothing new. In the Bible, Nehemiah faced ridicule when carrying out God's plan to rebuild the broken wall around the city of Jerusalem. Led by the Lord to return to Jerusalem after years of exile, Nehemiah faced a huge task and the negative harassment from enemies like Sanballat and Tobiah (Nehemiah 4). The secret of Nehemiah's success in rallying the workers and overcoming his enemies' discouragement is stated in verse 16a, "And it came to pass from that time forth, that the half of my servants wrought in the work, and the other half of them held both the spears, the shields, and the bows, and the habergeons." Praying to the Lord and setting their mind to work, Nehemiah grouped the people together to build the portion of the wall nearest their homes. With half of the people standing guard and half of the people building the wall, the work was soon finished in the face of those who opposed them.

As homeschoolers, we need to set our minds to the work of educating our children. Divide the task of homeschooling your children. Enlist the prayer support of your spouse, homeschooling friends, or others who will guard your back with the sword of the Spirit (Ephesians 6:17) against Satan's fiery darts of discouragement. God's strength is available to succeed, but you must set your mind to work and pray.

Father, the task of homeschooling seems huge, and the discouragement I am facing today seems even larger. Help me set my mind toward the work of homeschooling our children today, and send prayer warriors who are willing to defend me. In the name of Jesus, Amen.

No More

When we first started homeschooling, I was so excited to give my children the opportunity to experience every learning situation available. My schedule included lofty ideas of weekly field trips and my children's involvement in any sport, music, or church activity they wanted to attend after all, we wanted to make sure no one accused us of isolating our children. However, after homeschooling three to four months, I realized my sanity was at stake if I continued to run my four children out the door to each of their daily activities. The half completed projects and academic assignments that were left behind added additional proof we had a problem. That's when I decided: no more.

New changes were made at our house, and we began to reevaluate what was important to our children's education. Even worthwhile activities within our church and homeschool group had to be analyzed and prayed over. We simply did not have enough time to participate in everything that was available. "Simplify" became my theme, and I rediscovered the joy of homeschooling our children again.

Moses was a great leader in the Bible, but even he had to learn how to simplify his life. After leading God's people out of Egypt, Moses had the awesome responsibility of making this mass of people get along. Imagine dealing with the issues created by millions of people living together out in the wilderness. Moses was burning out fast trying to keep ahead of all the demands. Fortunately, Jethro, his father-in-law noticed what was happening and gave him some practical ideas to get his life back (Exodus 18:17-27).

What about your family? Are you running from activity to activity and missing the whole point of homeschooling—you know, the schooling you're supposed to be doing at home? Life already has enough demands on us to hurry and miss the joy of loving relationships. Don't let the world pull you off the track God has given you in homeschooling. Guard your time together and pray before you say "yes" to one more thing. Remember, we're not isolating. We're equipping our children to grow in their walk with Christ and that simply takes time. "See then that ye walk circumspectly, not as fools, but as wise, Redeeming the time, because the days are evil. Wherefore be ye not unwise, but understanding what the will of the Lord is" (Ephesians 5:15-17).

Lord, our family is on overload and we need Your help. Programs and activities have replaced people and relationships, and we need Your discernment to rediscover why we are homeschooling. Bring us back to our first loves—You and each other. In Jesus' name, Amen.

Daisy

December 8

What picture comes to your mind when you hear of a cow named Daisy? Do you see a soft-eyed jersey with a sweet, calm nature? That's what my son and I were hoping for when we adopted a baby twin calf from our neighbor one spring for a homeschooling project. Although she was not a jersey, she did have the sweetest face with big eyelashes that looked like the petals on a daisy. Thus she was named, and a new adventure in raising a baby calf began for my son.

My misconception of the nurturing abilities of small boys was blown away as my son faithfully cared for his new little friend. Dutifully, he mixed bottles of calf milk replacer for her to drink. Outings with friends were postponed to keep Daisy on a regular feeding schedule, and school assignments were done in the barn so she wouldn't feel alone. Like a mother hen with her chicks, my son proved to be the ideal parent of this little life.

However, Daisy didn't stay little. With all her expert care, she began to grow stronger. At 300 pounds, I knew Daisy needed to be taught how to lead, so we could take her out to the pasture to eat grass. Accomplishing this task proved to be successful at first, but then at 500 pounds, Daisy started to "push her weight around." Many times I watched my frustrated young son dragging and being half drug by Daisy, as he took her from the barn to the pasture. When Daisy's weight reached 900 pounds, we had a real problem. Daily, she would jump the pasture fences to be near our house. No matter if flowers or gardens were in her way, Daisy went wherever she wanted. The time had come to sell Daisy, so she could discover her own nurturing abilities. But one problem stood in the way—the love of my young son for this once little, but now huge cow. How do you sell your "child" and watch her leave?

Sending your children off into the world isn't easy for homeschoolers either. As we teach our children, we forget that someday they will need to leave our home. Keeping the right perspective and preparing yourself and your child for that day takes a determined effort. God's example of cutting the strings best demonstrates how we can face that day when our children need to leave. He sacrificed His only begotten son when Christ came to this sinful earth (John 3:16), so we could receive forgiveness. Praise Him, "That spared not his own Son, but delivered him up for us all" (Romans 8:32a).

Father, thank You for the blessing of homeschooling my children. Help me to remember they belong to You, and someday, they will serve You on their own. Give me wisdom to know when that time has come. In Jesus' name, Amen.

 Share your thoughts about this devotional at **aophomeschooling.com/**342

How Much Wood?

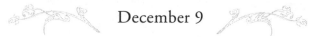

Living and homeschooling on one income forced our family to heat our old farmhouse with wood for the winter months. Although our money was limited, the endless supply of wood available in our grove and the groves of neighbors was not. One math lesson my children wished they could have skipped learning was the dimension of a true "cord" of wood—4' x 4' x 8'.

Since we needed seven or eight cords of wood each winter, we had to begin our work during the summer months. Working together as family included big hands, medium hands, and even little hands to put up our needed supply. But one year, our wood cutting plans were changed by an unexpected course of events. My husband, who was the first link in our wood cutting regime, was hurt when cutting down a tree. As the tree fell, it twisted and hit him in the head, knocking him unconscious and leaving a huge gash in his forehead. My children and I were able to get him to the doctor, but we now faced the chore of cutting wood alone.

I normally cry when I am faced with overwhelming responsibility, but there was no time for tears. That fall I forced myself to learn how to operate the chainsaw as proficiently as my husband. My children stepped up and took on my usual tasks, and somehow we completed all the work. We finished and stacked the last piece of wood just before the first snow.

Have you ever wanted to cry when facing the enormous challenge of homeschooling? Teaching our children, maintaining a home, and fulfilling the duties of being a wife can bring you to tears. The responsibilities are just too much! Where will the strength come from to knock down each day's work? God is the One who will pick you up and give you the skills you need to teach your children. Even when you face topics or concepts you don't know, He will lead you to the right person to help. God has a burning passion for His children, and He won't leave you out in the cold. "And not only so, but we glory in tribulations also: knowing that tribulation worketh patience; And patience, experience; and experience, hope: And hope maketh not ashamed" (Romans 5: 3-5a).

Lord, thank You for being bigger than any giant I may have to face in homeschooling. Teach me how to be the best possible teacher for my children. I love You. In Jesus' name, Amen.

Homeschool Hazard Signs

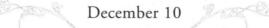

December 10

Like the road signs that warn us of impending danger, there are also warning signs for parents on the road of homeschooling. We can either take heed to the dangers that they clearly indicate lay ahead, or we can choose to disobey these common hazard signs and end up in a homeschooling wreck.

When you see the "Slippery When Wet" sign of tears in your discouraged child's face, chances are you're leaving out the loving encouragement needed when teaching academics. Pay attention to the "High Wind Warning" sign and give your child the godly correction and discipline he needs when you hear the floors pounding and the windows rattling from his rebellion. Don't ignore your child exceeding the posted "Speed Limit" sign. When you see him hurrying through schoolwork or skipping devotions to run to another extra-curricular activity, you will need to take your child to parental court to reevaluate what's important in his life. Rest assured, disregarding these hazards and setting your homeschool on cruise will cause an accident.

God tells us to watch for warning signs in our spiritual lives, too. When we start to see the evidences of "Adultery, fornication, uncleanness, lasciviousness, idolatry, witchcraft, hatred, variance, emulations, wrath, strife, seditions, heresies, envyings, murders, drunkenness, revellings, and such like" (Galatians 5:19b-21a), we are headed down the dangerous road of living life in the flesh. Before you are pulled over by the Holy Spirit, take the next exit and pray. Turn your heart back to the Lord, and heed His warnings to keep your life headed in the right direction.

Lord, help me to recognize the danger signs of evil in my life and turn back to You. Teach me to stay close to You and to Your Word, so I stay on the path that leads to righteousness. In Jesus' name, Amen.

The Cottonwood

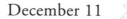

"For I am the LORD, I change not" (Malachi 3:6a).

The enormous cottonwood tree had stood for years outside the upstairs bedroom window of our farmhouse. As a young girl, I grew up playing in its branches and hiding behind its trunk during games of hide and seek. Its shade covered and cooled our house in the summer and its branches protected us from the fierce north winds of winter. Now, as an adult, I looked out the same window and watched as my young daughters played the same childhood games during recess from homeschooling. A third generation had come to this farm home, and somehow the cottonwood had remained the same—strong, protective, and majestic.

Very few things remain the same during one's lifetime. Perhaps that is why we feel insecure and uncertain many times. As Christians, however, we can find comfort in knowing, "Jesus Christ the same yesterday, and to day, and for ever" (Hebrews 13:8). No matter what difficulties we face or what changes may come, God's constant and faithful love will never be different than it is today. We can always depend on the promises of His Word and the power of the Holy Spirit to guide and direct our lives.

What things in life are you counting on to always be around—a loved one, your money, your health, your children, a home? My old farmhouse is now torn down, my children are grown and have moved away, and the cottonwood is no more. The most important homeschool lesson has taken twenty-five years for me to learn—the only thing that will ever remain the same is the Lord. "Of old hast thou laid the foundation of the earth: and the heavens are the work of thy hands. They shall perish, but thou shalt endure: yea, all of them shall wax old like a garment; as a vesture shalt thou change them, and they shall be changed: But thou art the same, and thy years shall have no end" (Psalm 102:25-27).

Father God, I stand before You with thanksgiving and awe for being such a great and mighty God. Thank You for being the one thing in life I can always depend on. I give You my worship and my praise today. In Jesus' name, Amen.

 Share your thoughts about this devotional at aophomeschooling.com/345

The Thorn

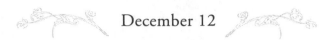

"To every thing there is a season, and a time to every purpose under the heaven: . . . and a time to heal" (Ecclesiastes 3:1, 3b).

The pain in my daughter's palm was first apparent while practicing her piano lesson for school one day. A small discoloration and swelling was visible, but they seemed insignificant against the healthy flesh. As time went on, however, I observed the difficulty my daughter had while holding her pencil during schoolwork. I applied my own home remedies to help with the discomfort, but they brought little change. Eventually, a cyst was diagnosed by a specialist, and surgery was scheduled to remove it.

The night before her surgery, my daughter and I got home late after spending the evening roller skating with a group of homeschooling families. As I came to say goodnight, I looked at her hand one last time, since she had fallen and bumped her hand while skating. Amazingly, a crack had appeared in the swelling. Gently pulling the skin apart, I could just see the tip of something. Grabbing my tweezers and a flashlight, I proceeded to do "surgery." I stared in amazement as the "cyst" turned out to be an inch-long cactus thorn.

The incorrect diagnosis of my daughter's pain made me realize that we also misdiagnose the emotional problems in people's lives. Many times we fail to address the deeper issues of "why" a person is acting a certain way and simply respond to their outward displays of unloving behavior. Perhaps if we saw their problem through the eyes of the "Great Physician," we would know how to help their healing process. Christ's actions illustrate this best when He didn't debate or argue with the Samaritan woman at the well in John 4:7-26. Instead, He saw into her heart and addressed the pain of her failed relationships with men and the need she had to be forgiven and loved.

Is there a prickly person God has placed in your life? You know, one of those people who can't be pleased no matter what you do. The behavior he is displaying could be the result of many hidden, painful experiences. Instead of reacting negatively or avoiding him, respond in love. If you ask the Lord for wisdom to see into his true problems, He will show you the loving "surgery" that may help heal his pain.

Father, please help me love the unlovely people You've put into my life. Give me understanding to see the real "thorn" that is causing their pain and the desire to reach out with Your love. In Jesus' name, Amen.

Time for Recess

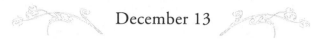

December 13

"Better is an handful with quietness, than both the hands full with travail and vexation of spirit" (Ecclesiastes 4:6).

Somewhere during my teaching career as a homeschooling parent, I came up with the brilliant idea (NOT) of cramming all our schoolwork into half days. By eliminating our mid-morning playtime, we could school for four to five hours straight and finish the day early. My reasoning for this decision was to provide "more" free time and field trips for my children, but later, I was forced to admit that my brilliant idea was really meant to make life more convenient for me. Every time we attempted this cramped schedule, my children became stressed out. Praise God, they were smarter than me on this issue and said the trade off was simply not worth the strain. Time for recess was just as important as school time.

God made us and He knows that the human body is frail (Psalm 103:14). I think He also knew that mankind would overextend itself, so He gave us the commandment for a Sabbath day to worship Him and rest from our labors (Exodus 20:8-11). This rest not only focuses our attention on our Creator God, but it also replenishes our body physically, emotionally, and spiritually. Like everyone else, homeschooling families are tempted to rob time from play and relaxation to keep up with the world's hurried pace.

Is your homeschooling schedule allowing time for breaks? Even homeschooling parents need time to walk away from the work for a few minutes. Don't just send your children outside to play—go with them. Let the Lord refresh you and take away the pressures of your homeschooling day. God is in control, and He will help you accomplish all that needs to be done. "There remaineth therefore a rest to the people of God. For he that is entered into his rest, he also hath ceased from his own works, as God did from his" (Hebrews 4:9-10).

Lord, show me again how to discipline myself with the right amounts of work and relaxation. Forgive me for making my day bigger than You've planned. Help me to pray and seek Your will each morning. In Jesus' name, Amen.

Dedicated Dads

December 14

"And, ye fathers, provoke not your children to wrath: but bring them up in the nurture and admonition of the Lord" (Ephesians 6:4).

If you're a homeschool mom, you've probably experienced the feeling of being unappreciated by the world, right? Imagine then, what your husband must feel like as he quietly contributes to your family's homeschooling day. Even though you get some credit for doing the majority of teaching, he usually receives no recognition at all. He remains unnoticed by both friends and family (sometimes his own). Perhaps it is time to consider some of the ways he faithfully supports your children's educational success, such as the following:

• Providing the working capital to keep your school from going in the red. Because of his hard-earned income, you are able to buy curriculum and go on field trips.

• Being the substitute teacher who gives you a breather. Without the extra support of reading stories, practicing spelling words, or teaching a particular subject area, you would certainly burn out as 24/7 mom and teacher.

• Serving as "principal of the school." Knowing that Dad is waiting to talk to them will provide that added discipline needed to curtail even the most disruptive or disrespectful child.

• Supplying an endless array of shop classes that will benefit your child later in life. Lessons in carpentry, mechanics, or plumbing will save your child the expense of having to pay for these services when he is an adult.

• Being the spiritual leader who guides your children into the most important truths they will ever learn—God loves them and sent His Son, Jesus, to be their Savior.

This Christmas, have your children show appreciation to their father. Why not give him the praise that's due and thank him for all his sacrificial acts of service and love with a thoughtful card or gift? Make this scripture true in his life: "As arrows are in the hand of a mighty man; so are children of the youth. Happy is the man that hath his quiver full of them" (Psalm 127:4-5a).

Lord, forgive me for taking my husband for granted and not acknowledging his homeschooling efforts as I should. Thank You for the countless hours of love and support he provides every day. In Jesus' name, Amen.

 Share your thoughts about this devotional at aophomeschooling.com/348

Dying to Self

December 15

"I am crucified with Christ: nevertheless I live; yet not I, but Christ liveth in me: and the life which I now live in the flesh I live by the faith of the Son of God, who loved me, and gave himself for me" (Galatians 2:20).

Homeschooling is not what you thought. Those images of perfectly happy children soaking in your words of wisdom have evaporated. You feel like you have bitten off more than you can chew. You are reevaluating. Homeschooling involves sacrificing more of your precious day than you intended. "What about time for me?" you ask.

God commands us to sacrifice all that we are to Him. Romans 12:1 states, "I beseech you therefore, brethren, by the mercies of God, that ye present your bodies a living sacrifice, holy, acceptable unto God, which is your reasonable service." Living to please yourself should no longer have a place in your life. God wants you to move beyond the immediate to the eternal and trust Him to lead you by faith. Your flesh will continue to cry out, "What about me?", but as you nail those fleshy desires to the cross, you will experience a new dimension to your homeschooling and your personal walk with God. His plan for you is much bigger than a new outfit, a new house, a trip, or whatever you think makes you feel content. Let Him teach you how to homeschool and bring those things into your life that will make you truly happy.

Lord, forgive me for thinking that this world is all about me. Show me how to say "No" to those things of the flesh that cause me to want my own way and give up homeschooling. In Jesus' name, Amen.

Share your thoughts about this devotional at aophomeschooling.com/349

Feeble Excuses

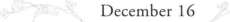

I was listening to my daughter as she gave me the feeble excuse, "But Mom, the rest of the homeschool group is going!" I already knew my answer was going to be "no" to this unchaperoned activity of co-ed young teens, but her words caused me to think about the need we all feel to be like everyone else. I remembered using the same poor excuse with my parents and hearing the same "would you jump off a cliff if everyone else did it, too" lecture. Why do we have such a need to be like others?

God had been leading His people ever since He first brought them out of Egypt. Why did they think they needed a king now? Moses, the judges, and the prophets had protected, exhorted, and provided directly for His people, but now the people wanted Samuel to find a king to rule over them so they could be like the other nations around them (1 Samuel 8:21-22). Samuel tried to warn them what having a king would do to their lives, but they wouldn't listen. God's response in 1 Samuel 8:7b is probably the answer to all the generations of young people who have ever used the "but everyone else is doing it" excuse: "For they have not rejected thee, but they have rejected me, that I should not reign over them."

What excuse are you telling God to justify your sinful actions? Do you find yourself caught up in activities and making purchases so "you can be like everyone else?" If you are His child, He has a different plan for your life than to go with the flow. He wants to set you apart to be holy unto Himself. "As obedient children, not fashioning yourselves according to the former lusts in your ignorance: But as he which hath called you is holy, so be ye holy in all manner of conversation; Because it is written, Be ye holy; for I am holy" (1 Peter 1:14-16).

Jesus, I stand convicted of my sinful selfishness. I yield my life to Your correction and ask You to cleanse me of those things that do not glorify You. My body is Your temple, and I give You all that I am today. In Your precious name, Amen.

Repeat Lessons

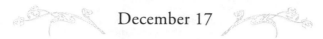

December 17

"Jesus Christ the same yesterday, and to day, and for ever" (Hebrews 13:8).

Young children love consistency in homeschooling lessons. Playing the same game or reading the same book repeatedly gives them a sense of accomplishment. Repetition helps them master letters, words, and mathematical operations and provides a strong foundation for their future learning. Because these foundational lessons are so important, we can be thankful young children are willing to learn through repetition.

God, too, repeatedly teaches us the same lessons in life. Just when we think we've mastered a spiritual truth such as obedience and submission, Satan comes and tricks us. We forget what we have learned from God's Word and we fall into sin. Because God never changes, He lovingly takes us back to the beginning and shows us again how to live for Him.

Are you finding yourself relearning an old truth you thought you'd never forget? Don't let prideful thinking cause you to ignore this repeated lesson. Humbly acknowledge again that you need His love and wisdom to win over sin's temptation. "Wherefore let him that thinketh he standeth take heed lest he fall" (1 Corinthians 10:12).

Father, sometimes I seem to continue to battle the same sins over and over. Thank You for Your forgiving love. Please help me to remain faithful in what You have taught, so I might glorify You today. In Your Son's name, Amen.

 Share your thoughts about this devotional at **aophomeschooling.com/351**

Dream Stealer

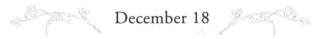

December 18

"No," I said again to my daughter for the hundredth time. "We don't have the money to buy a horse." As I heard myself saying the words, I felt like I was bursting her bubble, although I knew what I was saying was true. Any homeschooling family living on one income knows the careful planning and budgeting that has to be implemented just to pay for day-to-day living expenses.

But a heart without dreams is like a house without windows, and I was beginning to realize that every time I told my daughter "No, you can't have a horse." Then one day a thought came to my mind. I was limiting and superseding what God may want. Instead of automatically saying "no" to my daughter, I went with her to God in prayer. We placed her dream of a horse into His hands and waited for God's answer.

Two months went by, and then one day I received a call from a lady in our town. She wanted to know if she could have permission to give her grown daughter's old 4-H horse to my daughter as a Christmas present. I couldn't believe what she was saying and was humbled by both God and her offer. Needless to say, that Christmas was one my daughter never forgot. Not only did she receive a new horse, but this same lady also bought my daughter a new bridle, breast collar, halter, and matching saddle pad!

I don't know who learned the greater lesson that Christmas, my daughter or me. She had tenaciously hung on to her dream, and I had learned that God is much bigger than my faith or pocket book. What about you? Are you automatically saying "no" to your children, or are you leading them to the Lord and saying, "Let's pray." "Now unto him that is able to do exceeding abundantly above all that we ask or think, according to the power that worketh in us, unto him be glory" (Ephesians 3:20-21a).

Father, what a great and mighty God You are! Forgive me for failing to lead my children to You, the Creator and giver of every good and perfect gift. Thank You this Christmas for giving us the gift we needed most—Your son, Jesus. In His name we pray, Amen.

Arise, O Sleeper

December 19

"Wherefore he saith, Awake thou that sleepest, and arise from the dead, and Christ shall give thee light" (Ephesians 5:14).

Waking up my children in the wintertime usually brought an unwelcomed start to our homeschooling day. Most mornings my children were dead to the world because it was still dark outside. They responded like bears in hibernation—in lethargic slow motion. I felt like the evil stepmother in Cinderella as I forced them out of their beds to do their list of morning chores before breakfast. I was always glad for the change of seasons and embraced the longer and happier days of summer sunshine.

Waking up those who don't know the Lord can be a difficult task as well. Because they are dead in Christ, they can only be convicted of their sin by the power of the Holy Spirit. Our job, as Christians, is to shine the warmth of God's love on their lives and to enjoy the privilege of telling them what Christ has done for us. However, according to Jude 22-23, we may face resistance: "And of some have compassion, making a difference: And others save with fear, pulling them out of the fire; hating even the garment spotted by the flesh." Sometimes the Holy Spirit may use us to kick, pull, or drag people out of their beds of sinful stupor.

God is a loving Father, and He desires that none perish (2 Peter 3:9). As we listen to the Holy Spirit's leading, we must be careful to do exactly as He leads to help others know the forgiveness of sins. Has the Lord laid someone on your heart who needs awakening from his sinful state? Don't be surprised if he initially rejects the joyful Good News of Christ's salvation. Some people are as crabby as an old bear, but God wants to change their hearts, too. Don't give up. Keep shining the warmth of God's love and seek His guidance. He will show you how to win over their hearts.

Lord, use me this Christmas season to show Your love to my stubborn neighbor. Let Your love shine through me and warm the coldness of his hard heart. Show me what to do and give me the words to say that will challenge him to hear Your voice and change his ways. In Jesus' name, Amen.

The Christmas Bean

I'm not sure how the tradition got started. I think my daughter first started the idea since she was the best "cake baker" in our homeschool family. Every Christmas we baked a small cake for a birthday party in Sunday school for Jesus. Using only half the dough, my daughter decided to use the other half for individual cupcakes for our family. She thought decorating these cupcakes for each person at our Christmas Eve dinner would be fun, and then she had an inspiration. Why not hide an uncooked kidney bean in one of the cupcakes? The person who found the bean baked in their cupcake would then be the first to open his gifts at Christmas.

Even today my daughter continues this Christmas tradition. In fact, our family's Christmas wouldn't be complete without it. But that's how traditions get started, isn't it? Most times, traditions make our lives more meaningful. They give us a sense of security, and a sense of roots and familiarity.

But sometimes, traditions can sap the very life from us. When we allow the traditions and rituals in our worship to replace a vibrant relationship with Christ, we quench the Holy Spirit. Jesus rebuked the Pharisees for this sin when He said, "But in vain they do worship me, teaching for doctrines the commandments of men" (Matthew 15:9). God desires a circumcised heart that is tender and humble in worship. Paul warned the Colossians of the same problem, "Beware lest any man spoil you through philosophy and vain deceit, after the tradition of men, after the rudiments of the world, and not after Christ" (Colossians 2:8).

Any tradition can replace true love and heartfelt responses, but we must be especially careful not to approach our Holy God only with token rituals begun by man. Christ's response to the woman at the well says how we should worship best: "But the hour cometh, and now is, when the true worshippers shall worship the Father in spirit and in truth: for the Father seeketh such to worship him. God is a Spirit: and they that worship him must worship him in spirit and in truth" (John 4:23-24).

Lord, forgive me when I think I've worshiped You simply by going to church or offering up a prayer. Help me to remember that in the family of God, You desire a heartfelt love in my worship. I offer my love to You anew. In Jesus' name, Amen.

Broccoli Soup

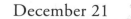

December 21

"A man's pride shall bring him low: but honour shall uphold the humble in spirit" (Proverbs 29:23).

The snow was gently falling as we sat down to enjoy our Christmas Eve supper of soup, sandwiches, and cookies. The candles were lit and the light from the flickering flames made each homemade Christmas ornament hanging from the windows twinkle. The house was cozy and warm from a full day of cooking, and the fragrant aromas tantalized our taste buds. Four young faces were eagerly anticipating opening their Christmas gifts after the meal, and my husband and I smiled in satisfaction at God's blessings. With Grandpa and Grandma's arrival earlier that afternoon, the perfect Christmas scene was now complete.

I had worked so hard to make everything just right and wanted to impress my in-laws with a memorable Christmas. I had made this meal many times and felt confident as I dished out the two different choices of soup—chili or broccoli-cheese. As we closed our eyes and my husband offered a prayer of thanks to God, I looked down at my bowl. I couldn't believe my eyes. There, swimming on top of my broccoli soup, were a dozen knat-like bugs. I whispered to myself in agony, "Where did they come from?" Then, I remembered. I had forgotten to wash the broccoli before putting it into the soup. I could feel my heart sink with embarrassment even before my husband finished his prayer. This was going to be a memorable Christmas, all right, especially for my mother-in-law who had just been served buggy, broccoli soup.

Many times our motives for wanting things are so wrong. We want to impress instead of bless, and pride is waiting to bring us to our knees. What about your petitions? Are you selfishly asking God for things just to make you look good? If you're doing most of the talking during your prayer time with God, there may be a problem. Let the Holy Spirit correct your attitude today and don't wait to be served your cup of humble "soup." "Every one that is proud in heart is an abomination to the LORD: though hand join in hand, he shall not be unpunished" (Proverbs 16:5).

Lord, give me the same attitude that was in Christ Jesus when He emptied Himself to be born a man and to die for my sins. Teach me again how to be a servant and to care more about others than myself. In Jesus' name, Amen.

 Share your thoughts about this devotional at aophomeschooling.com/355

Christmas Cheer

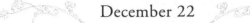

"She openeth her mouth with wisdom; and in her tongue is the law of kindness. Her children arise up, and call her blessed" (Proverbs 31:26, 28a).

"Let's go, Mom. Everyone is waiting for us in the car," cried my daughter as she ran out the door for the Christmas Eve program at church. I smiled at her enthusiasm and thought back to days when I was a young girl looking forward to Christmas. My Christmases were filled with relatives, oyster stew, chocolate covered cherries, Christmas programs at church, and opening gifts in knee-deep paper with my family of nine. But my most cherished memories of Christmas were the hours my mother and I spent beforehand wrapping gifts for my family.

My mother had an insatiable love for celebrating Christ's birth. She shared God's love through brightly lit decorations, great food, and presents. Yes, my mother loved to give presents, and she chose me to help her wrap them. Together we spent hours making perfect bows and wrapping "just one more box." I considered helping her a great honor because she trusted me not to tell my brothers and sisters what was in their packages.

When I grew older, I realized why my mother and I had so many gifts to wrap each year. Knowing she couldn't give us much, my mother cleverly wrapped each part of a gift into as many boxes as possible. She knew our young minds couldn't comprehend value, but we could count. To a young mind, the more presents you had, the better.

Tonight, I stood in my mother's place. My homeschool family was smaller, but our money to make Christmas special was just as short. As I turned to shut off the light and walk out the door, I smiled as I saw the huge pile of gifts waiting to be opened when we returned. My daughter and I had just finished wrapping them. Some Christmas traditions are just worth passing on.

Lord, thank You for the sacrificial love of mothers. Like the Proverbs 31 woman, give me wisdom to love my family with special acts of kindness. Teach me how to make every day a special gift with the same love that was given to me. In Jesus' name, Amen.

No Peeking

"The secret of the LORD is with them that fear him; and he will shew them his covenant" (Psalm 25:14).

Christmas is such a fun time for secrets. At our house, our four children were not allowed to look into the closets or under our bed until all the gifts were wrapped. Since we were home-schooling, enforcing this rule was not too difficult. However, even after the presents had been wrapped, determining what was inside was sometimes easy for my children to figure out, especially as they got older and smarter. I learned that if I wanted to surprise them at Christmas, I needed to cleverly disguise the box in which the gift was wrapped, even if disguising it meant adding a brick for extra weight.

Have you ever wondered why Jesus disguised His spiritual truths in parables when He lived on earth? Although He spoke to the multitudes, the gift of His truths about the kingdom of Heaven was hidden from those with hard hearts and ears that refused to listen (Matthew 13:10-15). The meaning of His message was only understood by those who sought the truth with repentant hearts.

Do the truths of God's Word seem hard to understand to you? When reading the Bible, you must come realizing the Scriptures "are spiritually discerned" (1 Corinthians 2:14b). That means unless you are born of the Spirit and filled with the Spirit, you will not understand God's Word. Ask the Holy Spirit to reveal the meaning of what you are reading in the Bible today. He promises to show you if you come with a repentant and obedient heart. "And ye shall seek me, and find me, when ye shall search for me with all your heart" (Jeremiah 29:13).

Father, open my mind to understand the truth of Your Word. I want to do Your will, but I need Your guidance. Speak to my heart in the power of the Holy Spirit and reveal what You are teaching me from Your Word today. In the name of Jesus, Amen.

Peace on Earth

December 24

"He hath delivered my soul in peace from the battle that was against me" (Psalm 55:18a).

The words on the Christmas card and the noise coming from our school room stood in stark contrast to one another. "Peace on Earth," the card read. "My, wouldn't that be nice?" I thought. I guess every homeschooling parent longs for a peaceful home, but hearing the crescendo in my children's voices, I knew that peace wasn't happening today at our house. But Christmas was coming, and I could hope, right?

As I thought more about peace on earth, I wondered what Christ meant in John 14:27 when He said, "Peace I leave with you, my peace I give unto you: not as the world giveth, give I unto you. Let not your heart be troubled, neither let it be afraid." Then, the truth of this verse dawned on me—true peace is not the absence of arguments, violence, or wars. True peace is experiencing God's love instead of His wrath because we receive the forgiveness of sins through the blood of Christ by the power of the Holy Spirit. That means fighting children, threats of war, and even interruptions to homeschooling days need not change to experience the presence of Christ's peace in my life.

Would you like to find peace this Christmas? Don't look for the absence of problems. Look instead to the peacemaker whose birth made the angels of heaven proclaim, "Glory to God in the highest, and on earth peace, good will toward men" (Luke 2:14). Let the power of the Holy Spirit fill you this Christmas and experience the peace of Christ within. Shalom! "These things I have spoken unto you, that in me ye might have peace. In the world ye shall have tribulation: but be of good cheer; I have overcome the world" (John 16:33).

Jesus, I praise You for the love, forgiveness, and peace You give to all who trust in You. Please walk with me this Christmas and give me the peace of Your presence in my life. In Your holy name, Amen.

 Share your thoughts about this devotional at aophomeschooling.com/358

A Love Letter

December 25

I see you sitting there—tired, worn out, and empty. Another year of homeschooling has used you up. You feel helpless like a baby. That's OK. I know all about being a baby. I was born one for you many years ago. I know the ache you feel to be held and loved, and that is why I came. I knew you would be sitting there, years in the future, praying and asking me to hold you, and I am dear one. Let me give you a special Christmas gift of love as I breathe new life into the very center of your soul.

Do you know that I think of you every moment of every day? I watch you patiently home-school the children I gave you, and I know how badly you feel when you fail and lose your temper. I forgive you, my child, just as you forgive your children when they make a mistake. "It's OK; we'll try again," you say to them, and I'm telling you the same thing, too. I'm so proud of you and how you've followed me when I asked you to teach your children about me at home. Your sacrifice says that you love me. I know all about that, too. I left everything that was mine when I came from heaven. I know how you feel when the Father asks so much of you.

Look at me, my child. You may feel beat up, but do you know that you are still beautiful? I see that smile. Yes, you're still as beautiful as the day I created you. I love who you are and I'm whispering your name. Can you hear me? Remember my child that this is not your home. You really belong here with me in heaven. But I want you where you are now to love this family I gave you. Don't give up. I want you to trust me. I won't let you down. Every promise I've made is true, and someday I'm coming back for you. But for now, rest in my love, and tonight and even tomorrow when you wake up, I'll be here watching over you. I love you. Merry Christmas.

"Seeing then that we have a great high priest, that is passed into the heavens, Jesus the Son of God, let us hold fast our profession. For we have not an high priest which cannot be touched with the feeling of our infirmities" (Hebrews 4:14-15a).

Jesus, thank You for the best Christmas gift I could ever receive—Your forgiveness and love. My heart sings with praise to You for understanding my every need. I love You, Jesus, and offer You my life again to use however You choose. In Your name I pray, Amen.

 Share your thoughts about this devotional at aophomeschooling.com/359

Greater Than, Less Than

December 26

I thought my daughter was going to pull out her hair when she said, "Mom, I just don't get this!" We were studying the concepts of greater than, less than, and equal to in math, and she simply couldn't remember which sign to use when there was a lesser value. I explained, "A simple way to remember is that the sign should point to the smaller value." My daughter smiled as she began to understand and exclaimed, "Mom, you're so smart!"

Unfortunately, the concepts of greater than and less than do not work in the spiritual matters of our lives. Many times we try to make our sins appear less by comparing them to other's sins. If we haven't murdered, stolen, or used drugs to harm our bodies, we may think we're not too bad. But comparing our sins to others doesn't make them less or greater. James 2:10 tells us, "For whosoever shall keep the whole law, and yet offend in one point, he is guilty of all." No matter if you've told a little white lie or if you've just robbed a bank, in God's eyes your sin is sin. We may try to point our finger at someone else to think we are better, but like the old story goes, pointing at the sins of others always leaves three fingers pointing back at you!

Do you try to justify your "little" sins by saying they're less than someone else's sin? According to the world, you might have the right answer, but not according to God. Christ died an agonizing death on the cross for you because His love was greater than any of your sins, big or small. Won't you stop comparing and start confessing your sin to Him today?

Jesus, forgive me for thinking there is such a thing as "little" sin. I know each of my sins nailed You to the cross, and I bow before You today in repentance. Please cleanse my heart and fill me with the Holy Spirit. In Your name, Amen.

Dying Hope

I found my daughter crying in her bedroom holding her cat for comfort. Lying on the bed was her literature workbook opened to the homeschool assignment she had been scheduled to complete that day. Not knowing the source of her pain, I offered a hug and waited for her to express her heartache. "Mom, that story was so sad," she cried. I looked at the page she had been reading and saw she had finished O. Henry's, "The Last Leaf."

Her compassionate heart had connected with the surprise ending for which O. Henry is noted. Seriously ill with pneumonia, a young woman lay in the hospital waiting to die. She knew she was near death and was determined to die when the last leaf fell from the vine outside her hospital window. Her close friend, roommate, and fellow artist had spoken to the doctor, and the doctor told her that her friend had little chance of surviving unless she could convince her dying friend to want to live. But no amount of encouragement would change the dying girl's mind.

Distraught, the friend went to the old man who lived in the apartment underneath theirs for help. This self-imposed guardian of these two young girls and washed-up artist, who was always "waiting to paint his next masterpiece," discovered the answer to give hope to the dying girl. However, in the process, the story takes a surprising turn of events.

We all like to read and hear stories of noble characters who remain faithful through difficult times with sacrificial love. Perhaps the most moving story is found in God's Word when Jesus faced death on the cross for our sins. As He stated to Peter in Matthew 26:53, He could have called on twelve legions of angels to spare Him from such a horrible death, but He didn't. Instead, He stayed on the cross through each nail that was hammered into his hands and suffered each agonizing breath, until He said, "It is finished" (John 19:30).

Does the story of Jesus' sacrifice on the cross move you to tears? Why not take a moment today to reread Luke, chapters 22 and 23 and remember what a loving Lord we serve. And don't forget to read the best surprise ending ever written in chapter 24—hallelujah, Christ arose!

Lord, like the faithful servant who invested his talents wisely, I want to be found faithful when You return. Help me sacrificially love and teach my children every lesson they need to learn to become people of character. In Jesus' name, Amen.

Robbing God

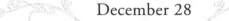

"Will a man rob God? Yet ye have robbed me. But ye say, Wherein have we robbed thee? In tithes and offerings" (Malachi 3:8).

When our children were young, we felt convicted by God to teach them the principle of tithing. We incorporated this lesson into our homeschooling and purchased little, white glow-in-the-dark church banks in which they could place their dimes, quarters, nickels, and pennies. When they earned money for chores or received money as gifts, we taught our children how to determine one tenth of the amount and place it into their bank. They loved the sound of the dropping coins and felt so grown up as they placed their own money into the offering plate each Sunday at church.

As time went by, we thought the habit of tithing had been firmly established in our children. We expected them to be diligent in giving part of their hard-earned money from part-time jobs to the Lord. But the temptations to buy new CD's, videos, clothes, and teenage toys proved to be too strong. One day I noticed all my son's new purchases, and I wondered where the money had come from to buy them. I questioned whether or not he had been tithing, and he sheepishly confessed that he had not.

Stealing from God isn't a new temptation. Years ago, the sons of Eli the priest in 1 Samuel 2 thought they could steal God's portion of the offerings being presented by the people of Israel. Although the priests were entitled to receive a portion of the offering for themselves (Leviticus 7), Eli's worthless sons were confiscating the choicest part of the offering which was to be given to God. God's rebuke for this sin was a judgment that was swift and sure—both of his sons would see death on the same day (1 Samuel 2:34).

What about you? Are you robbing God of His portion of your family's income? With all the bills and homeschooling expenses for each month, the temptation to steal what belongs to God is just as strong today. Why not take God at His Word instead and claim the promise of Malachi 3:10: "Bring ye all the tithes into the storehouse, that there may be meat in mine house, and prove me now herewith, saith the LORD of hosts, if I will not open you the windows of heaven, and pour you out a blessing, that there shall not be room enough to receive it."

Lord, give me strength this day to make a change in the way we spend our money. I know all the blessings we have are from You. Guard my heart against the temptation to take Your portion for myself, and let my actions and faith honor You. In Jesus' name, Amen.

 Share your thoughts about this devotional at **aophomeschooling.com**/362

Transformations

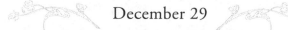

December 29

"When I was a child, I spake as a child, I understood as a child, I thought as a child: but when I became a man, I put away childish things" (1 Corinthians 13:11).

Everyone needs to grow up, including the children of homeschoolers. However, sometimes we make the homeschool nest so comfortable that our children stave off responsibilities they should be assuming as adults. We need to stop pacifying them with material comforts and encourage instead their desire to provide for themselves. After all, homeschooling means teaching our children to learn how to work, as well as how to think.

Sometimes we like our comfortable spiritual nest, too, and fail to grow up into mature believers. The Apostle Paul had much to say to the new Christians living in Corinth. He was looking for followers of Christ who were ready to feed on the meat of the Word, but instead he found selfishness, jealousy, and strife (1 Corinthians 3:1-2). The writer to the Hebrews was also concerned about the lack of spiritual maturity in believers when he penned: "For every one that useth milk is unskilful in the word of righteousness: for he is a babe. But strong meat belongeth to them that are of full age, even those who by reason of use have their senses exercised to discern both good and evil" (Hebrews 5:13-14).

What about you? Do you want just enough of Christ to get into heaven, or have you grown up in the Lord? The testimony of your salvation experience is not the only thing you should be sharing. If you are chewing on the meat of God's Word, your prayer life will be vibrant, and your testimony will reflect what God is teaching you in your life today! "But grow in grace, and in the knowledge of our Lord and Saviour Jesus Christ" (2 Peter 3:18a).

Lord, thank You for Your patient love that pushes me to trust You more. Give me a new hunger for You and Your Word today, so I will become the mature person in Christ that You desire. In Jesus' name, Amen.

My Unknown Angel

December 30

"Take heed that ye despise not one of these little ones; for I say unto you, That in heaven their angels do always behold the face of my Father which is in heaven" (Matthew 18:10).

We had been camped out for almost three hours waiting for the arena doors to open. We had come early to get in line for a free concert of our family's favorite Christian artist. Normally, I avoid crowds, especially when I have four small children to navigate through them, but this opportunity was too good to miss. My children had worked so hard homeschooling through the spring, and this outing was the rewarding finish to a productive school year. We were all looking forward to praising the Lord with wonderful music and meeting new Christian friends.

Finally, the time came for the doors to be opened. We were only twenty rows back from the entry, and we knew we'd get the choicest seats available. With thousands of people around us, my husband and I huddled the children between us as we inched our way forward. As soon as the doors opened, however, we felt a change come over the crowd. Like a crazed flock of sheep, everyone wanted to be the first into the building and began pushing their way forward. My husband and I looked at each other in panic and realized our children were getting crushed by the force of the crowd. We both tried to push back, but it was no use.

Then something happened that I'll never forget. An enormous man standing behind us saw the dilemma we were in. Making a barrier between us and the crowd with his huge, football-player frame, he turned and shouted at the crowd, "BACK OFF! You're hurting these children up here!" Immediately, everyone stopped their pushing, and we continued filing our way through the door. As we passed through the entrance, I turned to thank this wonderful man who had delivered us, but he was gone. I quickly scanned the crowd in both directions thinking he would be easy to spot, but I never saw him again.

I suppose some would say we exaggerated the details in our minds, or that this gentleman simply slipped by us without us seeing him. But I still believe, even to this day, that God used an angel to protect our children from being hurt. "For he shall give his angels charge over thee, to keep thee in all thy ways" (Psalm 91:11).

Lord, thank You for Your protective love that cares for my family each day. Even when I cannot see it, help me to remember that You will never lead us where Your love cannot keep us. In Jesus' name, Amen.

 Share your thoughts about this devotional at **aophomeschooling.com/364**

Meeting of the Minds

December 31

"The way of a fool is right in his own eyes: but he that hearkeneth unto counsel is wise" (Proverbs 12:15).

Our homeschooling days would never have survived without incorporating family meetings. Every week, we sat down for a discussion time with our children to ask for their feedback about our homeschooling schedule and activities. Curriculum choices that weren't working were replaced with options that met each child's learning style. Unrealistic goals based on prepackaged teacher's keys were adapted to fit the abilities of each child. The enlistment of our children's insightful and creative opinions helped to keep our homeschooling interesting, workable, and fun.

The early Christian church would never have survived if a meeting of the minds hadn't happened as well (Acts 15). There was a big division between the Jewish and Gentile believers about the matter of circumcision for salvation. The apostles and the elders in Jerusalem needed to agree to the truth of the Gospel message of Christ. Fortunately, several apostles kept the church from dividing by presenting Scripture that brought these two camps together (vs. 1-12).

Are you sensing some issues in your homeschool and the need for change in the new year? Plan a meeting of the minds with your children. You'll be amazed at their ideas and insights and find the unity in homeschooling that God desires for your family. "Without counsel purposes are disappointed: but in the multitude of counsellors they are established" (Proverbs 15:22).

Lord, forgive me for failing to counsel with my own children about homeschooling. Give me wisdom to hear Your voice as You speak through their heart-felt needs. In Jesus' name, Amen.

About the Author

Born in Iowa, Janet Tatman was raised on a country farm, the youngest of seven children. Attending public school, Janet graduated from high school with honors in 1973. One year later, she earned a secretarial diploma from a local community college and worked as an administrative assistant and an accountant. In 1976, Janet married her high school sweetheart and later had four children.

Answering God's call, Janet began homeschooling in the early 1980s. Moving to Nebraska in the mid 1980s, she continued to teach all her children from preschool through high school. During her homeschooling years, she often found encouragement in her favorite Bible verses:

> "Wherefore seeing we also are compassed about with so great a cloud of witnesses, let us lay aside every weight, and the sin which doth so easily beset us, and let us run with patience the race that is set before us, Looking unto Jesus the author and finisher of our faith" (Hebrews 12:1-2).

Now a veteran homeschool mom with over 25 years of experience, Janet is proud that all her children have received post-secondary degrees from a university or college. Her children's occupations include a registered nurse, an archeologist, a technical writer, and a Bible college graduate.

A life-long advocate of Christian education, Janet loves encouraging other homeschool families. Her pastimes include attending church, enjoying the outdoors, gardening, and spending time with family and friends, especially doting on babies. In 2006, Janet and her husband moved back to Iowa from Nebraska to care for their aging parents. She currently lives in the country near Sheldon, Iowa with her husband Steve, an English Springer Spaniel named Lucy, and two family cats. Janet is a beloved mother, teacher, wife, and friend. And I should know…because I am her daughter.

Switched-On®

Discover the Switched-On Advantage, and Make Homeschooling Easy with Worry-free Technology!

Do you ever wonder if there's a better way to homeschool? Well, there is! With the combination of a solid academic curriculum and an engaging, interactive, multimedia presentation, students learn efficiently, effectively, and have fun with Switched-On! Parents also benefit from loads of special features that shave time off administrative tasks such as lesson planning, grading, and record-keeping. Switched-On is a powerful tool for teaching and learning.

Take advantage of Switched-On today by visiting aophomeschooling.com or call 800-622-3070.

HomeschoolView™

A publication of **Alpha Omega Publications**®

Learn from the Ants

"Go to the ant, thou sluggard; consider her ways, and be wise: Which having no guide, overseer, or ruler, Provideth her meat in the summer, and gathereth her food in the harvest" (Proverbs 6:6-8).

The new school year will soon be approaching with all its demands and responsibilities. Keep the promise you've made to yourself and start planning early. Use some of your summer free time to acquaint yourself with your child's curriculum and formulate schedules and lesson plans for the new school year.

Eliminating the stress of last minute organization will launch you into a successful school year. Your children will follow your lead easier if you know what goals you hope to accomplish in each subject area. Here are some practical things you can do now to be a prepared homeschooling parent.

Order your curriculum. Most orders take three to four weeks for delivery, and if you wait, you may not receive your material in time. If you're still deciding on which curriculum to use, check out Alpha Omega Publications® and their great products, including Switched-On Schoolhouse®, LIFEPAC®, and Horizons.

Once you've received your curriculum, read the scope and sequence for each subject. Find the authors listed in your reading material and compile additional books for your child's reading list. Order the materials needed to conduct the science experiments in your course. Look for games and educational computer software that will compliment your math lessons. Purchase maps that will enhance your history, geography, and Bible classes. Decide on themes or topics for compositions. Choose daily devotional books for your children to use in their Bible instruction. The more you can accomplish in preparing how to use your curriculum to its best advantage, the better.

Organize field trips. Begin budgeting and scheduling trips to museums, zoos, weather stations, planetariums, or whatever compliments your child's subject areas. To make the trip pertinent, try to correlate the time of the field trips with the time of the school year you will be studying this information. See if you can save on expenses by car pooling with other homeschoolers. Plan extra-curricular activities.

To view the rest of this article visit our website:
www.aophomeschooling.com

The Homeschool View is a free monthly eNewsletter from Alpha Omega Publications that contains tips, stories, and information about products, special offers, events, homeschooling best practices, and more. Below are sample screenshots from a few of our Homeschool View eNewsletters.

Sign Up Now!

Visit aophomeschooling.com to sign up and receive the FREE monthly Homeschool View eNewsletter.

Horizons Preschool

Prepare Your Preschooler for Lifelong Learning with the Amazing Horizons Preschool!

Is it time for your preschooler to start his academic education? With Horizons Preschool from Alpha Omega Publications,® you'll get more than a preschool game or craft. You'll discover a comprehensive and captivating preschool curriculum that has everything you need! Biblically-based lessons and hands-on learning give children an introduction to social studies, language arts, math, phonics, science, and more.

Give your child a complete preschool education today by learning more at aophomeschooling.com or by calling 800-622-3070.

Switched-On®
ELECTIVES

Want Variety? Switched-On Has It with 20 Elective Courses!

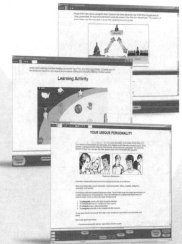

> American Literature
> British Literature
> Civics
> The Civil War
> College Planner
> Consumer Math
> Elementary French
> Elementary Spanish
> Essentials of Communication
> Health Quest
> High School Health
> Home Economics
> Secondary French
> Secondary Spanish
> Spanish I
> Spanish II
> State History
> The Story of the Constitution
> Trigonometry
> Vietnam Era

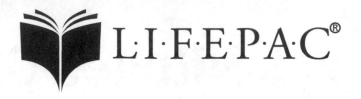